Big Book of
Scrapbooking

This is the photo I took for our Christmas cards in 1998. The oak grove across the street from our house was the perfect backdrop for my photo shoot. At the time I really didn't give much thought to the trees, other than thinking it would be nice to share the view with our family and friends. Now, as I look at this photo, I am reminded that we too often take the beauty in our everyday lives for granted. We no longer live in the house with this amazing view. I wish now that I had taken the time to learn more about the history of this land and the live oak trees planted there and how it came to be protected in a state where real estate is so valuable. I wish I had learned more about the Chumash Indians who held pow-wows there often. I wish I had learned more about these beautiful evergreen trees with leaves very different from oak trees I am more familiar with and their significance in this community. I wish I had taken more time to enjoy the view.

the view
of a thousand oaks

Thousand Oaks, California

MEMORY
MAKERS
BOOKS

contents

introduction

Are you looking for new ideas for your scrapbooks? Well look no further! This book has everything you need, from figuring out how to store all of your scrapbooking stuff to creatively cropping your photos and adding just the right embellishments to your pages. You'll find tons of new and different page ideas for all your projects. In addition, learn to use fabric, ribbon, tags, pressed leaves, wire, beads and buttons to make your pages perfect. You'll also learn all the latest photo cropping techniques, including photo tearing, weaving, mosaics and collages. And best of all, you'll learn the best way to store all your tools, no matter how many you have. This book has something for every scrapbooker, beginner and expert alike. Get started today!

MEMORY
MAKERS

SCRAPBOOK
EMBELLISHMENTS

M

MEMORY
MAKERS
BOOKS

Table of Contents

12 Organics

Bring nature to your pages with dried flowers and leaves, jute or hemp string, rocks, spanish moss, leather, wood, clay tiles, seeds, feathers, sea glass, raffia, pine needles, wheat straw, twigs and other elements from the great outdoors.

32 Textiles

Add texture, richness and depth to your scrapbook pages through the use of textiles—including nubby cotton or linen, shiny satin, the jewel or earth tones of fibers—twisted, tied or strung across a page. For a homey feel, a back-to-roots essence, textiles are the embellishment of choice.

54 Baubles

Dress up a page with jewelry that turns an everyday ensemble into something special. Tiny mico beads, glass pebbles, glitter and tinsel as well as other shiny embellishments catch the eye. String them, glue them to photos or photo mats for stunning effects.

76 Paper Crafts

With hundreds of colors and countless prints and textures, paper can be used to create an endless variety of scrapbook embellishments. Learn to weave, fold, punch, pleat, quill, cut and tear paper to create decorative elements for any page theme.

98 Metallics

Shiny, warm, malleable metals bring an earthy or masculine feel to many scrapbook pages. Perfect for tags, titles, journaling and photo corners, or used in the form of metal wire which is twisted and strung with beads, metallics are a wonderful addition to a scrapbooker's tool box.

Meet the
Memory Makers Masters

Valerie Barton

A scrapbooker for four years, Valerie Barton began with the intention of preserving her children's school memories in an album, a task which eventually evolved into a full-blown passion and creative outlet. Valerie cites the therapeutic nature of scrapbooking and its impact on the positive elements in life. In her own words, "If I'm having a bad day, all I have to do is work on my pages." Characterizing herself as an "out-of-the-box" scrapbooker, Valerie adds that her approach to scrapbooking favors the dimensional, where layers, paper craft and fibers create texture and dimension that are often considered "shabby chic." Being a Memory Makers Master for Valerie has meant having the opportunity to interact with other women who have the same passion. She says being a Master has also been motivation for her to strive to become a better journaler. When not hard at work scrapbooking, Valerie works as an elementary school counselor in Flowood, Mississippi where she lives with husband Mark, daughter Kaitlyn and son Addison.

Katherine Brooks

Katherine began scrapbooking six years ago after the birth of her daughter. Initially scrapbooking with the primary purpose of documenting her family's overall history and special times, Katherine soon discovered scrapbooking to be the perfect outlet for creative expression. Describing her style and approach to scrapbooking, Katherine says, "I like adding simple detail to my layouts. As for my style, I love country décor and find that it transfers into my layouts." A proud mom, Katherine most enjoys creating layouts of her family. For the sake of her children, she strives to scrapbook more about herself. For Katherine, being a Memory Makers Master has given her an opportunity to correspond with other women who share her enthusiasm for the craft, and has led to new friendships. When not scrapbooking, Katherine is busy as an instructor and product designer for Deluxe Designs, and has recently released an idea book titled, *Tagging Along*. Katherine lives in Gilbert, Arizona, with husband John and children Meghan and Matt.

Brandi Ginn

Although Brandi Ginn began scrapbooking as a child, married life and motherhood proved to be the motivation for her taking up the craft on a consistent basis four years ago. For Brandi, scrapbooking is the natural form for her interests in photography and the overall creative process to take. As Brandi describes, scrapbooking affords her the rewarding and unique opportunity to create something meaningful and lasting from the perspective of both an artist and mother. "There's a great sense of accomplishment that comes from preserving our family's history." Describing her style as fairly traditional, Brandi most enjoys documenting the life and times of her family in her scrapbook pages. Evolving as a crafter and pushing herself to turn out innovative work characterizes Brandi's experience as a Memory Makers Master. When not conceptualizing her next layout, Brandi is at work as a freelance writer and designer, and lives in Lafayette, Colorado, with husband Nathan and daughters Alexa and Brinley.

Diana Graham

Diana Graham's interest in scrapbooking actually began more as an obsession with scrapbooking products than with scrapbooking itself. Until being invited to a crop by a local scrapbook store owner, Diana was content with simply shopping for the embellishments that would later adorn her pages. "I was in love with picking out paper and stickers and new gadgets and tools," she says. Four years later, Diana now enjoys scrapbooking for the relationships it promotes, as well as the smiles on her children's faces when they look at her scrapbooks. In describing her style and approach to scrapbooking, Diana says she favors using a lot of product on her pages. She says that being a Memory Makers Master has given her the opportunity to explore new themes and products, and the Masters challenges have forced her to push her creativity to new levels. In addition to to her crafting endeavors, Diana is a stay-at-home mom who lives in Barington, Illinois, with husband Brad and children Jeremy and Ella.

Diana Hudson

Diana Hudson began scrapbooking 11 years ago, after the arrival of her first child. Recognizing the opportunity to combine her interests in needlework, paper art and journaling, Diana began scrapbooking in order to create timeless keepsakes for future generations of her family. For Diana, scrapbooking provides a unique opportunity to remember what is important and share it with others, particularly through journaling. "The photos are a treasure, but the written word is equally important to me," says Diana. Describing her style as clean, classic, as well as eclectic, Diana enjoys trying new styles in order to continuously evolve as a scrapbooker. As a Memory Makers Master, Diana has appreciated the friendships forged with other Masters who, like her, have viewed the experience as a springboard for exploring new products and techniques. In addition to her artistic endeavors, Diana is a stay-at-home mom who revels in caring for her family. She lives in Bakersfield, California, with husband Curtis and children Ryan and Sydney.

Torrey Miller

Torrey Miller has been scrapbooking for the past three and a half years, after having been invited by a friend to a crop. Instantly, the craft became the creative solution for artistically uniting all the things Torrey enjoys best. In her own words, "Scrapbooking offers me a single medium in which I can expressively combine my poetry, photography, art and writing, all in a beautiful package." A self-described "artsy" and "eclectic" scrapbooker, Torrey particularly enjoys scrapbooking loved ones as well as the scenic photographs she takes. Over the course of her Memory Makers Masters tenure, Torrey says that in addition to building friendships, she has been challenged to scrap outside her comfort zone and experiment more in her layouts, leading to a willingness to try most any technique. When not planning her next project, Torrey works as a pediatric registered nurse and freelance writer, and enjoys the creative influences of friends and family members. Torrey lives in Thornton, Colorado.

Kelli Noto

Having scrapbooked in high school, Kelli Noto renewed her interest in the craft after the arrival of her first child 11 years ago. For Kelli, her scrapbooking is a tribute to her children as well as a special form of family documentation for future generations. In characterizing her style, Kelli notes that her color choices and favoring of bold, graphic lines are the result of the masculine influences from raising two sons. As for her approach, Kelli says, "I believe that scrapbook pages should start with the photos. I try to keep my pages photocentric and use embellishments only as enhancements." Kelli's most prized photo opportunities and favorite scrapbooking subjects are catching her children hard at play and engaged in sports. As a Memory Makers Master, Kelli has enjoyed exchanging techniques with her newfound friends and fellow Masters artists, and has been inspired to continuously evolve in page design. In addition to being a busy scrapbooker, Kelli owns a photography business and lives in Centennial, Colorado, with husband John and children Eric and Kevin.

Heidi Schueller

Having kept a scrapbook during her high school and college years, Heidi Schueller returned to her former hobby two and a half years ago while working as a Creative Memories consultant. It was this experience that Heidi says instigated her passion for "modern" scrapbooking and her enthusiasm for its resurgence. Characterizing her approach to scrapbooking as "resourceful," Heidi always strives for originality in her layouts and works to create pages that invite personal interpretation. "When people look at my pages, I want the photos and artwork to tell a story. The whole page should give an emotion and feeling to the onlooker," says Heidi. As for favorite scrapbooking subjects, Heidi enjoys creating layouts based on her children and her travels. As a Memory Makers Master, Heidi has most appreciated the additional opportunities to create new art based on the Master's challenges, meeting her fellow Masters, and serving as a Camp Memory Makers instructor. When not working at her craft, Heidi is a stay-at-home mom and scrapbook instructor and lives in Waukesha, Wisconsin, with husband Bill and daughters Isabel and Claudia.

Trudy Sigurdson

Trudy Sigurdson began scrapbooking two and a half years ago after a trip to replenish her rubber stamping supplies led her into a scrapbooking store. She was hooked after taking one class. Now a scrapbook designer and instructor, Trudy describes her style of scrapbooking as textured and dimensional, where her love for paper scrunching, distressing, and machine sewing all converge. In describing her approach of utilizing fewer photos and incorporating reflective journaling, Trudy says, "I think that I am more of an emotional scrapbooker than an event scrapbooker. I prefer to write and record poems or quotes that show how much I love my children." According to Trudy, being a Memory Makers Master has pushed her creatively, leading her to new products and the assignments have helped her expand her style. In addition to her regular teaching and designing, Trudy served as a Camp Memory Makers instructor in the summer of 2003. Trudy lives in Victoria, British Columbia, with children Aysha and Alex.

Holle Wiktorek

A scrapbooker since high school, Holle Wiktorek has 13 years of scrapbooking and five years of teaching scrapbook classes to her credit. What began as a school assignment grew into a much-loved pastime for documenting both life-changing and everyday events. Holle notes that scrapbooking has become a way for her to close the distance between far away friends and family, namely her often-deployed U.S. Army officer husband. "When my husband is deployed, scrapbooking keeps us close as I relive our moments together," says Holle. Hesitant to categorize her scrapbooking style due to its constant evolution, Holle continuously works to find new techniques using paper tearing and chalking and her favorite products of cardstock and embellishments. As a Memory Makers Master, Holle has challenged herself to try new products and improve with each featured layout, enjoying the exchange of ideas with fellow Masters. In addition to instructing scrapbook classes, Holle is a public school teacher and lives in Clarksville, Tennessee, with her husband, Thomas.

Embellishments Library

The scrapbooker who was once concerned about how to fill a white page need worry no longer. The exponential growth of scrapbooking has resulted in a plethora of extraordinary embellishments that turn one-dimensional layouts into canvases of creative expression. Scrapbook toolboxes now hold beautiful threads, sparkling beads, whimsical buttons and much more. While not all embellishments are safe to bring into contact with photos and memorabilia, it is still possible to place them on pages in ways that avoid close proximity, or to encase them in pockets, 3-D keepers and shaker boxes. Enjoy exploring both design possibilities and the array of stunning embellishments on the market today.

Organics

Hemp, jute and string were the forerunners when it came to organic embellishing. The lumpy nature of these embellishments concerned some scrapbookers, however. As scrapbooks became more 3-D, these products were perceived as less obtrusive. They were joined by objects such as pressed flowers and leaves, skeleton leaves, grasses, shells and seeds. In the future more people may wish to press their own flowers and leaves or pound flowers into pulpy colorants for shadowing and enhancing art. Organics are perfect embellishments for earthy pages including vacation and outdoor themes and they are sure to fit in well on "altered" page collage-like spreads.

Textiles

Years ago, the recognition that fabrics and sewing techniques could support scrapbook page themes led scrapbookers to create faux sewing in their albums. However, rather than reach for true sewing supplies, they "quilted" together pieces of paper and created penned "stitch" lines. More recently scrapbook artists have been browsing their local fabric stores for supplies such as fabrics, ribbons, zippers, embroidery floss, threads and quilting patterns. The result? Scrapbook pages with softer edges, more dimension, a homey feel and texture to spare.

Paper

Paper, in all its variations, is a staple of scrapbooking. While today's scrapbookers continue to reach for cardstock and patterned papers, they are growing increasingly excited about the novelty and specialty papers such as mulberry, waushi, velvets, embossed and metallic papers. They are tearing, sculpting, folding, ironing, pleating, wetting, painting, crimping and embossing them to create awesome embellishments for pages across all themes. In looking forward, scrapbookers are also looking back toward ancient paper arts such as origami and iris folding to embellish their pages. All it takes is a bit of research and daring.

Baubles

While glitter has found a home on scrapbook pages for some years, other forms of glitz such as beads, tinsel and sequins are more recent additions to the scrapbook toolbox. Tiny micro beads and marbles, sequins, glass pebbles, rhinestones, gems and other decorative elements add sparkle as well as dimension to today's pages. Scrapbookers continue to expand, visiting non-scrapbook related aisles in their hobby stores for inspiration and products that push the envelope such as tiles and mirrors. While no one can predict exactly what the future holds, many scrapbook professionals expect to see increasingly intricate beadwork designs on pages.

Metallics

Metallic papers, first popular a handful of years ago, opened the door for the use of other metallics on scrapbook pages. They were followed by freeform wire titles and embellishments, created by wrapping thin wire around pegs. Paper clips, eyelets, brads and page jewelry as well as metallic leafing products have become increasingly popular to dress up elegant layouts. Many of the available metallics have been made in silver but the future is sure to offer more gold, copper and bronze-colored embellishments as well as adhesives created specifically to hold them to pages.

Organics

Through the ages man has celebrated nature's beauty by decorating with organics…elements found in the environment or made from natural materials. From flower arrangements on end tables to rock gardens, wood carvings, clay vessels, seashell collections and much more, man has brought nature home. Organics are used functionally as well as cosmetically to make rope, string, tiles, dinnerware and clothing.

Over the years scrapbookers have explored ways to incorporate organics into their art. Organic embellishments such as dried flowers and leaves, jute or hemp string, rocks, spanish moss, leather, wood, clay tiles, seeds, feathers, sea glass, raffia, pine needles, wheat straw and twigs bring nature's voice to scrapbook spreads. They reflect and support the theme when placed beside meaningful journaling and outdoor photos. Used in their natural state, or stamped, cut, stained or layered, these gifts from the great outdoors can be used to embellish tags, envelopes, titles, borders, photo mats or as stand-alone page embellishments. Organic embellishments are sold in scrapbook or hobby stores. Pick up your favorites, or take a walk around the block. You're sure to find elements that just beg to be showcased in your album.

Until I Saw the Sea

Frame a photo with sea treasures

Valerie adds an organic element to a seaside photo with a partial border of small seashells nestled inside of a fabric frame. Tear four blue vellum strips; horizontally layer at top and bottom of page. Mount embellished padded fabric frame over photo matted on blue cardstock and torn mulberry paper. Add small seashells inside of frame with glue dots. Write title on vellum tags. Tear hole in one vellum tag; embellish with beaded wire. Print journaling on vellum; crop into tag shape. Cut second tag from blue textured cardstock; punch small square at bottom of tag. Embellish tag with lace and seashell. Tie tags together with thin satin ribbon; mount vellum tag to page and let top tag dangle free.

Valerie Barton

Deep Thoughts

Collage textured elements

Valerie adds texture to collaged elements with jute string woven through meshed paper. Freehand tear tan cardstock; crumple, flatten and brush with brown chalk. Mount over blue background cardstock that has been lightly brushed with sandpaper. Cut black corrugated cardstock into photo corners and decorative strip; tear edges and mount on photos. Attach mesh strip to page with eyelets; weave jute string through mesh. Print journaling on vellum; cut to size and tear edges before layering on page. Die cut title letters from textured cardstock. Stamp remaining title letters on tan paper with brown ink. Freehand cut frame for title word from suede leather; layer over title word and mount on page. Attach silver star brads. Layer small tan paper torn square over brown corrugated cardstock torn into triangle shape and attach large silver eyelet before mounting on page.

Valerie Barton

Super Scrappin' Getaway at Cowichan Bay

I like my embellishments to capture the mood of the photos on the page. A spread of a misty and rugged sea coast was a good place to try a new technique that involved ironing folds and creases into background paper before scrunching it. The vellum and pale blues help carry a peaceful feeling.

Trudy Sigurdson

Trudy Sigurdson

Super Scrappin' Getaway

Stitch a netted border

Trudy catches starfish and sand dollars in a stitched coastal netting border. Spray light blue cardstock with water; randomly crease paper and iron fold. Repeat process until creases are evenly distributed throughout. Lightly crumple cardstock; flatten and horizontally tear at bottom. Stitch large and small pieces over a 2" strip of coastal netting to a dark blue cardstock background. Gently curl edges of light blue cardstock with fingers; brush edges with black chalk. Mount starfish and sand dollars along coastal netting border. Tie hemp string into knots at 3" intervals; mount along bottom of page. Mat photos on dark blue cardstock. Print title and journaling on vellum. Tear journaling into 1" strips; insert strips in between jute string loops knotted at 1¼" intervals. Tie vellum journaling block with jute string before mounting on page.

I've Been Working on the Railroad

Accent sticker with natural elements

Small, black crystallized rocks look like a mound of coal atop a locomotive sticker on Kelli's thematic layout. Print title words on tan cardstock; silhouette cut with a craft knife before layering on matted title strips. Trim edges of large photo with corner rounder; double mat and mount railroad track die cut around edges of photo. Attach eyelets at corners of title blocks and upper corners of photo mat. Link together with jute string. Print journaling on tan cardstock; mat and detail with a ¼" strip of red cardstock. Mat smaller photos on tan and red cardstock. Mount a few photos with self-adhesive foam spacers; wrap corners of photos with jute string. Adhere locomotive sticker at bottom of page; mount small black crystallized rocks atop sticker with heavy two-sided tape.

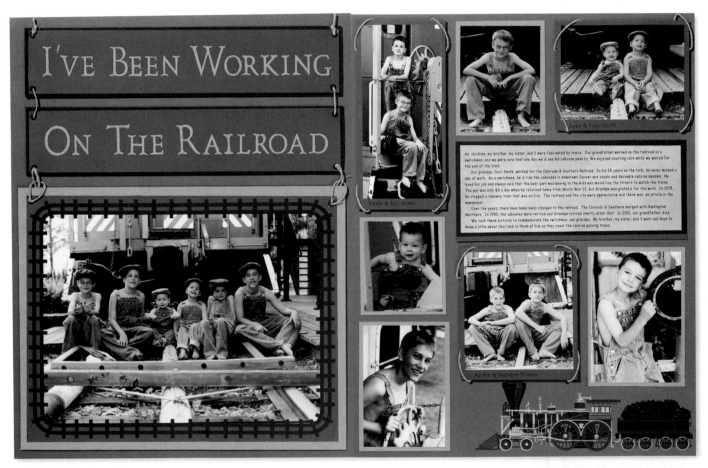

Kelli Noto

I really feel that black-and-white photos allow you to focus more on the faces of your subjects because you don't have the distraction that color generates. I actually shoot in black-and-white about 25 percent of the time. But on other occasions I'll shoot in color or shoot digital pictures and may print them in black-and-white afterwards.

Kelli Noto

Patriot

Antique cardstock with tea stains

Tea-stained paper enhances Diana's sepia-toned photos. Stain cardstock with plain brewed tea applied with an eye dropper; dry. Cut title letters, tag and photo mat from tea-stained cardstock. Mat title letters on navy blue cardstock; silhouette cut. Cut tag; scrape edges with scissor blade. Attach eyelet; tie fibers. Mount fabric tag and sticker to tag. Slice four ½" tan cardstock strips; tear one side of each strip. Chalk torn edges in brown and red. Mount strips around edges of photo; layer photo corners over torn strips. Print journaling onto tea-stained cardstock. Crumple, wet and iron journaling block. Add distressed details by rubbing black and gold chalk over cardstock. Tear and curl edges before mounting under red thread secured to page with copper nailheads.

Diana Graham

Time

Stamp hugs and kisses on pebbles

Diana stamps a message of love on small rocks collected by her daughter. Layer cropped photos on red mesh cardstock and dark blue rectangles torn around the edges. Cut photo corners from dark blue cardstock; tear edges before mounting on one photo. Freehand cut title letters from red mesh cardstock; mount on clay art tiles. Layer tiles over paper-torn cardstock squares; stitch to page with tan embroidery thread. Mount large copper eyelets on page; hang folded tan and red mesh cardstock over jute string strung through eyelets. Print journaling on tan paper; cut to size and mount inside folded cardstock. Stamp sentiment on copper tag; tie clay lettered tile at one end before layering with dark blue torn cardstock strip. Stamp "X" and "O" on small rocks and "MOM" on background with red ink at bottom of page. Mount rocks on page with liquid adhesive.

Diana Graham

Heidi Schueller

Garth/Faith

Twist "barbed wire" Accents

Heidi adds rustic country elements to her page with "barbed wire" accents. Slice two 2" border strips from tan cardstock. Print title letters onto green cardstock. Cut letters into approximately 1 x 1½" sections. Pierce top and bottom of each section; stitch sections together with hemp string. Mount sections on border strips; attach silver star nailheads. Mat photos on tan cardstock. Attach green eyelets to border strips and photo mats. Craft barbed wire embellishments by twisting small pieces of wire around two strands of wire using needle-nosed pliers. Feed "barbed wire" through eyelets; secure at back of border and photo mat. Print journaling on vellum; cut to size and mat on green cardstock. Secure to page with hemp string looped through green eyelets on border strips. Mount silver star nailheads along lower edge of bottom photo. Attach shrunken plastic designs to nailheads with linked jewelry jump rings.

Gone Fishing

Dangle die-cut fish on a rope border

Heidi shows off the catch of the day with die cut fish layered over a rope border. Print title and journaling on tan cardstock; mount on green cardstock background. Cut green corrugated cardstock to fit inside title letters. Freehand cut trees; add chalk details before mounting at the bottom of the page. Freehand draw fishing net pattern. Cut pattern pieces from cardstock. Crop photos to fit net design. Cut two pieces of rope. Mount on sides of pages. Mount die-cut fish with self-adhesive foam spacers over rope for dimension.

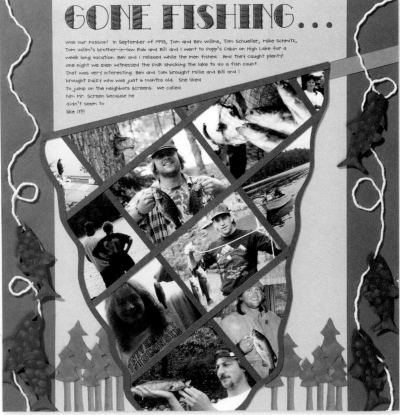

Heidi Schueller

Feed the Birds

Enhance die cuts with spanish moss

Brandi's spread features "tweet" birdhouses embellished with dimensional details. Mat photos on green and blue cardstock. Print title words and journaling on tan cardstock. Cut out title letters; mat on blue, red and green cardstock. Tear around the edges of a few; detail with eyelets and small brads. Mat journaling on green cardstock textured with a crimper. Punch small holes at top of journaling block; tie jute string through holes before "hanging" on page from a small brad. Layer birdhouse die cuts over black and red cardstock so color shows through cut-outs. Punch heart from tan cardstock; mount on red birdhouse. Add spanish moss at top of birdhouses to resemble nests. Mount two birdhouses with self-adhesive foam spacers over strips of jute.

Brandi Ginn

I do take it into consideration, but I'm truthfully not as concerned today about archival issues as I once was because I do such a good job of archiving my negatives. I figure that if a supply—the moss on a page perhaps, or something else—hurts my photos twenty years down the road, then I'll just make prints and replace the damaged ones.

Brandi Ginn

Miss Aysha

Layer organic elements for a border

Trudy layers a variety of elements for an interesting border. Mat mustard-colored textured cardstock on rust cardstock. Tear two 1" strips of rust cardstock for border strips; brush dark brown chalk along torn edges. Attach eyelets at top and bottom of torn paper strip. String metal hearts and stars on raffia before mounting on border strips. Tie hemp string on metal hearts and stars; tie key charm to one heart. Layer dried leaves, vintage stamps and mica tiles on background; mount border strips atop layered design. Secure raffia ends to back of page. Print journaling on transparency; layer over dried leaf, mica tile and stamp. Secure to page with flat eyelets. Wrap and tie twigs with raffia; mount on border strip and journal block. Mat photos on rust cardstock; mount on page.

Trudy Sigurdson

I have always felt comfortable working with color, but recognize that not everybody feels that way. When determining the colors to use on my pages, I draw from the background elements in photos and take cues from things like the way the sun throws warm gold highlights on hair.

Trudy Sigurdson

Branded by the Effects of Nature

Add rustic appeal with textured fabric

Stamped leather and burlap add rustic charm to Valerie's page. Tear two 3" patterned paper strips; mount horizontally near the bottom of page. Mat two photos on golden yellow cardstock; tie one with hemp before matting. Layer both on patterned paper strips. Craft plastic frame by watermark stamping onto transparency; sprinkle with golden yellow embossing powder and heat set. Tear edges and inside of transparency to create frame and decorative strip. Mount embossed transparency frame to page over large photo with eyelets. Attach burlap strip to bottom of one photo with eyelets. Mount on page; layer with embossed transparency strip. Stamp title letters with brown ink on distressed leather remnant; press brown ink pad around the edges. Cut three tags from patterned paper; tear bottom edges of tags. Print balance of title letters on vellum; tear into strips and layer over torn yellow cardstock strips. Cut small pieces of burlap into top of tag shape; mount atop tag with eyelets. Punch two small holes at bottom corners of leather piece; tie jute through holes connecting title tags together. Print journaling on vellum; tear around edges and layer with torn paper strip and dried leaf. Stamp name on torn piece of patterned paper; layer metal frame attached with eyelets. Layer on page with burlap remnant, leather strip and button.

Valerie Barton

Queen Victoria's Memorial

Create subtle decoration with pressed flowers and leaves

Dried and pressed flowers and leaves enhance Trudy's monochromatic layout. Horizontally layer and mount ivory spring roll strips with tan eyelets on patterned paper. Double mat photos, using crumpled and flattened tan cardstock for the second mat. Stitch matted photos to page; gently curl edges of tan matting with fingers. Print title and date on ivory cardstock; cut title block to size. Mount pressed leaves and flowers on title block; pen border around edge. Mat title block on crumpled and flatted tan cardstock embellished with buttons and hemp string layered on an ivory paper strip. Cut date into tag shape; attach eyelet. Tie tag to decorative square embellished with flowers, leaves, hemp and buttons. Stitch matted title block and decorative square to page.

Trudy Sigurdson

Adonis Narcissus Diggs

Add charm with wooden embellishment

A pre-made wooden fence adds simple charm to Torrey's heritage page. Double mat patterned paper with solid colored cardstock. Double mat photo. Cut oval in cropped vellum to highlight subject in photo. Cut oval frame from solid-colored cardstock; layer on vellum. Mount vellum to top of matted photo with gold brads. Mount wooden picket fence along bottom of page. Print journaling on vellum; cut to size and mount on fence.

Torrey Miller

Mother's Day

Highlight dried flowers with pre-made paper frames

Delicate dried daisies encapsulated in memorabilia pockets make a fresh springtime border. Print journaling on textured cardstock background. Cut strip of meshed paper; mount horizontally at bottom of page. Place pressed flowers in memorabilia pockets to keep them from crumbling. Layer pre-made paper frames over encapsulated flower before mounting on page. Mat one photo on dark green textured cardstock. Frame smaller photo with pre-made paper frame. Print title on vellum; cut to size before layering over protected pressed daisy. Mount pre-made frame over vellum title block.

Diana Hudson

Captured

Add a textured touch with fringed mesh

A solitary photo layered over fringed mesh gives a contemporary look to Diana's layout. Cut a 6 x 12" piece of patterned paper; print title. Print journaling on solid green cardstock. Mount patterned paper with title over solid green cardstock and mat on brown speckled cardstock. Cut a 14" strip of mesh. Wrap around the middle of the page and attach on the back of the page. Mount enlarged photo over mesh strip. String button on green satin cording; tie at ends and mount over mesh and photo.

Diana Graham

Year of the Dress

Build a balsa wood "dressing room"

Heidi designs a "dressing" room to showcase paper dolls of her daughter. Tear a 2" strip of black cardstock and patterned paper; horizontally layer at bottom of page over background patterned paper. Craft "dressing room" from lightweight pieces of balsa wood mounted on patterned vellum and cardstock. Place magnetic sheet behind windows. Mount lightweight hobby hinges to the back of "dressing room" and doors. Paper fold vellum pockets; mount over torn paper strips. Silhouette cut photos; mount on magnetic sheets and crop. (Dolls may sit in windows after page completion). Print title on yellow and journaling on rust cardstocks. Silhouette cut title letters; mat on black cardstock and silhouette again. Paper tear around balance of title; punch flowers from vellum and cardstock and layer. Mount journal blocks behind "dressing room" doors.

Heidi Schueller

Uniquely You

Stamp and emboss a clay tile

Katherine crafts a unique clay title block. Cut a 5" piece of patterned paper; vertically layer over rust cardstock. Layer green gingham ribbon at edge of patterned paper strip; mat background with dark green cardstock. Print journaling on ivory cardstock; cut to size and gently curl right edges with fingers. Ink edges of journaling blocks. Mount on page with small brads at left side of journal blocks. Mat large photo with tan cardstock; wrap bottom with knotted copper wire. Create the clay title tile by first molding polymer clay into a rectangular block. While still malleable, press in title letters and flower stamps. Heat the clay block with an embossing gun; color with metallic rub-on's. Heat again; sprinkle with clear ultra thick embossing enamel and emboss.

Katherine Brooks

Pure Country

Use mesh for textured dimension

Katherine's embossed elements give rustic charm to a country page. Using a craft knife, cut a ¼" frame from brown cardstock; mount over matted mesh background with foam tape. Crumple, flatten and iron patterned paper; mat on brown cardstock. Attach flat eyelets at corners before matting again on layered mesh background. Mat all photos on blue cardstock. Emboss metal tag with ultra thick embossing enamel; while embossing powder is still warm, press in black inked letter stamps. Attach jump ring to tag; string on twine wrapped around matted photos on left page. Emboss paper clip with copper powder; clip photo to background at bottom of page. Cut title letters from corrugated cardstock; emboss with copper powder. Print balance of title and journaling on tan cardstock; cut to size and tear bottom edge. Ink edges of title and journal blocks and mesh scraps. Staple title block to patterned paper. Slice ½" border design in brown cardstock on right page using a craft knife and metal straightedge ruler. Layer over green mesh and green cardstock with foam tape. Emboss small metal tag in same way as described above; attach tag to mesh with jump ring. Double mat one photo with distressed patterned paper; attach flat eyelets on second mat. Double mat small photos; use embossed corrugated cardstock for second mat. Layer journaling block over sliced blue cardstock strips; attach flat eyelet at lower right corner over mesh scrap.

Katherine Brooks

Full of Beans
Craft a shaker box full of beans

Special treasures found in a boy's pockets are packaged in Katherine's homemade shaker box tags. Unwrap tan paper yarn; horizontally mount along bottom of page with silver brads at 2½" increments on olive green cardstock. Mat with dark green cardstock. Single and double mat photos on light and dark green cardstock. Wrap two matted photos with dark green waxy flax. Crimp three 1½" strips of light green cardstock; emboss with green ink and ultra thick embossing enamel. Mount photo over crimped and embossed strips with self-adhesive foam spacers. Print title letters; silhouette cut. Mat large letters on tan cardstock and silhouette again. Print journaling on ivory cardstock; cut to size and brush the edges with brown chalk. Cut tag shape from stamped and crumpled light green cardstock. Punch window in tag with square punch; attach screen to back of window. Punch circles for tag holes; tie with fibers. Sculpt "beans" from polymer clay; bake as directed on packaging. Adhere foam tape on back of tag around edges; before sealing to page, add clay beans.

Katherine Brooks

I knew I wanted to use beans on the page but I didn't have beans in the cupboard—it's just too hot in Arizona to heat up the stove so I seldom cook. I made these beans out of polymer clay, and they look absolutely perfect.

Katherine Brooks

Amigo at the Denver Zoo

Layer a unique textured background

Think outside the box when looking for organic textures to enhance your pages. Brandi's use of a latch-hook rug mesh gives a unique textured background to her zoo spread. Mount latch-hook rug mesh on tan cardstock with sticky dot adhesive. Single and double mat photos on yellow and green cardstock; detail mats with black fine tip pen. Print title letters on green cardstock; silhouette cut. Print journaling on tan cardstock; cut to size and mount.

I first started scrapbooking for my children. Although I still do it for my children I also do it for myself. There's a great sense of accomplishment that comes from preserving our family's history.

Brandi Ginn

Brandi Ginn

Gardening 101

Plant a flowerpot

Heidi plants seeds of knowledge within this flowerpot of pressed flowers and curled wire stems. Print title on ivory cardstock; cut to size, chalk edges and mount vertically over tan cardstock. Punch squares from cardstock in shades of pink and red; mount along edge of title strip. Mat photos on red and pink cardstock; attach eyelets at corners. Frame photos with hemp strung with seed and letter beads. Mat again on cardstock, leaving room for photo captions. Print photo captions on ivory cardstock; brush pink chalk around the edges before mounting on second mat. Freehand cut and layer flowerpot; detail edges with chalk. Laminate pressed flowers; silhouette cut. Punch teardrop shapes for leaves from green cardstock; mat on lighter green cardstock and silhouette cut. Wrap green wire around a pencil to curl; remove and bend to shape. Mount flowerpot, pressed flowers and leaves on page with self-adhesive foam spacers over curled wire.

Heidi Schueller

Holle Wiktorek

Destin, Florida

Scatter sea glass

Holle's warm memories of a seaside vacation come to life with sandy letters and sea glass. Tear two 1¼" strips of tan cardstock; chalk torn edges and press tan ink pad on strips. Horizontally layer over blue cardstock at bottom of page. Freehand cut palm tree trunk from corrugated cardstock and leaves from green cardstock. Crumple and chalk leaves. Place double-sided adhesive sheet on cardstock before die cutting title letters. Cut through both layers; coat with decorative sand. Mount die-cut letters on torn paper strips among mounted sea glass. Double mat photo; mount on background. Cut tags from tan cardstock; stamp sand dollar and family names on tags with brown ink. Stamp sentiments on light green cardstock with brown ink; paper tear and layer on tags.

Punch hole at top of tags; layer and mount to page with star brad.

Seeking Shelter

Layer a distressed collage

Diana captures the essence of an imaginative day of military play with rustic layers. Mat one photo on green cardstock; tear edges of matting and rub with black chalk. Roughen edges of photo by scraping with blade of scissors; mat. Crumple, flatten and chalk tan cardstock. Tear distressed paper into thirds; randomly tear holes into cardstock. Layer and mount torn strips with mesh pieces and photos over patterned background paper. Wrap copper wire through mesh and around torn cardstock. Attach eyelets; loop and tie jute through eyelets. Print title word and letters on tan and green cardstock; tear paper and chalk around edges. Wrap title word block with copper wire before mounting on page. Print journaling on green cardstock; tear around edges and add chalk for dimension. Tie small piece of jute at upper right-hand corner; mount journal block on page with self-adhesive foam spacers.

Diana Graham

Valerie Barton

Fishing

Create an accent with handmade paper strips

Valerie uses textured handmade paper to provide interest to a simple layout. Slice a 3" strip of rust cardstock, a 3½" strip of tan cardstock and a 4" strip of brown cardstock. Slice three 1¼ x 2½" rectangles in rust cardstock with a craft knife and straightedge ruler; layer over larger cardstock strips and stitch together. Layer photo with torn edges over torn handmade paper strip before mounting at center of stitched border. Tear two 1" strips of handmade paper; horizontally layer on page about 4" apart. Mat large photos on tan cardstock; layer one over rust torn cardstock strip before matting. Tear edges of small photo; mount on vellum tag. Mount all photos on page. Stamp title word with green ink on bag. Embellish "tag in a bag" with unique items; layer and mount corkboard strip, mesh square, torn paper pieces, swirled paper clip and buttons. Wrap embellished tag with fishing line; mount on page. Journal on tag and tie fibers before sliding into embellished bag. Tie button with jute; mount on torn handmade paper strip.

Pinewood Derby
Build interest with wood paper

Kelli documents what it takes to build a car with a border showing creative progression steps. Cut a 2½ x 10¾" piece of wood paper for right-hand page border. Punch five square "windows" in border strip. Mount on red cardstock strip of the same size; mat on black cardstock. Freehand cut visuals from cardstock and wood paper for "windows" showing how to build a handmade car. Attach black eyelets as car wheels in fourth window. Punch scalloped circle from blue cardstock; layer over freehand cut "ribbons" for last window. Slice two 1¾" strips of preprinted photo strip; horizontally mount at bottom of red cardstock background. Die cut title letters from wood paper; mat on black cardstock and silhouette cut around words. Cut two frames from wood paper; mount over matted photos with self-adhesive foam spacers for dimension. Crop and mount balance of photos; write photo captions with black fine-tip pen.

Kelli Noto

Uninvited Grill Guests

Scatter feathers for a nature accent

Nature inspired Holle's layout documenting the hatching of ten baby birds in her backyard barbecue. Single and double mat photos on light blue, tan and brown cardstock. Print journaling on tan cardstock; cut to size and tear two edges. Double mat on cardstock with torn edges and torn mulberry paper. Cut a few title words from black and blue cardstock; mount on cardstock, cut to size and mat. Adhere letter stickers to matted cardstock strip for one title word. Write the last title word on matted cardstock strip. Freehand draw, cut and papercraft camera, hands and barbecue from cardstock; detail with black and white pens and brush with chalk. Craft nest from cut pieces of paper yarn mounted atop unwrapped paper yarn strips. Cut or punch ovals for eggs; detail with black pen and mount at center of nest. Randomly mount feathers around title and journaling blocks.

Holle Wiktorek

I am strongly into non-event scrapbooking. Events such as Christmas and birthdays come only once a year, but the smaller events are what make up the bulk of our lives. Those are the things that I want to celebrate in my albums. Scrapbooking them allows me to throw myself into the daily blessings.

Holle Wiktorek

Textiles

Early production of fabrics and fibers began around 5,000 B.C. when flax was first spun into a fine linen used for ancient burial shrouds. Other natural fibers, including cotton and wool, were spun into fabrics by the Egyptians several thousand years later, and the Chinese introduced silk as a precious commodity in about 1725 B.C. Until the Industrial Revolution, which brought the invention of the cotton gin and flourishing of factories in the early 19th century, fibers were produced on smaller spinning and weaving looms. Things changed in the late 1890s when manufactured fibers, like rayon, nylon and polyester, came on the textile scene, providing greater comfort, durability and colorfastness.

The immense versatility in color and texture of natural and man-made textiles have made it a choice embellishment for scrapbookers. Ribbon, with its many colors, patterns, textures and widths, can be crafted into dimensional shapes or layered as a simple and elegant design element. Lace, which was a popular fashion embellishment in the 15th century, is now used for photo mats, borders and other scrapbook adornments. Other fabrics can be cut, torn, woven, sewn, layered, embroidered, stuffed, collaged and beaded and tied for unique effects in albums. However you implement textiles into your layouts, you're sure to increase visual appeal by adding a textured touch to your page.

And Tia Makes Three

Add warmth with fringe and fibers

Trudy adds warmth to a rich monochromatic layout with fringed fabric that invites the onlooker to touch the page. Cut two 7 x 11¾" pieces of fabric; mount on textured paper. Stitch around three edges onto dark brown cardstock. Wrap bottom of page with monochromatic fibers; secure to back of page. Mat photos with dark brown cardstock; double mat large photo on mesh before mounting on page. Die cut tags from metallic paper; punch hole and tie fibers. Embellish tags with mesh square and themed buttons. Print title and journaling on transparency; cut to size. Mount journaling blocks on page with small brads. Embellish title and journaling blocks with themed buttons.

Trudy Sigurdson

Letters to My Son

Wrap journaling in charming details

A mother-to-son conversation resounds on this beautiful spread. Mat light green cardstock with olive green cardstock. Cut two 2" strips of mesh; horizontally mat along bottom of pages. Mount knotted hemp string at top edge of mesh strip. Mat photos on olive green cardstock; mount along bottom of page. Attach flat eyelets to background between photos. Tie key charm and Chinese coin with beaded hemp; vertically wrap around large photo. Mount on page with photo corners. Print journaling on putty-colored cardstock; tear edges and brush with chalk. Cut two large tags from olive green cardstock; detail edges with fine-tip black pen. Punch circle; mount at top of tag and attach eyelet. Layer torn journaling blocks on tags and mesh. Wrap beaded jute string around top and bottom of tags. Tie jute at top of tag and around key before mounting on journal block. Stamp title words on putty cardstock; paper tear edges and brush with chalk. Layer paper-torn title words over mesh onto tag (created as described above); wrap title tag with hemp.

Trudy Sigurdson

Sepia-toned photos are beautiful but they can look flat. I love to use them on scrapbook pages but, when doing so, I like to use textiles on the spreads to add dimension and texture that the photos lack.

Trudy Sigurdson

Pumpkin Patch

Embellish preprinted papers with fibers

Brandi adds charm with seasonal dimensional details and fibers. Embellish preprinted paper tags with fibers by slicing the angled end; gently lift and punch a small hole to attach fibers. Cut coordinating patterned paper in shape of tag; tear in half and mount on first and third tag. Embellish with buttons layered over torn cardstock; mount cork scrap. Mat two photos on patterned paper; tear top edge before mounting on page. Tear out the middle of a shaded section; gently curl edges outward. Mount photo behind paper-torn "window." Crop small photos; mount on shaded areas. Mat large right-hand page photo on patterned paper; tear bottom edge. Punch holes at upper corners; tie fibers. Mount on page with self-adhesive foam spacers. Cut large tags from yellow cardstock; detail edges with chalk and pen. Attach eyelet at top of tags over punched leaf shape; tie fibers. Stamp title. Print journaling on yellow cardstock; detail edges with chalk and pen.

Brandi Ginn

Witchie, Witchie

Spin a fibered web

Diana catches the spirit of Halloween with a fiber web. Tear lower right corner of patterned paper; mount over orange cardstock. Punch large circle from orange cardstock; shade edges with purple chalk. Punch small holes in circle; tie sheer black ribbon before layering on black torn cardstock corner. Mat photo on purple paper; tear edges and brush with black chalk. Mount under black torn corner over patterned paper. Craft web from black embroidery thread; mount on lower right page corner. Tuck ends under torn patterned paper edge. Mount buttons, tied with purple and black embroidery thread, along torn pattered paper edge. Cut tag from patterned paper with printed journaling. Attach eyelet and tie fuzzy fiber; mount over crafted web. Layer die-cut spider over embroidery thread strip; mount on page with self-adhesive foam spacers. Write title on torn vellum block. Print journaling on vellum; cut and mount on page. Embellish title and journaling block with seed beads.

Diana Graham

Arizona Fall

Collect fibers in fall colors

Katherine ties together colors of the season with fibers and photos of a colorful Arizona autumn. Tear one edge of gold cardstock; mat on dark brown cardstock for background. Crumple and flatten light brown cardstock; apply metallic rub-ons with cotton swab. Double mat large photo; use textured cardstock for second mat. Punch leaf from thin copper square; emboss and stamp name and date in leaf and square. Tie copper leaf to fibers; wrap around photo mat. Print title on dark gray cardstock; silhouette cut and apply copper metallic rub-ons with fingertips. Double mat letter "O" on light and dark brown distressed cardstock. Slice ¼" strips of rust cardstock; cut into ½" pieces. Mount around "O" to look like a sun. Mat series of three photos on a single cardstock strip; mount at bottom of left page. Double mat photo series on right page; mount the center photo on strip with self-adhesive foam spacers. Print title word and journaling on ivory cardstock; detail edges with black pen and tan chalk. Cut title block to size; mount on page with small brad. Slice a 1" strip of textured cardstock; mount at top of right page. Attach eyelets at each end. Tie fibers to each side of punched copper square; string through eyelets.

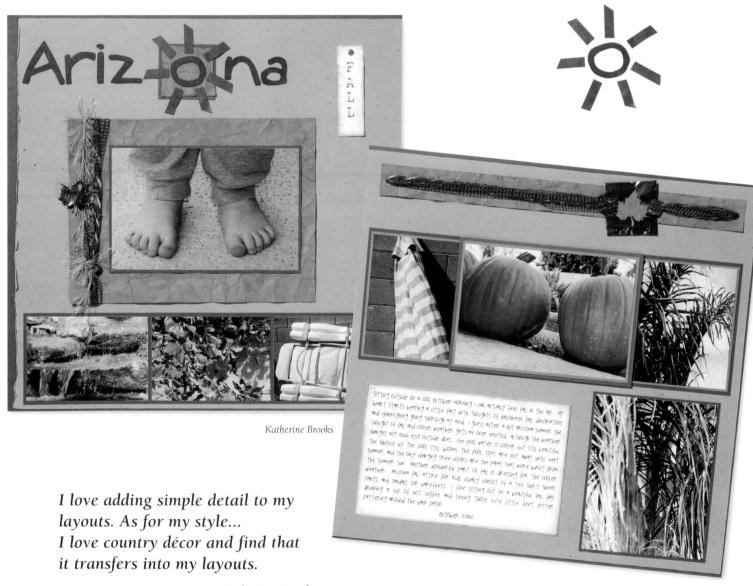

Katherine Brooks

I love adding simple detail to my layouts. As for my style...
I love country décor and find that it transfers into my layouts.

Katherine Brooks

A Mother's Pride

Add monochromatic texture with fiber and seashell borders

Subtle, textured details call attention to Trudy's black-and-white seaside photos. Print title, journaling and poem on light blue cardstock; cut to size. Crumple and flatten title; mat on blue cardstock and mount at top of page with small silver brads. Cut poem into small squares to fit inside die-cut vellum envelopes. Attach silver eyelets to poem tags and tie fiber at top. Single and double mat photos. Using a craft knife and straightedge ruler, slice two windows in light blue cardstock larger than the large matted photo and printed journaling block. For left-hand page, lay cardstock with sliced window over darker blue cardstock. Mount fibers and small seashells behind window. Wrap light blue cardstock with fibers before mounting on dark blue cardstock background. Repeat the process for right-hand page journaling block. Stamp descriptive words and location on light blue cardstock; cut to size, crumple and flatten. Mount with small silver brads.

Trudy Sigurdson

Within You I See Myself

Wrap a pretty page in ribbon

A shiny hair ribbon ties up this feminine page while metallic details reflect the shine of a mother's love. Mat blue cardstock with darker blue cardstock. Slice two 5" strips of patterned paper; vertically mount at outside edges of each page. Knot ribbon; vertically mount along edge of patterned paper strip. Single and double mat photos on light green cardstock. Emboss edges of double-matted photos with green ink. Attach eyelets at upper corners of second mat. Print journaling on green cardstock; cut into four journaling blocks. Press edges of journaling blocks on tan stamp pad. Print descriptive words on transparency; cut to size and mount over bottom of large photos with small silver brads. Stamp title letters at bottom of page with black ink. Print date on green cardstock; insert into concho and mount on page.

My daughter is a "pink" girl, but I find it difficult to buy scrapbook papers in the shades of pink that she most often wears. So I often choose to photograph her in black-and-white so that I can select the colors without worrying about matching her outfits. These are also the colors I love best and those that support my page theme.

Katherine Brooks

Katherine Brooks

When a Child Is Born

Collage textiles for decorative effect

A collection of sheer, metallic and natural elements are collaged on textured paper tiles for a soft monochromatic layout. Pink crumpled, flattened and ironed cardstock is cut into 3¾" squares and mounted on rose cardstock. Horizontally layer paper lace across top of page. Stitch matted photo secured with photo corners to page over paper lace. Print journaling and date onto pink cardstock. Paper tear pink and white cardstock strips; mount at top of journaling block before stitching on page. Collage skeleton leaves, mica tiles, metal heart, buttons, dried flowers and leaves on page. Wrap bottom of page with tied sheer ribbon; tuck ribbon under edges of paper tiles.

Trudy Sigurdson

The Perfect Dress

Layer lace for a feminine look

Soft details enhance Holle's story of what it takes to find the perfect wedding dress. Print journaling on patterned vellum; tear edges and mount at upper left corner of mauve cardstock. Die cut title letters from felt and cardstock. Heat emboss cardstock letters with silver embossing powder. Layer title letters over vellum and lace strips; border with sparkled yarn. Stamp title word on pink cardstock; cut into ribbon shape and mount at top of page. Mat two photos together; mount over lace strip. Adhere dimensional stickers around photo.

Holle Wiktorek

Katherine Brooks

You Can't Hide Beautiful

Accent a border with ribbon

Gingham ribbon adds a textured touch to Katherine's feminine borders. Slice four 3" strips of patterned paper; horizontally mount at top and bottom of pages. Mount gingham ribbon over pink ½" torn paper strips at patterned paper's edge; wrap around to back of page and mount. Using craft knife and straightedge ruler, slice two cardstock photo frames, one larger than the other from mauve and green cardstock. Heat emboss mauve cardstock frame with pink metallic embossing powder; press heart stamp at top while still warm. Mount on green cardstock frame; layer over large photo. Mat balance of photos on green cardstock. Print title and journaling on vellum; tear edges of title block. Mount with embossed silver brads over pressed flower. Remove center of metal framed tag; layer over vellum journal block. Heat emboss small tag, stamp with heart while warm. Mount on photo with small silver brad.

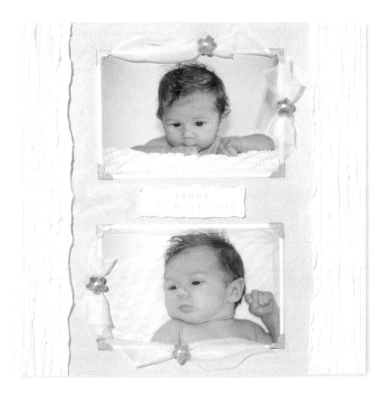

Jenna

Stitch a torn fabric background

Sheer fabric softly frames photos of this newborn. Mount photos on pink cardstock background with photo corners. Cut fabric to size of background cardstock; stitch around mounted photos. Cut out center of fabric over photos; gather on two sides and secure with stitched ceramic buttons. Tear two 1½" strips of white textured cardstock; gently curl edges. Vertically mount at outside edges of page. Stitch around entire page ¼" from edges. Wrap fibers on paper-torn borders, securing to back of page. Stamp title on white cardstock with lavender ink; tear edges and gently curl. Stitch around edges at center of page.

Trudy Sigurdson

Muriel

Stitch a floral bouquet

Torrey draws inspiration from dress details in a heritage photo with an embroidered silk ribbon bouquet. Using a craft knife and straightedge ruler, slice window $\frac{1}{2}$" smaller than photo into 12 x 12" light green cardstock. Mount photo behind light green cardstock. Slice a slightly larger window into $11\frac{1}{4}$ x $11\frac{1}{4}$" dark green cardstock. Freehand draw floral design on dark green cardstock with pencil. Pierce holes into cardstock before stitching with silk ribbon using a variety of embroidery stitches. Mount stitched cardstock frame over light green cardstock frame. Die cut letters into white cardstock. Rub letters on a watermark stamp pad and dip in gold ultra thick embossing powder. Heat from the underside with embossing gun until melted. Mount at bottom of dark green cardstock.

Torrey Miller

Torrey Miller

Dian Frybarger

Craft a memory board with fabric and ribbon

Torrey nestles vintage photos on a fabric-covered french memory board. Cut fabric to size of cardstock; mount, securing edges to back of page. Cut pieces of grosgrain ribbon to border and criss-cross on page. Layer ribbon as shown; wrap edges around back of page and secure. Mount small buttons at ribbon intersections. Print title and date on yellow cardstock; trim with decorative scissors and mat. Freehand craft fruit and leaves from colored cardstock to match fabric design; detail with chalk. Mat photos on gray, coral and yellow cardstock trimmed with decorative scissors. Nestle title block and photos under ribbon on page.

A Pinch of Sugar

Stitch designs on vellum tags

Simple designs stitched on vellum tags are a sweet addition to Heidi's page that tells the tale of two girls. Print journaling on tan cardstock. Use printed card-stock as first mat for two double-matted photos. Write balance of title on vellum tags with brown pen. Punch hole at top of vellum tags; string brown ribbon through hole; mount under double-matted photos. Tie brown ribbon into small bows; mount at bottom of vellum title tags. Trace leaf and butterfly design onto vellum tags with pencil. Carefully stitch with tan and brown embroidery thread. Punch small holes in vellum tags; tie together with ivory ribbon.

Heidi Schueller

My pages are original to the core. I may use idea books as a start, but when I'm done, nothing is the same as the idea I looked at.

Heidi Schueller

First-Grader

Tie fibers to a colored slide mount

Katherine twists fibers together to secure a colored slide mount holding the title to her page. Mat green cardstock with burgundy cardstock. Slice a 2" piece of patterned paper; tear bottom edge. Create a second patterned paper by rubbing a brown ink pad over neutral card-stock. Slice a 1½" strip of inked patterned paper; tear bottom edge. Horizontally layer patterned papers together; mount at top of green cardstock. Attach two eyelets ½" from edges of page. Color slide mount with pigment powder and adhesive; detail edges of slide with gold leaf pen. Punch small holes at sides of slide mount; attach eyelets. Print title on vellum; cut to size and mount behind colored slide mount. Tie fibers to eyelets on slide mount; string through eyelets on page. Secure fibers on back of page. Mount photos at page center. Horizontally and vertically mount green ribbon around photos. Attach small brads at ribbon intersections. Print journaling on neutral cardstock; cut to size. Press edges of journaling block onto brown ink pad; mount at bottom of page.

Katherine Brooks

Spring
Embellish with embroidered stickers

April showers brought May flowers to Holle's layout with colorful embroidered stickers. Slice a 3¼" strip of patterned vellum and a 3¾" strip of white cardstock; tear one edge of each strip. Horizontally layer at top of page over teal cardstock. Mount embroidered sticker as title over torn layered strips. Horizontally wrap fibers around page securing at back. Crop small photos into tag shapes. Mat tag-shaped photos on pink cardstock. Mount flower eyelet at top of tags; tie with fibers. Mount photo tags at top of page. Mat cropped photo on patterned paper. Print journaling on white cardstock; cut to size. Mat on pink cardstock with paper-torn edge. Embellish photo and journaling mats with flower embroidery stickers.

Holle Wiktorek

For me, the highlight of becoming a Memory Makers Master was watching my mom have so much fun with it. When we go to a scrapbook store together she insists on telling everyone. I tell her that no one cares, but she keeps on talking!

Diana Graham

Diana Graham

How Sweet It Is
Layer tag with textured details

Diana's memo board holds a tag layered with textured papers and dry embossed die-cut flowers. Diagonally layer yellow ribbon across patterned paper; wrap ends around edges and mount to back of page. Mount stitched buttons at ribbon intersections. Mat photos on solid and patterned paper. Stamp flower photo corners; silhouette cut and mount on one photo. Print title and journaling on vellum; cut to size. Paper tear edges of journaling block; mat on patterned paper and mount on page with fibers and beaded hat pin. Layer title block with mesh, untwisted paper yarn and paper-torn patterned paper on tag. Attach flower eyelet; tie with fibers. Stitch bottom of tag and mount small button. Die cut flowers and leaves from magenta, orange and green paper; dry emboss around the edges. Layer flowers and title tag on page.

Love...

Illustrate a lasting bond with stitching

Diana uses a common metaphor to reflect a strong bond between friends. Mat two photos on one piece of pink cardstock. Horizontally tear matting under bottom photo. Stitch torn pieces back together with black embroidery thread in a zigzag formation, leaving space between the pieces. Print title and journaling along right side of dark pink cardstock background. Cut a piece of printed vellum into square; mount on page. Pierce holes in vellum with paper piercer to ensure even stitches. Stitch around vellum square with black embroidery thread. Brush pink chalk on journaling to highlight specific words.

I'm not a shy person and my pages are a reflection of my personality. I've tried to work with other styles, but it seems that most often, whatever I create turns out colorful!

Diana Hudson

Diana Hudson

Do Not Peek

Add texture with a sheer element

Sheer mesh fabric tied with colored ribbons becomes a textured border on Valerie's page. Mat two photos on pink and green cardstock. Circle cut large circle from white cardstock. Press edge of circle on watermark stamp pad; heat emboss with silver embossing powder. Circle cut third photo; mat on embossed circle. Attach eyelet at top of embossed circle; tie with fringed fibers. Stamp flower design on vellum; print journaling over stamped design. Cut to size and tear top and bottom edges. Mount on page with colored eyelets. Rub colored chalk on metal-rimmed tags; tie with blue yarn. Mount alphabet beads on tags. Cut large piece of mesh fabric. Mount on left side of page, leaving slack in the fabric. Gather together at center and tie with sheer, colored ribbon. Cut out center of square metal rimmed tags; layer with flower button over mesh fabric scrap. Mount metal frame over blue cardstock scrap; write date at center with blue pen.

Valerie Barton

Brandi Ginn; Photos Cummings, Aliso Creek, California

Beach Bums

Mat photos with stitched fabric squares

Brandi brings the crisp, clean look of California's relaxed lifestyle to her layout with photos matted on stitched pieces of blue linen fabric. Slice a 3¾" strip of patterned paper; tear one side and mount as a border over light blue patterned paper. Gently curl edges. Cut a 5 x 7" piece of patterned paper; tear two edges before mounting at bottom right corner of right page. Stamp title words on background paper with gold ink and heat emboss. Mat photos on pieces of blue stitched fabric. Stamp seashell designs on white cardstock; detail with colored chalks and silhouette cut. Randomly mount on page, use self-adhesive foam spacers on a few for dimension. Encapsulate seashells under watch crystal; wrap fiber around the edge. Stamp "sand" with blue ink on white cardstock; mount large glass pebble over word on border strip. Print journaling on vellum; cut to size and mount over stamped seashell design. Tie fibers to swirl clips; attach to matted photos and border strip.

Sailing at Lake Granby

Craft thematic embellishments from fabric

Kelli takes inspiration from a day out on the lake with maritime accents crafted from fabric, eyelets and twine. Single and double mat a few photos on red and blue cardstock. Freehand cut photo corners from red cardstock for two photos. Craft sailboat sails from white fabric with stitched edges. Attach gold eyelets; string pieces together with twine. Mount atop freehand cut boat layered under freehand cut waves. Craft life preserver from white fabric cut into circle. Mount rectangles cut from red cardstock and twine over fabric circle. Freehand cut waves from blue cardstock; mount along bottom of second page. Die cut letters from red cardstock. Attach eyelets at left side of letters; stitch with frayed twine. Embellish first letter of title word by layering on stitched fabric and cardstock detailed with eyelets and twine.

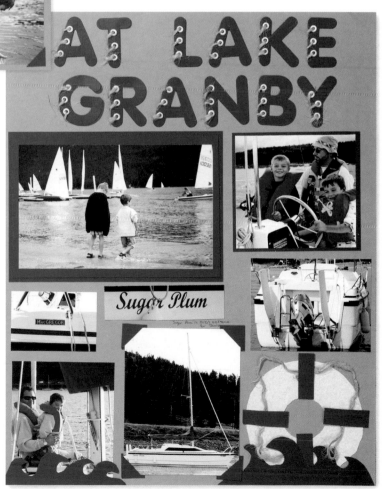

I'm not a seamstress, in fact I can't sew at all. So, when I use fabric on my pages I need to look for shortcuts. For example, I'll cut material from a piece of clothing or maybe an old ironing board cover in a way that allows me to utilize an edge that has already been stitched. Then I completely cover the material with adhesive to prevent other edges from unraveling.

Kelli Noto

Kelli Noto

Zoo Crew
Hide journaling under tied tags

Heidi's page hides journaling under buttoned tags tied together with embroidery thread. Slice ¾" and 1" strips of brown and golden yellow cardstock; tear one edge. Horizontally layer at top of page over rust cardstock background. Cut title letters; mat two times on brown and black cardstock and silhouette cut. Punch a small hole at top of each letter and in layered torn paper strip. Dangle title letters with small wire pieces curved into "S" shape through small punched holes. Double mat smaller photos on freehand cut tag shapes; score right side of tag ¼" from ends. Apply strong adhesive at scored edge of tags only so tags can lift to reveal journaling; mount on page. Mount buttons stitched with embroidery thread on tag; tie a 2½" piece of embroidery thread to buttons. Mount stitched buttons on page to the left of buttoned tag. Print journaling on cardstock; cut to size and mount under tags. Wrap 2½" piece of embroidery thread around button stitched to page to secure. Mat large photo on golden yellow cardstock; apply foam tape adhesive along three edges of photo mat. Mat again on blue cardstock. Print journaling; cut to size to fit inside of space between mattings. Stitch tied button to 1 x 2" strip of cardstock; mount strip behind journaling block with strong adhesive. Slide buttoned journaling block into space between mattings. Tie small buttons with embroidery thread; mount as a border on right side of page.

Heidi Schueller

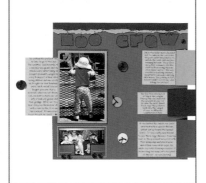

Funny Face
String fringed fibers through eyelets

Colorfully fringed fibers strung across Valerie's photos add an artistic and textured element to her layout. Tear a 4½" strip of mustard cardstock; mount vertically on yellow cardstock as a border. Gently roll edges with fingers. Mat photos on purple cardstock; mount on page. Stamp title words with blue and purple inks. Stamp letters and shape on small yellow cardstock strip; mount metal frame atop strip. Print journaling on golden yellow cardstock lightly stamped with square design. Tear all edges; mount on border. Attach eyelets on border and background cardstock. String fringed fibers through eyelets; secure at back of page. Mount purple buttons on page and border strip. Mount small golden yellow punched squares a bottom right corner.

Valerie Barton

Busy Bee

Stitch the whimsical flight of a busy bee

Heidi photojournals the happenings of her favorite busy bee with colorful clip art and stitched flight lines. Double mat photos on solid cardstock and patterned paper; mount on black cardstock background. Print title words and clip art; mat on yellow cardstock and silhouette cut around shapes and words. Print journaling on yellow cardstock; cut to size and mount alongside photos as shown. Pierce holes in cardstock with paper piercer; stitch flight lines with white embroidery thread.

I love stitching, in fact I'm teaching a class for scrapbookers who want to learn how to sew on their pages. I've enjoyed mixing mediums in my art ever since I was encouraged to do so when I attended the University. Mixing mediums adds dimension and interest.

Heidi Schueller

Heidi Schueller

Memphis

Detail border with sheer ribbon

Sheer ribbon strung through eyelets gives a delicate accent to Valerie's journaling and photos. Mat three photos on green cardstock; mount on patterned paper background. Mat one photo over torn vellum strip before matting on green cardstock. Tie sheer green ribbon at bottom of matted photo. Mat two landscape photos together to look like one panoramic photo on one large piece of green cardstock. Print title and journaling on vellum. Paper tear edges; mount on green cardstock. Attach silver eyelets at top and bottom of journaling block as well as on cardstock border with photos. String sheer green ribbon through eyelets; tie.

Valerie Barton

How much embellishing is enough? I generally take my cue from the photos. When they are streamlined and elements in the pictures are more linear, I tend to make my embellishments look the same. Here, a few strips of ribbon was enough to carry the theme and feel of the layout.

Valerie Barton

Being Your Mom

Dangle charms on fibers

Valerie's "charm-ing" photo mat dangles seashell charms tied to textured fibers. Slice three 2½" strips from two colors of green cardstock and green vellum. Paper tear one edge; vertically layer and mount at left side of page. Attach silver brad at top and bottom of layered border; vertically wrap fibers around brads. Double mat photo; tear second matting along bottom edge. Wrap fibers along bottom of second mat; tie silver seashell charms to fibers with thread. Print journaling on vellum; paper tear along top and bottom edges. Mount to page under matted photo and over torn vellum strips with silver eyelets. Print title; silhouette cut with craft knife. Cut tag from green cardstock. Attach eyelet; tie with fibers. Embellish tag with torn paper strip and die-cut seagull.

Valerie Barton

The Smile on Your Face

Embellish with buttons and lace

Valerie adds a feminine touch to patterned paper segments with dainty embellishments. Double mat photo on peach and tan cardstock; tear the top edge of peach mat. Brush torn edge with tan chalk. Wrap satin fiber around photo; tie together with button. Print title words on peach cardstock; mount 12 x 12" embossed vellum over peach cardstock. Using a craft knife, carefully slice a diagonal strip into embossed vellum; slide double matted photo into strip and adhere. Print title word on peach cardstock; silhouette cut. Paper tear a 5½ x 7½" piece of peach cardstock; brush tan chalk around torn edges. Using a craft knife and straightedge ruler, slice square and rectangular windows into cardstock. Mount vellum strip and photo behind cut windows; journal on vellum strip with peach gel pen. Tie fibers to buttons; mount under rectangular window. Layer torn cardstock with windows over vellum strip before matting on tan cardstock. Tie horizontally and vertically with lace and fibers. Cut two squares from patterned paper; mat one on torn cardstock square brushed with rose chalk and double mat the other. Slice a 1" strip from patterned paper; mat on tan cardstock. Stitch buttons to matted strip. Horizontally mount at bottom of page over lace strip.

Valerie Barton

Dressing alike...

...it's a sister thing.

Diana Hudson

I love heritage scrapbooking. I enjoy documenting previous generations for future generations.

Diana Hudson

Dressing Alike
Sew up fond memories

Diana documents her mother's love of sewing with machine-stitched journaling tags and photo mats. Print title onto lavender cardstock. Horizontally stitch a 7½" piece of vellum to patterned paper and mount at the center of the lavender cardstock. Mat lavender cardstock on green cardstock for background. Double mat one photo on purple solid and green patterned papers. Stitch buttons to purple patterned paper strip; mount at top of first matting. Mat photo on folded purple patterned paper; stitch around edges. Tie two photos together with sheer purple ribbon; mount stitched button where photos meet. Print journaling onto purple paper and vellum. Cut large journaling into tag shape. Mat on purple patterned paper; stitch around edges. Attach eyelet; tie fibers. Embellish with stitched buttons at lower right corner. Cut journaling on vellum to size; layer over purple patterned paper with sheer ribbon strips stitched around the edges. Attach vellum to ribbon-trimmed paper with beaded hat pin. Embellish with stitched buttons at lower right corner.

Cut small tag from purple patterned paper; mat on solid purple paper. Stitch around edges and attach eyelet. Tie sheer ribbon to tag; loop over button on journaling block as shown. Cut journaling for small tag to size; layer on tag under dimensional heart sticker.

Fringies
Stitch dimensional flowers

Stuffed and stitched flowers reflect the snugly comfort of a treasured blanket. Divide background into four quadrants; cut colored cardstock to fit quadrants and mount together on the back. Print title words on paper; trace onto 12 x 12" vellum with purple pen. Mount vellum over color-blocked background. Print large title word on vellum; color with brush pens. Stitch around edges of letters with purple embroidery thread; silhouette cut leaving a small border around stitched edge. Mount at top of page with self-adhesive foam spacers. Lightly pencil flowers, stems and leaves on vellum. Cut flowers out of vellum-layered background. Pierce along penciled design to ensure even stitches. Stitch layers together with purple embroidery thread along design lines. Mount gingham fabric behind cut-out flowers over fiber fill for dimensional flowers. Triple mat photo; color block third mat with two colors of cardstock. Attach beaded ribbon at the bottom of third mat. Mount embellished and matted photo at center with self-adhesive foam spacers.

Heidi Schueller

To Dance the Dream
Create fantasy with fringed fibers and embossed snowflakes

Torrey creates a sparkling winter fantasy with large and small snowflakes stamped and silhouette cut into unique designs. Stamp background with snowflake design using watermark stamp. Apply clear embossing powder and heat. Stamp more snowflake patterns and dust with pigment powders. Stamp snowflake designs on vellum. Heat emboss two snowflakes with lavender embossing powder and another with silver embossing powder; silhouette cut. Add sparkling details to another with glitter glue. Print title word on paper; trace onto vellum using watermark pen. Heat emboss with purple embossing powder. Silhouette cut around letters; layer on page over fringed fibers mounted on background. Write smaller title words on vellum with watermark pen; heat emboss with silver embossing powder. Cut to size and mount on page. Double mat largest photo; use torn mulberry paper for second matting. Mat remaining photos on white cardstock. Print journaling on vellum; tear edges and mount between photos.

Since I don't have my own kids, I love scrapping my "adopted" kids...my nephews and my best friend's daughter. I also love to scrap my artistic photos of "stuff"...scenery, textures...stuff...

Torrey Miller

Torrey Miller

frolicking

Malibu, California - 2002

Let a joy keep you. Reach out your
hands and take it when it runs by.

~Carl Sandburg

Baubles

Humans dating back to the Neanderthal have adorned their bodies and clothing with small objects such as animal bones and teeth, seashells and colorful stones. In the ancient world, beads were viewed as status symbols and were used for bartering in international trade. Stones, bone and other adornments were worn to ward off bad spirits and "lucky charms" dangled on bracelets and necklaces. In the early 20th century the popularity of decorative fashion jewelry boomed. Small lockets, trinkets, glass beads and family crests hung on bracelets and necklaces of the masses.

Flash forward to the art of scrapbooking, where baubles, trinkets and other unique embellishments are helping tell the story behind the photos and are adding their special brand of visual appeal. A large selection of baubles is available at craft stores. But other embellishments such as jewels, beads, buttons, ceramic tiles, charms, glass pebbles, lockets and old jewelry can be found everywhere from fabric stores to garage sales and dusty attics. Use baubles to embellish photo frames, string them to create borders, decorate photos, use them in a collage or in one of the other creative ways you'll find in this chapter.

Diana Graham

The Dance of the Leaves

Detail title with stitched buttons

Stitched buttons, in shades of orange and green, add a homespun touch to Diana's page. Tear edges of mustard paper; mat on orange cardstock with eyelets for background. Horizontally mount panoramic photo as border at top of left page. Print title words on vellum; cut to size. Attach eyelets at title block corners; tie together with fibers and mount on photo border. Mount stitched buttons on title blocks as shown. Single and double mat photos. Die cut frame from vellum; mount over photo on right page. Attach eyelets at corners; string fibers through eyelets and tie. Print journaling on tags; tie fibers and embellish with stitched buttons. Scrape edges of tags with scissors blade; add dimension to edges and around journaling with chalk.

Holle Wiktorek

Best Friends

Add decorative jewels and beads

There are many reasons Holle's mom is her best friend and they are clear in this loving page. Slice a 2" strip of blue cardstock; tear one edge and vertically mount at left side of page. Die cut hearts from red cardstock and title letters from cork. Embellish hearts with tinsel, beaded wire, glitter glue and fibers. Layer embellished hearts with letters on border strip with self-adhesive foam spacers. Paper tear tan and blue cardstock pieces; collage on page. Mount torn tan cardstock piece at upper right corner over tinsel shreds. Die cut title letters from red cardstock; mount on torn cardstock with small mesh scrap. Die cut frame from red cardstock; embellish with glitter glue, mesh scrap, fiber and swirl clip before mounting over photo. Circle cut two photos; mount on die-cut red cardstock circles. Attach blue fiber at back of photo circles; "hang" from flower brad attached to page. Print journaling on mulberry paper; tear edges and mat on red cardstock with torn and curled edges. Die cut wavy frame from red cardstock; embellish corners with blue jewels before matting on corrugated cardstock.

Joy in Blytheville

Add a touch of glitter to punched shapes

Holle decorates holiday memories with punched holly leaves in a variety of textures and shine. Use large letter stickers to create "Joy" title; embellish with ribbon and punched holly leaves. Mount letter stickers on black cardstock trimmed with gold glitter glue. Die cut small title letters from gold cardstock; mount along bottom of title block. Mat oval cut photo on green cardstock oval. Attach metal holly leaves with red eyelets above oval photo. Mat photos on green cardstock; apply gold glitter glue around edges of green matting. Layer matted photos on brown suede paper detailed with gold glitter glue dots. Adhere dimensional wreath sticker at bottom of suede paper between photos. On right page, mat photos on green cardstock. Craft a layered embellishment with punched oak and holly leaves. Mount photo at bottom of right page. Frame photo with punched holly leaves layered over punched oak leaves detailed with gold glitter glue. Mount small red beads at stems of holly leaves to look like berries. Print journaling on tan cardstock; cut to size and mat on green cardstock. Embellish with holly leaves punched from gold cardstock and tied together with red ribbon.

My favorite person to scrapbook is my husband. He makes me happy, and he has shown me things I would never have experienced. Although I scrapbook many events like birthdays, holidays, vacations and seasons, my favorite event to scrapbook is our anniversary.

Holle Wiktorek

Thomas and I stopped by his parents' house in Blytheville on the way to our last adventure before he left the country. We surprised Dad and Ma Cel with a new computer, monitor, and internet service. They surprised us with two accessories to our Snow Village collection: Hershey truck and moving van/movers figures. These were perfect because I love chocolate, and we have lived in three houses within the past year. They also allowed me to choose two new outfits at The New York Store as my Christmas gift. We enjoyed Dad's famous chicken wraps for dinner and a trip to the Dixie Pig during our visit.

Holle Wiktorek

My Little Man

Stitch a button border

Layers of torn paper are stitched together and secured with buttons to create a soft, textured background for Trudy's black-and-white photos. Tear eight 1½" strips of light blue paper; horizontally mount on light blue background matted with ivory cardstock. Machine stitch around three edges of page. Punch squares from blue paper; mount along outside edges of page at 2½" increments and machine stitch around square. Stitch buttons over squares to complete border. Mat photos on ivory cardstock; mount on page. Print title and journaling on transparencies; cut to size and mount in between torn strips on page. Embellish title and journaling blocks with stitched buttons. Print descriptive words on vellum. Cut vellum and white and blue cardstock into tag shapes. Layer printed vellum over diagonally torn blue cardstock layered on white tag. Stitch around edges of tag. Mount eyelet over punched square; tie fibers. Mount die-cut star to tag; embellish with button threaded with silver wire. Mount tags on page with self-adhesive foam spacers.

Trudy Sigurdson

58

friendship

braids

Friendship Braids

Dangle beads from braided embroidery thread

Diana re-creates her daughter's favorite hair embellishment as the perfect accent to dangle from a large slide frame. Print title and journaling on blue background cardstock. Mat photos on patterned paper. Trace slide frame onto patterned paper; cut out shape and mount on top of slide frame. Braid four colors of embroidery thread large enough to wrap around slide; leave ends long to dangle beads from. Add beads at loose ends and knot.

Michelle
Sydney
Rachel

I like to use large photos. I am photo-driven and think nothing should take away from the photos. When you enlarge a great photo it draws your eye and automatically takes center stage.

Diana Hudson

As I look back, I realize now that this was a defining moment in the friendship of these six-year-old girls. As constant companions for over two years, I had the pleasure of watching their friendship grow. On this day as they sat together having their hair braided alike, it occurred to me how intertwined their lives had become. The braiding was uncomfortable, yet they were determined to get through it together.

Diana Hudson

Light of My Life

Embellish tags with beaded wire

Valerie adds color and texture to hanging metal-rimmed vellum tags with beaded wire. Cut teal cardstock into a 7¾" square; tear two edges and mount on patterned paper background. Die cut title letters from teal cardstock; mount on page above torn cardstock square. Print balance of title words and journaling on vellum; tear into strips. Tear seven more strips of vellum; chalk torn edges with pastel colors. Layer title vellum strip over die cut title letters. Weave together printed and plain vellum strips over torn teal cardstock square in an under/over fashion. Slide cropped photo under a few vellum strips to secure. Attach eyelet at lower right corner of second photo; mount at an angle next to title words. Tear a hole from center of vellum and metal tag; wrap tag with beaded wire and punch hole at top of tag through remaining vellum. String fiber through small hole and and attach through eyelet on photo. Embellish other vellum and metal tag with beaded wire bent into "K" shape. Punch hole in vellum; attach fiber through hole and loop around vellum strip. Complete page by wrapping fibers around top of page; secure ends at back of page.

Valerie Barton

Layout design comes fairly easily for me. I find journaling more difficult. I keep a notebook close by to sketch ideas and I've started to write little excerpts in it also. It helps me to write a little and come back a day or two later and write some more.

Valerie Barton

After running in and out of the house for an hour, watching her <u>Snow White</u> video, and lining her babies up on the couch, Jayce watered the flowers Honey and I worked three hours to plant and arrange. Although our flowers are bright and beautiful, my excitement is watching Jayce grow and learn everyday!

Holle Wiktorek

Flowers

Embellish patterned paper with beads

Holle adds sparkling gold beads to flowers silhouette cut from patterned paper. Slice a 3½" strip of blue patterned paper; tear one edge and horizontally mount over pink patterned paper background. Silhouette cut flowers from patterned paper. Embellish center of flowers with gold beads. Mat photos on green patterned paper. Silhouette cut green leaves from patterned paper; embellish leaves with glitter glue. Mount leaves with self-adhesive foam spacers at bottom of matted photos. Print journaling on patterned vellum and embossed cardstock; cut to size and tear edges. Mount vellum journaling block on gold textured paper with small brads. Cut title letters from green cardstock using letter template.

A Treasured Time
Display heart-shaped trinkets

Diana stitches together a pocket full of treasures. Stamp words on ivory cardstock with pink ink. Cut vellum to fit on top of ivory background; tear top of vellum to form pocket before stitching three sides to page. Mount photos on ivory and pink cardstock. Texture edges of matting by scraping with scissors blade. Stamp photo corners; silhouette cut and mount at two corners of one matted photo. Mount eyelet at the top and slightly off-center of one photo; tie sheer ribbon through eyelet. Mount one photo behind vellum pocket; mount others atop vellum. Mount one small photo behind silver frame. Tear stamped heart; crumple and shade with pink and tan chalk. Mount silver letter over stamped word. String sequins on embroidery thread; mount under stamped word. Stitch heart button to stamped heart with pink embroidery thread. Stamp title on torn ivory cardstock strip; chalk edges. Layer over large patterned heart tag with dangling charms tied with fibers. Print journaling on ivory cardstock; tear edges and chalk. Mat on pink paper with torn edges. Stuff a small chalked envelope with a silver heart charm, vellum and patterned paper heart. Tie silver heart charm with beaded embroidery thread. Punch heart from ivory cardstock; ink around edges and heat emboss with ultra thick embossing enamel. Gently bend and crack when cooled to give the look of antiqued broken glass. Layer at bottom right corner under photo and mount.

Diana Graham

You
Shape title letters with baubles

It's all about "her," on this bright page on which beaded wire, buttons and sequins are shaped into title letters. String fibers at top and bottom of green cardstock background; wrap around edges and secure to back of page. Mat photo on blue cardstock. Cut six ½" slices at top of mat; weave torn patterned vellum strip through slices. Embellish with beads on matting. Print journaling on plain and patterned vellum. Paper tear around specific words; mount torn pieces on vellum with journaling. Tear edges of vellum title block; layer over torn patterned vellum strip on top of blue cardstock. Mount dimensional hearts on square metal-rimmed tags before layering on patterned vellum. Attach small brad at right edge of vellum title block. Heat emboss two or three layers of copper ultra thick embossing enamel on precut mini-mat; stamp flower design with black ink in last layer while still warm.

Valerie Barton

Torrey Miller

When taking photos of children, I like to use a zoom lens. I stand halfway across the backyard and snap away without interfering in their space and ruining the spontaneity. Often, when you get up close and personal with kids, they stop what they are doing and just give you cheese.

Torrey Miller

Bubbles

Create iridescent bubbles

Torrey captures unburstable bubbles on her page by mounting watch crystals over small circles of patterned vellum. Mount pieces of patterned vellum over lavender cardstock before mounting on page. Cut squares of colored cardstock into various sizes; layer over a purple cardstock background. Mat photos on white cardstock. Cut circles from patterned vellum to fit under watch crystals; randomly mount vellum under watch crystals on page as shown. Use a template to create title letters from blue and lavender cardstock. Mount one letter with self-adhesive foam spacers for dimensional interest. Mount bubble blower die cut; add details with black pen. Mount watch crystal atop die cut.

Bubbly, Sudsily

Craft dimensional bubbles

Heidi creates her own sparkling bubbles with computer-generated art coated with clear micro beads. Horizontally and vertically mat photos on vellum with torn edges. Attach six eyelets to vellum between photos. String beaded wire through eyelets; wrap ends of wire into swirls and bend over vellum to secure. Mount embellished photo mats on blue patterned paper background. Cut title letters from purple cardstock using lettering template. Mat on silver metallic cardstock; silhouette cut. Horizontally and vertically mount under torn vellum strips attached to page with eyelets. Silhouette cut computer-generated bubbles; mount clear micro beads with two sided adhesive tape. Randomly mount beaded bubbles on page. String clear beads on wire; pierce small holes into patterned paper background and attach.

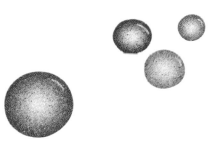

Micro beads are messy to use so if you don't like working with messy stuff, you're going to find them a challenge. Working with micro beads is a bit like adding sprinkles to a sugar cookie. But unlike sprinkles, beads aren't sticky, don't dye your fingers and clean up easily!

Heidi Schueller

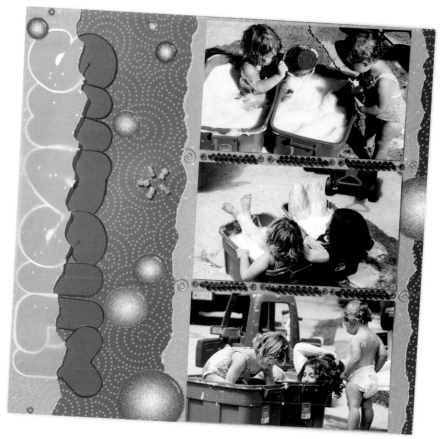

Heidi Schueller

Diana Graham

You Make My Heart Leap!

Capture frogs in a shaker box

Diana captures small ceramic amphibians in a tag-shaped shaker box. Mat 4¼" patterned paper strip on white cardstock; vertically mount on patterned paper background with eyelets. Single and double mat photos on yellow, white and green cardstock. Silhouette cut preprinted die cuts; embellish hearts with buttons. Mount title block, heart and frog die cuts with self-adhesive foam spacers. Print journaling on transparency; cut to size and mount under title block. Cut two tags from white cardstock for shaker box; detail edges with green pen and green and yellow chalk. Punch "window" in one tag; mount piece of transparency behind punched window. Mount die cut heart to top of tag with eyelet; embellish with small buttons. Adhere two layers of foam tape on back of embellished tag around edges. Mount frogs to plain tag making sure they will show through window of embellished tag when mounted together. Seal shaker box. Mount eyelet to patterned paper strip; string embroidery threads through eyelets on page and tag. String letter beads on embroidery thread; mount to page through eyelets attached to background between photos.

Kids

Add realistic details with pre-made embellishments

Dragonflies land among a collection of real twigs and hand-crafted leaves and grass. Mat green patterned paper with dark green cardstock. Mount large strip and small square of mesh over patterned paper. Mat photos on ivory cardstock and layer on page over mesh. Print journaling on vellum; tear around edges and mount at bottom right corner of page. Cut title letters from light green cardstock; mat and silhouette cut. Freehand cut leaves and grass from green cardstock. Lightly score along leaf and grass vein lines, bend gently. Mount on page with self-adhesive foam spacers among real twigs and pre-made dimensional dragonflies.

Torrey Miller

You Are My Sunshine

Dangle beaded tags

A collection of seed beads in shades of yellow are adhered to dangling metal-rimmed vellum tags as a visually interesting border embellishment. Slice a 2½" strip of yellow cardstock; crumple and flatten for a textured look. Paper tear one edge; attach eyelets before mounting at top of blue cardstock as a border. Cut tags from green cardstock using template; stamp leaves and title before embellishing with buttons. Print journaling on ivory cardstock; cut to size and mount over green vellum strip with one torn edge. Punch hole through vellum metal-rimmed tag; mount beads with liquid adhesive. String sheer ribbon through hole and tie to eyelet on border. Freehand cut leaves from vellum; emboss line down leaves and gently curl edges together for dimension. Mount at center of pages as shown. Tear yellow mulberry paper into petal shapes; mount together to make a flower. Using a craft knife, slice an ultra thin strip of yellow cardstock; mount as flower's stamen. Double mat photos on blue and yellow cardstock; detail second mat of one photo with beads.

I started scrapbooking to keep a record of my children's events from school. It soon became a creative outlet for me personally. Now I use it as therapy. If I'm having a bad day all I have to do is work on my pages and the problems don't seem as impending doom.

Valerie Barton

Valerie Barton

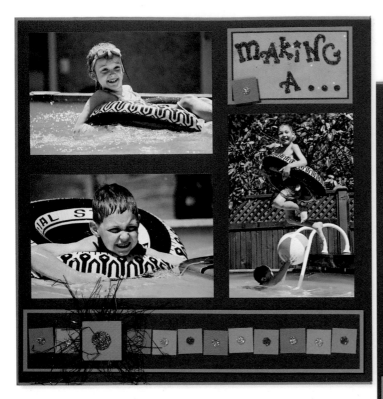

Trudy Sigurdson

Making a Splash

Add a sparkling splash of color

Trudy's striking choice of colors is enhanced with glittered geometric designs layered on a black background. Slice three 1¾" wide strips of black cardstock; mat on teal cardstock. Mount at bottom of two pages as a border and at the center of third page. Craft sparkling geometric embellishment from layered punched shapes: punch 31 small squares from colored cardstock. Adhere blue, silver and teal glitter to white cardstock with double-sided adhesive. Punch 31 small circles from glittered cardstock; mount glittered circles on small punched squares. Punch four large circles from blue glittered cardstock; mount on large teal punched squares. Mount large and small squares on border strips as shown; mount large squares over black tinsel for extra pizazz. Print journaling on speckled vellum; cut to size and double mat. Embellish top of journaling block with two small and one large punched squares with glittered circles layered over tinsel as shown. Mount photos on page. Print title words on cardstock; silhouette cut and embellish with glitter. Mount on double-matted speckled vellum. Embellish title block with geometric designs.

Jewel of the Pool

Accent elements with jewels

Diana showcases her little mermaid with a paper-piecing kit embellished with sparkling jewels. Assemble paper-piecing kit into mermaid; embellish crown with jewels and mount at bottom of page over patterned paper. Mat one photo on vellum; freehand cut edges in wavy shape and embellish with jewel. Cut title letters from blue cardstock; mount on page and embellish with jewels. Mount cropped photos on right page. Punch circles from blue patterned paper to fit inside metal-rimmed tags. Adhere sticker letters on circle tag; mount in between large title words. Attach eyelet to second tag; tie with ribbon. Make a shaker box out of a metal-rimmed tag by first cutting out the white center. Cut two clear circles from transparency; mount one to back of metal rim. Use two circle punches, one larger than the other, to make a circle frame out of foam. Mount foam frame to back of transparency; fill with beads and mount second transparency to back of foam frame. Finally, mount shaker tag to page with clear adhesive. Print journaling on vellum; cut to size and mount on page. Embellish with jewels at corners.

Diana Hudson

I'm not a trendy kind of woman. I tend to dress in khakis and white shirts. The most "out there" I get is to add a splash of red or blue. I think that monochromatic color schemes more closely reflect my personal style.

Diana Hudson

Moo La La

Feature jazzy and jeweled die cuts

Trudy gives her page Las Vegas shine with glittered die cuts and sparkling jewels. Tear eight 2" strips of black cardstock. Lightly rub torn edges with liquid adhesive before dipping in black glitter. Brush off excess glitter; horizontally mount on black cardstock background. Mount two torn strips at top of page with self-adhesive foam spacers for a dimensional title block. Print title letters on black cardstock; silhouette cut letters. Lightly spray letters with spray adhesive; coat with lavender glitter. Mount title on torn cardstock strip at top of page. Single and double mat photos; mount on page. Print journaling on blue vellum; cut to size and layer on white cardstock before mounting on page. Die cut flowers from colored cardstock; spray with adhesive and coat with glitter. Mount star jewels on glittered flowers before layering on page. Randomly mount jewels on page as shown.

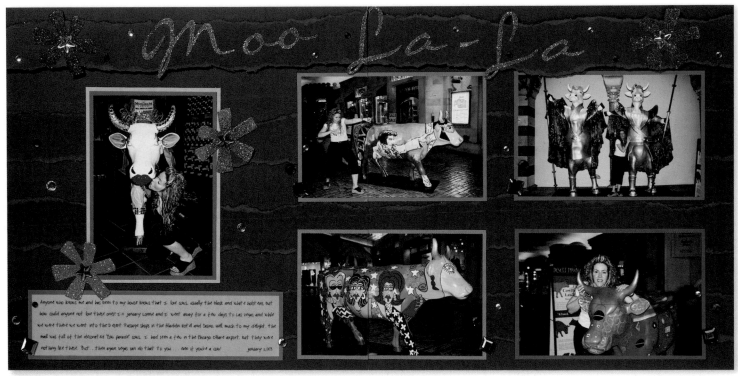

Trudy Sigurdson

A black background is a wonderful backdrop for brightly colored photos. It also allows jewels and glitter to shine vibrantly. It doesn't work for all spreads, but certainly is the perfect canvas to show off something like the glitz of Las Vegas.

Trudy Sigurdson

beaver lake school
grade four
september two thousand two

Trudy Sigurdson

First Day of School

String beads on wire

Thin wire, sparsely strung with delicate beads, adds an elegant touch to Trudy's page. Slice a 7" strip of lavender cardstock; vertically mount over purple cardstock for background. Mat photos on white cardstock; mount on page as shown. Print title on white cardstock; cut to size and add pen detail around edges. Color empty spaces in title letters with pencil crayons. Mount title block over lavender cardstock strip. Slice 1" strips of patterned vellum; layer and mount at top of page and on white cardstock strip. Mount button tied with fibers atop layered vellum strips. Stamp name on title block. Punch small hole at top of vellum tag; tie with string and "hang" from vellum strip over stamped name. Embellish title block with buttons and silver star. Stamp journaling at bottom of page. String wire with beads. Lay beaded wire on page; pierce small holes in cardstock at one end. Feed wire through hole and bend ends toward page to secure; wrap other wire end around edge of page and secure with tape.

Winter

Shake up seasonal fun

Diana frames title and journaling blocks with sparkling snow-filled windows. Mount $11\frac{1}{2}$ x $11\frac{1}{2}$" piece of patterned vellum paper over white cardstock of the same size; mat on purple cardstock. Attach eyelets at corners. Mount photos on purple cardstock. Create title and journal shaker boxes: Print title and journaling on vellum; cut to size. Cut purple paper, patterned vellum and transparency to size of title and journal blocks. Tear out window at center of purple paper; mount transparency to back of torn window. Adhere foam tape to back of top layer; mount to patterned vellum, making sure to fill with shaved ice before sealing. Embellish outsides of shaker boxes with beads and punched snowflakes layered with jewels. Cut two tags from stamped cardstock. Slice window in one tag; mount transparency behind window. Rub edges of tag onto blue ink pad; attach eyelet to tag and tie fibers. Adhere double-sided foam tape around edges of window on back of tag; fill with punched snowflakes and beads before sealing. Write date on small tag; tie with fiber and hang from punched and embellished snowflake.

Diana Graham

Sweet n' Sour

Mount real dimensional embellishments

Torrey's thematic page offers good fortune with real Chinese coins and chopsticks layered amongst a die-cut fortune cookie. Stamp blue cardstock with Chinese lettering; mat stamped cardstock with dark blue cardstock. Tear a 1" strip of dark blue cardstock; horizontally mount at top of page with self-adhesive foam spacers. Heat emboss cardstock with copper embossing powder; freehand cut triangles to shape into title letters. Mount title letters on torn cardstock strip at top of page. Tear a 2½" strip of pink paper; horizontally mount over background near the bottom of the page. Tear a 1" strip of dark blue cardstock; layer over pink torn paper strip. Mat photos on white cardstock; mount atop torn cardstock strips. String fibers with Chinese coins; mount over torn pink paper strip securing ends at back of page. Print "fortune" journaling on white cardstock; cut to size. Mount die-cut fortune cookie and chopsticks on page with self-adhesive foam spacers and glue dots. Slide fortune into fortune cookie.

Torrey Miller

Torrey Miller

Fish

Embellish fish tales with colorful lures

Colorful fishing lures embellish special memories of a dedicated fisherman. Rub black, yellow and red cardstock over texture plates for a subtle dimensional look. Slice a 2½" strip of yellow and red textured cardstock; paper tear one edge before vertically mounting at sides of page. Gently curl edges with fingers. Cut title letters using template from red textured paper; paper tear around edges of letters. Mount atop torn yellow cardstock border with self-adhesive foam spacers. Weave jute string around letters on border. Using an oval cutting system, cut two oval frames from yellow and red cardstock. Vertically tear red oval cardstock frame in half as shown; layer over yellow cardstock frame with self-adhesive foam spacers. Mount photo behind oval mat. Mount colorful fishing lures on border strips and photo mat; mount fishing pole on red border strip. Print journaling on white cardstock; tear edges and gently curl with fingers.

Bathtub
Frame a photo with ceramic tiles

Kelli's unique family portrait, set in a bathtub full of bubbles, is framed with with rows of shiny ceramic tiles as a thematic dimensional embellishment. Mat photos on black cardstock. Double mat large photo, leaving room for border embellishment. Mount tiles at top and bottom of second matting. Print title and journaling on gray cardstock; mat on black cardstock. Mount matted photos and journaling on blue background cardstock.

I hide behind the camera and collect little 4 x 6" slices of life to call my own. I put these little rectangles into scrapbooks so I can show my children how much they are loved. There are very rarely any photos of me, unless I accidentally shoot my own shadow.

Kelli Noto

Why a Picture in The Bathtub?

There was this big, blank wall right above the bathtub in the master bathroom. I looked and looked for some art that would work, but came up empty handed. The classic art seemed too formal for such a utilitarian space, and more modern pieces didn't work in the art-deco styling of the room either. Nothing seemed to fit. We had teased before that the bathtub would be big enough for the whole family to bathe at the same time. So, I thought, "Why not?" We all put on our swimsuits, filled the tub with bubbles, and snapped away. The neighbors must have thought we were crazy when they saw the camera's flash, but I was happy with the resulting photographs.

Kelli Noto

Swim
Hook a fish border

Tiny fish charms playfully dangle from small metal hooks under a beaded wire frame. Mat photos on light blue cardstock; mount at bottom of page. Mount two photos on one piece of light blue cardstock, leaving room for title and embellishment. Punch title letters; heat emboss with blue embossing powder. Mount title letters between two photos. Cut wire long enough to frame around both photos; string with beads. Mount beaded wire around photos as shown. Secure beaded frame with ½" pieces of wire bent into a U-shape; place wire over beaded wire and push ends through cardstock to back of page. Twist wire together on back of page to secure; press ends and flatten against page. Attach fish charms to metal hooks; mount under beaded frame with glue dots.

Kelli Noto

I love clay! It's economical and versatile. I can control its bulkiness as well as color it with rub-ons, embossing powders, stamp it, leave it plain. It's great for a title, like the "Baby" on this page or for other embellishments.

Katherine Brooks

Baby

Mold embossed clay letters

Embossed and stamped letters formed from clay headline Katherine's story. Double mat a $10\frac{7}{8}$" square piece of patterned paper on green and mustard cardstock; attach small brads at corners of patterned paper. Mat photos and mount on patterned paper. Stamp upper left and lower right corners of left page with geometric pattern. Print journaling on cream cardstock; cut to size. Press edges on ink pad and detail with black pen. Mat small photos on green cardstock; mount at bottom of journaling block. Using a craft knife and straight-edge ruler, slice a $\frac{1}{2}$" frame from green cardstock; slice a $\frac{3}{8}$" frame from patterned paper. Layer together and wrap with copper wire. Mount over large photo with self-adhesive foam spacers. Mold polymer clay into a large rectangle. Cut title letters from clay. Heat emboss with copper ultra thick embossing enamel; while enamel is still warm press in patterned stamp. Mount on page above journaling block.

Katherine Brooks

Sea Glass Beach

Sculpt wire into freeform designs

Torrey incorporates contemporary wire designs embellished with glass beads. Stamp seashells and dots on background with watermark stamp for a subtle patterned background; mat on teal cardstock. Mat photos on white cardstock; mount on page. Print title and journaling on patterned vellum. Tear strips of blue and green vellum. Cut wire and bend and curl into freeform shape; string beads as you proceed. Mount atop torn vellum strips as shown. Using a craft knife, slice a window for 3-D keeper; fill with collected sea glass and seal on back. Cut a frame to fit around 3-D keeper from green cardstock.

Most often, a page theme and photos dictate the embellishments on a spread. However, there have been times when I knew that I wanted to try a new embellishment technique and shot photos that would work specifically with it. You use a different part of your brain when you work in that direction.

Torrey Miller

Torrey Miller

Scrapbooking allows me to combine all the crafts I love, including needlework and paper arts, resulting in a page I will treasure forever.

Diana Hudson

Home

Collage decorative elements

Diana's collection of decorative elements is displayed on a crafted memo board. Cover matte board with color copied blueprints; wrap around edges and mount to back of board. Cut ribbon strips; mount diagonally, securing ends to back of board. Attach flower nailheads at ribbon intersections. Before matting black background cardstock on gray cardstock, paper press edges in gold ink. Mount memo board to top of black cardstock. Stamp house design on white cardstock with blue ink; cut to size and press edges onto blue ink pad. Mount metal letter at lower left corner before securing under ribbon. Tie clock charm with embroidery thread; dangle from ribbon. Mount laminate chips, fabric swatch and clipped paint color cards on board, securing under ribbon as shown. Mount glass "love" pebble atop small tassels. Print part of title on gray cardstock; cut into tag shape. Cut large title letters from burgundy cardstock; mount on tag. Press edges of tag onto blue ink pad for decorative edging. Attach eyelet over small blue cardstock strip; tie with burgundy ribbon. Mount small photos behind metal frames; tie with burgundy ribbon before mounting to page. Punch photos into square and rectangle shapes; mount on right page.

Diana Hudson

He's Leaving on a Jet Plane

Embellish a torn frame with baubles

Words could not describe how hard it was for Holle to say goodbye to her husband for a year of service overseas. She does her best with a collage of photos, thematic patterned paper pieces and strips of torn cardstock. Cut pieces of patterned paper along design lines; collage with torn pieces of colored cardstock over burgundy and brown cardstock backgrounds. Die cut title letters from brown and blue cardstock; assemble at the top of both pages. Mat photos on blue and tan cardstock; tear one edge before mounting on collaged background. Print journaling; paper tear edges and mount on page with silver star brads. Tear out center of corrugated cardstock; adhere focal photo behind torn window. Embellish with letter pebbles, beads and patterned paper strips. Wrap corners with wire before mounting at center of right page.

Holle Wiktorek

I don't care if others see a page as "busy" as long as I like it. We all view art through different eyes. I believe that what is really important is making sure that you have a strong title and focal picture on every spread.

Holle Wiktorek

live

love

laugh

Alex at Beckwith Park, July 1st, 2001

Children will not remember you for the material things you provided,

but for the feeling that you cherished them.

- Unknown

Paper

The art of paper making dates back to over 5,000 years ago when Egyptians experimented with cutting and layering thin, softened strips of a plant called Cyperous Papyrus. The plant's strips were pounded into a thin sheet and left in the sun to dry, becoming the perfect medium for record keeping, spiritual texts and works of art. Paper-making techniques progressed throughout the years and continents, working its way through Asia and the Muslim world, Europe and then westward to America. Johann Gutenberg, in the late 15th century, is credited with the birth of "modern paper." Paper making became industrialized in the 19th century and as it became more easily accessible, it proved to be a versatile medium for writers, artists, educators and designers.

Modern scrapbookers are now graced with a large variety of papers for both backgrounds and embellishments. The number of colors and textures available, let alone quality, makes paper THE invaluable source for scrapbookers. Linen, mulberry, vellum, textured or handmade, its uses are limited only by the imagination. We can roll it, texture it, tear it, distress it, layer it, weave it, fold it, stitch it, punch it and emboss it! Enjoy what the Masters have done with paper and see what unique designs you can be inspired to create.

Maize Maze

Layer a-mazing paper crafted cornstalks

Torrey's paper crafted corn maze opens up to reveal two pages of photos. Create the cover with a 12 x 12" piece of moss green cardstock. Cut a 10 x 12" piece of green cardstock; trim top into a wavy line. Vertically layer with 1¼" strips of light green cardstock mounted at ¾" increments; trim tops along wavy edge. Vertically slice entire page 7½" from left edge, creating the doors for page. Reposition pages together until cover is finished. Freehand cut leaves and corn husks from green cardstock. Bend leaves; mount some with self-adhesive foam spacers. Detail corn husks with chalk; mount atop each other with self-adhesive foam spacers. Mount fibers behind tops of husks. Cut title letters from mustard cardstock; mount on 5¾ x 2¾" moss green cardstock strip. Vertically slice title block down the middle before mounting on both sides of cover with self-adhesive foam spacers. Set cover "doors" aside. Slice 7½" and 4½" strips of green cardstock for insides of page "doors." Starting with the "door" panels, freehand slice maze design from mustard cardstock using a craft knife and straight-edge ruler. Print journaling on vellum; paper tear and mount over maze design on left "door" panel. Mount torn vellum strips over maze design with single matted photo on right "door" panel. Quadruple mat photo; tear top edge of last mat. Vertically mount fibers alongside photos on both panels. Cut date, names and balance of title from mustard cardstock. Mount date alongside photo. Single and double mat photos for center of fold-out page; tear one edge of second matting. Horizontally mount fibers at middle of page under title words on green cardstock strip. Mount names over torn vellum strips. Attach three 1 x 3" strips of light green cardstock to each side of back of center panel; position at top, center and bottom of page to serve as hinges. Mount front and back panels of left and right "doors" together over hinge strips.

Torrey Miller

Remember
Pave a pebbled pathway

Valerie crafts a detailed pebble pathway. Mat photos on tan cardstock; tear edges and brush with rust chalk before mounting on page. Stamp title on cream cardstock; embellish with torn cardstock, mulberry and handmade paper strips, mesh and freehand cut pebbles detailed with chalk. Wrap title block with fibers. Tear tan cardstock into path; layer over feather cut torn green cardstock to resemble blades of grass. Detail feathered edges with yellow chalk. Freehand cut pebbles from cardstock in shades of brown; shade with rust and brown chalks and mount along paper-torn pathway.

Valerie Barton

I have learned not to be afraid to expand my horizons beyond traditional scrapbooking. I belong to a local rubber stamp club and get so many new and unique ideas to use in my scrapbooks. When we share and learn creatively from each other, we all come out the better for it.

Valerie Barton

No Yucky Stuff

Layer an intricate freehand-cut design

Torrey re-creates the cow from a yogurt container into a clever design element. Slice large brown and blue cardstock strips; tear one edge. Vertically and horizontally layer over mustard cardstock matted with blue cardstock for background. Freehand draw cow head on brown velveteen paper; silhouette cut. Cut darker areas from cardstock and velveteen papers in shades of brown; layer pieces together to shape cow's face. Mount completed cow at left side of left page with self-adhesive foam spacers. Freehand cut spoon from silver cardstock; add shaded details cut from gray cardstock. Print title and journaling on cream cardstock and vellum. Cut title on cream cardstock into conversation bubble; mat and silhouette cut. Mount on page above cow with self-adhesive foam spacers. Cut journaling block to size; mount on page with small brads at corners. Die-cut "m's" from blue, mustard and brown cardstock. Slice a few and layer colors together for a visually interesting border. Single and double mat photos. Silhouette cut large photo; mount at bottom of page amongst die-cut "m's".

Torrey Miller

My entire family supports me in my scrapbooking obses-sion...my dad, sister and aunt faithfully and eagerly anticipate all my creations. And above all, none of this would be possible without the gifts that God has so graciously given me.

Torrey Miller

Dandelions

Punch and layer dimensional flowers

Torrey Miller

Torrey illustrates the life of a dandelion with punched shapes. Mat photos on yellow cardstock; mount atop mustard cardstock background. Write poem on yellow cardstock; cut to size and mount on page. Craft dandelion flowers from sun and flower shapes punched from yellow, tan and green cardstock and vellum. Freehand cut stems from brown cardstock. Layer among freehand cut cardstock leaves and grass. Punch large sun shapes; layer with punched flower shapes using self-adhesive foam spacers between layers. Gently bend top layer of punched flowers. Punch small leaves from green cardstock; layer and mount over small sun punched from vellum and yellow cardstock for flower buds. Craft vellum dandelion fly-aways from punched sun shapes; trim off segments with small scissors and layer with freehand-cut brown cardstock stems. Randomly mount dandelion fly-aways on pages.

Holle Wiktorek

Holle's Hobbies

Texture and distress cardstock

Holle's hobbies include scrapbooking those hobbies, as seen on this diverse page. Cut one 4½ x 12" piece of brown paper using a wavy template on one side; mount at top of patterned background paper. Cut one side of a 1¼" strip of brown paper using wavy template; mount atop large brown paper strip. Distress rust cardstock by crumpling and flattening; rub with brown and black chalk. Slice two 3½ x 12" strips of distressed cardstock; layer at bottom of page. Attach eyelets 1" from edge of each side and 4" from the top and bottom of page. String fibers through eyelets; secure at back of page. Crop photos into squares; mount at top and bottom of page. Print title, journaling and photo captions on tan paper; cut to size. Mount photo captions on photos. Crumple and flatten journaling block; tear bottom edge and distress with chalk and ink before matting on brown cardstock. Cut title letters into small tags; punch hole at top; tie with twine and chalk edges. Mount tags on 4¼ x 7¾" piece of black cardstock. Cut large title letters from brown cardstock; mount under title tags. Attach title block to page with large gold brads at corners.

Clara

Dry emboss on vellum

Dry embossed leaves enhance Torrey's heritage photos. Punch twelve 1" squares from blue cardstock and eight 1" squares from teal cardstock; punch decorative corner at one corner of each square. Layer patterned paper with decorative punched corners over blue decorative corners and mat on teal cardstock for background. Using a craft knife and straightedge ruler, slice a $2\frac{1}{2}$ x $5\frac{1}{2}$" window in a $5\frac{1}{2}$ x 9" cream cardstock frame. Slice a 3 x 6" window in a $4\frac{3}{4}$ x $8\frac{1}{2}$" patterned paper frame and a 5 x $8\frac{5}{8}$" blue cardstock frame. Layer patterned paper frame and blue card-stock frame together over decorative punched corners at insides of window; mount atop cream cardstock frame and photo. Print title on vellum and cut to size; mount on blue card-stock trimmed with decorative corner punches and photo slots. Using a graduated template, cut ovals into cream and teal cardstock and patterned paper to frame photo. Slice windows into mat as described above for photo on right page slightly off-center; mount together over blue decorative photo corners. Print journaling on cream vellum trimmed with decorative scissors. Freehand dry emboss leaves to match patterned paper design on cream vellum. Use a stylus and a mouse pad to emboss. Trim around leaves with decorative scissors. Mount leaves on blue cardstock with decorative punched corners; layer atop blue decorative punched corner squares before mounting on pages.

Torrey Miller

Peter Rabbit
Re-create a storytime favorite

Torrey crafts a picture book hero from paper. Triple mat photo on white, cream and beige cardstock. Punch decorative corner into cream cardstock mat before layering over small teal squares. Mount matted photo on teal cardstock matted with beige cardstock with punched decorative corners. Punch two 1½" square from beige cardstock; trim corners with decorative corner punch. Slice in half and embellish cream photo mat. Print title block on cream cardstock; cut to size and punch decorative corners. Mat on beige cardstock before mounting on page. Freehand draw rabbit, jacket and carrots on colored cardstock. Silhouette cut drawn pieces; detail with pen and chalk. Piece together and mat on tan cardstock; silhouette cut around design. Weave basket from ¼" strips of brown and tan cardstock. Freehand cut, bend and mount basket handle. Trim woven rectangle into basket shape and detail with pen and chalk. Layer carrots behind basket. Mount rabbit and basket around title block with self-adhesive foam spacers.

Torrey Miller

The View
Layer patterned papers

Diana layers patterned vellum and paper together for a muted background that brings focus to the photo. Print partial title and journaling on patterned paper. Cut a 6 x 12" piece of patterned vellum; mount on top half of patterned paper for background. Print journaling on 7¾ x 10" olive green cardstock; mount photo and layer on background papers. Slice a ¼" strip of patterned vellum; horizontally mount 1¼" from bottom of page. Adhere letter stickers on photo/journaling block and patterned paper background as shown. Mount plastic window over dried leaf and mesh scrap with copper brads.

Diana Hudson

Wedding Memories

Fold decorative paper frames

Holle's pleated photo frames add a subtle decorative element to wedding photos. Silhouette cut preprinted frames; write journaling with gold and green pens. Print journaling on printed vellum; cut to size and mount on pink paper before mounting atop preprinted frames. Craft folded photo frames from patterned paper by first cutting a 2¼ x 3½" window into a 4¼ x 5½" piece of patterned paper. Miter corners with a straightedge ruler and craft knife, cutting a ½" slice at a 45 degree angle toward the outside of the frame. Fold pleats at ¼" increments in a back and forth fashion after scoring with a bone folder and straightedge ruler.

Holle Wiktorek

Brandi Ginn

Family

Paper tear title and photo mats

Paper-torn photo and journaling mats keep Brandi's page looking soft while adding a textured accent. Slice a 4½" strip of patterned paper; tear one edge and mount vertically over pink paper background as a border. Print title and journaling on ivory cardstock; cut to size and mat on patterned paper with paper-torn edges. Link title letters together with small pieces of wire pushed through page and secured at back. Layer ivory cardstock over patterned paper; tear edges and use as photo mat.

I know that my scrapbooking style has been called "shabby chic." While that's often the case—I like to create pages that include scrunched and rolled paper, stitching, a weathered look and nontraditional elements, I don't think that this page fits the definition. It's not "shabby," just "chic"!

Trudy Sigurdson

Tia and Trudy

Weave wavy strips

Trudy constructs a textured background with loosely woven wavy cardstock strips. Freehand cut wavy strips from pink and mauve cardstock. Weave together over white cardstock, starting at the upper left corner. Secure ends; attach eyelets at corners. Double mat photos on pink and mauve cardstock. Mount large photo on left page with photo corners; outline with black fine-tip pen. Print journaling on pink cardstock; cut to size, mat and outline with black fine-tip pen. Cut tags from white cardstock; stamp names, adhere heart stickers and outline with black fine-tip pen. Attach eyelet and tie sheer ribbon. Mount glass pebble atop heart stickers. Attach swirl clip to tag with dragonfly charm. Layer skeleton leaves, mica tiles, dragonfly charms, metal heart and star, and embellished tags over woven background and around photos and journaling blocks.

Trains in a Bubble

Punch a landscaped border

Heidi re-creates the charming atmosphere of a model train yard with punched flowers and leaves layered as a border accent. Slice two ¼" strips of burgundy cardstock; vertically mount at edges of forest green cardstock background. Print title and journaling on cream and brown cardstock. Cut title border strip; mat on brown cardstock. Horizontally mount on background. Cut small title words on brown cardstock to size; mount on title strip and embellish with punched flower. Silhouette cut photo element; mount at end of title strip. Double mat photos on cream and brown cardstock, leaving room on first mat for embellishments. Paper tear brown and gray "pebbles" from cardstock; mount on title block and photo mats as shown. Adhere train tracks on photo mats with strong adhesive. Punch flowers, leaves and grass from colored cardstock; layer and mount at top and bottom of page as a border.

Heidi Schueller

Punches are an expensive investment, so when I buy a punch (and I only own 9-10), I select those that I'm sure I'll use over and over. For example, I own a couple of snowflake punches because I live in Wisconsin and I'm certain I'll have plenty of winter pages to create.

Heidi Schueller

Tootsie

Punch a colorful flower lei

Torrey adds an elegant punched lei around a vintage photo as a decorative element. Double mat burgundy cardstock with green and yellow cardstocks; punch corners of burgundy and green cardstocks with decorative corner punch. Quadruple mat photo with white, purple and green cardstocks. Craft photo corners with 1¾" squares cut from purple cardstock. Punch opposite corners with decorative corner punch; layer punched design over lavender cardstock. Diagonally slice square in half; mount decorative corner over photo and fold edges behind matting and secure. Mat photo two more times on green cardstock with punched decorative corners and yellow cardstock. Print title and journaling on lavender cardstock; cut to size and trim edges with decorative scissors. Double mat title block and mount atop multi-matted photo. Punch flowers from colored cardstocks; layer and mount to form a flower lei.

My dad's cousin, Sammie Yvonne "Tootsie" Ochs, circa 1944 - about age 7. The outfit was a gift from her dad, purchased in Hawaii during his tour of duty in the Pacific.

Torrey Miller

A Sweet Proposal

Feature torn flowers

Valerie's paper-torn flowers add elegance to her page. Tear a 4" strip of patterned paper; horizontally mount at top of light green cardstock. Freehand cut tag from green and blue cardstock, sizing one tag just larger than the other; stamp title letter with burgundy ink. Print second title word and journaling on light yellow vellum. Circle cut title word; mount atop metal-rimmed tag and embellish with paper torn flower petals. Attach eyelets to tags and tie fibers. Die cut last title word from burgundy and dark green cardstock. Tear a 3½"-wide strip of patterned paper; vertically mount at right side of right page. Tear a 1" strip of dark blue and burgundy cardstock; vertically mount on either side of patterned paper strip. Mat photo and mount over torn border strips. Tear edges of vellum with printed journaling; tear small hole in vellum to highlight photo element before layering over torn border. Attach eyelets at top and bottom of vellum; string with fibers and tie. Double mat large photo on burgundy and dark green cardstock with torn edges. Double mat photos for right page; tear second mat of two photos. Freehand tear flower petals from colored cardstock and assemble to look like flowers in patterned paper. Layer on page with freehand sliced stems and torn leaves.

Valerie Barton

She's Got Personality

Embellish journaling tags

Diana nestles embellished journaling tags inside of decorative envelopes. Mat blue paper on green paper for background. Layer a 7 x 11½" piece of patterned paper with one torn edge over background. Mat photos on teal, purple and green papers. Print part of title and journaling on white cardstock. Cut title words into small tag shapes. Attach eyelets and tie with embroidery thread. Die cut title letters from white cardstock; mount at top of page and detail with blue chalk. Cut journaling blocks into large tag shapes; add pen details around the edges. Attach eyelets at tops of tags; tie embroidery threads with beads and number charm. Embellish tags with flower eyelets before nestling in embellished vellum envelopes. Fold vellum into envelopes using template. Stitch to page with white embroidery thread. Embellish envelopes with flower stickers, ricrack and torn patterned paper strips.

Diana Graham

It's easy for me to scrapbook about my kids, but I have difficulty scrapbooking about myself. I guess I'm a little intimidated by the prospect. I know it will be difficult and take time, so I find myself setting the task aside until I feel that I can do it "right."

Diana Graham

Holle Wiktorek

Springtime Smiles

Layer dimensional flowers

Holle picks pre-made dimensional flowers and layers them into pretty springtime bouquets on her photo mats. Mat two photos on purple cardstock; layer third photo under preprinted cardstock frame. Mount on patterned paper background. Print journaling; cut to size and mat on purple cardstock. Wrap bottom of journaling block with fibers before mounting on page. Die cut title letters from purple cardstock; mount at top of page and on photo frame. Layer pre-made embellished flowers at corners of photo mats.

Sugar & Spice

Add a soft touch with torn mulberry

Gently torn mulberry paper contrasts with sharp photo corners, reflecting the two sides of Heidi's little girl. Mat two 10½" squares of navy cardstock on lavender cardstock. Layer over patterned background paper, leaving inside edge flush with patterned paper. Cut two 1" squares from yellow patterned paper; slice diagonally and mount as corners of matted navy cardstock. Double mat photos on yellow patterned paper and pastel colored mulberry paper, tearing edges by using a thin paintbrush and small amount of water to paint a line along mulberry paper. Gently pull apart to create feathered edges. Cut or punch 1" squares from patterned paper and 1¼" squares from lavender cardstock; slice all diagonally and layer as photo corners. Print title and flower clip art from computer; silhouette cut. Layer a few flowers with vellum; silhouette cut around shape and mount at photo corners and along bottom of navy cardstock. Mount title letters at top of navy cardstock. Layer preprinted butterfly die cuts with vellum; silhouette cut and mount on page.

I come from a long line of artists. My grandma wanted to be a fashion designer and my mother earned her degree in Fine Arts. I earned my degree in Fine Arts as well and continue to draw and paint whenever I get the chance. But since I have little girls, I can't help adding to their beauty by creating memorable scrapbook pages around their photos!

Heidi Schueller

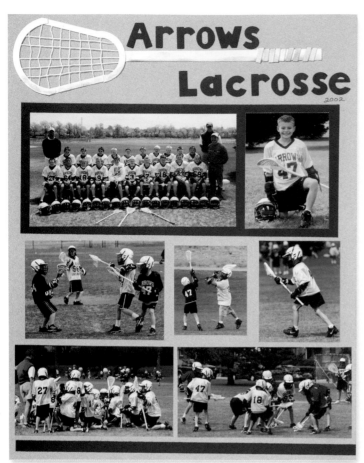

Arrows Lacrosse

Craft realistic sports equipment

Kelli gives realistic detail to a paper crafted lacrosse hook with string and dimensional chalking. Mat two photos on one black mat. Slice a $\frac{1}{4}$" strip of black cardstock; horizontally mount at bottom of page. Crop remaining photos and mount on gray cardstock background. Punch title letters from black cardstock; mount at top of page. Craft lacrosse hook from paper and string. Freehand cut curved and straight pieces for net; mount rows of string behind assembled hook pieces as shown. Slice $\frac{1}{8}$" and $\frac{3}{8}$" strips of white cardstock; wrap $\frac{1}{8}$" strip around end of $\frac{3}{8}$" strip as shown. Shade with gray chalk. Crop photos for right hand page. Lay sections of mesh on gray cardstock background page. Mount photos and journaling block on mesh, allowing portions of the mesh to show.

Kelli Noto

I've found that if I want action shots of a sports event I get better pictures when I shoot the warm-ups than the game itself. When photographing the warm-ups I can get closer and it is easier to anticipate the action and know where the ball is going to be. That makes it easier to follow it with my camera.

Kelli Noto

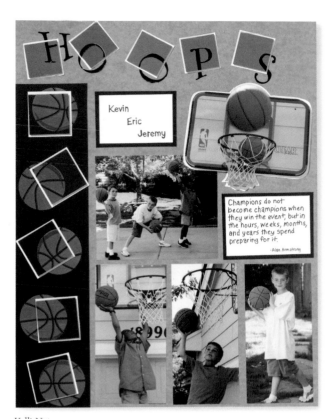

Kelli Noto

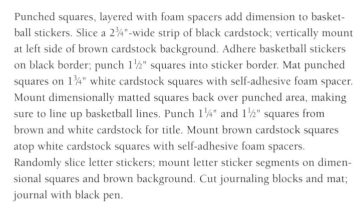

Hoops

Give basketball stickers a little bounce

Punched squares, layered with foam spacers add dimension to basketball stickers. Slice a 2¾"-wide strip of black cardstock; vertically mount at left side of brown cardstock background. Adhere basketball stickers on black border; punch 1½" squares into sticker border. Mat punched squares on 1¾" white cardstock squares with self-adhesive foam spacer. Mount dimensionally matted squares back over punched area, making sure to line up basketball lines. Punch 1¼" and 1½" squares from brown and white cardstock for title. Mount brown cardstock squares atop white cardstock squares with self-adhesive foam spacers. Randomly slice letter stickers; mount letter sticker segments on dimensional squares and brown background. Cut journaling blocks and mat; journal with black pen.

Tough Yet Tender

Weave a simple border design

Valerie adds visual interest to title borders with a woven design. Slice a 2½" x 11¾" strip from blue cardstock and a 2½ x 9¼" strip from burgundy cardstock; set burgundy strip aside. Using a craft knife and straightedge ruler, slice into blue cardstock to prepare for weaving. Starting ¼" from side edge and 3" from one end of blue cardstock, slice nine 3" strips at ¼" increments, cutting all the way to end of cardstock strip. Slice seven ¼ x 3½" strips of burgundy cardstock. Weave burgundy strips into blue cardstock in under/over fashion, leaving ¼" between each woven strip. Secure ends with adhesive and trim off excess. Vertically mount completed woven border strip at left side of page as border on black cardstock background; horizontally mount burgundy border strip at bottom of page. Cut title letters from crumpled and flattened brown cardstock; detail with gold metallic rub-ons and black chalk around the edges. Attach eyelets to a few letters; mount title word on blue cardstock strip. Die cut shadowed title word from brown and white mulberry paper; layer and mount on burgundy cardstock. Write remaining title word on small tag; shade tag with chalk and tie with jute string. Mount with small clothespin where two border strips meet. Print journaling on vellum; paper tear edges. Layer with cropped photos on page. Slice ⅜" burgundy strip and ¼" blue cardstock strip; frame one photo with strips as shown. Paper tear strip of brown distressed cardstock. Insert one corner of mounted photo into sliced paper strip. Freehand craft dandelion from white mulberry paper. Cut small squares of mulberry paper; dampen one edge with water and pull out center to fray edges. Mount pieces together in circle as shown over thin strip of green cardstock.

Valerie Barton

Torrey Miller

Lucky Fish
Hang vellum paper lanterns

Illuminated paper lanterns hang at the top of Torrey's page documenting a visit to Boston's Chinatown. Double mat gray cardstock with mustard and burgundy cardstock. Double and triple mat photos; mount on page. Print journaling on vellum; cut to size and mount on page with small brads at corners. Freehand craft lanterns from crimped vellum cut into shapes; cut lantern handles and bottoms from brown cardstock. Mount with crimped vellum shapes over freehand cut and layered flames with self-adhesive foam spacers. "Hang" lanterns on fiber; horizontally mount fiber across top of page. Freehand cut triangles to shape into title letters; mount on lanterns and sliced vellum strip. Freehand cut and color large fish from tan cardstock. Detail with pen and chalks; mount on page with self-adhesive foam spacers.

Reflections of Albuquerque
Assemble a mosaic from punched shapes

Torrey re-creates a detailed mosaic from punched shapes. Mat blue cardstock on brown cardstock. Cut a 5¼" strip of beige cardstock; horizontally mount at center of page. Slice ¼", 1" and 2¼" strips of tan vellum; mount at top of page and above and below beige cardstock. Punch squares, rectangles and triangles from colored cardstock. Assemble on vellum strips in a mosaic design similar to that in photo. Triple mat photos on white, rust and brown cardstock; mount on page. Print journaling on vellum; cut to size and mount on blue cardstock background. Freehand draw and cut design from rust and beige cardstock; layer with punched circles at bottom of journaling block.

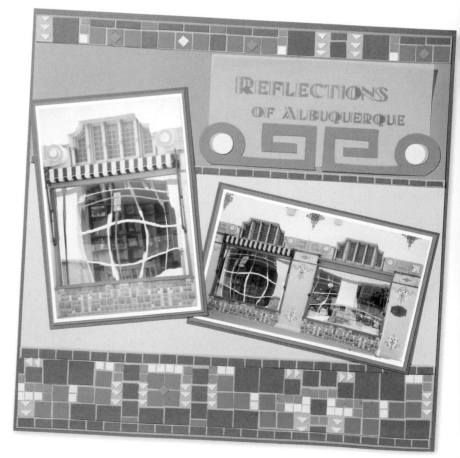

Torrey Miller

Valentine's Day Weekend

Roll torn edges of photo mats

Holle layers matted photos with torn and rolled edges over strips of stamped and torn cardstock for a rustic look. Stamp state name on yellow and brown cardstock and vellum with brown inks. Tear stamped cardstock and vellum into large pieces; collage over blue background cardstock. Single and double mat photos on brown and green cardstock; tear edges of first mat. Gently curl torn edges. Frame one photo with frayed material scrap mounted on page. Mount stitched buttons around fiber framed photo and at top of page with cork strip. Paper tear hearts from red cardstock; brush edges with brown and black chalk. Die cut title letters from dark green cardstock; layer over paper-torn hearts. Cut last title word from corrugated cardstock using template; mount along bottom of page. Print journaling on rust cardstock; tear edges and mount on page.

When I started teaching I realized I changed my bulletin boards more than any teacher in the school. When scrapbooking was introduced professionally in Tennessee I realized my scrapbook pages were "mini bulletin boards."

Holle Wiktorek

Holle Wiktorek

It's the Little Moments

Texture a multilayered photo frame

Katherine highlights a favorite photo behind multilayered, textured and inked photo mats. Slice two ¼" strips of olive green and brown cardstock and one ½" strip of rust cardstock. Horizontally mount at bottom of pages. Mount brads on rust strip at 3" increments. Crumple and flatten an 8½ x 11" piece of green cardstock; dab brown and bronze ink over cardstock with a crumpled paper towel. Using a craft knife and straightedge ruler, cut a 6 x 8½" window in textured and inked cardstock. Cut smaller windows in rust, olive green and tan cardstocks; tear inside edges of olive green frame. Mount green textured frame over smaller frames with foam tape. Curl inside torn edges of olive green matting toward outside of page. Print title on vellum; cut into strip and mount at bottom of multi-matted photo with brass clips. Double mat photos for right page. Print journaling on tan cardstock; cut to size. Punch holes in three journaling strips; tie with fibers and mount all on page.

I kept all of my scrapbooking supplies in a small plastic bin when I first started. Now, several years later, I have my own room along with several cabinets in the kitchen!

Katherine Brooks

Katherine Brooks

Christmas in the Desert

Ink edges of cardstock

Katherine adds a bit of color to page elements by carefully pressing their edges on a colored ink pad. Mat moss green cardstock with brown cardstock. Mat three photos on olive green cardstock; cut to size, leaving room for title blocks. Press edges of matting on ink pad to shade. Mat four photos on brown cardstock; mount two at bottom of left page and two at top of right page. Freehand cut tag from tan cardstock; press edges on ink pad to shade. Punch hole in punched tan cardstock circle at top of tag; tie with fibers. Stamp date on small white tag, crumple, flatten and rub with chalk. Tie string to top of small tag and attach to present. Crumple, flatten and shade die-cut cactus; mount with pre-made present atop large tag. Print title and journaling on light and olive green cardstock. Cut title blocks to size; press edges on ink pad. Mount at bottom of large photo mat with small brads. Cut journaling into a 2¾" strip; horizontally mount at right side of right page. Using a craft knife and ruler, slice a 5½ x 3⅝" window in a 6¼ x 4¼" piece of olive green cardstock. Press outside edges of frame on ink pad. Cut a 5¼ x 3⅜" window in a 6 x 4" piece of light green cardstock. Mount olive green frame over light green frame; tie with fibers on right side. Mount frame over photo on page with self-adhesive foam spacers.

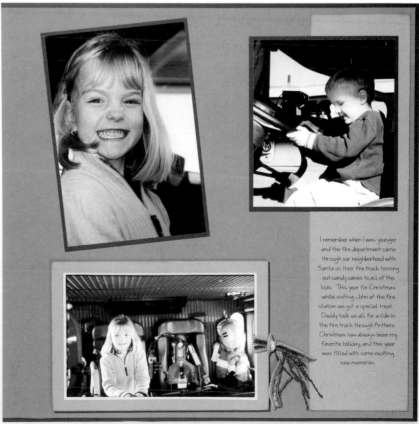

Katherine Brooks

Friday's Child

Embellish torn cardstock strips

Torrey assembles a simple monochromatic page to accentuate striking photos. Stamp chicken wire design on light green cardstock with watermark stamp ink for a subtle background pattern; mat with dark green cardstock. Print journaling on light green cardstock strip; horizontally tear and mount as a 2½"-wide border strip near bottom of page. Tear another 2½" strip of light green cardstock; vertically mount over stamped cardstock background as shown. Print title on green vellum; tear into strip and layer on page wrapping one end around stamped background. Mount sheer ribbon atop torn cardstock strips; wrap ends around to back of page and secure. Punch hearts from light and dark green cardstock; mount on torn border strips with self-adhesive foam spacers for dimension. Mat photos and layer on page.

Torrey Miller

Valerie Barton

Our View of Canoeing the Okatoma

Craft a textured river

Valerie creates a textured river bank and hidden journaling blocks on a page documenting a memorable trip on the Okatoma River. Punch 1½" squares from colored cardstock; assemble at top of page in two rows as a border. Mount journaling blocks on cardstock strips. Attach two or four punched squares from border to top of each strip. Slice opening in cardstock background; slide journaling strips through openings. Mount remaining punched squares to background. Stamp title words on squares with brown ink as shown; mount 1" square punched photo vignettes on remaining squares. Mat two photos on blue cardstock over torn light green cardstock strip; tear top and bottom edge of matting. Using a bone folder and straightedge ruler, horizontally score cardstock just under photo and fold up over photo. Machine stitch across photo. Mat remaining photos on colored cardstock; tear bottom edge of one mat. Mount on page over torn blue cardstock strips. Piece together a mosaic river from small paper-torn cardstock scraps layered together. Craft textured river banks with liquid adhesive mixed with pigment powder; mix together on wax paper and sprinkle with sawdust. Let dry overnight; peel off in segments and assemble on either side of mosaic river.

Grant's Farm

Embellish tags with dimensional elements

Brandi stamps and embellishes a series of tags with buttons, wire, paper yarn and a sunny quilled design. Mat two sets of three photos on one strip of brown cardstock; mount at bottom of pages over tan cardstock background. Mat two photos on green and brown cardstocks. Print title and journaling on cream cardstock; cut to size and press edges on ink pad. Stamp designs on precut tags and ink around edges before embellishing. On first tag, mount buttons embellished with curled wire over green torn-paper strips; attach eyelet. For second tag, quill sun from yellow cardstock strip; mount at center of punched flames. Attach eyelet over punched green cardstock circle. Mount buttons over distressed cardstock strip on third tag; attach eyelet over punched brown cardstock square. Glue stitched button over paper yarn looped into flower shape; layer over torn green cardstock on fourth tag. Attach eyelet.

I'm having to buy albums much more often than I used to because the popular bulky embellishments fill them so quickly. Tags are a great way to embellish without bulk, and that saves me money!

Brandi Ginn

We love Grant's Farm! It's so much fun to watch Alexa experience the goats! We learned that when you go in the spring they are so tiny–perfect size for a two year old. The goats barely came up to her waste and they haven't learned to jump on their hind legs and attack anyone with food! Alexa even shared her string cheese with the older goats. Brinley was comfortably asleep in her sling and missed out on everything. Although at 2 months I'm not sure she cared.   April 2001

Brandi Ginn

Metallics

Man first used metals such as gold, copper, lead and silver to create practical items such as weapons and eating utensils. As early as 6,000 B.C., Ancient Egyptians used lead in liquid form as eye paint because of its shiny metallic appearance. The use of metals expanded throughout the Medieval and Renaissance periods in which it was utilized to create armor, to the Gothic period when it was used for architecture, and on to the Art Nouveau arts and crafts movement. Each metal holds its own fascination for man. Gold, symbolic over the ages as a measure of wealth, is malleable and glows with luster. Copper, with its rich tones, is a good conductor of heat and electricity. Lead, the easiest metal to bend and shape while maintaining its strength, is ideal for nuts and bolts. Silver, a softer metal, is perfect for fashioning decorative ornaments, chains and jewelry.

Scrapbookers have recently recognized the many qualities metal can bring to their pages. It reflects and adds color and texture as eyelets, beads, embossing powders, clips, sequins, glitter, pins or studs and brads. Metals can be used for fastening and securing items on a page or simply as an embellishment. You can coil it, form it, emboss it, bend it, shape it, bead it...even wrap it! We're sure that you'll be able to find plenty of metallic inspiration in the following pages to get you thinking about how you can add its shining elements to your layouts.

Torrey Miller

Sand Between Her Toes

Wrap metal hearts with beaded wire

Torrey adds a rustic decorative element with beaded wire wrapped around "rusty" metal hearts. Crumple and flatten brown cardstock for texture; rub with coarse sandpaper for a wind-swept look similar to the sand dunes in the photo. Mat enlarged photo on patterned cardstock, leaving room for embellishments; tear edges and gently curl toward photo with fingers. Vertically slice matted photo to be mounted on both pages. Print journaling on vellum, leaving room for highlighted words. Stamp words on colored cardstock with brown ink; cut or paper tear to size. Mount atop printed vellum, at the side of and on photo mat with self-adhesive foam spacers. Mount vellum on left page; mount matted photo with self-adhesive foam spacers on both pages as shown. Wrap metal hearts with beaded wire as shown; mount over torn teal cardstock strip at right side of photo mat.

A Cherished Love

Add a golden touch with embossing powder

Katherine adds a golden touch to unique page embellishments by embossing with gold embossing powder. Tear a 4½" strip of patterned paper; layer over a larger strip of torn khaki paper. Vertically mount on tan cardstock matted with black cardstock; gently roll torn edges with fingers. Mat photo on black cardstock; layer over layered torn strips. Attach eyelets on either side of photo as shown. Heat emboss metal-rimmed vellum tag with gold embossing powder; stamp letters while embossing powder is still warm. Punch holes in sides of embossed tag; string gingham ribbon through tag and eyelets and tie. Ink edges of premade tags; stamp with title words. Heat emboss metal clock with gold embossing powder; mount on one tag. Tie tags with gingham ribbon; mount at top of page with self-adhesive foam spacers. Print journaling on cream cardstock; cut to size and press edges on ink pad to shade. Punch flowers from white cardstock; attach brads in center and press edges of flower petals on ink pad to shade. Mount flowers atop curled wire as shown.

Katherine Brooks

Explore, Discover
Emboss metal letters

Katherine heats a few layers of ultra thick copper embossing powder to add dimension and shine to metal title letters. Cut moss green cardstock in half; mount over dark green cardstock for background. Horizontally attach mesh strip at center of page; wrap around ends of page and secure on back. Double mat large photo on left page; use textured cardstock for second mat. Press edges on ink pad to shade. Turn down upper left corner and secure with silver metal star stud. Single and double mat photos on brown, green and textured cardstock. Attach brads between two photos matted on one piece of brown cardstock. Mount double matted photos on page with foam tape for a bit of dimension. Crop remaining small photos into squares and rectangles; lightly distress the edges with sandpaper and mount along the top of both pages as shown. Heat emboss metal letters by pressing letter on an embossing pad; sprinkle with copper embossing powder. Repeat until desired thickness is achieved. Heat from underneath until bubbly; mount on page when cooled. Press ink pad on white cardstock; print journaling on inked white cardstock. Cut to size and tear edges; gently curl torn edges with fingers. Stamp date at bottom of right page with black ink.

Katherine Brooks

I love trying new techniques and capturing not just major events, but those fun silly moments I never want to forget.

Katherine Brooks

Two Little Souls...

String beads on coiled wire

Brandi adds sparkle and shine that is second only to the smiles on her daughters' faces with strands of beaded coiled wire. Mount photos together across bottom of one page and across the top of the other. String large and small beads on coiled wire; mount along photos. Secure large beads to page with glue dots. Mount small photos behind metal frames; layer over beaded coiled wire strands. Single and double mat remaining photos on blue cardstock and mesh fabric; mount at corners. Print journaling; cut to size and mount below one matted photo on fabric.

Brandi Ginn

I am the granddaughter of a photographer and grew up in front of the camera. Winning a camera (in a photo contest in 1992) sparked my interest in taking pictures. Scrapbooking, for me, was the natural extension of the creative process.

Brandi Ginn

Trudy Sigurdson

I consider myself visually, rather than verbally creative, so I often can't come up with words that express what I feel. That's why I use poems and quotes on my pages. I often know what kind of thing I want to say, but it may take me hours to find the right verse. I think that the poem I pick is equally as important as the photos and can make or break a page.

Trudy Sigurdson

Cherished

Add dimension to metallic stickers

Trudy gives extra dimension to pewter stickers by mounting them on wooden blocks before adding them as an embellishment to her page. Double mat photos with light and dark blue textured cardstock; mount over light blue matted cardstock background with photo corners. Print title and date on light blue textured cardstock and poem on vellum. Cut title and journaling strip to size, crumple and flatten. Mat on dark blue cardstock strip; attach small silver brad on one side. Mount both on page over skeleton leaf. Cut printed vellum to size. String pewter beads on fibers; mount at top and bottom of printed vellum strip. Adhere pewter stickers atop small wooden blocks; mount at one side of title and journaling blocks and over skeleton leaves on vellum.

Diana Graham

By the Shore

Tell a story with metal word eyelets

Diana assembles a sentiment about a father-son relationship with metal word eyelets attached to a large handcrafted and embellished tag. Mat patterned paper with green cardstock. Single and double mat photos with blue cardstock and green patterned paper. Mount metal photo corners on double matted photo. Layer single matted photo with mesh scrap. Print part of title and journaling on blue and white cardstock. Cut title word block to size and mount behind metal frame next to metal title letters. Cut date journaling to size; mount under green glass pebble at bottom right corner of page next to metal number eyelets. Freehand cut tag from green patterned paper; attach eyelet at top over circle punched screen. Tie unwrapped paper yarn to tag. Tear small holes in tag; mount mesh behind torn holes. Mount metal frame on tag over cropped photo. Assemble metal word eyelets with printed and cut words into sentiment on tag. Shade pail and shovel die cuts with chalks for dimension. Cover torn paper strips with decorative sand using two sided tape; mount above and below sand pail with sand dollars and sea stars.

Grandma

Dangle metal frame charms

Miniature gold frames dangle from a decorative metal plaque as an elegant page embellishment. Mat enlarged photo on patterned paper; layer with frame sliced from green cardstock over cream cardstock background. Print journaling on vellum and title on green cardstock. Silhouette cut title and mount at top of page. Cut journaling block to size; mount alongside photo as shown. Write journaling on light green cardstock; cut to size to fit behind small metal frame charms. Tie frame charms with thin green ribbon; secure ends under decorative metal plaque mounted on page.

My grandmother is full of spirit. She laughs easily, likes telling dirty jokes, and can bake up a storm. . . She used to win radio contests on a weekly basis. When my father and his brother were young, they'd run from her when they were in trouble. She chased them down, hurdling over fences with her red hair and skirt flying behind her. She always caught them. Grandma has a very full life. She is so busy with her various activities that it is hard to find a time to take her to lunch. She survived the Great Depression, World War II, raising two rambunctious boys and a spirited daughter, breast cancer, and losing her husband of sixty years. She is a remarkable woman and I am blessed to have her as my grandmother.

Kelli Noto

It's Not Fair!

Dangle wire stars from eyelets

Valerie bends wire into dangling stars that hang from a cut and folded window secured with silver eyelets. Using a decorative ruler, draw a 4½ x 5½" zigzag frame on green cardstock. Slice along penciled lines with a craft knife and straightedge ruler. Bend pointed ends back and secure with eyelets. Paper tear a small window in upper right corner of green cardstock before mounting on gray cardstock background. Adhere pewter sticker at center of torn window on gray cardstock. Mat photo on green cardstock; mount at center of decorative window on gray cardstock. Bend wire into star shapes using a jewelry jig; dangle from eyelets with freehand crafted wire hook. Print journaling on green cardstock; cut to size and mat on gray cardstock before mounting on page.

Valerie Barton

Diana Graham

Fuzzy Caterpillar

Layer metal screen on vellum tags

Metal screen scraps add texture and shine to Diana's layered title tags. Single and double mat photos on green cardstock and vellum; mount metal photo corners on one single matted photo. Scrape edges on first mat of double matted photo with scissors blade. Mount photos on patterned paper background; layer one over metal screen mounted with small silver brads. Punch a 1" square into a 1¼" punched square of green cardstock; layer on metal-rimmed vellum tag over metal screen scrap. Attach metal letter on layered tag with silver brad. Print title words and journaling on green vellum. Paper tear around edges and mount title words next to layered tags at top of page. Tear around edges of journaling block; layer over metal screen secured to page with silver brads. Attach a safety pin embellished with a button and beads at top of journaling block.

Topsy Turvy

Incorporate household items into layout

Unusual household items are incorporated into Kelli's layout, providing both subtle and bold metal accents. A stainless steel outlet cover frames title letters while a scrap of window screen becomes a subtle second mat for an enlarged photo. Slice a 1" strip of black cardstock; attach metal letter nailheads as title before horizontally mounting across top page of on gray speckled cardstock. Mat small photo on black cardstock; mount at right side of title border strip. Double mat enlarged photo on black cardstock and window screen frayed around the edges. Print journaling; cut to size and mat on black cardstock. Place stainless steel outlet cover on page; mark holes with pencil on cardstock for placement of eyelets and holes to punch. Set outlet cover aside; punch small holes on markings using a hole punch and attach eyelets. Mount letter nailheads on black cardstock to show through window of outlet cover. Secure outlet cover on page over nailhead letters with wire tied through eyelets and holes.

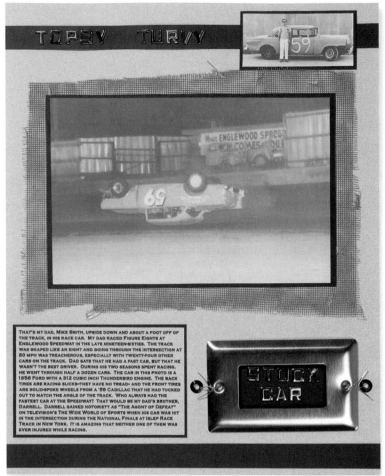

Kelli Noto

Torrey Miller

The Blues Diner

Create faux "hammered tin" photo corners

Torrey creates the look of antique "hammered tin" accents by stamping designs into silver metallic embossing enamel. Double and triple mat photo on white, blue and silver cardstocks; mount photos on blue matted cardstock background. Print title and journaling on silver cardstock and vellum. Cut title block to size; mat with blue cardstock. Cut journaling block to size; mount on page with eyelets at corners. Stamp and heat emboss toasters on colored cardstock; silhouette cut and mount along bottom of page. Create faux "hammered tin" accents by pressing embossing pad onto cardstock and sprinkle with silver metallic ultra thick embossing enamel. Heat cardstock from underside with embossing gun until powder liquifies. Add a second and third layer of enamel. While enamel is still warm, press in stamped design. Cut design into squares when cool; diagonally slice into triangles. Mount at corners of triple matted photo and title block.

In the Pits

Stamp design into embossed title letters

Katherine stamps a design into warm metallic embossing enamel giving the look of tire tracks imprinted in silhouette cut title letters. Print title font, silhouette cut. Press letters onto embossing pad; heat emboss with silver and clear embossing powders. While still warm, press in stamp design. Mount on blue cardstock background. Slice two ¼" strips of navy cardstock; vertically mount at outside edges of background. Single mat photos on teal and navy cardstock; mount all on page. Attach screw eyelets at corners of largest photo as shown. Freehand cut small rectangular strips from colored cardstock. Mount along bottom of page with square punched photos matted on white cardstock as a border design. Print journaling blocks on white cardstock. Cut large journal block to size; tear bottom edge. Add pen and chalk details around edges. Craft pocket for memorabilia with navy cardstock mounted on page with foam tape adhered around the edges. Punch square "windows" in navy cardstock; mount square punched matted photo behind one window before adhering pocket to page. Mount journaling block atop navy cardstock; slip memorabilia behind dimensional pocket. Cut small journal block to size; mount on screen scrap with small silver brads. Cut tag from light blue cardstock using template; crumple, flatten and brush with tan chalk for a distressed look. Slice window in center of tag; mount screen with journaling behind window. Attach eyelet; tie with fibers. Add the shine of hardware with washers tied to tag fibers.

Katherine Brooks

I have been scrapbooking more layouts and albums having to do with myself. I want my children to know that I'm not just "Mom" and that I have fears, dreams and goals in my life.

Katherine Brooks

Riding the Range

Incorporate chicken wire into background design

Trudy creates a visually arresting background with torn cardboard layered over chicken wire. Tear windows from large cardboard; layer atop chicken wire mounted on tan cardstock. Mat photos on brown cardstock. Print title, journaling and photo captions on tan cardstock. Cut title blocks to size and chalk edges; mount with self-adhesive foam spacers over chicken wire in largest window. Cut journaling and photo captions to size; mount under and around photos. Wrap rusty metal hearts with hemp string; mount in torn windows over chicken wire.

Diana Graham

Giddy-Up

Wrap a frame with charms and beads

Charming silver accents wrap around a weathered photo frame and dangle from a faux suede tag. Scrape edges of brown cardstock background with scissors blade for a distressed look. Vertically mount photo border on brown cardstock background. Attach silver brads at corners of background. Scrape pre-made frame die cut with sandpaper; attach silver brad at left side. Tie hemp string embellished with silver beads, western charms and metal letter charm to brad and wrap around left side of photo frame. Mount embellished frame over photo layered on blue jean patterned paper. Double mat photo on beige and brown cardstocks; distress edges. Mount over photo border. Print journaling on ivory cardstock; cut into tag shape. Antique tag with shades of brown ink blotted with a cotton ball; scrape edges. Attach decorative eyelet; tie fibers and hemp string embellished with silver beads. Mount tag below double-matted photo. Tear strip of tan cardstock for title block. Sand paper, sticker and die cut letters. Mount with barbed wire die cut on title strip; adhere dimensional bandanna and rope stickers.

108

Fascinated

Add simple silver accents for an elegant touch

A solitary silver star serves as a hanger for a velvet matted photo frame. Slice large window in red velveteen paper to frame enlarged photo. Wrap crushed velvet around pre-made matte board; mount over framed photo. Cut ribbon strip; secure ends behind framed photo. Mount large silver star over ribbon to look like frame is hanging on page. Mount pewter letters under framed photo. Write date on red velvet paper; cut to size and mount behind metal frame secured with silver brads. Pen journaling at bottom of page.

Kelli Noto

I Must

Dangle journaling tags from beaded clips

Katherine's list of things she "must do" are crafted into tags dangling from beaded swirl clips. Stain velvet paper with ink; cut velvet and wrap around a die cut cardstock frame. Mount over photo; embellish with micro beads. Stamp copper strip in ink, dry emboss with letters and heat to discolor. Punch hole in copper strip with eyelet setter and attach to frame with copper brads. Tear a 3½" strip of patterned paper and a 4" strip of brown cardstock; paper tear one edge and vertically mount at left side of cardstock background. Gently roll torn edges of brown cardstock with fingers. Cut small copper strips; fold in half; punch hole with eyelet setter and mount on torn strips with small brads. Attach beaded swirl clips to copper loops. Print journaling on cream cardstock; cut into strips. Press edges of journaling strips onto ink pad to shade and punch small hole at one end. Attach jewelry jump rings through holes and dangle on swirl clips. Print title on brown cardstock; silhouette cut and mount at top of page.

Katherine Brooks

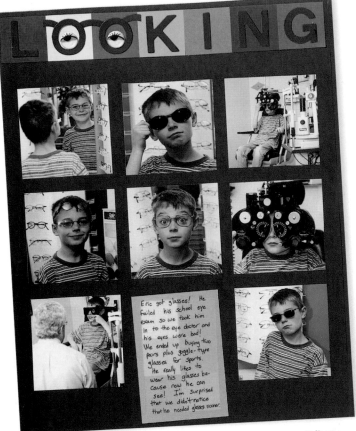

Kelli Noto

I don't carry my camera everywhere, although some people certainly think I do. I limit myself because I found that I was feeling like a spectator in my children's lives instead of a participant. It tends to isolate me from others because I'm only seeing a limited perspective—like when my son was knocked unconscious during a lacrosse game. I didn't see it happen because I was looking through my camera and he was outside my view.

Kelli Noto

Looking Spectacular

Embellish a good lookin' page with playful vellum journaling tags

Kelli creates a dramatic layout with vibrant colors set against a solid black background. Crop photos. Mount eight photos on the left-hand page directly onto black cardstock background. Attach silver brads to the remaining six photos; mount photos on right-hand page. Cut small vellum journaling tags: journal on tags. Set a silver eyelet in each tag. Wrap wire through eyelets and around set brads. Use a template to create the colored title letters. Mount letters on the first page on colorful cardstock blocks. Connect the "O's" in the word "LOOK" with freehand cut paper strips to form glasses. Attach googly eyes inside "O's." Journal on vellum block and attach to page over cardstock colorblock.

What You Do At 2

Dress up an occasion with a touch of elegant silver

Brandi adds a touch of class to her page with silver frames, adornments and photo corners. Mat one photo on rectangular sand-colored cardstock block. Mat two photos on torn sand strip, gently ripping and curling on edge; mount. Layer vellum over stamped sand paper and cut through both sheets to create title tag. Adhere pieces together. Wrap small rectangular piece of cardstock around one end of tag. Set eyelet through cardstock and tag; tie with fibers. Write title. Mount to background paper. Create journaling tag on the right-hand page in similar manner. Mat remaining photos on stamped paper; mount on background page. Embellish with silver photo corners, paper clip and adornment. Journal sentiment on separate small piece of vellum. Cut to size and mount behind silver frame.

Brandi Ginn

I've been scrapbooking on and off since I was about 10 or 12, and it looked really cheesy. I started to have more fun with it when I got married, almost 7 years ago. I think my overall style is pretty traditional but I love trying new things so my albums, as a whole, can be really eclectic.

Brandi Ginn

Fathers Build Dreams

Mount metal with metal

Katherine layers screen under matted photos for a masculine touch to a sentimental page. Stamp dark green cardstock with ink pad for a subtle pattern. Slice two ½" strips and two ¼" strips of inked cardstock and two ¼" strips of light green cardstock. Horizontally mount across top and bottom of rust cardstock background. Mat photos on light green cardstock; layer two matted photos on inked cardstock and large screen scrap. Tear bottom edge of screen; mount on page with flat eyelets. Print journaling on brown cardstock; cut to size and press edges on ink pad to shade. Mat on inked green cardstock. Attach screen scrap at bottom of journaling block with flat eyelets. Mount matted photo with self-adhesive foam spacers at bottom right corner of page. Punch squares into faux leather paper; mount at right side of journaling block. Stamp title letters at bottom of page with brown ink. Heat emboss first title word with silver embossing powder.

Katherine Brooks

Lately, with working and traveling, I find that I can't keep up with my normal 12 x 12" layouts and have started to create smaller albums for each trip.

Katherine Brooks

Haley

Shape wire into freeform flowers

Free-formed flowers shaped into wire embellishments are intertwined with embossed die-cut title letters. Divide burgundy cardstock background into quadrants; cut colored cardstock to fit sections. Double mat photo; trim second mat with decorative scissors and mount on colorblocked background. Die cut letters from burgundy cardstock; outline with embossing pen and heat emboss edges with copper embossing powders. Freehand form wire flowers from thin gauge wire; wrap wire around mounted and embossed title letters. Shape wire into numbers for date. Secure flowers and date to page with small pieces of wire bent into a "U"-shape; pierce holes through cardstock background and insert "U"-pins over wire embellishments. Twist "U"-pin wires together on back of page and flatten to secure wire.

Torrey Miller

Torrey Miller

Timeless

Embellish a paper crafted watch

Torrey paper crafts an antique pocket watch showcasing photos using an interactive spinning template. Slice a 1½" strip of patterned paper; vertically mount at right side of matted patterned paper background. Cut large circle from gold paper; embellish edges with swirl, fleur-de-lis and border punched shapes punched from matted gold cardstock. Cut smaller circle from beige cardstock for watch face. Layer gold sticker strips into Roman numerals around clock face; heat emboss small gold dots drawn with watermark pen between numbers. Attach gold clock hands with brad at center of clock face. Cut oval and arched window for photo and journaling. Complete clock face with gold letter stickers and punched border design. Assemble interactive spinning wheel with photos (following directions on template package). Freehand cut top of timepiece from gold cardstock; texture with paper crimper before layering over large oval ring with self-adhesive foam spacers. Oval cut 15 rings using cutting system; slice each ring at one end and link together on page. Oval cut fob from rust and gold cardstock; hang from chain. Embellish with fleur-de-lis and border design punched shapes; adhere sticker numbers at center of framed oval. Mount sheer gold ribbon across bottom of page, securing ends on back. Print title on red cardstock; silhouette cut and mat on burgundy cardstock. Silhouette cut again and mount on sheer ribbon strip intertwined with gold embroidery thread. Snip backs off of decorative gold buttons and mount on sheer ribbon strip.

Katherine Brooks

Greener Grass
Add a bit of shine with metal details

Katherine creates a textured background by rubbing metallic pearl colorant over a photo mat. Double mat photo on coral cardstock and textured cardstock. Texture second photo mat by laying tulle on coral cardstock collaged with patterned paper strip. Brush on a thin layer of liquid adhesive; dry. Add pigment paint over mounted tulle. Mount matted photo on textured mat; attach eyelets on either side of matted photo. String knotted wire through eyelets, securing at back of matting. Cut tag from patterned paper; press edges on ink pad to shade. Attach eyelet at one end and tie with fibers. Layer small date stamped tag, square punched photo and handmade tag under wire on matted photo. Print journaling on vellum; cut to size and tear one edge. Vertically mount at right side of matted red cardstock background with small eyelets. Slice a $^3/_8$" photo strip; ink edges. Mount over torn journaling strip with small brads. Cut vellum out of metal-rimmed tag. Press frame on embossing pad; sprinkle with gold embossing powder. Heat emboss with embossing gun. Print title on vellum; cut to size and layer with cropped photo under embossed metal tag rim. Attach eyelet and tie with fibers. Tie letter charm to fiber.

I Hope You'll Always...
Reflect color and light with metallic embellishments

Trudy's combination of metallic embellishments reflects color and light, adding dramatic dimensional interest to her page. Machine stitch sheer lavender fabric over lavender cardstock around edges; mat on white cardstock for background. Punch or cut squares into spring roll strip; machine stitch spring roll around edges near bottom of page as shown. String metal flowers with fibers, attaching bead through center of flower. Mount strung flowers and fibers atop spring roll border, centering flowers in punched window; secure flowers with glue dots. Stamp name on small white cardstock strip with lavender ink; slide into clear plastic tab and set aside. Mat photo on white cardstock; lightly adhere on background to determine placement and measure for machine stitched border. Remove matted photo; machine stitch border. Cut material away from inside of machine stitched border with sharp scissors. Mount matted photo with photo corners inside stitching lines where material has been cut away; layer on page over clear tab and purple vellum die-cut flower embellished with bead. Stamp date on background next to photo. Craft dragonfly from wire and beads; mount at side of photo. Slice a 4"-wide strip of lavender cardstock; layer with white mesh and mat on white cardstock. Print title words on white cardstock and vellum. Paper tear edges of words on white cardstock; brush edges with purple chalk. Cut title word on vellum to size; attach to matted strip with eyelets. Mount metal letters over die-cut vellum flower. Stamp title word on metal-rimmed vellum tag. Die cut two small tags from white cardstock. Adhere sticker heart under glass pebble and border with black fine-tip pen. Attach eyelet and tie together with metal-rimmed tag; hang from metal letter "a." Mount spring roll scrap to second white tag; border with black fine-tip pen. Attach eyelet and hang from small brad with string. Attach metal letter snaps to tag and along bottom of matted strip.

Trudy Sigurdson

Birthday Tea

Detail photo mat edges with gold paint pen

Katherine paints photo mat edges with a gold leaf pen, adding a bit of elegant shine to richly colored papers. Print title; silhouette cut. Heat emboss with gold embossing powder before mounting over matted patterned paper background. Heat emboss swirl clip with gold embossing powder; when cool, mount over "i" in title word. Horizontally mount three photos on right page; horizontally and vertically border photos with ribbon strips. Mount brads at ribbon intersections. Tear patterned paper and green cardstock strips; layer and mount at lower corner of right page. Single mat two photos on green cardstock; paint edges with gold leaf paint pen. Let dry; mount. Triple mat one photo on green cardstock and patterned paper; tear bottom edge of second mat. Paint edges of last mat with gold leaf paint pen. Let dry and mount with foam tape. Stamp letters on small tag cut from brown cardstock. Shade edges with ink. Punch hole at top and tie with ribbon and string; mount tag at upper right corner of triple matted photo. Paper fold tea bag from vellum using template; fill with tiny circles punched from brown and tan cardstocks. Punch hole at top of tea bag, tie with string and wrap around bottom left corner of triple matted photo. Print journaling and date on ivory cardstock; cut journal block to size. Shade edges with ink. Press metal frame on embossing ink pad; sprinkle with gold ultra thick embossing enamel; heat emboss. Layer trimmed date behind gold embossed frame; mount on paper-torn corner with brads.

Meghan had been planning my birthday surprise for over a month. I was shocked that she could keep it a secret from me for so long, especially since I am known for never being able to keep a secret. To celebrate my 33rd Birthday Meghan brought me to Abbey Gardens for afternoon tea and lunch. I love anything old and Victorian, and the restaurant was beautifully decorated. I was delighted that Meghan shared my birthday with me in such a special way. I am very lucky to have such a thoughtful daughter to plan such a wonderful afternoon for her mother.

Katherine Brooks

I had a good friend who told me about this cute little scrapbook store that I just "had" to visit. Upon my first visit I was hooked!

Katherine Brooks

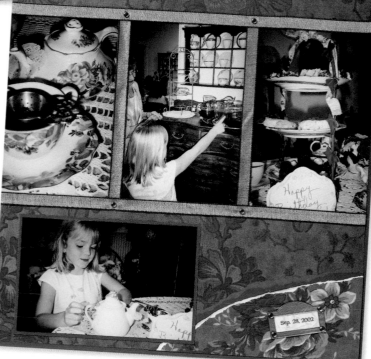

Kindergarten Hair

Keep it simple with silver accents

Diana's use of small silver brads works well with the simplicity of her monochromatic color-blocked page. Mount enlarged photo on preprinted patterned paper; attach brads at corners. Print title and journaling on vellum and preprinted tag die cuts. Write date on vellum; cut to size and layer behind silver frame mounted with silver brads. Cut journaling on vellum to size; mount on page with silver brads over tag detailed with eyelet and fibers. Cut title and descriptive words into strips; mount title word over enlarged photo with silver brads. Layer descriptive words printed on vellum over metal-rimmed tag layered with collaged colored paper strips; attach eyelet and tie with embroidery thread. Fold vellum envelope using template; attach eyelet. Insert written letter over patterned paper strip into envelope. Layer on page with silver brads over printed die-cut tag embellished with eyelet and embroidery thread. Cut journaling tag to size; mount atop photo with large brad allowing tag to move from side to side, showing hidden photo.

Diana Graham; Photos, Grins group Portraits, Palatine, Illinois

Diana Hudson

Too Two Cute

String stars on wire strand

Diana's freehand crafted stars dance across the page secured on a curled wire strand. Print journaling on white cardstock and part of title on blue cardstock. Cut journaling block into strip and adhere candle and present stickers at bottom. Mount two photos behind preprinted frames on blue cardstock background. Double mat two photos on white and blue cardstock. Freehand cut stars from colored cardstock to match design on preprinted frame. Attach eyelet at center of stars and border with colored pens. String wire through stars; curl wire ends and mount at center of pages. Unwrap paper yarn; mount on white cardstock. Cut title letters from paper yarn cardstock using template. Attach eyelet at center of "o" before mounting on page.

No More Training Wheels

Dangle an embellished tag from a beaded chain

Diana utilizes chains on her page to dangle a layered tag and link title blocks together. Mat green cardstock on blue cardstock for background; detail edges of green cardstock with black chalk pencil. Mat three photos on white cardstock; mount at left side of page. Mat single photo on blue cardstock. Print part of title and journaling on white cardstock. Cut journaling to size; detail edges with black chalk pencil. Attach four jump rings together; link to small punched hole in title blocks. Mat linked title blocks on red mesh. Cut journaling block to size; detail edges with black chalk pencil. Mount with red mesh scraps on tag cut from black cardstock. Tie red and blue raffia through punched silver circle at top of tag. Tie bicycle charm to tag with white embroidery thread. Cut large title letters from colored cardstock using template. Detail and shade edges of letters with white milky pen and black chalk; mat on black cardstock and silhouette cut. Attach red brad to top photo. Hang journaled tag and metal-rimmed tag layered with mesh and torn-paper scrap from beaded chain. Secure tag with glue dots over third photo.

Diana Graham

Katherine Brooks

Play Hard

Mount metal title letters with brads

Katherine captures reflected light with metal title letters that pop off of a dark background. Cut window screen into 1¼" strip; mount at top of brown matted cardstock background with flat eyelets. Sculpt clay into stone shape; press letter stamps into soft clay and shade with metallic rub-ons. Mount metal title letters over window screen strip with black brads. Mat two photos on blue cardstock strip; mount at bottom of page. Mat one photo on blue cardstock; mount with self-adhesive foam spacers over enlarged photo sliced into 1¼" strips. Print journaling on vellum; cut to size and draw frame around edges with black fine-tip pen. Mount on page with tiny silver eyelets.

Through Great Love

Document a true love story

Torrey retells a memorable love story through journaling and an artistic assembly of metal letters and hearts. Cut squares and rectangles of colored cardstock into various sizes; layer over a white cardstock background. Print title and journaling on vellum. Cut title blocks to size; mount on page over cardstock squares with silver eyelets. Mount metal letters and heart shapes on page with colored eyelets. Bend wire into heart-shaped hanger to hold memorabilia; mount to page with "U"-pins and secure at back of page. Punch hearts from pink and blue cardstock. Layer with two-sided tape before covering with clear micro beads. Mount on page with self-adhesive foam spacers. Mat large journaling block on blue cardstock with eyelets; mount on page. Punch four more hearts from pink and blue cardstock; layer on border strip with metal letters and hearts secured with colored eyelets.

Torrey Miller

Grandpa's Girls

Clip fibers to photo

Brandi ties textured fibers to a swirl clip adding a bit of whimsy to a photo mat. Stamp designs on green and ivory cardstocks with watermark and colored inks. Tear edges of light green cardstock; crumple, flatten and layer together. Machine stitch on stamped green cardstock background. Mat photo on ivory cardstock; tear edges. Print journaling on stamped ivory cardstock; tear all edges. Machine stitch journaling block to page. Stamp design and title on metal-rimmed vellum tag; layer over ivory cardstock strip. Punch hole at side and tie with fibers. Mount on page with self-adhesive foam spacers. Tie fibers to swirl clip; attach to mat. Glue fibers into place.

Brandi Ginn

Alex at Beckwith Park

String metallic beads on a fiber border

Trudy strings metallic beads and weaves fibers into a beautiful border design. Tear large and small vellum strips; vertically mount largest strips at sides of pages as a border on matted green cardstock background. Create fiber design by stringing two fibers through one metallic bead, alternating and crossing fibers atop another. Wrap fiber ends around top and bottom of green cardstock; secure at back. Mat page with darker cardstock. Mat photos on green cardstock; mount over layered vellum strips. Print journaling on vellum; cut to size and mount at bottom of pages. String beads on fibers; feed through small pierced holes above and below vellum journaling blocks.

Trudy Sigurdson

I am an emotional scrapbooker. I don't scrapbook to record events, although that is a natural part of the art form. More important, I want to record the emotions. Because of that, I care less about getting all of my photos scrapbooked than working with those special photos that speak to my feelings.

Trudy Sigurdson

Tis the Season

Add shine with metallic tinsel

Holle's holiday page gets sparkle from wire and tinsel embellishments. Cut two 2½" strips of green cardstock; tear one edge and horizontally mount at top and bottom of blue cardstock. Die cut large and small title letters from gold paper and red cardstock. Mount green metallic tinsel at top right corner of page. Punch tags from dark blue cardstock; mount red title letters on tags. Punch hole; embellish and wrap with wire. Mount tags on page with self-adhesive foam spacers. Print journaling on ivory cardstock; cut to size and mount over red metallic tinsel with self-adhesive foam spacers. Complete page with pre-made 3-D embellishments.

We decorated our house on November 1 this year, very early because Thomas was leaving on December 4 for Kuwait. He was a great help getting the boxes down from the attic, helping me set up and decorate the trees, and putting lights on the outside of the house. I carefully placed the Santas Mama painted, set the table with Christmas dishes, decorated the top of the kitchen cabinets, bathrooms, and our bed. Thomas made the bed with our snowmen flannel sheets and helped me hang ornaments. Teamwork can ease the workload. Thanks Babe!

Holle Wiktorek

Heidi Schueller

Her Eyes, How They Twinkled

Hang tags and photos from sewing notions

Sewing hooks and eyes are used to "hang" embellished tags and photos with fuzzy fibers on Heidi's holiday page. Punch swirls from tan cardstock; detail punched shapes with chalk: mount on tan cardstock background. Slice three ½" strips of red cardstock; horizontally and vertically mount as shown. Double mat photos on colored cardstock. Craft hanging loops by slicing ½ x 2" strips of cardstock. Fold in half over top of double-matted photo; punch hole through loop and photo mats with eyelet setter. Attach brad through hole. Feed fiber through loops; tie ends to sewing hooks attached to page with "U"-pins made from wire. Mount fabric Christmas trees on metal-rimmed vellum and colored tags. Attach eyes to top of tag with wire "U"-pins. String with fiber and hang from hooks attached to page. Print title on plain and yellow vellum; circle cut to fit inside round metal-rimmed tags. Hang title tags from top of page.

Christmas Eve

Embellish with sequins for sparkle and shine

Holle adds colorful shine to her page with sequined photo corners. Mat green embroidered cardstock with red cardstock for background. Mat photos on green vellum. Cut corrugated cardstock into 1½" squares; diagonally slice and mount as photo corners. Embellish corners with sequins. Cut a 1¾" strip of corrugated cardstock for title block; tear top edge. Mount die-cut title letters and embellish with sequins. Print journaling on green vellum; cut to size. Mount one journaling block on left page with red and holly-shaped eyelets at corners. Mount second journaling block on right page; border with red fibers. Embellish die-cut Christmas tree with sequins and star brad. Layer metal ornaments on red cardstock; embellish with twisted and curled red wire. Mount on page with self-adhesive foam spacers.

Holle Wiktorek

When I started teaching scrapbook classes at our local scrapbook store and at conventions, I found true happiness. I am constantly learning and staying challenged with new trends and techniques in the industry.

Holle Wiktorek

Additional Instructions

To My Beautiful Daughter

Embellish tags with pressed flowers and leaves (Page 12)

Delicate pressed flowers and leaves adorn Trudy's layered and stitched tags, lending an organic element to an outdoor portrait. Horizontally and vertically stitch a 2½ x 12" piece of vellum across bottom of purple cardstock background, forming pockets as shown. Mount sheer ribbon atop vellum pockets adhering to back of page. Vertically tear 3" strips of pink and purple cardstock; brush pink chalk along top, bottom and left edges. Layer atop another and curl right edges gently with fingers. Stitch to background cardstock along untorn edges as shown. Mat photo on dark purple cardstock; tear bottom edge of mat before mounting on background. Die cut six large tags; two each from white cardstock, vellum and lavender paper. Tear vellum and lavender tags into thirds. Layer top third of vellum tag and bottom third of lavender tag over white tag as shown; stitch around all edges. Mount pressed leaves and flowers on tags with glue dots; wrap tags with white floral wire. Mount silver eyelet at top of tags over punched purple rectangle. Tie sheer ribbon at top of tags to complete. Computer print title words on pink and white cardstock. Crop into geometric and tag shapes; detail with pink chalk and black pen outline. Mount silver eyelets and floral wire before layering on page.

Trudy Sigurdson

Oh Boy

Wrap a precut matte board with fabric (Page 32)

Diana frames an expressive photo of her son with a fabric covered matte board and unique matting that defines what it's like to be a boy. Wrap precut matte board with linen fabric; secure fabric to back of matte board with tacky tape. Print two copies of dictionary page containing "boy" definition from The Century Dictionary Online (after obtaining permission to copy the text). Mat photo with dictionary definition page. Print title words in red ink over second dictionary definition page. Cut to fit inside metal tag; tie metal tag with gingham ribbon around bottom of fabric frame. Mount frame to patterned paper background with strong adhesive. Adhere leter stickers to metal tag; mount to background with silver brads.

Diana Hudson

Frolicking

Frame colored tiles with metal conchos (Page 54)

Diana uses a simple embellishment to add a bit of color to sliced panoramic photos. Print journaling on textured paper for background. Vertically slice panoramic photo at random increments; reassemble across page, leaving space between each slice. Cut first and last photo strip into squares; mount on page leaving space for tile embellishments. Adhere letter stickers for title above photos as shown. Mount colored tiles to page with strong adhesive; layer conchos atop tiles piercing page with pointed ends. On back of page, bend concho prongs down toward page to secure.

Diana Hudson

Live, Love, Laugh

Tie rolled cardstock strips (Page 76)

Trudy rolls cardstock into unique embellishments. Crumple and flatten light blue cardstock; mat on darker blue cardstock. Machine stitch horizontally and vertically at $2\frac{1}{2}$" increments and around edges. Gently curl torn edges toward inside of page. Mat photo on tan cardstock; mount on darker blue cardstock with torn edges. Print journaling on vellum; cut to size and double mat on brown and dark blue cardstock with torn edges. Machine stitch double matted photo and journaling block over mesh strips to page; gently curl torn edges. Punch small stars from tan and blue cardstock; crumple, flatten and outline with black pen. Layer stars on page near photo and on journaling block. Die cut small tags from blue cardstock; punch hole at top and tie with hemp. Mount heart snaps on tags and outline with black pen. Layer with wooden blocks stamped with title words. Die cut large tag from tan cardstock; mount circle punched from brown cardstock at top of tag. Punch hole at center of brown punched circle and tie with hemp. Layer tag with large punched star outlined with pen and mesh; wrap with hemp and attach metal heart snap. Mount on page with self-adhesive foam spacers. Roll $1\frac{1}{4}$ x 5" torn paper strips and tie with hemp; mount alongside double-matted photo.

Trudy Sigurdson

American Dreamers

Stamp and emboss a gold metallic frame (Page 98)

Katherine adds a textured touch to a heat embossed frame with stamped stars and letters. Mat navy cardstock with burgundy cardstock. Tear $5\frac{1}{2}$" and 6" strips of patterned paper; horizontally layer and mount at center of page. Attach eyelets at upper corners of matted background; string with knotted gingham ribbon. Create photo frame by cutting a $7\frac{1}{2}$ x $5\frac{1}{4}$" window out of a $8\frac{1}{2}$ x $6\frac{1}{4}$" piece of cardstock. Press frame on embossing pad; sprinkle with gold and clear embossing powders. Heat emboss; repeat steps. While second layer is still warm, stamp stars and letters into frame. When cool, mount frame over photo with foam tape. Cut vellum out of metal-rimmed tags. Heat emboss metal rim with gold embossing powder. Print title and journaling on vellum; cut to size and layer with cropped photos under embossed metal tag rims.

Katherine Brooks

SUPPLY LIST

The following supplies were used to create the art featured in this book.

Page 12 To My Beautiful Daughter
Tag template (Accu-Cut), small tag die cuts (Accu-Cut), heart eyelets (Creative Impressions), dried flowers and leaves, cardstock, vellum, ribbon, floral wire, eyelets, chalk, black fine tip pen

Page 14 Until I Saw the Sea
Metal-rimmed vellum tags (Making Memories), textured cardstock, cardstock, vellum, mulberry paper, fabric, seashells, lace, ribbon, wire, beads, square punch, blue fine tip pen

Page 14 Deep Thoughts
Corrugated cardstock (DMD), die cut letters (Accu-Cut), stamps (Plaid), eyelets, netting, cardstock, vellum, jute, leather scraps, sandpaper, chalk

Page 15 Super Scrappin' Getaway
Cardstock (Bazzill), vellum (Scrapbook Sally), netting, hemp string, sand dollars and starfish (Magic Scraps), chalk (Craf-T)

Page 16 I've Been Working on the Railroad
Locomotive sticker (Mrs. Grossman's Paper Co.), train track die cut (Deluxe Designs), cardstock, jute string, eyelets, rocks

Page 17 Patriot
Patterned paper (K & Co), letter template (source unknown), tag template (Deluxe Designs), corner stamp (source unknown), cardstock, hemp string, fibers, nailheads, chalk, fabric tag

Page 17 Time
Mesh paper, clay tiles (source unknown), letter stamps (source unknown), cardstock, copper strip, eyelets, button, embroidery thread

Page 18 Garth, Faith
Star brads (Creative Impressions), shrink plastic (Grafix), clip art (clipart.com), cardstock, vellum, wire, eyelets, hemp string, jump rings

page 18 Gone Fishing
Corrugated cardstock (DMD), die cut fish (Creative Memories), cardstock, string, chalk

Page 19 Feed the Birds
Birdhouse die cuts (Heartland Paper Co.), heart punch (EK Success), cardstock, brads, eyelets, jute string, spanish moss

Page 20 Miss Aysha
Metal hearts and stars (Provo Craft), dried leaves (Nature's Pressed), key charm (Rubba Dub Dub), flat eyelets (Making Memories), hemp string (American Hemp), cardstock, eyelets, raffia, chalk

Page 21 Branded by the Effects of Nature
Patterned paper (Paper Loft), stamps (Hero Arts), tag template (Deluxe Designs), transparency (Pockets on a Roll), cardstock, vellum, eyelets, embossing powder, leather, button, twine, burlap leaves, metal frame

Page 22 Adonis Narcissus Diggs
Patterned paper (Keeping Memories Alive), wooden fence (Darice), cardstock, vellum, brads

Page 22 Queen Victoria's Memorial
Patterned paper (Colorbök), dried flowers and leaves (Nature's Pressed), spring roll (Magic Scraps), tag die cuts (Accu-Cut), hemp string (American Hemp), eyelets, buttons, pigment pen

Page 23 Mother's Day
Textured cardstock (Bazzill), mesh (Magenta) paper frames (Leeco), memorabilia pockets (Therm O Web), pressed daisies (Pressed Petals), vellum

Page 23 Captured
Patterned paper (source unknown), cardstock, mesh, satin cording, button

Page 24 Uniquely You
Patterned paper (Colors By Design), polymer clay (Polyform Products), stamps (Hero Arts, PSX Design), metallic rub-ons (Craf-T), cardstock, inks, brads, wire, ribbon, embossing powder

Page 24 Year of the Dress
Patterned papers and vellum (Over the River), dragonfly stamp (source unknown), flower punches (Family Treasures), cardstock, wire, balsa wood, hinges

Page 25 Pure Country
Patterned paper (Keeping Memories Alive), corrugated cardboard (DMD), lettering template (Scrap Pagerz), stamps (PSX Design), square stamps (Making Memories), flat eyelets (The Stamp Doctor), embossing powder (UTEE, Ranger), cardstock, chalk, ink, square punch, paper clips, jump rings, staples, screen, hemp twine

Page 26 Full of Beans
Tag template (Deluxe Designs), polymer clay (Polyform Products), stamps (PSX Design), fibers (EK Success), embossing powder (UTEE, Suze Weinberg's), waxy flax (Scrapworks), screen (ScrapYard 329), paper yarn (Making Memories), cardstock, circle punch, brads

Page 27 Amigo at the Denver Zoo
Cardstock, pigment pen, latch hook rug, mesh

Page 28 Gardening 101
Letter beads (Westrim), seed beads (JewelCraft), cardstock, eyelets, chalk, red hemp twine, pressed flowers, wire

Page 28 Destin, Florida
Corrugated cardstock (DMD), sand dollar stamp and inks (Stampin' Up), letter stamps (Hero Arts, PSX Design), alphabet die cuts (QuicKutz, Sizzix), cardstock, sea glass, chalk, star brad, decorative sand

Page 29 Seeking Shelter
Patterned paper (Creative Imaginations), mesh (Magic Mesh), cardstock, wire, chalks, eyelets, jute string, self-adhesive foam spacers

Page 29 Fishing
Handmade paper (Graphic Products Corp.), corkboard (Magic Scraps), stamps (Hero Arts), vellum tag (Making Memories), stickers (Paper Adventures), brown mini bag (DMD), cardstock, fibers, buttons, fishing line, metal screen, swirl paperclip

Page 30 Pinewood Derby
Patterned paper (source unknown), pre-printed photo strip (source unknown), faux wood paper, die cut letters, scalloped circle punch, cardstock, square punch, eyelets, fine tip black pen

Page 31 Uninvited Grill Guests
Mulberry paper (Pulsar Paper), lettering template (EK Success), sticker letters (EK Success), paper yarn (Making Memories), cardstock, chalk, feathers, black fine tip pen, white gel pen, brown marker pen

Page 32 Oh Boy
Patterned paper (Chatterbox), square and oval metal tags (Making Memories), ribbon (Offray), letter stickers (Creative Imaginations), linen fabric, pre-cut matte board, silver brads

Page 34 And Tia Makes Three
Textured cardstock (Bazzill), textured gold paper (Emagination Crafts), transparency (IBM), die cut tags (Accu-Cut), mesh (Magenta), fibers (Rubba Dub Dub), buttons (Jesse James) cardstock, fabric, brads

Page 35 Letters to My Son
Letter stamps (PSX Design), cardstock (It Takes Two, Bazzill), mesh (Magenta), hemp string (American Hemp), fibers (Rubba Dub Dub), eyelets (Scrapbook Source), photo corners (Canson), gray ink, chalk, circle punch

Page 36 Pumpkin Patch
Patterned paper (All My Memories), tag (All My Memories), leaf punch (EK Success), cardstock, fibers, buttons, chalk, wire, square punch, eyelets, cork

Page 36 Witchie, Witchie, Screamie, Screamie
Patterned paper (Design Originals), tag template (Deluxe Designs), spider die cut (source unknown), cardstock, circle punch, sheer ribbon, chalk, embroidery thread, buttons, fibers, black fine point pen

Page 37 Arizona Fall
Letter stamps (PSX Design), metallic rub-ons (Craf-T), copper (American Art Clay Co.), leaf punch (Emagination Crafts), fibers (EK Success), cardstock, eyelets, chalk, brad, inks

Page 38 A Mother's Pride
Letter stamps (PSX Design), fibers (Magic Scraps, Rubba Dub Dub), envelope die cuts (Accu-Cut), cardstock (Bazzill, It Takes Two), vellum, eyelets, brads, shells, ink

Page 39 Within You I See Myself
Patterned paper (C-Thru Ruler), conchos (Scrapworks), transparency (Staples), stamps (Barnes & Noble), ink, embossing powder, eyelets, brads, picture hanger, wire, ribbon

Page 40 When a Child is Born
Silver hearts (Provo Craft), cardstock (Bazzill), mica tiles (USArtQuest), dried leaves and flowers (Nature's Pressed), chalk (Craf-T), buttons (Jesse James), paper lace, skeleton leaves, ribbon, photo corners

Page 40 The Perfect Dress
Die cut letters (Sizzix), patterned vellum (Anna Griffin), dimensional stickers (EK Success), letter stamps (Plaid), cardstock, lace, felt, embossing powder, sparkle yarn

Page 41 You Can't Hide Beautiful
Patterned paper (source unknown), silver framed tag (Making Memories), heart stamp (Hero Arts), small tag (DMD), cardstock, vellum, brads, embossing powder, pressed flower, ribbon

Page 41 Jenna
Fibers (Rubba Dub Dub), letter stamps (PSX Design), date stamp (Office Depot), photo corners (Canson), cardstock, ink, fabric, ceramic buttons, embroidery thread

Page 42 Muriel
Silk ribbon (Plaid), die cut letters (QuicKutz), cardstock, embossing poweder (UTEE, Ranger)

Page 42 Dian Frybarger
Cardstock, fabric, ribbon, buttons, chalk

Page 43 A Pinch of Sugar
Leaf and butterfly pattern (Lasting Impressions), patterned paper (EK Success), vellum tags (Making Memories), cardstock, ribbon, embroidery thread, brown fine tip pen

Page 43 First Grader
Fibers (Rubba Dub Dub), eyelets (Making Memories), patterned paper (K & Co.), slide mount (Scrapworks), cardstock, vellum, ink, gold leaf pen, brads, ribbon

Page 44 Spring
Patterned vellum (EK Success), embroidery stickers (EK Success), fibers (EK Success), tag template (Deluxe Designs), cardstock, eyelets

Page 44 How Sweet It Is
Patterned paper (Karen Foster Design), flower die cuts (source unknown), corner flower stamp (source unknown), flower eyelet (Creative Impressions), cardstock, vellum, buttons, embroidery thread, ink, fibers, straight pin, ribbon, paper yarn, mesh

Page 45 Love...
Printed vellum (Posh Impressions), cardstock, embroidery thread, chalk

Page 45 Do Not Peek
Alphabet beads (Darice), silver-edged tags (Making Memories), flower stamp (Hero Arts), versamark pad (Tsukineko), cardstock, vellum, chalk, embossing powder, buttons, ribbon, mesh, fabric, fibers

Page 46 Beach Bums
Patterned paper (Frances Meyer), seashell stamps (Hero Arts), letter stamps (Hero Arts), sea shells (Magic Scraps), fibers (Rubba Dub Dub), cardstock, ink, chalk, embossing powder, glass pebble, watch crystal, spiral paper clip, fabric

Page 47 Sailing At Lake Granby
Cardstock, eyelets, twine, fabric

Page 48 Zoo Crew
Lettering template (Memories to Keep), embroidery floss (DMC), cardstock, wire, buttons

Page 48 Funny Face
Letter stamps (Stampin Up!), square stamp (Hero Arts), frame (Making Memories), cardstock, ink, eyelets, fiber (Fibers by the Yard), buttons (Magic Scraps), square punch, metal

Page 49 Busy Bee
Patterned paper (Provo Craft), embroidery thread (DMC), bee and flowers (Provo Craft), cardstock, clip art title

Page 50 Memphis
Patterned paper (PrintWorks), ribbon (Robin's Nest), cardstock, vellum, eyelets

Page 51 Being Your Mom
Tag template (Provo Craft), seashell charms (JewelCraft), seagull die cut (EK Success), cardstock, vellum, eyelet, silver brads

Page 51 Smile
Patterned paper (K & Co.), cardstock, vellum, buttons, lace, fibers, chalk

Page 52 Dressing Alike
Patterned paper (Anna Griffin), fibers (FK Success), embroidery thread (Making Memories), dimensional heart sticker (EK Success), vellum (Autumn Leaves), buttons (Making Memories), cardstock, sheer ribbon, eyelets, straight pin

Page 52 Fringies
Beaded ribbon (Hirschberg Schutz & Co.), embroidery thread (DMC), cardstock, vellum, gingham fabric, fiber fill, colored brush pens

Page 53 To Dance the Dream
Snowflake stamp (Holly Berry House), fiber (On The Surface), cardstock, vellum, mulberry paper, pigment powder, glitter glue, embossing powders

Page 54 Frolicking
Textured paper (Bazzill), letter stickers (Creative Imaginations), mini tiles (Magic Scraps), square conchos (Scrapworks)

Page 56 Best Friends
Corrugated cardstock (DMD), die cut letters, circles, frames and hearts (Sizzix), fibers (EK Success), beads (JewelCraft), jewels (Westrim), sparkle powder, (Z Barten Productions), flower brad (Idea Tool Box), swirl clip (Boxer Scrapbook Productions), cardstock, mulberry paper, tinsel, wire, mesh, cork

Page 56 The Dance of the Leaves
Tag templates (Deluxe Designs), buttons (Making Memories), cardstock, vellum, eyelets, chalk, fibers, embroidery thread

Page 57 Joy in Blytheville
Suede paper (Wintech), beads (JewelCraft), gold and silver paper (Canson), die cut alphabet (QuicKutz), "JOY" stickers (Meri Meri), holly leaf punch (Family Treasures), pine cone punch (Emagination Crafts), dimensional wreath sticker (Westrim), cardstock, glitter glue, eyelets, ribbon

Page 58 My Little Man
Transparency (IBM), fibers (Magic Scraps, On The Surface), buttons (Hillcreek Designs), star die cut (Sizzix), wire (Artistic Wire), cardstock, vellum, eyelets, embroidery thread, square punch

Page 59 Friendship Braids
Patterned paper (Creative Imaginations), beads (Rubba Dub Dub), slide frame (Scrapsahoy.com), letter stickers (Creative Imaginations), embroidery floss (DMC), cardstock (Bazzill)

Page 60 Light of My Life
Patterned paper (source unknown), die cut letters (Accu-Cut), eyelets (JewelCraft), metal and vellum tags (Making Memories), fibers (Cut-It-Up), cardstock, vellum, chalk, beads

Page 60 Flowers
Patterned and embossed paper (Anna Griffin), beads (Westrim), gold textured paper (Emagination Crafts), lettering template (Wordsworth), cardstock, vellum, glitter glue, brads, self-adhesive foam spacers

Page 61 A Treasured Time
Patterned vellum (Autumn Leaves), metal-rimmed heart tag (Creative Imaginations), heart charm (source unknown), key charm (source unknown), metal frame (Making Memories), metal letter (Making Memories), metal heart tag (Making Memories), photo corner stamp (source unknown), heart punch (Emagination Crafts), clear ultra thick embossing enamel (UTEE, Ranger), cardstock, sequins, button, ink, sheer ribbon, eyelet, chalk

Page 61 You
Patterned vellum (Paper Garden), beads (JewelCraft), metal-rimmed tags (Making Memories), fibers (Cut-It-Up), hearts (DoJiggies), flower stamp (Stampendous), cardstock, wire, sequins, embossing powder, small brad

Page 62 Bubbles
Patterned vellum (Wubie Prints), letter template (Scrap Pagerz), bubble wand die cut (Deluxe Designs), cardstock, watch crystals (twopeasinabucket.com)

Page 63 Bubbily Sudsily
Patterned paper (Paper Adventures), clear microbeads (Halcraft), silver metallic cardstock (Canson), cardstock, vellum, wire, beads, eyelets

Page 64 You Make My Heart Leap!
Patterned paper (Karen Foster Design), pre-printed die-cuts (source unknown), plastic frogs (source unknown), letter beads (Westrim), tag template (Deluxe Designs), transparency, cardstock, buttons, embroidery thread, eyelets

Page 64 Kids
Patterned paper (Provo Craft), mesh (Magic Mesh), dragonflies (Traditions), cardstock, vellum, twigs

Page 65 You Are My Sunshine
Beads (JewelCraft), sheer ribbon (Robin's Nest), buttons (Making Memories), metal-rimmed vellum tags (Making Memories), tag template (Deluxe Designs), letter stamps (Hero Arts), leaf stamp (Plaid), cardstock, vellum, mulberry paper, eyelets

Page 66 Making a Splash
Tinsel (Magic Scraps), glitter (Magic Scraps), vellum (Scrapbook Sally), square punch, circle punches, cardstock

Page 67 Jewel of the Pool
Beads (Halcraft), jewels (Hirschberg Schutz & Co.), eyelet (Creative Impressions), patterned paper (Cut-It-Up), lettering template (Scrap Pagerz), letter stickers (Provo Craft), paper-pieced mermaid (Cut-It-Up), metal-rimmed tags (Avery), vellum (Hot Off The Press, HOTP), cardstock, ribbon, foam board, transparency, circle punches

Page 68 Moo-La-La
Star jewels (Magic Scraps), square and round jewels (JewelCraft), die cut flowers (source unknown), cardstock, vellum, glitter

Page 69 Winter
Jewels (JewelCraft), beads (JewelCraft), shaved ice (Magic Scraps), patterned vellum (EK Success), snowflake stamp (source unknown), snowflake punches (Carl, Marvy/Uchida), cardstock, vellum, ink, eyelet

Page 69 Ayasha's First Day of School
Buttons (Making Memories), fibers (On The Surface), beads (On The Surface), wire (Artistic Wire), patterned vellum (Autumn Leaves), letter stamps (PSX Design), metal-rimmed tag (Making Memories), metal stars (source unknown), cardstock, ink, pencil crayons, fine tip pens

Page 70 Fish
Lettering template (C-Thru Ruler), texture plates (Fiskars), fishing pole and lures (Crafts Etc.), cardstock, jute string

Page 70 Sweet 'n Sour
Chopsticks (Pier 1 Imports), Chinese stamp (Hero Arts), fiber (EK Success), Versamark (Tsukineko), fortune cookie die cut (Deluxe Designs), cardstock, embossing powder, Chinese coins

Page 71 Swim
Beads (JewelCraft), wire (Artistic Wire), letter punches (EK Success), Versamark ink (Tsukineko), fish charms (source unknown), cardstock, embossing powder, hooks, marker, glue dots

Page 71 Bathtub
Ceramic tiles (Plaid), cardstock

Page 72 Baby
Patterned paper (Karen Foster Design), polymer clay (Polyform Products), metallic rub-ons (Craf-T), lettering template (source unknown), stamps (Postmodern Design), cardstock, ink, embossing powder, brads, wire

Page 73 Sea Glass Beach
Beads (Blue Moon Beads), patterned vellum (HOTP), memorabilia keeper (C-Thru Ruler), versamark ink (Tsukineko), shell stamps (JudiKins), dots stamp (Stamps by Judith), cardstock, wire

Page 74 Home
Patterned paper (Club Scrap), letter sticker (Paper House Productions), letter stamps (PSX Design), lettering template (Wordsworth), stamp (Club Scrap), glass pebble (Making Memories), metal letter (Making Memories), flower nailheads, clock charm, frame charms, cardstock, gold ink, matte board, ribbon, tassel, gold embossing powder, square and rectangle punches, eyelet, fabric

Page 75 He's Leaving on a Jet Plane
Patterned paper (Autumn Leaves), beads (JewelCraft), corrugated paper (DMD), alphabet die cuts (QuicKutz), alphabet pebbles (Making Memories), star brads (Creative Imaginations), cardstock, wire

Page 76 Live, Love, Laugh
Cardstock (Bazzill, Paper Adventures), letter stamps (PSX Design), small star punch (Emagination Crafts), large star die cut (Sizzix), heart snaps (Making Memories), tag die cuts (Accu-Cut), mesh (Magic Mesh), vellum, ink, hemp (American Hemp), photo corners (Canson), circle punches, chalk, black fine tip pen

Page 78 Maize Maze
Lettering template (Scrap Pagerz), cardstock, vellum, fibers, chalk, self-adhesive foam spacers

Page 79 Remember
Mulberry paper (Paper Garden), handmade paper (Graphic Products Corp.), letter stamps (Plaid), coastal netting (Magic Scraps), transparency, cardstock, black ink, fibers, walnut ink, chalk

Page 80 No Yucky Stuff
Die cut letters (Accu-Cut), velveteen paper (Wintech), cardstock; silver cardstock, vellum, brads

Page 81 Dandelions
Sun punch (Carl), flower punch (Emagination Crafts), small sun (Punch Bunch), small flower (All Night Media, ANM), small leaf punch, cardstock, vellum, self-adhesive foam spacers

Page 81 Holle's Hobbies
Patterned paper (EK Success) lettering template (EK Success), tags (HOTP), large gold brads (ACCO), rubon's (Lil Davis Designs), eyelets, chalk, twine

Page 82 Clara
Patterned paper (source unknown), corner punches (ANM), cardstock, vellum, decorative scissors, oval cutting system

Page 83 Peter Rabbit
Decorative corner punch (ANM), cardstock; chalk, black fine tip pen

Page 83 The View
Patterned paper (Chatterbox), mesh (Magic Mesh), sticker letters (EK Success), plastic window (Chatterbox), cardstock, vellum, dried leaf (Hirschberg Schutz & Co.), brads

Page 84 Wedding Memories
Patterned paper and patterned vellum (Anna Griffin), printed frame (Anna Griffin), gold marker

Page 84 Family
Patterned paper (Northern Spy), wire (Darice), cardstock

Page 85 Tia and Trudy
Letter stamps (PSX Design), mica tiles (USArtQuest), tag die cut (Accu-Cut), heart stickers (Colorbök), dragonfly charms (source unknown), metal star (source unknown), cardstock, photo corners, ribbon, glass pebbles; swirl clip, eyelets, skeleton leaves

Page 86 Trains in a Bubble
Flower, leaf and grass punches (EK Success, Family Treasures), cardstock, wire, train tracks (source unknown)

Page 87 A Sweet Proposal
Patterned paper (Colors by Design), fibers (Cut-It-Up), die cut letters (Accu-Cut), tags (Impress Rubber Stamps), cardstock, vellum, eyelets

Page 87 Tootsie
Flower punch (Family Treasures), decorative corner punch (Family Treasures), cardstock

Page 88 She's Got Personality
Patterned paper (source unknown), tag template (Deluxe Designs), letter beads (Westrim), vellum flower stickers (EK Success), flower eyelets (Doodlebug Design), cardstock, vellum, embroidery thread, beads

Page 88 Springtime Smiles
Patterned paper (EK Success), die cut letters (Sizzix), die cut frame (EK Success), fibers (EK Success), flowers and leaves

Page 89 Sugar & Spice
Patterned paper (source unknown), vellum accents (Cherished Memories), cardstock, mulberry paper

Page 90 Arrows Lacrosse
Letter die cuts (source unknown), cardstock, chalks, string

Page 91 Hoops
Letter stickers (Creative Imaginations), basketball stickers (Frances Meyer), cardstock, square punches, black fine tip pen

Page 91 Tough Yet Tender
Mulberry paper (Paper Garden), lettering template (Provo Craft), die cut letters (Accu-Cut), tag (Impress Rubber Stamps), cardstock, vellum, metallic rub-ons, eyelet, jute string, chalk

Page 92 Lucky Fish
Vellum (Paper Adventures), crimper (Fiskars), cardstock, chalks, brads, brush pens

Page 92 Reflections of Albuquerque
Cardstock, vellum, square punches, triangle and rectangle and circle punches

Page 93 Valentine's Day Weekend
Corrugated cardstock (DMD), die cut letters (Sizzix), lettering template (Cock-A-Doodle Design), buttons (Westrim), state stamp (Destination Stickers and Stamps), cardstock, chalk, cork, ink, fibers

Page 94 It's the Little Moments
Cardstock, clips (Scrapworks), fibers (Rubba Dub Dub), vellum, chalk, ink, brads

Page 95 Christmas in the Desert
Date stamp (Staples), small tag (American Tag), fiber (EK Success), cactus die cut (Deluxe Designs), cardstock, circle punch, ribbon, brads

Page 96 Friday's Child
Sparkled cardstock (Club Scrap), cardstock, vellum (Paper Adventures), heart punches (Emagination Crafts), chicken wire stamp (Art Impressions), watermark ink pad (Tsukineko), ribbon

Page 96 Our View of Canoeing the Okatama
Cardstock, square punches, letter stamps (source unknown), pigment powder, bone folder

Page 97 Grant's Farm
Stamps (Hero Arts), sun punch (EK Success), 3-D sticker (EK Success), ink (Tsukineko), chalk, buttons, wire, eyelets

Page 98 American Dreamers
Metal rimmed tags (Making Memories), eyelets (Making Memories), stamps (Hero Arts, PSX Design), patterned paper (K & Co., Mustard Moon), embossing powder (UTEE, Suze Weinberg), metallic rub-ons (Craf-T), ribbon, cardstock, chalk

Page 100 Sand Between Her Toes
Metal hearts (Darice), wire (Darice), beads (Blue Moon Beads), letter stamps (Plaid), cardstock, vellum, self-adhesive foam spacers

Page 100 A Cherished Love
Patterned paper (Anna Griffin), eyelets (Making Memories), metal clock (7 Gypsies), wire (Artistic Wire), letter stamps (PSX Design), flower punch (Family Treasures), pattern stamp (Anna Griffin), date stamp (Staples), tags (Making Memories), cardstock, ribbon, inks, brads, embossing powder

Page 101 Explore, Discover
Textured paper (Memory Lane), metal star stud (Scrapworks), metal letters (Making Memories), screen (ScrapYard 329) letter stamps (PSX Design), versamark ink (Tsukineko), cardstock, mesh, inks, brads

Page 102 Two Little Souls...
Metal frames (Making Memories), wire (Darice), patterned paper (All My Memories), cardstock, mesh fabric, bead

Page 103 Cherished
Pewter stickers (Magenta), pewter beads (source unknown), wooden blocks (source unknown), fibers (Rubba Dub Dub), photo corners (Canson), cardstock, vellum, skeleton leaves, brads

Page 104 By the Shore
Patterned paper (source unknown), metal letters (Making Memories), metal photo corners (Making Memories), metal frames (Making Memories), metal word eyelets (Making Memories), pail and shovel die cuts (Deluxe Designs), cardstock, decorative sand, glass pebble, chalk, mesh, paper yarn, eyelet, metal mesh, circle punch

Page 104 Grandma
Patterned paper (Anna Griffin), metal frames (source unknown), metal plaque (Boutique Trims), cardstock, vellum, satin ribbon

Page 105 It's Not Fair!
Eyelets (Doodlebug Design), pewter sticker (Magenta), wire (Artistic Wire), cardstock

Page 105 Fuzzy Caterpillar
Patterned paper (Creative Imaginations), metal photo corners (Making Memories), metal rimmed tag (Making Memories), metal screen (source unknown), cardstock, silver brads, beads, button, square punches, safety pin

Page 106 Topsy Turvy
Silver nailhead letters (JewelCraft), eyelets (Creative Imaginations), cardstock, window screen, stainless steel outlet cover, wire

Page 106 The Blues Diner
Rubber stamps (Hero Arts, Stampa Rosa-no longer in business), cardstock, vellum, embossing pad, embossing powder, sterling silver high gloss embossing granules, eyelets

Page 107 In the Pits
Stamps (Hero Arts), eyelets (Making Memories), fibers (Rubba Dub Dub), snaps (Making Memories), screen (ScrapYard 329), washers, cardstock, square punch, ink, brads, embossing enamel

Page 108 Giddy-Up
Letter stickers (source unknown), pre-printed die cut letters (source unknown), metal letter (Making Memories), pre-printed photo frame (My Mind's Eye), western charms (source unknown), 3 dimensional stickers (EK Success), barbed fence die cut (source unknown), pre-printed photo strips (source unknown), cardstock, silver beads, hemp string, fibers, small silver brads, self-adhesive foam spacers

Page 108 Riding the Range
Large and small metal hearts (Provo Craft), cardboard, cardstock, hemp string, chicken wire

Page 109 Fascinated
Velveteen paper (source unknown), pewter letters (source unknown), metal frame (Anima Designs), metal star, cardstock, ribbon, crushed velvet, silver brads, black fine tip pen

Page 109 I Must
Patterned paper (K & Co.), brads (Hyglo/American Pin), swirl clips (Clipiola), copper strip (Art Emboss), walnut ink (Postmodern Design), cardstock, jump rings, microbeads, inks

Page 110 Looking Spectacular
Eyelets, brads, wire (Artistic Wire), die cut letters (Accu-Cut), cardstock

Page 111 What You Do At 2
Metal plaque (Boutique Trims), paper clip (Scrap Arts), stamp (Hero Arts), fibers, ink, cardstock

Page 112 Father's Build Dreams
Leather handmade paper (Memory Lane), snaps (Making Memories), letter stamps (Barnes & Noble), square punch (Family Treasures), cardstock, inks, embossing powder, screen

Page 113 Haley
Wire (Artistic Wire), lettering template (Scrap Pagerz), decorative scissors (Fiskars), cardstock, copper embossing powder

Page 113 Timeless
Patterned paper (source unknown), gold metallic cardstock (HOTP), gold sticker letters (Pioneer), interactive template (Scrapbook Specialities), swoosh punch, fleur de lis punch, heritage border punch all (Family Treasures), gold sticker strips (Mrs. Grossman's Paper Co.), clock hands (Crafts Etc.) cardstock, gold buttons, gold embroidery thread, gold embossing powder

Page 114 I Hope You'll Always...
Wire (Darice), metal letters (Making Memories), metal flowers (Making Memories), metal rimmed tag (Making Memories), eyelets, brads, spring roll (Magic Scraps), fibers (Rubba Dub Dub), tags (Accu-Cut), beads (On The Surface), letter stamps (PSX Design), heart stickers (Colorbök), chalk, cardstock, fabric, ink, photo corners

Page 114 Greener Grass
Metal rimmed vellum tag (Making Memories), charm (Memory Lane), postalz (Art Accents), wire (Artistic Wire), embossing powder (UTEE, Suze Weinberg), date stamp (Staples), small pre-made tag (DMD), cardstock; vellum, fibers, ink, brads, tulle

Page 115 Birthday Tea
Patterned paper (Daisy D's), letter stamps (PSX Design), vellum envelope (Ink It!), swirl clip (7 Gypsies), metal frame (Making Memories), cardstock, inks, ribbon, thread, gold leaf pen, brads, embossing powder

Page 116 Too Two Cute
Lettering template (EK Success), wire (Artistic Wire), eyelets (Doodlebug Design), pre-printed photo frames (My Mind's Eye), paper yarn (Making Memories) cardstock

Page 116 Kindergarten Hair
Patterned paper (SEI), metal-rimmed vellum tag (Making Memories), vellum pocket, cardstock, vellum, brads, metal frame, eyelets, embroidery threads

Page 117 No More Training Wheels
Mesh (Magic Mesh), lettering template (source unknown), metal-rimmed tag (Avery), bicycle charm (source unknown), tag template (Deluxe Designs), cardstock, chain, jump rings, chalk, white milky pen, black chalk pencil, raffia, foam tape

Page 117 Play Hard
Letter stamps (Barnes & Noble), eyelets (Making Memories), brads (Hyglo/AmericanPin), snaps (Making Memories), metallic rub-ons (Craf-T), polymer clay (Polyform Products), cardstock, vellum, embossing powder, screen

Page 118 Through Great Love
Metal letters (Making Memories), metal heart eyelets (Making Memories), wire (Artistic Wire), heart punch (Emagination Crafts), microbeads (Magic Scraps), eyelets, cardstock, vellum

Page 118 Grandpa's Girls
Metal-rimmed vellum tag (Making Memories), stamp (Raindrops on Roses), cardstock, ink, chalk, fibers

Page 119 Alex at Beckwith Park
Cardstock (Bazzill), fibers (On The Surface), beads. vellum, embroidery floss

Page 120 Tis the Season
Gold paper (Canson), wire (Artistic Wire), metallic tinsel (Z-Barten Productions), die cut letters (QuicKutz, Sizzix), 3-D Christmas embellishments (Westrim), tag punch (EK Success), cardstock

Page 120 Her Eyes, How They Twinkled
Metal-rimmed tags (Making Memories), flat eyelets (Doodlebug Design), fabric trees (source unknown), swirl punch (EK Success), cardstock, vellum, chalks, hooks & eyes, fibers

Page 121 Christmas Eve
Corrugated cardstock (DMD), embroidered paper (Creative Imaginations), die cut letters (QuicKutz), silver ornament charms (Making Memories), holly eyelets (Eyelet Factory), star brad (Creative Imaginations), tree die cut (Deluxe Designs), metal charms (Making Memories), cardstock, sequins, eyelets, wire, fibers

Sources

The following companies manufacture products showcased on scrapbook pages within this book. Please check your local retailers to find these materials. We have made every attempt to properly credit the items mentioned in this book and apologize to those we may have missed.

7gypsies™
(800) 588-6707
www.7gypsies.com

ACCO Brands, Inc.
(800) 989-4923
www.acco.com

AccuCut®
(800) 288-1670
www.accucut.com

All My Memories
(888) 553-1998
www.allmymemories.com

All Night Media
(see Plaid Enterprises, Inc.)

American Art Clay Co., Inc.
(800) 374-1600
www.amaco.com

American Hemp—a division of Earth Goods, LLC
(800) 469-4367
www.hemptwine.com

American Tag Company (wholesale only)
(800) 223-3956
www.americantag.net

Anima Designs
(412) 726-8401
www.animadesigns.com

Anna Griffin, Inc. (wholesale only)
(888) 817-8170
www.annagriffin.com

Art Accents
(See Provo Craft)

Artistic Wire Ltd.™
(630) 530-7567
www.artisticwire.com

Art Impressions, Inc.
(800) 393-2014
www.artimpressions.com

Autumn Leaves (wholesale only)
(800) 588-6707
www.autumnleaves.com

Avery
(800) GO-AVERY
www.avery.com

Barnes & Noble
www.bn.com

Bazzill Basics Paper (wholesale only)
(480) 558-8557
www.bazzillbasics.com

Blue Moon Beads (wholesale only)
(800) 377-6715
www.bluemoonbeads.com

Boutique Trims, Inc. (wholesale only)
(248) 437-2017
www.boutiquetrims.com

Boxer Scrapbook Productions LLC.
(888) 625-6255
www.boxerscrapbooks.com

Canson, Inc.®
www.canson-us.com

Carl Mfg. USA, Inc. (wholesale only)
(847) 956-0730
www.carl-products.com

Chatterbox, Inc.
(888) 416-6260
www.chatterboxinc.com

Cherished Memories- no contact information available

Clipiola- no contact information available

Club Scrap™, Inc.
(888) 634-9100
www.clubscrap.com

Colorbök™, Inc (wholesale only)
(800) 366-4660
www.colorbok.com

Colors By Design
(800) 832-8436
www.colorsbydesign.com

Craf-T Products (wholesale only)
(507) 235-3996
www.craf-tproducts.com

Crafts, Etc.
(800) 888-0321
www.craftsetc.com

Creative Imaginations (wholesale only)
(800) 942-6487
www.cigift.com

Creative Impressions
(719) 596-4860
www.creativeimpressions.com

Creative Memories®
(800) 468-9335
www.creativememories.com

C-Thru® Ruler Company, The (wholesale only)
(800) 243-8419
www.cthruruler.com

Cut-It-Up™
(530) 389-2233
www.cut-it-up.com

Daisy D's Paper Company
(888) 601-8955
www.daisydspaper.com

Darice, Inc.
(866) 432-7423
www.darice.com

Deluxe Designs
(480) 497-9005
www.deluxecuts.com

Design Originals
(800) 877-7820
www.d-originals.com

Destinations Stickers and Stamps, Inc. (wholesale only)
(866) 806-7826
www.stateofminestickers.com

DMC Corp.
(973) 589-0606
www.dmc-usa.com

DMD Industries, Inc.
(800) 805-9890
www.dmdind.com

Doodlebug Design, Inc.™
(801) 966-9952
www.doodlebugdesigninc.com

DoJiggies- no contact information available

EK Success™,Ltd. (wholesale only)
(800) 524-1349
www.eksuccess.com

Ellison®
(800) 253-2238
www.ellison.com

Emagination Crafts, Inc.
(866) 238-9770
www.emaginationcrafts.com

Eyelet Factory, Inc. (wholesale only)
(503) 631-8864
www.eyeletfactory.com

Family Treasures
(949) 457-2258
www.familytreasures.com

Fibers by the Yard™
(405) 364-8066
www.fibersbytheyard.com

Fiskars, Inc.
(800) 500-4849
www.fiskars.com

Frances Meyer, Inc.
(800) 372-6237
www.francesmeyer.com

Grafix® Graphic Art Systems (wholesale only)
(800) 447-2349
www.grafixarts.com

Graphic Products Corporation (wholesale only)
(800) 323-1660
www.gdcpapers.com

Halcraft USA, Inc.
(212) 367-1580
www.halcraft.com

Heartland Paper Co.
www.heartlandpaper.com

Hero Arts® Rubber Stamps, Inc.
(800) 822-4376
www.heroarts.com

Hillcreek Designs
(619) 562-5799
www.hillcreekdesigns.com

Hirschberg Schutz & Co. (wholesale only)
(800) 221-8640

Hot Off The Press, Inc.
(888) 300-3406
www.craftpizazz.com

Holly Berry House, Inc.
(800) 735-2752
www.hollyberryhouse.com

Hyglo®/AmericanPin
(800) 821-7125
www.americanpin.com

IBM®
www.ibm.com

Idea Tool Box, LLC
(801) 224-5910
www.ideatoolbox.com

Impress Rubber Stamps
(206) 901-9101
www.impressrubberstamps.com

Ink It!- no contact information available

It Takes Two®
(800) 331-9843
www.ittakestwo.com

Jesse James and Co., Inc.
(610) 435-0201
www.jessejamesbutton.com

JewelCraft
(201) 223-0804
www.jewelcraft.biz

JudiKins
(310) 515-1115
www.judikins.com

K & Company
(888) 244-2083
www.kandcompany.com

Karen Foster Design™ (wholesale only)
(801) 451-9779
www.karenfosterdesign.com

Keeping Memories Alive™
(800) 419-4949
www.scrapbooks.com

Lasting Impressions for Paper, Inc.
(800) 9-EMBOSS
www.lastingimpressions.com

Leeco Industries, Inc.
(800) 826-8806

Li'l Davis Designs
(949) 838-0344
www.lildavisdesigns.com

Magenta Rubber Stamps
(800) 565-5254
www.magentarubberstamps.com

Magic Mesh™
(651) 345-6374
www.magicmesh.com

Magic Scraps™
(972) 238-1838
www.magicscraps.com

Making Memories
(800) 286-5263
www.makingmemories.com

Marvy® Uchida (wholesale only)
(800) 541-5877
www.uchida.com

Memories to Keep- no contact information available

Memory Lane- no contact information available

Meri Meri
(650) 525-9200
www.merimeri.com

Mrs. Grossman's Paper Co. (wholesale only)
(800) 429-4549
www.mrsgrossmans.com

Mustard Moon
(408) 229-8542
www.mustardmoon.com

My Mind's Eye™, Inc.
(801) 298-3709
www.frame-ups.com/mme

Nature's Pressed
(800) 850-2499
www.naturespressed.com

Northern Spy
(530) 620-7430
www.northernspy.com

Office Depot
(800) GO-DEPOT
www.officedepot.com

Offray
www.offray.com

On The Surface
(847) 675-2520

Over The River- no contact information available

Paper Adventures (wholesale only)
(800) 727-0699
www.paperadventures.com

Paper Garden, The (wholesale only)
(435) 867-6398
www.mypapergarden.com

Paper House Productions
(800) 255-7316
www.paperhouseproductions.com

Paper Loft, The (wholesale only)
(801) 254-1961
www.paperloft.com

Pier 1 Imports
(800) 245-4595
www.pier1.com

Pioneer Photo Albums, Inc.
(800) 366-3686
www.pioneerphotoalbums.com

Plaid Enterprises, Inc.
(800) 842-4197
www.plaidonline.com

Pockets on a Roll- no contact information available

Polyform Products Co.
(847) 427-0020
www.sculpey.com

Posh Impressions
(800) 421-POSH
www.poshimpressions.com

Postmodern Design LLC
(405) 321-3176

Pressed Petals
(800) 748-4656
www.pressedpetals.com

PrintWorks
(800) 854-6558
www.printworkscollection.com

Provo Craft® (wholesale only)
(800) 937-7686
www.provocraft.com

PSX Design™
(800) 438-6226
www.psxdesign.com

Pulsar Products LLC
(877) 861-0031
www.pulsarpaper.com

Punch Bunch, The
(254) 791-4209
www.thepunchbunch.com

QuicKutz®
(888) 702-1146
www.quickutz.com

Raindrops on Roses
(307) 877-6241
www.raindropsonroses.com

Ranger Industries, Inc.
(800) 244-2211
www.rangerink.com

Robin's Nest Press, The
(435) 789-5387
www.robinsnest-scrapbook.com

Rubba Dub Dub Artist's Stamps & Supplies
(209) 763-2766
www.artsanctum.com

ScrapArts
(503) 631-4893
www.scraparts.com

Scrapbook Sally
(866) SBSALLY
www.scrapbooksally.com

Scrapbook Specialties™
(702) 456-6661
www.scrapbookspecialties.com

Scrap Pagerz™
(435) 645-0696
www.scrappagerz.com

Scrapworks, LLC
(410) 255-5227

ScrapYard 329, LLC
(866) 242-2742
www.scrapyard329.com

SEI, Inc.
(800) 333-3279
www.shopsei.com

Sizzix
(877) 355-4766
www.sizzix.com

Stamp Doctor, The
(866) 782-6737
www.stampdoctor.com

Stampendous!®
(800) 869-0474
www.stampendous.com

Stampin' Up!®
(800) 782-6787
www.stampinup.com

Stamps by Judith
www.stampsbyjudith.com

Staples
(800) 3-STAPLE
www.staples.com

Suze Weinberg Design Studio
(732) 761-2400
www.schmoozewithsuze.com

Therm O Web, Inc. (wholesale only)
(800) 323-0799
www.thermoweb.com

Traditions- no contact information available

Tsukineko®, Inc.
(800) 769-6633
www.tsukineko.com

USArtQuest
(800) 200-7848
www.usartquest.com

Westrim® Crafts
(800) 727-2727
www.westrimcrafts.com

Wintech International
(800) 263-6043
www.wintechint.com

Wordsworth Stamps
(719) 282-3495
www.wordsworthstamps.com

Wubie Scrapbook Paper Products
(888) 256-0107
www.wubieprints.com

cutting edge
Photo cropping
for scrapbooks, book 2

wave chaser

Joshua

Laguna Beach

The boys love being on their boards
so much that they will endure the
often chilly Pacific Ocean for hours.

MEMORY
MAKERS
BOOKS

"Though we travel the world over
to find the beautiful,
we must carry it with us
or we find it not."

Ralph Waldo Emerson

introduction

Our photos are the heart and soul of our scrapbooks, and thousands of scrapbookers and photo enthusiasts have discovered the joy of creative photo cropping. If you are hungry for new photo-cropping ideas, we are excited to provide more innovative ways to communicate using your photos. As you experiment with and explore this special niche of scrapbooking, you will learn that there are many ways you can use a single photograph. Conversely, there are certain photos that just beg for a specific type of photo cropping.

To answer every need, we feature dozens of ideas in this book—from simple to complex—all equally intriguing and inspiring. The first chapter includes brand-new ideas for cropping photos into slices and segments and mats and frames. It also introduces the art of photo tearing. The next chapter explores never-before-seen ways to crop photos using shapes—from tags and template shapes to letters, symbols and punched shapes.

The final chapter reveals innovative ways to showcase photo weaving, mosaics and collage, and ends with whimsical ways to bring movement to your photos. Easy-to-follow instructions and illustrated step shots make these photo projects appealing and doable. As always, we recommend that you work with duplicates (see page 138) and not your original photos. Or, at least have a negative on file for backup. The use of photo-safe paper and adhesives will help ensure the longevity of your photo art.

Our goal with this book is to inspire you to push your photo cropping beyond the boundaries of traditional scrapbooking. We hope you enjoy this fresh generation of cutting edge cropping techniques sure to trigger personal, highly individualized results with your own images. Take a few minutes to sharpen those scissors, put a new blade in your craft knife and let the creativity begin!

Michele

Michele Gerbrandt
Founding Editor
Memory Makers magazine

getting started

Photo "cropping" or cutting begins with photographs. Famed photographer Ansel Adams once said, "Twelve significant photos in any one year is a good crop." Mr. Adams was a bit more discerning than the average picture-taker. He had a keen eye for cropping photos through the lens with breath-taking results. Today's savvy scrapbookers are creating quality photos with the added indulgence of physically cropping a photographic print to manipulate its composition for eye-pleasing effects.

when to crop

A photo can tell many stories depending on how it is cropped. As you experiment with photo cropping, you will become keenly aware of what types of photo cropping techniques work best for certain types of photo compositions. And for those photo blunders, photo cropping allows you to remedy the situation in many cases. Put creative photo cropping to use in the following situations for eye-pleasing results:

Command Focus

Busy photos, with lots of people and unnecessary background, take attention away from the photos' subjects. Framing, slicing and silhouetting can isolate and focus attention on your subject.

Correct Flaws

Cropping allows you to remove photo blemishes, such as flare from flashes, closed eyes, strangers in your pictures, out-of-focus elements, lab printing errors and more. It even allows you to use "junk" photos from the beginning of a roll of film!

Boost Style

Add style and variety to your page by cropping your photos into a shape. There are many shapes with which to experiment, and changing the shape will also change the final effect. Give your cropped photo breathing room, however, so that the photo's content is not lost.

Design New Art

Herein lies the reason behind this book and the allure of creative photo cropping—the "shear" fun and enjoyment of cropping a photo into a new piece of photo art.

Using Photo Scraps

Save your photo scraps and snippets as you are cropping. Most will be reassembled back into the new piece of art but you can also use photo scraps to create custom-coordinated photo frames, put in photo shaker boxes, make "illuminated" lettering or title letters, form interesting borders or a mini mosaic, incorporate into a photo collage or use for matting journaling blocks.

when not to crop

As entertaining as photo cropping can be, there are some types of photos that should not be cropped. Before you begin cropping, keep these tips in mind:

Heritage Photos

Consider the value to future generations if one-of-a-kind family heirloom or other old photographs are left intact. Crop duplicates of historic photos instead of cropping the originals.

Artistic Photos

Cropping can minimize the artistic composition of a photograph. Perhaps the photographer's out-of-focus foreground lends a perspective that would be lost if you cut it out. Maybe the extra space around the subject was deliberately composed to evoke a certain mood. Before cropping, consider the drama of a photo's imagery.

Polaroid Prints

A Polaroid "integral" print (above; noted for its thickness and ¾" lower white border) should not be cropped. The positive and negative sides of the print stay together, and cutting the print exposes the chemical layers. Instead of cutting an integral print, use a color copy of the print for cropping.

Polaroid "peel apart" photos (above) are safe to crop. The final print is separated from the reactive chemicals and the negative when the photo is peeled apart.

Photo and Negative Handling and Storage

Photo cropping relies on ordering reprints and enlargements from negatives or photos. Use these tips for easy access and preservation of photos and negatives:

- Wash and dry hands before handling negatives, then wear cotton gloves to prevent scratching the negatives.
- Avoid cutting negative strips, which ruins the emulsion and the negative.
- Keep negatives and photos organized chronologically or by subject or theme for quick access.
- Prior to ordering reprints, clean negatives with a commercial-grade emulsion cleaner, such as PEC-12® (Photographic Solutions).
- Use 100 percent acid-, lignin- and PVC-free negative sleeves, storage binders and storage boxes.
- If storing negatives in an acid-free envelope, separate strips with acid-free paper to prevent sticking.
- Store away from dust, bright light and excessive heat or high humidity; store in temperatures between 65-70 degrees with 30-50 percent humidity.
- Store negatives separately from photos, ideally in a safe-deposit box.

photo duplication

The easiest way to duplicate your photos is by having reprints or enlargements made from your negatives. However, we often have photos for which we have no negatives. Fortunately, there are ways to duplicate photos without the use of negatives.

Color Copy Machines

The least expensive duplication option is to use a laser color copier, which is sensitive to the different shades in photographs. Color copiers allow you to change the size of the image. For preservation purposes, use acid-free, 28-pound or heavier, smooth white paper. Color photocopy toner is known to be more stable than inkjet dyes, so choose color copying over printing with an inkjet printer when possible. In addition, use a mat or other barrier between layered photos and color copies of photos when possible. Color copy machines can be found at select scrapbook stores or office supply stores.

Take a Picture of a Picture

The biggest benefit of this method is that it creates negatives for your photos. A manual 35mm SLR camera—with an inexpensive, close-up or macro lens set—works great for this purpose. Simply place your photo on a flat surface or tape it to a wall in bright, even light, then focus and snap!

Digital Photo Machines

Digital, print-to-print photocopy machines (shown is Kodak's Picture Maker) are user-friendly, self-service machines that can be found at your local discount, photography, drug store or supermarket. Some popular standard features include the ability to make enlargements and reductions, custom cropping, rotating and zooming in, and the ability to sharpen and adjust color and brightness of images. Some allow you to convert a color print to a black-and-white or sepia-toned photo. Many digital photo machines have the ability to write images to floppy disks and print from CD-ROMS.

KODAK Picture CD and KODAK Picture Maker are registered trademarks of © Eastman Kodak Company, 2003. Used with permission.

Scanning Photos or Printing Digital Images

To scan your photos at home, use the TIFF file format for high-resolution images. The quality of your duplicated photos will depend on the quality of your scanner, scanning software, printer and the photo paper you print on (shown is Epson's Glossy Photo Paper made specifically for scrapbooking). If do-it-yourself scanning is not for you, you can have high quality photo scans put on a CD-ROM at a camera store, mini lab or professional lab. To print images from a CD-ROM, a high-quality color printer and photo-quality printer paper will give the best color results.

cropping tools & supplies

The tools listed below are used time and time again throughout this book to create photo art. Little extras, such as acid-neutralizing wipes for hands and photo fingerprint and adhesive cleaner, keep photos in quality condition before and after cropping. An embossing stylus or photo-safe wax pencil can be used for tracing cutting lines onto photos. Use a fine-grained sandpaper nail file, with a light and careful touch, to smooth cropped, curved photo edges.

Cropping Essentials

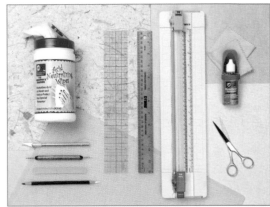

- Acid-neutralizing hand wipes
- Craft knife
- Cutting mat
- Embossing stylus
- Fine-grained sandpaper nail file
- Graphing ruler
- Metal straightedge ruler
- Paper trimmer
- Photo fingerprint and adhesive cleaner
- Photo-safe wax pencil
- Small, sharp scissors

Photo-Safe Adhesives

We recommend the use of archival-quality adhesives for mounting your new photo art onto acid- and lignin-free paper and scrapbook pages. The adhesives most widely used are:

- Adhesive application machine
- Double-sided photo tape
- Glue sticky circles
- Photo tab mounting squares
- Removable artist's tape
- Repositionable adhesive dots
- Self-adhesive foam spacers
- Self-adhesive foam tape
- Tape runner
- Terrifically Tacky Tape™

Additional Cropping Tools

The following items are used randomly throughout this book to complete specific photo-cropping techniques. In many cases, you may apply or substitute a specific tool that you already have on hand for one used in a given project.

- Decorative scissors
- Dies
- Eyelet-setting tools
- Foam core board (not shown)
- Piercing tool or sewing needle
- Plastic foam cutting mat
- Punches
- PVC-free page protectors (not shown)
- Shape cutters
- Swivel-blade craft knife
- Templates

"The thing that's important to know is that you never know. You're always sort of feeling your way."
–Diane Arbus

basic cropping

It's amazing how the most fundamental cropping techniques can bring dazzling results to your photo art. With a few little cuts here and a few snips there, your photos will take on a whole new look. Some of the things you will learn in this chapter include how to:

- Cut and reassemble slices for interesting effects
- Combine vertical and diagonal slices for visual appeal
- Layer silhouettes atop slices for impact
- Combine vertical and horizontal slices with photo segments
- Slice oval- or circle-cropped photos into new art
- Curve panoramic photos to fit an 8½ x 11" page
- Slice slots for inserting photo accents
- Curl slices to create movement
- Slice reverse-image photos to create reflections
- Create sliced photo under- and overlays
- Frame mini photos with cropped photos
- Use partial silhouetting for a degree of separation
- Cut a foam core photo shadowbox
- Crop a self-framing photo shaker box
- Pierce and shadow-cut self-framing photos
- Tear photos in a number of ways for amazing aftereffects

These fresh and basic photo-cropping techniques are guaranteed to spark a creative fire with easy-to-achieve outcomes. Once you feel comfortable with these basic yet striking ideas, you'll feel empowered to bring more of your scrapbook tools and supplies into use to crop photos creatively.

slices & segments

All you need is a sharp craft knife and a metal straightedge ruler to crop photos into slices and segments. The strategic placement of your cropped slices and segments is what gives your photos flair when reassembled. Watch for straight lines in photo images; they provide obvious and natural cutting lines. Or, experiment by cropping random slices and segments across photos for a unique surprise upon reassembly!

Slice horizontally on a vertical panorama

Kelly Angard (Highlands Ranch, Colorado) brings focus to her son by cutting random-sized slices into a vertical panoramic photo. Use removable artist's tape to hold photo down onto cutting mat. Cut slices into photo with a craft knife and metal straightedge ruler. Assemble slices, leaving even spaces between the slices, and mount onto page. Try this simple vertical-slice technique on a horizontal panoramic photo for the same framing effect.

Offset a sliced corner

Jodi Amidei (Memory Makers) gives an interesting twist to a photo framing effect. First, slice the right or left corner from a vertical photo using a craft knife and metal straightedge ruler. Reassemble the picture onto your page, offsetting the cropped corner at an angle. Experiment with slicing both the upper right and lower left corners from a horizontal picture and reassembling onto the page at opposite angles for a more dramatic effect. Photo Kelli Noto (Centennial, Colorado)

Stack corner photo slices

Cutting the corners from duplicate photos is a clever technique that Melanie Fischer (Centennial, Colorado) uses to make this cool pool layout. To start, remove a ⅛" wide inset corner from your original photo. Continue by slicing ⅛" wide corners from the duplicate photos, making smaller corners as you go. Stack the corner slices on your layout by mounting away from your center photo, mounting the slices from largest to smallest. This technique pulls your eyes into the focal point of the layout—the photo subject.

Slice randomly and reassemble

Take some great photos, add an eye-pleasing photo cropping technique, and you get a fabulous layout like this one by Kelly Angard (Highlands Ranch, Colorado). When cutting your own pictures, keep a pattern to your slices. For example, crop ¼" slices on one picture, ½" slices on another and combine the two measurements to crop ¾" slices on yet another photo. Slices can be vertical or horizontal, based on the position of the subject in the photo, as long as the slices leave the main photo subject intact. Reassemble slices on page with even spacing for added drama. Photos Jeff Neal (Huntington Beach, California)

Combine offset vertical with diagonal slices

To make this visually pleasing frame that focuses on the majesty of her pet, Karen Wilson-Bonnar (Pleasanton, California) combined vertical offset segments at one end of her photo with diagonal slices at the other end. Keeping the diagonal slices at just one end of the photo helps draw the eye through the entire picture. Crop the vertical slices in random sizes and assemble and mount offset onto page. Assemble and mount diagonal slices onto page leaving even spaces between the slices.

Combine different photos to impact horizon

When Sue Nunamaker (Villa Park, Illinois) made a mistake on a photo she cropped for a layout, she unwittingly stumbled upon a new photo-cropping technique. Sue placed the slices of a miscropped photo onto a similar, uncut photo and realized the neat effect it had. To accomplish this technique, gather two photos with similar horizons. Use removable artist's tape to hold one photo down to a cutting mat. Crop ⅜" slices from the photo with a metal straight-edge ruler and craft knife. Mount the slices ¼" apart on the uncut photo. This technique would be a beautiful way to enhance photos of grassy hills, snowy mountainsides and other gorgeous landscape shots. The key is to use a background photo that is very similar to the sliced photo, yet different enough in color to see the difference between the two.

Couple horizontal and vertical slices

Brandi Ginn (Lafayette, Colorado) uses a combination of horizontal and vertical slices on two different photos to give the illusion that they are one, while using the same effect to frame a picture mounted on a tag. Use removable artist's tape to hold photos down onto cutting mat while cropping ½" slices with a metal straightedge ruler and craft knife. Assemble slices onto page leaving space between each slice while placing photos directly next to each other. For a twist on the tag, cut horizontal slices from parts of a photo to frame the photo subject and mirror the cropping technique on the page. Photos Brian Cummings (Aliso Creek, California)

Join vertical- and diagonal-sliced photos

The visual impact of this technique comes from the placement of the diagonal photo slices. To do this, Jodi Amidei (Memory Makers) used a photo of a flowering tree, sliced it vertically and then joined it with a diagonally sliced photo of a sports car. The slices are alternated when reassembled onto the page. Crop the right and left side of the first photo into ⅛" slices. Cut the rest of the photo into ¼" slices. Follow the same measurements when cutting a second photo, only this time cut diagonally. Assemble, alternating slices from both photos onto page, first with a temporary adhesive then permanently when satisfied with the arrangement. Photos Erica Pierovich (Longmont, Colorado)

Shredding Photos

Put that handy little office appliance, the paper shredder, to use cropping photo slices for you. If desired, first apply adhesive to the back of the photo with an adhesive application machine. After shredding, some assembly will be required.

1 To crop a photo into vertical or horizontal slices, feed either the photo's vertical or horizontal straight edge into the shredder.

2 To crop a photo into diagonal slices, hold the photo by one corner and feed the opposite corner into the shredder.

Combine diagonal segments with silhouette

Silhouetting gives any picture interest and "popping" the silhouette adds to the spectacle. To add drama to this silhouette-cropped butterfly, Jodi Amidei (Memory Makers) sliced diagonal lines in the original picture for a dazzling background. Begin with two copies of the same photo. Mount first photo to a cutting mat with removable artist's tape and crop photo into ⅜" diagonal slices with a craft knife and metal straightedge ruler. Silhouette crop the subject from the second photo as shown and mat on white cardstock. Assemble slices evenly spaced on a piece of cardstock. Trim the photo-laden cardstock with a paper trimmer to a smaller size so it is "borderless." Apply the silhouette-cropped image atop its original image on the first photo, using self-adhesive foam spacers for lift. This technique works well for page layouts as well as the cover piece for handmade cards.

1 Use small, sharp scissors to silhouette crop around contours of the photo subject. Cut slowly, following each outline, being careful not to lob off any necessary features. Use a sharp craft knife to crop around tiny parts that are not easily accessible with scissors.

Accent horizontal slices with crimped silhouette

Using a crimper on a silhouette-cropped American Flag, Diana Hudson (Bakersfield, California) gives the flag a very realistic look—as if it is waving in the wind. Slice a background photo into equal segments to break up the pattern of the sparks for a wavy look. Adhere the crimped and silhouette-cropped flag with self-adhesive foam spacers over the slices. For variation, try crimping the background segments also.

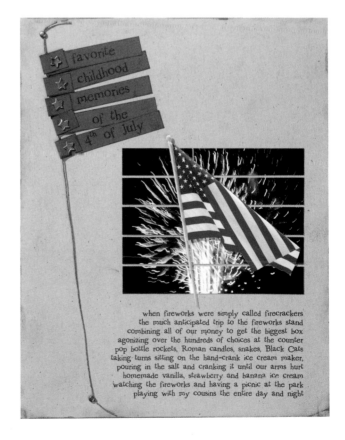

Mix random vertical slices with linear segments

Using slices and segments together is what Heidi Schueller (Waukesha, Wisconsin) did with a hot air balloon picture. First, use a photo-safe wax pencil and graphing ruler to mark the cutting lines for slices and segments onto photo. This will allow you to experiment with how you would like to showcase the highlights of the photo by simply wiping off misplaced lines. When satisfied with the look, crop the slices and segments with a craft knife and metal straight-edge ruler, wiping off the wax pencil residue as you go. Assemble on page like a mosaic—leaving spaces in between the slices and segments. Try this technique on garden, travel and architectural photos, making slices and segments around key elements of the photos' subjects.

Combine random horizontal slices with linear segments

Cutting random horizontal slices into bowling photos gives Heidi Schueller (Waukesha, Wisconsin) the result she was looking for—the illusion that the bowling ball is breaking apart the photos wherever it hits. Mark cutting lines and "cut-in" depths with a graphing ruler and photo-safe wax pencil. Tack photos onto cutting mat with removable artist's tape. Use a metal straightedge ruler and craft knife to slice on the marked lines, adding a diagonal cut at each end. Wipe off any pencil residue with a soft cloth. Reassemble and mount photos on layout, pulling slices out randomly for a jagged look.

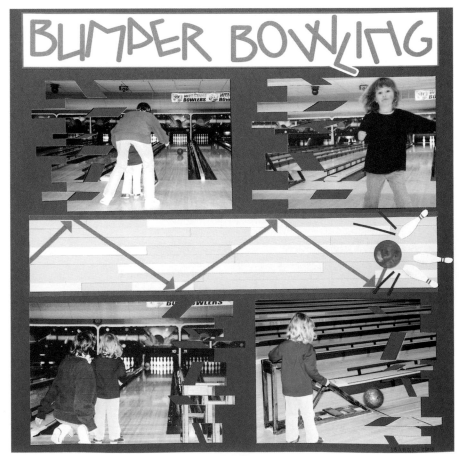

Add variety to circle- or oval-cropped photos

Slicing a casual pattern into circle- or oval-cropped photos adds visual impact to these fun-filled amusement park photos of Kelly Angard (Highlands Ranch, Colorado) with her daughter. Start with a circle- or oval-cropped photo. Follow the step below to crop slices. For variation, experiment with different slicing patterns as shown in the illustrations. Reassemble and mount slices on brightly colored cardstock, if desired.

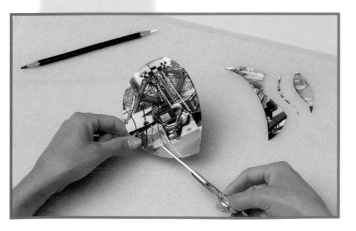

1 Use a photo-safe wax pencil to freehand draw random cutting lines on photo. Use small, sharp scissors or a craft knife to cut on the cutting lines. Use a soft cloth to wipe off any pencil residue from photo slices.

Sean, Cameron & Amber Stutzman
Maui ~ July 2000

Curve a panoramic photo

Some photos, such as these Maui panoramas, deserve to be showcased in a unique way.
But panoramas can be hard to fit on an 8½ x 11" page layout. Jodi Amidei (Memory Makers)
made an interesting layout by slicing and visually "curving" the photos upon reassembly.
This technique is unique in that it mimics the effect of a "fish eye" camera lens and you feel as
though you are out there on a boat yourself. Follow the instructions on the next page to apply
this technique to panoramic photos. Inspiration Corinne Cullen Hawkins (Walnut Creek,
California); Photos Pennie Stutzman (Broomfield, Colorado)

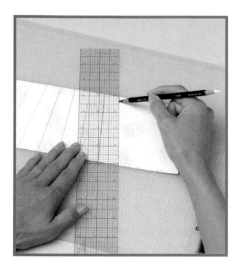

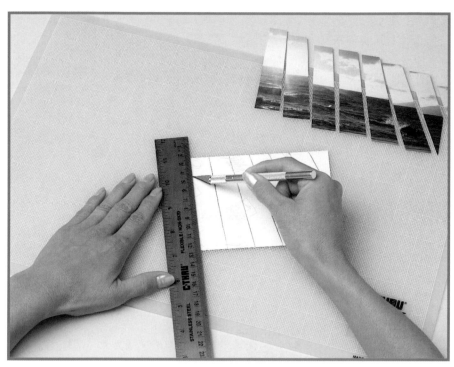

1 Flip photos over. Along the lower edge of the bottom photo, use a graphing ruler and a pencil to make "tick marks" at 1" intervals, beginning at the photo's center and working outward. Along the upper edge of the photo, make tick marks at ¾" intervals, beginning at the center and working outward. Use a pencil to connect the upper and lower marks (shown) to create the cutting lines, starting with a vertical line at the center and working outward. Repeat this step for your top photo, this time making ¾" interval tick marks on lower edge and 1" interval tick marks on upper edge of photo.

2 Use a craft knife and metal straightedge ruler to slice on the cutting lines, keeping photo slices in order for easier reassembly. Repeat this step for top photo.

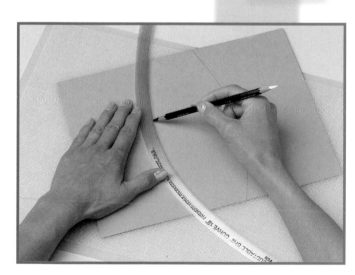

3 Measure up 4½" from lower edge of 8½ x 11" inch cardstock background and make tick marks on both the right and left sides of the cardstock at this point. Place a curve ruler (Hoyle) on these two points, allowing the ruler to curve slightly down in the center. Use a pencil to draw a slight curve to serve as a placement guideline for reassembling the photo slices. Rotate the cardstock 90 degrees and repeat this step on the top of the cardstock for the top photo.

4 Reassemble the lower photo slices, beginning with the center slice placed directly at the center, working from the center outward. Use a removable adhesive (Hermafix) in case you need to pick up a slice for better placement. When reassembling, overlap photo slices slightly on upper edges to help form the curve, picking up and replacing slices as needed. Repeat this step with top photo.

basic cropping ■ 151

Insert page accents into sliced slots

Beverly Sizemore (Sulligent, Alabama) came up with an innovative way to accent a seaside photo. She replicated the sea grass in the photo, and inserted the grass into cropped slots in the foreground to make it look as though the grass was growing from the photo! Follow the step below to apply this technique. For variation, use a craft knife to slice the sides of individual grass blades directly on the photo, leaving a portion of the grass blades still connected to the photo (shown at right). Curl the sliced photo grass blades forward around a pencil to add dimension. Experiment with this technique on any photo that has easily replicated objects in the foreground or background, such as leaves, rocks, etc.

1 Use a craft knife to freehand cut short slots into the foreground at the base of the sea grass in the photo. Tuck freehand-cut paper sea grass into the slots and secure grass blades on the back of the photo with tape to hold in place.

Curl wavy slices for movement

Jodi Amidei (Memory Makers) applies an easy slicing technique to effectively mimic the rolling waves of the ocean in the photo. Secure the photo onto a cutting mat with removable artist's tape. Use a craft knife and a wavy ruler to slice the waves into the photo. Apply adhesive around the outside edges only of the photo and mount on page. After the adhesive is dry, use the tip of your craft knife to lift up the sliced edges and gently "roll" them forward. Apply liquid adhesive to the underside of the slices that stay in contact with the page for added firmness. Photo Leslie Aldridge (Broomfield, Colorado)

Slice half circles for spherical dimension

This serene photo of MaryJo Regier's (Memory Makers) three little seldom-serene boys bounces to life when half-circle slices are cut into the blown bubbles and curled forward slightly for a realistic look. MaryJo used a block-printing cutter (Speedball) with a curved, half-moon blade to puncture the photo strategically on one side of each bubble in the photo. This technique can be applied to any small, orb-shaped objects in photos—such as the balls in a ballroom, baseball or tennis balls in flight, a polka-dot dress or buttons on a shirt. Remember, the key to the realistic look is to curl the sliced half-circles forward slightly to shape.

Slice and curl to mimic waves

Kelly Angard (Highlands Ranch, Colorado) wanted to give the feel that you were right in the raft with her son. To accomplish this technique, flip photo over and mark a small "s" pattern repeatedly into the water portion of a photo with a wax pencil. Tape your photo onto a cutting mat with removable artist's tape and cut the "s" pattern with a craft knife. Turn photo over again and lift the cuts slightly, bending them gently forward. Mount photo on a watercolor background to accent the openings of the cuts. A variation on this technique is to cut random-sized "s" patterns into the water—making larger-sized patterns where the waves in the water are bigger, and smaller-sized patterns where the waves are smaller.

Slice waves to imitate breeze

Slicing quick-and-easy waves across a photo can create the feeling of a breeze. Cynthia Anning (Virginia Beach, Virginia) used a wavy ruler and craft knife to slice across the upper and lower edges of this photo, highlighting the autumn fun of her active young son. Try this with any outdoor activity photos where wind or waves are part of the subject matter, whether real or imagined! Assemble slices to background paper, leaving space in between each segment.

Join scenic photos with random slices

Most scrapbook pages are made with photos, but Kathy Graham (Miamisburg, Ohio) made a travel album cover page from extra scenic photos that might have otherwise gone unused. For an 8½ x 11" layout, select 6-8 photos. Layer photos randomly on a cutting mat and rearrange until you are pleased with the new scene. Use a craft knife to freehand cut random slices into photos, using each previously cut photo as a visual pattern for cutting the next photo. Don't worry about not getting the slices to match perfectly; cutting imperfections here lend to the allure of the finished artwork. Cut into the finished art to accommodate paper-pieced art, if desired. Use a lettering template and additional photos or photo scraps to create a page title for extra pizazz.

Slice a reverse image to create a reflection

When a luxury liner came to port in her neighborhood, Alison Lindsay (Edinburgh, Scotland) had to go see it. Alison was so impressed with the ship that she wanted a dramatic visual effect to help convey that. Slicing a reverse image of the ship gave her just what she was looking for. To start, obtain a reverse-image reprint of your original photo. To get a reverse image, the photo print operator should flip the negative so that the emulsion side is opposite of the correct printing method normally used. Request that the original image and the reverse image are an exact match. Turn reverse-image photo upside down so top of ship is at bottom of photo. Use a wavy ruler and craft knife to crop photo into slices. Reassemble slices on page so that ship is upside down to create a reflection. This is a great mirroring effect that could be used for just about any photo, not necessarily just those around water.

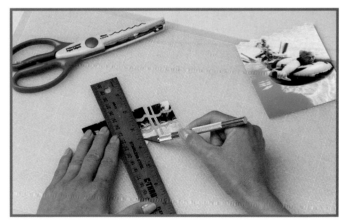

1 Crop slices in desired widths from edges of photo with decorative scissors. Reassemble slices and mount with temporary adhesive directly on cutting mat. Use a metal straightedge ruler and craft knife to crop ⅛" wide vertical segments from slices at 1" intervals; discard the small slices. Reassemble photo segments onto cardstock, lining up edges and leaving even spaces in between each segment.

Try decorative-scissor-sliced segments

Torrey Miller (Thornton, Colorado) shows a great new use for decorative scissors on this wet-and-wild photo. Follow the step above to use wave-patterned scissors (Fiskars) to slice segments that will draw your eye to a photo's focal point. Try this technique on any activity photos where a little implied movement is desired. For variation, try cropping vertically down the sides. Photo MaryJo Regier (Memory Makers)

Combine partial circles with random slices and segments

Cutting random slices and segments from an enlarged photo, and matting it the way Julie Mullison (Superior, Colorado) did, gives it the conceptual feel of looking into a stained-glass window. To apply this technique, pay special attention to where you are cutting and where you put your cut-out pieces so as not to "lose" them when reassembling the pieces back onto your cardstock. The illustrated steps below depict how to turn a photo into a stained-glass work of art.

1 Use a circle scissor (EK Success), circle cutter or circle template to cut a partial or quarter circle from one corner of a photo.

2 Mount partial circle on corner of cardstock. Use scissors or a craft knife to freehand slice or crop random slices and segments from the remainder of the photo, reassembling with temporary adhesive as you go. Use a craft knife to cut a theme-related symbol into the photo, if desired.

Interlock sliced half circles

Sometimes we design our pages to flow with our photos, like Trudy Sigurdson (Victoria, British Columbia, Canada) did in these pictures of her daughter playing in the wind. By cutting and tucking sliced half circles in the photos, Trudy re-created the feeling of movement depicted in the photo. First, use an adhesive application machine to apply lightweight, complementary-colored cardstock to back of photo. Follow the steps below to create photo art. To add visual contrast, mat finished photo art to a deeper shade of the same color cardstock.

1 Use a graduated circle template (Coluzzle® by Provo Craft) and a swivel craft knife or the outer edge of the brass stencil (Cut-N-Tuc® template by Stamporium) to crop the photo into a circle the same size as the outer edge of the brass stencil.

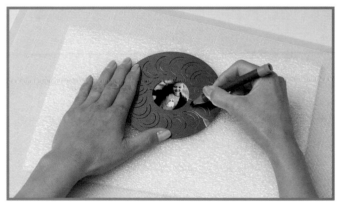

2 Place brass stencil atop circle-cropped photo; hold in place with removable artist's tape (3M), if desired. Use a craft knife to slice the photo, slicing through all slots or channels on the brass stencil.

3 Fold slices up and tuck behind each consecutive slice to form a ringed frame around the photo subject.

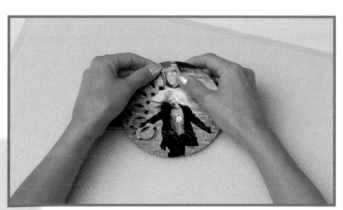

"Old hat, NEW HAT..."

Michaela just loves hats! Seeing these pictures of her wearing all of her hats reminds of the Berenstain Bear book my mom used to read to me ,"Old Hat, New Hat."

Slice and fold photo-framing accents

To add triangle accents to her photos, Julie Mullison (Superior, Colorado) used a template (Incire™ by Avec/Ecstasy Crafts) to cut them into her photos. To make the contrast in the slices, Julie used a yellow ink pad on the back of the pictures and then mounted them to purple cardstock after they were cut. Use a medium sandpaper to lightly sand the back of the picture to remove any of the photo's processing information and to hold the ink better. Secure your photo with removable adhesive and lay the template on the photo and center. Use a craft knife to slice through the template's slots or channels and the photo. Pull back gently on the sliced areas to expose the colored backing of the photo.

Crop a vertical-segment overlay

Kelli Noto (Centennial, Colorado) used vertically cut and overlaid photo segments to give a casual portrait added intrigue. Slice photo in half vertically. Cut 1" off the top of the left side of the photo, and 1" off the bottom of the right side of the photo. This will give the illusion that you have mounted them offset. Mat the cut photos to cardstock, lining up facial features in the portrait. Mount the right side of your photo directly onto your layout. Mount the left side with self-adhesive foam spacers.

Use horizontal segments for comparison

Holle Wiktorek (Clarksville, Tennessee) came up with an interesting way to compare the facial features of her family members. This technique would be a fun thing to do between siblings, parents, or even between close friends! Choose or take close-up photos of the people you want to compare features with. Make duplicate copies of your photos. Slice the photos into segments that feature just the eyes, noses or mouths in horizontal strips. Mount them by category and in the order the original photos appear on the page. Consider photographing and cropping other parts of the body as well—such as hands, feet, eyebrows or ears—for making amusing studies in genetic anatomy. Use this technique with photos of friends to accentuate differences and to identify possible similarities.

the tree which moves some to tears of joy

is in the eyes of others

only a green thing that stands in the way.

some see nature all ridicule and deformity,

and some scarce see nature at all

but to the eyes of the man of imagination,

nature is imagination itself.

Separate segments with journaling

Try this simple yet engaging way to break up an image without losing the image's full content—separate the photo segments with journaling or page accents. By cutting her picture into segments and separating the segments, Trudy Sigurdson (Victoria, British Columbia, Canada) "lengthens" the photo and gives the illusion that this is a panoramic photo. Slice vertical photo into three to four segments and mount separated from each other. For variation, experiment with this technique on a horizontal photo.

Reassemble cut segments with eyelets

Kelly Angard (Highlands Ranch, Colorado) found a riveting technique that works great for photos with a lot of background. Kelly does a great job of keeping your eye on the boys, but makes the whole photo more playful by the way it's reassembled. Slice photo into equal or random segments, being careful not to cut through any faces or important objects in your photo. Number the pieces on the back for easier reassembly. Mount the pieces onto cardstock leaving space in between the segments. Set eyelets (see page 165) into the connecting corners of the segments. String paper yarn or fiber in a crisscross pattern through the eyelets and around the outer edges of the cardstock and secure from behind with tape.

Slice a duplicate to make an over- and underlay

Jodi Amidei (Memory Makers) uses an over- and underlay technique with two different colors of the same photo to give all new angles to the original photo. Start with one color and one black-and-white copy of the same photo. Lay the black-and-white photo on a cutting mat and secure with removable artist's tape. Make a diagonal cut with a craft knife and metal straightedge ruler all the way across the photo. Use a temporary adhesive to mount your original photo onto paper. Then, using the removable adhesive, experiment with the way you want your black-and-white photo to lay under and over the original color photo. Once satisfied, mount in place with permanent adhesive. This technique also gives some great new angles when done with horizontal photos. Photo Bruce Aldridge (Broomfield, Colorado)

Alternate color with black-and-white photo segments

Combining color with segments of a duplicate black-and-white photo is a captivating way to make any layout more appealing. Ruthann Grabowski's (Yorktown, Virginia) cropping technique successfully keeps the emphasis on the boys in the photo while playing up the beauty of Pennsylvania countryside in the background. To create this effect, select a color photo with nice scenery in the background. Make a black-and-white duplicate of the photo. Layer photos together front to back and hold together with temporary adhesive. Use a metal straightedge ruler and craft knife to crop random, triangular segments across photo. Separate photo segments; wipe off any adhesive residue. Reassemble into original image, alternating color with black-and-white photo segments. Use remaining set of segments for a second piece of photo art ready-made for gift giving!

A BRIGHT SPOT
IN THE DAY

The serenity of the Pennsylvania country side is broken by the sound of my boys at play: racing their scooters down the steep walking path. Timothy and Jeffrey can brighten up a dull day with their endless activity and enthusiasm!

summer 2001

mats & frames

In and out of the scrapbooking realm, some photos just beg for special mat and frame treatments. What makes these captivating mats and frames so spectacular is that they're all made with photos. You may be so impressed with the final results that you'll be tempted to hang them in your home instead of tucking them away safely in a scrapbook!

Time is made up of captured moments.
The things shared and the moments spent
together become gifts that the heart never forgets.

- Author Unknown

Crop mini frames from spare photos

Mini photo frames are all the rage. So Trudy Sigurdson (Victoria, British Columbia, Canada) came up with the idea of making her own style of mini frames from spare photos! First, punch or cut a 3" square from spare photo. Use decorative scissors around the edges of the square for accent, if desired. Remove a 2" square from the middle by using a punch or a metal straightedge ruler and craft knife. Mat frame, if desired. Crop a piece of a page protector for the "glass" in the frame and mount to the back of the frame. Trim featured photo to size; center and mount behind frame with self-adhesive foam spacers for depth. "Hang" your photo from wire and a brad fastener when mounting on page. Close-up photos of objects and landscapes work well for frames or try this technique with enlarged photos, using a duplicate copy for the frame.

Mat color photos with black-and-white enlargement

When you look at this layout by Diana Hudson (Bakersfield, California), you get the feeling she matted her pictures with a beautifully painted canvas background—which is actually a black-and-white photo printed on canvas paper (Fredrix). A simple variation to this technique is to print a color enlargement on canvas paper for mat and mount black-and-white photos on it. Photos Mona Payne (Henderson, Nevada)

California dreamin'

Joshua and Jordan really look forward to their annual summer vacation in Laguna Beach. After spending all day in the water, they like to walk around town in the evenings to visit their favorite shops and restaurants. The trip is not complete until they get ice cream and make a trip to the candy store. They think of Laguna as their second home.

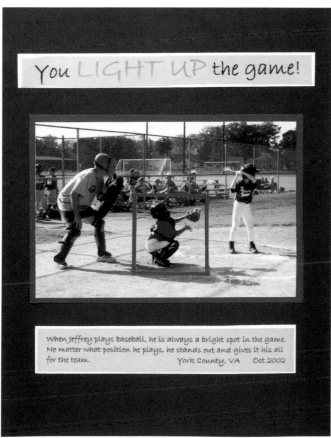

You LIGHT UP the game!

When Jeffrey plays baseball, he is always a bright spot in the game. No matter what position he plays, he stands out and gives it his all for the team.   York County, VA   Oct 2002

Spotlight with a black-and-white background

When Ruthann Grabowski (Yorktown, Virginia) watches her son Jeffrey play baseball, he is all she sees during the game. To express this in her layout, Ruthann features a color photo segment atop a black-and-white duplicate photo to make him the focal point. Begin by making a black-and-white copy of a color photo. Use a metal straightedge ruler and craft knife to cut the desired focal subject from a square segment of the color photo; mat with cardstock. Mount the color image directly on top of the black-and-white copy in its original position. This technique is a great way to focus attention on a single person, or a small group of people in a crowd. For variation, use a black-and-white photo segment atop a color photo background and experiment with placing photo subject off-center.

wave chaser

Joshua

Laguna Beach

The boys love being on their boards so much that they will endure the often chilly Pacific Ocean for hours.

Mat a framed photo overlay on a photo background

Diana Hudson (Bakersfield, California) takes a playful photo and turns it into a charming layout by slicing and matting her main photo to a similar-themed photo, then mounting that to an enlarged version of the original. Use a window pattern cut from cardstock to help crop the frame overlay following the steps below. Photo Mona Payne (Henderson, Nevada)

1 Cut one 2¾" square from cardstock to form a window pattern. Cut one 3¼" square from cardstock to form window pattern. Discard resulting cardstock squares. Place smallest window pattern atop photo, center photo subject and trace lines of square on photo with a wax pencil. Repeat this step using the larger square, center over previously drawn small square, resulting in a set of square cutting lines that will form a frame on the photo.

2 Use a metal straightedge ruler and a craft knife to slice on cutting lines; remove resulting interior square frame and discard. Use a piercing awl or sewing needle to pierce holes in both frame and photo at all four interior corners. Thread fiber from back of photos, add a bead and tie in a knot on top of photo. Repeat for three remaining corners. To finish, mount new photo art atop background photo of similar subject for dimension.

Embellish a punched photo mat

Using an enlarged photo to serve as a mat for smaller photos gives any layout "eye appeal." But to take it to the next level, embellishing the mat is the way to go! Kelly Angard (Highlands Ranch, Colorado) does just that by adding baseball charms to go with her baseball photo layout. This would be a great idea to do with a larger event photo for a mat—and smaller snapshots of loved ones or friends at the event—with charms, punched shapes or beads to dangle as accents. Follow the steps below to create your own embellished photo mat.

1 Punch squares of desired size from cardstock. Arrange squares on back of photo, turning squares so they are in a diamond shape in desired position and leaving enough room between diamonds for setting an eyelet. Trace around diamonds with pencil. Use a craft knife and metal straightedge ruler to crop diamonds into photos to form windows.

2 Punch ⅛" holes between the diamond windows, insert the tubular end of an eyelet—one at a time—into each hole. Flip photo over. Insert eyelet setter into eyelet opening and tap firmly with a hammer until eyelet is almost flat. Remove setter, cover the eyelet with a soft cloth and tap hammer again to "finish" the set of each eyelet.

3 Cut a 1" length of wire. String wire through charm and through eyelet, wrapping wire around itself to "tie off." Use nylon jaw pliers to help flatten a bit, if desired. Cut excess wire with cutters. Repeat until all punched windows are accented with dangling charms.

Frame a color photo with a black-and-white photo

Trudy Sigurdson (Victoria, British Columbia, Canada) adds depth to her picture by cropping a frame out of a black-and-white copy. Start with a same-sized, black-and-white duplicate of a color photo. Use a ruler and a photo-safe wax pencil to mark the frame outline on the black-and-white photo. Secure the photo to cutting mat with removable artist's tape and crop out the center marked area with a metal straightedge ruler and craft knife. Double mat the color photo. Mount the black-and-white frame with self-adhesive foam spacers atop the color photo. You may also cut a piece out of a page protector to sandwich between the frame opening and matted photo for a faux glass look.

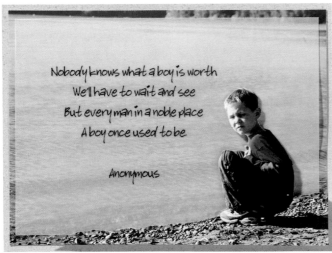

Nobody knows what a boy is worth
We'll have to wait and see
But every man in a noble place
A boy once used to be.

Anonymous

Frame a partial silhouette against a photo background

By using the partial silhouetting technique and a vellum piece over a photo background, Trudy Sigurdson (Victoria, British Columbia, Canada) makes her son look three-dimensional! Begin with two duplicate photos; the color and size of your reprints is not as important as having a photo subject that falls along one of the photo's edges. Using small, sharp scissors or a craft knife, partially silhouette crop the subject from one photo, leaving some of the foreground intact to become part of the frame. Print title or journaling on vellum; trim vellum into rectangle that is ⅛" smaller than photo size. Adhere vellum atop second photo and mat photo. Adhere partial silhouette atop vellum-laden photo, in its proper position in original image, with self-adhesive foam spacers for lift. For additional depth and variation, mount a frame cut from an additional copy of your photo atop the completed piece with foam tape doubled in thickness. This technique can be used whenever you desire to make a subject look as if it is coming right out of the photo.

Create a shadowbox photo frame

Shadowbox frames are an attractive way to display several different items all in one spot. The shadowbox concept is a natural for cropping photos creatively, as shown by MaryJo Regier's (Memory Makers) photo art. As you can see, a shadowbox photo frame gives you the ability to display several smaller pictures behind a sectioned photo frame. To make your own shadowbox photo frame, follow the instructions below. Complete the new photo art by adhering smaller, trimmed photos behind frame, centering photo subjects in cut squares. For variation, experiment with the placement of your square "windows" on the enlargement, or introduce sepia-toned or black-and-white photos into the project. You may also cut a piece out of a page protector to sandwich between the frame openings and smaller photos for a faux glass look.

1 Trace same-sized template squares atop photo enlargement using a photo-safe wax pencil, leaving equal distance between all squares. Use a craft knife and metal straightedge ruler to cut out squares.

2 Place photo on top of an 8 x 10" sheet of ⅛" thick foam core board, holding photo in place with a temporary adhesive. Trace photo windows onto foam core with a pencil.

3 Use a craft knife and metal straight-edge ruler to cut windows into foam core, cutting ⅛" outside of the traced lines so that foam core edges won't show through photo windows. Mount and adhere cropped enlargement to foam core with permanent adhesive.

Combine shadowboxes with partial silhouetting

Monique McCloskey (Oceanside, California) took her son Dylan to celebrate his birthday at California's LegoLand and not only came home with souvenirs but also some great photo memories. To incorporate the souvenirs into photo art, Monique used a layout with foam core for the shadow box. For special effect, a partial silhouette of the family helps draw the eye across the photo, into its recesses, and back to the family again. Although it may look like there are two copies of this photo, it is really just one. First, crop two segments from one enlarged photo as shown below to create the recesses in which to place mementos.

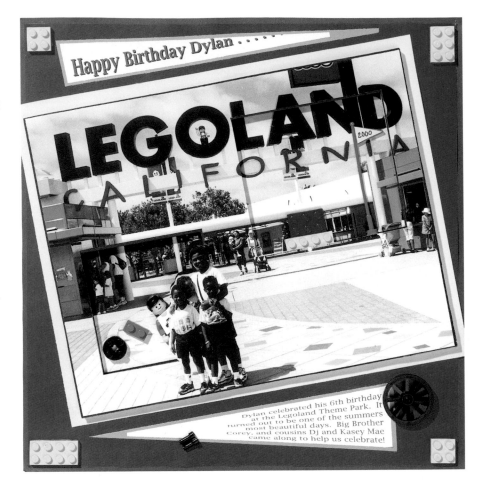

1 Use a photo-safe wax pencil and a graphing ruler to trace squares in the desired sizes based on the position of the photo subject you wish to crop into a partial silhouette. Use a craft knife and metal straightedge ruler to cut on straight lines. Use small, sharp scissors to crop around the photo subjects in a partial silhouette, leaving the outer edges of the bodies attached to the uncut photo. Wipe off any pencil residue from photo segments.

2 Place cropped photo on foam core board and trace squares, including shape of partial silhouette, onto foam core. Set photo aside. Use a craft knife and metal straightedge ruler to cut outside of traced lines. Use scissors to crop outside lines of partial silhouette. Cropping outside of traced lines ensures the foam core board won't show in finished art.

3 To assemble photo art, mount photo on top of foam core in its proper position, mat with black cardstock. Mount and adhere photo segments in the cut out recesses. Mount and adhere mementos as desired.

Crop a photo shaker box frame

Shaker boxes have become a very big thing in the scrapbooking world. To put a fresh twist on the trend, Kelly Angard (Highlands Ranch, Colorado) uses a photo as the top frame of her shaker box. Begin with two same-sized, subject-related photos—one for the frame and one for the background. To make a photo shaker box, follow the instructions below. Try this technique with birthday, baby, wedding, heritage, travel or holiday photos and add themed confetti, charms, punched shapes, beads or buttons in the shaker. Photos Chrissie Tepe (Lancaster, California)

1 Use a craft knife and metal straightedge ruler to cut a 1" frame from the top photo; discard resulting photo rectangle.

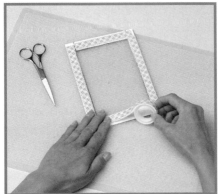

2 Cut a page protector ¼" larger than frame opening for "windowpane." Mount windowpane on back of photo frame. Cover outer edges of frame back with double-sided foam tape, making sure all edges are sealed completely.

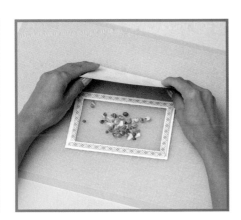

3 Sprinkle some shells (U.S. Shell, Inc.) atop windowpane. Remove the foam tape backing; discard. Place and center background photo atop exposed foam tape to create shaker box.

Tole a photo silhouette

To give these pictures a 3-D effect, Jodi Amidei (Memory Makers) used silhouette-cropped flowers from duplicates of the original photo and an embossing stylus to curl the flowers just enough to give them the look she was after. Start with three duplicates of the same photo. Use small, sharp scissors to silhouette crop the flowers from first photo; save the scraps for title letters. Crop out the center of the flowers from the second photo. Follow the steps below to "tole" the flowers and flower centers. Mount flowers, then their centers, in their original positions on the third photo with self-adhesive foam spacers for lift. Try this with any curved photo subject to add dimension. Photo Sandra Yanisko (Barto, Pennsylvania)

1 Place silhouette-cropped photo pieces face down on a mouse pad. Rub an embossing stylus or the round tip of a bone folder around outer edges using a circular motion to curl. Rub lightly around entire photo. Repeat on all photo pieces to achieve tole effect.

Template-cut a self-framing photo

When Kelly Angard (Highlands Ranch, Colorado) looked at this adorable picture of her daughter, she was distracted by some of the background. Her solution? Kelly used a template and a craft knife to cut out the distractions while successfully framing the photo with itself. Follow the instructions shown to apply this technique to your photos. It's a super technique for all those pictures that you don't use because of the distracting backgrounds!

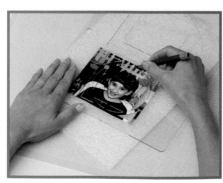

1 Place template (EZ2Cut Shapemakers by EZ2Cut/Accu-Cut) on photo and plastic foam cutting mat. Hold photo and template down with removable artist's tape, if desired. Insert a swivel blade knife into cutting channels to slice template pattern into photo. Discard resulting scraps.

Pierce an ornate, self-framing photo

To add more beauty to this happy picture, Jodi Amidei (Memory Makers) used a brass stencil to pierce a pretty pattern into a self-framing photo. Follow the illustration shown to create a self-framing photo using a brass stencil (Ornare™ by Ecstasy Crafts). Try varying the holes to make your own design. Make the holes slightly bigger and mount on contrasting paper for diversity. Photo Pam Klassen (Reedley, California)

1 Secure photo face up, centering focal point, to back of brass stencil with temporary adhesive. Cut slots from photo with a craft knife and discard. Place photo and stencil atop piercing mat or mouse pad. Use a piercing awl or sewing needle to pierce holes into photo following the design provided by the holes on the stencil.

1 Secure photo face up to back of brass stencil with temporary adhesive. Use a craft knife to carefully cut out stencil's pattern on photo. Set aside resulting frame. Place remaining photo center on plastic foam cutting mat and top with oval graduated template and center image. Use swivel blade knife to crop photo into an oval shape. Reassemble center in frame on cardstock.

Shadow-cut a self-framing photo

Shadow cutting a frame is an excellent way to draw your eye right into the focus of the photo while adding some interest to the framing effect itself. Jodi Amidei (Memory Makers) uses a brass "shadowing" stencil to create the butterfly pattern, and an oval graduated template (Coluzzle® by Provo Craft) to crop out the center. Follow the step at right to apply this technique to your photo. For variation, mat photo pieces with vellum, mulberry or textured paper. Photo Chrissie Tepe (Lancaster, California)

tearing

Once thought to be taboo in the world of scrapbooking, tearing photos is now enjoying popularity. Tearing can add drama or a soft and subtle look to photos, depending on the look you're trying to achieve. Removing the clear plastic backing from a photo can make tearing easier. Tear slowly to stay in control of the tear's direction.

Tear photos for a dramatic effect

MaryJo Regier (Memory Makers) gives an enticing picture a dramatic twist by tearing around the outer edges and matting it on black cardstock. Lay your picture face up for the tear to show rough, white edges (face down for tear to show smooth, clean edges). Place your left hand on the picture using your index finger as a guide for the tear. Use your right hand to tear around all of the edges of the photo, turning the photo as you go. Mat on black cardstock to emphasize torn edges.

Tear a unifying line across multiple photos

Making a unified tear across the top line of a photo series draws your eye right across the page and the story told in the photos. It also allows you to use more pictures on a single page layout as shown here by MaryJo Regier (Memory Makers). For a 12 x 12" layout, select five pictures from the same event. Trim the four that will go on the bottom of the page to 3" wide. For an 8½ x 11" layout, select four photos and cut three for the bottom 2¾" wide. Lay photos face down in reverse order; tape them all together making sure that you do not run tape along the "tearing edge." Turn taped photos right side up and tear the top edge toward you all the way across the top edges. Tear the top from the fifth photo also. Try using this technique with any photo sequence, such as sports photos, a toddler getting dressed, a baby rolling or a birthday party.

Every child is a different
kind of flower...
And all together, they make this world
a beautiful garden
~anonymous

Rachel & Jake

Soften torn edges

Torn photo edges lend an easygoing feel to scrapbook pages, but you can soften a torn edge even more with chalk. Kelly Angard (Highlands Ranch, Colorado) turned vivid color photos of her children into tender mementos of a sibling relationship by simply rubbing chalk onto the torn edges of the photos. First, tear photo edges—tearing pictures with the photo lying face up so that you will get the rough white edge on which to chalk. Then use your fingertip, a cotton swab or a sponge-tip makeup applicator to apply complementary-colored chalk on photo edges. To make the color deeper, add more chalk; to make the color softer, use less.

Burnt and faux-burnt torn edges

It has always been a favorite—dressing up and taking "old time" pictures. Adding a burnt edge to Kelly Angard's (Highlands Ranch, Colorado) picture of her son, gives it the conceptual feeling of it really being an old picture! There are two ways to do this technique. The first way is to use matches (above left). Tear photo edges leaving "burning room." Light a match and hold it to the edge of the picture. Blow it out when desired burnt look is achieved. Repeat this in small increments until all of photo and mat (if desired) are complete.

To create the look without the matches (which is safer in a scrapbook), brush tan, black and gray chalk onto the torn edges of the picture and mat (above right). For the final touch, use a fine-tip black marker to draw all along the edge of the tear.

Offset assemble a torn photo

Jodi Amidei (Memory Makers) proves that you can play a trick on the eye by taking a photo, tearing it and reassembling it offset for an effect deserving of a second look. Hold down a photo with your left hand using your index finger for your tearing guide. Tear toward you until it is torn all the way through the photo. Then tear the other side in the same way so that you have two larger end segments and one small center segment. Reassemble and mount offset so that the middle segment is higher or lower than the side segments, with each segment overlapping each other ever so slightly. Photo Torrey Miller (Thornton, Colorado)

Unite photos with diagonal tears

When you think football, you think rough and tough! MaryJo Regier (Memory Makers) does a fantastic job of giving you that feeling with the diagonal tears on the photos of her coach husband and ball-playing son. The photos—shot on different rolls of film on different days—stand united by the mirrored, diagonal tears. Tear photos toward you diagonally into three sections. Reassemble on page, leaving slight gaps in between the segments. Note how the direction of the torn lines leads the eye across the first photo and onto the second photo without missing a beat. Try it. A few well-placed tears can put the viewer's eyes right where you want them!

It's not flesh and blood, but the heart that makes us fathers and sons.

S. Chiller. Jake, age 10 darpi, age 41 Bear Creek Bears October 2002

Layer a torn photo

Diana Hudson (Bakersfield, California) takes a photo that, in its original form, may have had the focal point lost in all of the water in the background. By layering a torn copy with chalked edges, she adds interest while keeping the focus on the boy. Start with two copies of the same photo. Cut the first photo down to a more manageable size to handle when tearing. Tear around the focal point, making sure to tear toward you to get the rough edge. Chalk the torn edges lightly. Use self-adhesive foam spacers to mount the torn piece on the second photo, lining up the image in its proper position in the original photo. This technique is useful whenever you are looking for a way to bring the focal point to the forefront of the photo. Photo Mona Payne (Henderson, Nevada)

Tear a peek-a-boo window

MaryJo Regier (Memory Makers) captures a very sweet moment in black-and-white and frames it with a bold-colored peek-a-boo frame. The frame was a junk photo from the beginning of a roll of film that otherwise would have been tossed out. To make the frame, layer the two pictures together and place on a light box. If you do not have a light box, a brightly lit window will do. Mark four tearing points on the top photo with a photo safe wax pencil. Place the top photo onto a cutting mat and use a craft knife to start a cut large enough to get your fingers into to begin tearing the frame opening. Remember to leave some room for tearing. Start at one end of the cut and move around the entire shape tearing toward you. Mount the frame atop the peek-a-boo photo.

Tear a frame from an enlarged photo

Kelly Angard (Highlands Ranch, Colorado) uses an enlarged, snowy photo to make a frame for the photo of these sled dogs. She tears and rolls the opening of the frame to make it look as if it was torn back just to expose the sled dogs. To apply this technique, start with an 8 x 10" photo enlargement for the frame. Measure the peek-a-boo photo for an approximate opening size for the frame. Place enlarged photo on a cutting mat and cut out a general shape for the frame leaving enough room to then tear the opening. Tear around the cut-out shape and roll the torn edges back slightly with your fingers. Mount the second photo underneath the frame opening. For variation, try this technique with an old black-and-white copy underneath and burn the torn and rolled edges (see page 174).

Create a torn photo series montage

Expect the unexpected when you combine straight-cropped photos with randomly torn photos into a new photomontage. MaryJo Regier (Memory Makers) uses a photo series—one horizontal and three vertical shots—to capture a rugged, yet tender moment between father and son. Begin with one horizontal photo for the background. Use a craft knife and metal straight-edge ruler to cut the photo's subject into a square; mat with black paper and adhere back on photo. Tear three vertical photos into strips. Reassemble onto background photo to create the photomontage, lining up and matching photo subjects while tucking torn edges behind cropped and matted photo at center. For this type of photo art, shoot with camera from the same spot, pivoting left to right and overlapping some shots to capture movement in the scene. Turn camera horizontal and then vertical to get both types of shots, with elbows at the same height against your body (or use a tripod) while shooting to keep the subjects the same proportion with each progressive shot. A great technique for any photo series!

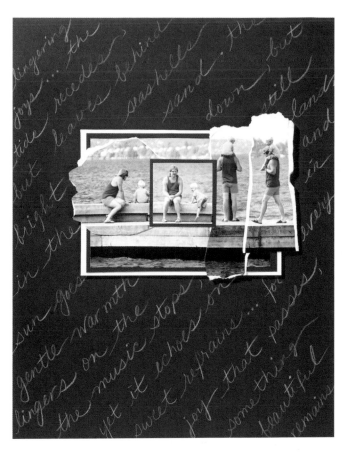

Tear photos to contrast positive and negative space

Brandi Ginn (Lafayette, Colorado) wanted to do a layout that showcased how much her family loves the snow. Cutting a heart shape from cardstock first for a pattern ensures a perfect torn photo heart. To create a torn heart and heart-shaped frames, see the step below. For a variation, try putting a picture underneath the torn heart frames or hang charms from the cutouts (see page 165).

1 Freehand cut a heart from cardstock. Use a photo-safe wax pencil to trace the heart pattern onto the photo. Make a small slit on the photo to begin a tear. Tear around drawn heart. Remove any pencil residue with a dry, soft cloth.

You've taught me many things in life.
· how to speak my mind
· when I roam, I can still come back home
· there is no stronger bond than to love someone
· you're never too old to be a child
· wisdom comes from trial and error
· family ties may stretch but they never break

"All I need is my brains, my eyes and
my personality, for better or for worse."
–William Albert Allard

Autumn

A dream is a path to the future
A quiet belief in the heart
A small secret wish nurtured deep in a spirit
where all great accomplishments start.

A dream is an endless horizon
That only a dreamer can see.
A dream is a challenge...
A promise of all you can be.

KELLIE

shape cropping

Now that you have learned all about the basic, linear cropping of photos, shape cropping is a natural progression. With the wide array of theme-shaped templates and punches available, you may have a hard time deciding which ones to use to bring visual contour to your photographs! Here, you will discover how to:

- Crop photos into tags

- Frame a tag shaker box

- Slice shape pull-aparts

- Layer nested template shapes

- "Art deco" a panoramic photo series

- Switch shapes for positive/negative effect

- Use photos to create page titles

- Wrap lettering around a photo

- Crop reflected lettering

- Cut symbols into photos

- Lift randomly punched squares

- Punch and layer several photos

- Punch a thematic vignette or funky border

- Punch and slice interlocking photo tiles

- Combine circles and squares for a fold-out gallery

- Curl punched shapes for lift

- Punch a delicate or artsy edge

- Dangle a photo embellishment

- Stitch a suspended photo border

These well-defined cropping techniques will lend curvaceous structure and distinctive form to your photos and page layouts. In no time at all, you'll feel at ease and more than prepared to conquer cutting edge photo cropping techniques.

tags

There are limitless possibilities for incorporating photos into tag designs, which greatly increases the versatility of these much-loved page accents. Whether tags are freehand cut or cropped using a template, pattern or punch, one thing's for certain: These little photo accents have a huge impact!

Slice vertical strips

Jodi Amidei (Memory Makers) vertically slices a photo to feature her daughter's face and fade out the photo's background. See page 250 for tag pattern which can be used to create any of the tags on this spread. Mount pieces on tag leaving space between each slice. Slice a large or small photo either in equal or random segments depending on the tone and theme of your photo.

Punch a simple design

Add understated elegance to a photo tag with a punched design that doesn't overpower the photo. MaryJo Regier (Memory Makers) uses a punch (Missing Links Paper Shaper by EK Success) to punch a simple design. Use a decorative punch around the border of a photo or just at the corners for a delicate design.

Punch a vellum window

Trudy Sigurdson (Victoria, British Columbia, Canada) crops a window into a vellum overlay to highlight her daughter's face. Crop a photo into a tag shape either with a template or cutting system (Accu-Cut). Cut a piece of vellum into the same shape. Lay vellum over photo tag to determine where to cut or punch the "window." Cut out window; mount vellum over photo tag before adding embellishments and journaling. For extra interest, punch a single large window or a number of smaller windows to highlight various areas of a photo.

Layer a torn photo tag

A torn photo, layered with vellum on a tag, creates the perfect space for Trudy Sigurdson's (Victoria, British Columbia, Canada) thematic title. Cut two photos and one piece of vellum into a tag shape. Mount vellum on one photo tag. Diagonally tear a strip from second photo tag; mount over vellum, leaving space between the pieces as shown.

Frame a tag shaker box

Diana Hudson, (Bakersfield, California) makes use of two photos on a cleverly crafted tag shaker box. Use a template or die-cut system to cut two photos and a piece of foam core board into a tag shape. Follow the steps below to create a shaker box photo tag. Try this technique with any photo theme, including wedding, baby, school, travel and more. Finish tag by tying fibers, raffia or ribbon into hole and mount on page.

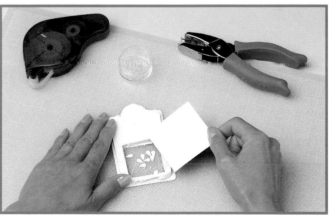

1 Cut tag shape into the photo using a tag template (Coluzzle® by Provo Craft) to form the front of the shaker box. Punch square (Emagination Crafts) in center of photo along lower edge to form "window." Trace tag template onto foam core board and cut out slightly inside traced marks with a craft knife to form shaker backing. Cut the foam core square portion slightly larger than the square window. Cut a square ¼" larger than window opening from a page protector to form shaker "glass." Center and adhere over picture tag with tape.

2 Adhere foam core piece to back of photo tag, placing adhesive around all sides of the window. Sprinkle beads and punched teardrops (Fiskars) atop window. Mount precut square background photo on back of window, adhering all sides completely to prevent beads and punched shapes from spilling out.

template shapes

The myriad of template shapes and types available provide a myriad of photo-cropping possibilities. Experiment with theme-shaped, geometric-shaped, graduated or nested, or panoramic-sized templates for stunning results that'll get more use out of your templates than ever before.

Slice a vertical background design

Jodi Amidei (Memory Makers) elaborates on a photo's theme with a vertically sliced palm tree with the help of a shape template. Trace shape with template on photo background. Cut apart with a continuous scissor stroke. Mount pieces, leaving space between each shape as shown. Photo Bruce Aldridge (Broomfield, Colorado)

1 Position template (Stamping Station) shape atop photo and trace shape with a wax pencil. If template shape is not long enough to reach from upper and lower edges of photo, draw two parallel lines about ¼" apart, connecting the drawn shape and forming continuous cutting lines.

2 Use small, sharp scissors to cut along drawn lines, making sure to use one continuous stroke of the scissors for a clean cut. Similar to silhouette cropping, have patience and move the photo in and out of the scissor blades instead of moving the blades around the shape.

3 Place the cut-apart photo slices in order on cardstock of choice, making sure to pull segments apart to allow background paper to show through. Adhere segments in place.

Slice a pull-apart design

Kelly Angard (Highlands Ranch, Colorado) horizontally slices stars and stripes into a large photo to reflect its patriotic theme. Trace a shape template onto a photo enlargement in desired positions with a wax pencil. Draw two horizontal lines about ¼" apart connecting the drawn shapes and forming continuous cutting lines. Cut along drawn lines using one continuous scissor stroke for a clean cut. Mount the cut-apart segments to background leaving a generous amount of space between pieces. Offset the cropped shape over segments with self-adhesive foam spacers for dimension as shown. Change the template shape to coordinate with your page and photo themes as desired. Photos JoAnn Petersen (Parker, Colorado)

Garden Girl

Step into my garden
Step in and you'll see
a measure of peace
and tranquility.

It's the scent of the blossoms
the buzz of the bees
the sweet song of birds
as they sing in the trees.

The sweet scent of roses
their petals so new
as they glisten and sparkle
with the fresh morning dew.

Run your toes through the grass
beneath a canopy of trees
hear the rustle of leaves
as they blow in the breeze.

Let the beauty of springtime
Fill your soul with great peace
Take it with you and share it
with each one you meet.

Create a kaleidoscope of color

Brandi Ginn (Lafayette, Colorado) adds a kaleidoscope of colors and shapes to her page with layers of floral photos cut from "nested templates." Follow the steps below to create layered photo page accents. Experiment with different photo themes, paper colors and layered shapes for varied results. Photos Michele Gerbrandt (Memory Makers)

1 Use a wax pencil to trace different nested template (Hot Off The Press) shapes atop photo duplicates. Use small, sharp scissors to cut out different shapes.

2 Mat cropped photo shapes with complementary-colored cardstock and reassemble to re-create original photo, using self-adhesive foam spacers between photo layers for dimension.

Layer nested template shapes

Kelly Angard (Highlands Ranch, Colorado) layers colorful sunset photos in designs cut from a nested template to achieve an elegant and dimensional embellishment. Trace template shapes onto different photos with the same theme. Mat each cropped photo on complementary-colored paper and silhouette around shape. Layer atop another with self-adhesive foam spacers for dimension.

Alternate black-and-white with color photo layers

Add visual appeal to a nested template design with black-and-white photos interspersed with color photo layers. Kelly Angard (Highlands Ranch, Colorado) achieves this look with two black-and-white and two color copies of the same photo. Trace nested template shapes onto photos, alternating color and black-and-white layers. Remount cropped shapes atop original image. Photo Erica Pierovich (Longmont, Colorado)

we left our hearts in san francisco, summer 2002

Slice a deco design in a panoramic photo

MaryJo Regier (Memory Makers) adds an interesting perspective to a panoramic skyline photo with a sliced and reassembled deco design. Follow the steps below to apply this technique to a panoramic photo. Experiment with this fun techniques using different photo themes and by varying the segments that you give dimension to with self-adhesive foam spacers.

1 Place template (Scrapbook Magic) atop panoramic photo; hold both in place on cutting mat with removable artist's tape. Use a craft knife to cut out the template's different sections; set resulting photo pieces aside.

2 Use extended reach punches, if needed, to cut out the template's small circles, ovals or triangles. Trim ⅛" from outer edges of larger photo pieces using small, sharp scissors. Reassemble photo, mounting various photo shapes with self-adhesive foams spacers for dimension.

Swap color and black-and-white punched shapes

Jodi Amidei (Memory Makers) adds visual variation to a sliced and reassembled color and black-and-white photo with the swapping of punched shapes. Begin with a color and black-and-white copy of the same photo. Follow the steps below to create the photo art. After cropping, use all of the leftover photo triangles and punched circles to create a second piece of photo art for a gift! This simple technique works well for any photo theme.

You've taught me many things in life,
- how to speak my mind
- when I roam, I can still come back home
- there is no stronger bond than to love someone
- you're never too old to be a child
- wisdom comes from trial and error
- family ties may stretch but they never break

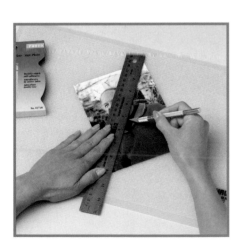

1 Layer color photo atop black-and-white photo and tape together with removable artist's tape. Use a metal straightedge ruler and craft knife to cut diagonally across the photos.

2 With photos still taped together, trace various template circles randomly onto photo triangles with a photo-safe wax pencil. Use a craft knife to carefully crop circles from layered photos. Or, use various-sized circle punches instead.

3 Separate layered photos. Reassemble large photo using one color and one black-and-white triangle. Adhere color circles in their original spot atop black-and-white photo. Adhere black-and-white circles in their original spot atop color photo.

letters

It's quick and easy to incorporate letters into your photo art. Whether you're cropping letters directly into your photos, revealing the negative space left behind by cropped letters or cropping letters from photo scraps, photo lettering provides custom-coordinated page accents.

Watch for opportunities within a photo

Sometimes a photo will unwittingly provide you with title letters that you can build upon as Jennifer Whitten (Stephenville, Texas) discovered with a poolside photo of her children. Round corners of photo. Cut P and L letters and arrange with photo to spell "pool." Experiment with posing people in photos in certain ways or with certain objects to help create lettering that could prove useful on a scrapbook page.

Crop photo into title letters

Build on the theme of your page and make a bold statement with photos cut into title letters. MaryJo Regier (Memory Makers) humorously incorporates photos of her sons' marble collection into a dimensional title that looks like it's ready to roll off the page. Use a template or die-cut system to cut letters from photos. This technique makes good use of photo scraps, extra photos or preprinted photo strips. Consider photographing the items being used in a photo to create title letters. Inspired by Angelia Wigginton (Belmont, Mississippi)

Minnesota:
Land of 10,000 Lakes
and not a single fish today...
But there's always lots of sand!

West Battle Lake

June 22, 1996

Jake (4) and Dylan (7)

Punch a title into a photo

A creative use of negative space is achieved with the help of letter punches. MaryJo Regier (Memory Makers) punches a vertical title into the background of a treasured photo of her son, saving space and personalizing the photo at the same time. Punch title letters horizontally or vertically in a photo depending upon background space available. Set punched photo letters aside or mount elsewhere on the page for an extra embellishment.

Reveal letters in negative photo space

Pamela Frye Hauer (Denver, Colorado) makes a bold statement with large letters carefully cut into a photomontage. Create this look by first composing a photomontage; adhere photos together and tack down on cutting mat with a temporary adhesive. Use a large lettering template or create your own letter pattern by printing letters from the computer. Place pattern over area to be cut out. Trace with wax pencil and carefully slice out shape with a craft knife, making sure to hold photos together when slicing. Mount photos onto contrasting colored cardstock to make letters stand out.

Slice numbers into photomontage

Terri Sharp (Hillsborough, New York) illustrates how fun it can be to incorporate sliced numbers into a photomontage to commemorate a Disney anniversary during her family's travels. Begin by assembling the photomontage and tack down on cutting mat with a temporary adhesive. Use large number templates or create your own numbers pattern by printing numbers from the computer. Place pattern over area to be cut out. Trace with wax pencil and carefully slice out shape with a craft knife, making sure to hold photos together when slicing. Mount photos onto contrasting colored cardstock to make numbers stand out.

Carve letters into photos

Holle Wiktorek (Clarksville, Tennessee) integrates part of her page's title with images on her page by "carving" the letters into a series of five photos. Crop a series of vertical photos to fit page, making sure each photo is wide enough for its intended letter. Use a template to trace the letter onto the photo with a wax pencil; select an area in the photo that doesn't interfere with its focal point. Using a craft knife, carefully carve the letter into the photo.

As terrorists strike and there is threat of war with the Middle East, I am reminded of good times in my life. Attending family gatherings, bowling on lazy afternoons, building snowmen, climbing on Daddy's shoulders, and decorating for Christmas...these are the things that matter. If terrorists would spend more time focused on family and happiness, they could enjoy the true power of peace. I wish they would take control of their own happiness instead of hurting others. If it could only be that easy...all I can do is pray.

We cruised in the Corvair for nine glorious summers. Wind in our hair, sun on our faces, and the AM radio blaring oldies made us feel young again. We knew we wanted a classic, something that could hold a couple car seats, and it had to be a convertible. But the lack of shoulder harnesses meant that we only took her on short trips down slow streets.

She reigned over the garage instead of the road. There was a woman in Ohio who had been having her own dreams of Corvair summers with open sky above. She made an offer and a trucking company picked up the car. We never regretted buying the Corvair, but we knew it was time to let go.

1966 Corvair Corsa Convertible

Highlight negative space of carved letters

A classic black-and-white photo provides the perfect backdrop for Kelli Noto's (Centennial, Colorado) steady hand and talent for using a craft knife. Create a pattern for title words by printing letters from the computer; silhouette cut. Place letters on top of photo and trace. Carefully cut out letters with a craft knife. Mount carved photo over monochromatic-colored cardstock to highlight words.

Crop and layer letters onto enlargement

This creatively cropped page requires three 8 x 10" prints of the same photograph and can be accomplished using just about any photo theme. First, mat one uncropped 8 x 10" photo with paper or cardstock. Create photo letters from additional 8 x 10" prints as described below. Art by Pam Klassen (Reedley, California); Based on a submission by Sharon Kropp of C-Thru Ruler Co. (Bloomfield, Connecticut); Photo Kris Perkins (Northglenn, Colorado)

1 Using a lettering template (Better Letter by C-Thru Ruler Co.), position a letter on an 8 x 10" print. Trace and cut out with a craft knife.

2 Repeat Step 1 for each letter, cutting the 1st and 3rd letters from one photo and the 2nd and 4th letters from the other. Use paper letters for positioning.

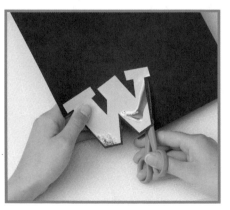

3 Mount each photo letter on cardstock. Use small, sharp scissors to cut around the mat edges. Leave about ⅛" margins.

4 Carefully layer each photo letter on the uncut 8 x 10" photo so that the images are aligned with the background photo.

Enhance carved letters with soft details

Letters carved out of an enlarged photo provide a window for Kathleen Childers' (Christiana, Tennessee) soft paper torn strip. Create this layered look by following the tips below. Try this with any photo subject—or better yet, make a deliberate effort to photograph objects in close-up that appear in your people shots.

1 Use a wax pencil and graphing ruler to measure and draw a vertical line down the center of photo and a horizontal line across the center of photo to help pinpoint the photo's exact center. Place lettering template (EZ2Cut Shapemakers by EZ2Cut/Accu-Cut) on photo and starting at the center of the photo, insert swivel craft knife into appropriate letter's channel and cut. Repeat step, working from center and going outward, until entire title is spelled out with even spacing between each letter.

Wrap photo letters around photos

Scenic title letters wrap around Kelly Angard's (Highlands Ranch, Colorado) camping photos, adding smaller creative and visual elements to the larger photos. Cut letters using a template and craft knife. Mount photo letters around photos in an eye-pleasing manner. Experiment with horizontal, vertical or diagonal placement for variation.

Assemble a reflective title

A reflective title cut from a collection of thematic photos makes for an interesting showcase of images. Kim Rudd (Idledale, Colorado) assembled her reflective title with photos that contained still water reflections, but any photos containing mirrored images or reproduced with a reverse image will work. Follow the tips below to create this look with your photos.

1 Trace letters with a wax pencil and use a craft knife and scissors to cut them out. To create reflected lettering, simply flip the template (Better Letter by C-Thru Ruler Co.) upside down on photo directly below original letter and trace and cut.

Watch for surname in photographed signs

A fun-filled trip to Disney Adventures theme park had Jeanne Ciolli (Dove Canyon, California) thinking in terms of the perfect scrapbook page. While at the theme park, she posed her family around the large letters of the entrance sign with creative thoughts brewing in her mind. Silhouette-crop photo letters and nestle amongst a colorfully collaged background for a unique title. Watch for your surname within the decorative lettering of signs while traveling for one-of-a-kind page titles!

Use leftover photos for illuminated letters

It's easy to incorporate photo scraps into page title lettering like Pam Klassen (Memory Makers) did for these custom-coordinated, illuminated looks. Simply crop or punch the photo scrap into a shape, then back or mat with cardstock or additional photo scraps. For variation, try mounting cardstock letters on top of the cropped photo scraps.
Photos Debbie Mock (Memory Makers), Pamela Frye Hauer (Denver, Colorado), Sandra De St. Croix (St. Albert, Alberta, Canada), Lora Lee Dischner (Denver, Colorado)

symbols

Symbols offer a universal language all their own, and when cropped into photos, the message can be twice as effective. Use dies, templates, patterns or freehand to cut symbols into photos for token appeal!

Craft a photomontage symbol

Holle Wiktorek (Clarksville, Tennessee) found a clever way to announce the sex of her friends' unborn child by piecing together a photomontage into the international female symbol. To create your own photo symbol, follow the tips below. Use a light box or a keen eye to lay photos over the symbol one at a time, making sure the desired images won't be trimmed off. Be creative with other symbols that relate to the theme of your photos like a heart, international male symbol, cross or other religious symbol.

1 Enlarge and photocopy female symbol pattern on page 250. If desired, cut pattern into as many pieces as the number of photos you wish to include in the new photo art. Position pattern pieces over photos randomly to capture desired images; cut with scissors. Reassemble new art on cardstock background.

Slice a related symbol into a photo

A spiritual symbol freehand cut into a photo by Jodi Amidei (Memory Makers) enhances a drab background while maintaining religious reverence. Freehand draw (or use the pattern on page 250) of any related symbol onto a photo with a wax pencil before slicing with a craft knife. Wipe any remaining wax residue from photo surface with a soft cloth. Photo Brenda Martinez (Lakewood, Colorado)

Die cut a symbol

Jodi Amidei (Memory Makers) makes a bold statement of patriotic peace with an international symbol die cut into an enlarged photo. Use the photo die cut elsewhere on your page to reinforce its intended meaning without the use of words.

1 Place photo face up on foam side of die (Accu-Cut) and center die beneath area of photo where you wish to cut symbol. Place die foam side up on die tray; roll through machine (Accu-Cut) to cut the symbol's shape.

punches

Punch manufacturers continue to launch new punch shapes and styles, providing scrapbookers with a never-ending supply of photo-cropping tools. Give punches a try on your photos—it's a punch of fun!

Exaggerate elements in a photo series

Cropped segments of an enlarged photo are reassembled in MaryJo Regier's (Memory Makers) photo series, adding an exaggerated element to her athletic son. Reprint photos in a variety of sizes for an interesting way to highlight desired elements in a photo. Punch photo images into square, geometric or free-form shape and reassemble in a vertical or horizontal line. Try this with any photo where magnification of an element in the photo could be funny, such as that big fish catch or an eye-popping expression.

Add a delicate corner touch

Torrey Miller (Thornton, Colorado) softens a photo of delicate yet hardy pansies with a simple punched corner treatment. Use a small square punch to punch two diagonal squares from one photo corner. Mount the punched photo and photo square stair-stepped diagonally as shown. Experiment with this technique using different geometric-shaped punches on different photo corners or borders for variation. Photo Jodi Amidei (Memory Makers)

Add dimension to randomly punched squares

Trudy Sigurdson (Victoria, British Columbia, Canada) gives a portrait of her children a "lift" with randomly punched squares mounted back in place with self-adhesive foam spacers. Turn punch over and insert photo to capture desired image before punching. Mount punched photo squares back in place with self-adhesive foam spacers in a variety of thicknesses for dimensional interest.

Punch a duplicate photo

Trudy Sigurdson (Victoria, British Columbia, Canada) uses a different approach to the above technique but basically achieves the same effect. Punch details into a duplicate photo with square punches in a variety of sizes. Mount squares over original images with self-adhesive foam spacers. Reprint duplicate photos either in black-and-white, sepia or a colored tone for a contemporary graphic look.

Punch a scenic border

Pam Kuhn's (Bryan, Ohio) visual ensemble of Boston's cityscape is featured with punched "windows" and dimensional details. Stack three different cityscape photos for the background. Cut ½" off each end of a duplicate set; cut or punch window in the center of each photo before matting on one piece of patterned paper. Cut or punch a smaller square in the center of each matted photo; mount over background photos with self-adhesive foam spacers for dimension. Punch four other city scenes; mat and mount on top layer of stacked photos.

Punch a thematic vignette

Kelly Angard (Highlands Ranch, Colorado) used a square punch to focus in on elements of interest and showcase a number of photos in her thematic vignette. Punch square shapes into photos. Turn punch over and insert photo to capture desired image. Single and double mat photos; place around large photo of the same theme as shown. Try this with wedding, baby, school, travel and heritage photos for a unique photo essay.

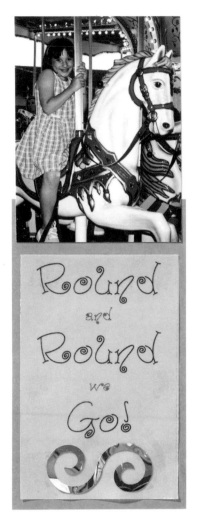

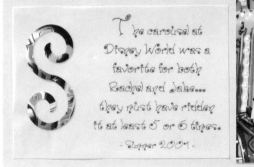

Create a frame with punched photo pieces

Decorative shapes, punched from duplicate photos, enhance Kelly Angard's (Highlands Ranch, Colorado) photo frame with a kaleidoscope of color. Turn punch shape over to capture desired images from photo background. Select shapes that work with the theme of your photos. Experiment with other punched shapes for variation.

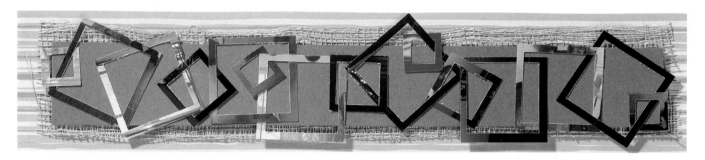

Punch a geometric photo border

Jill Tennyson's (Lafayette, Colorado) punched geometric border makes good use of leftover photo scraps. Square shapes, in a variety of sizes, are punched and then re-punched to achieve a thin photo frame. Slice through one edge of punched square frames to link shapes together. Mount linked shapes in an asymmetrical, eye-pleasing fashion.

Punch interlocking photo tiles

MaryJo Regier (Memory Makers) links together punched photo shapes representing the symbolic bond between sisters. Follow the instructions below to create the interlocking photo tiles. This is a great technique to use on photos of family or friends. If you use photos that all have different-colored backgrounds, the small half-diamonds that result from interlocking will be more prominent.

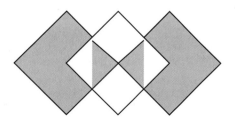

1 Punch a number of large square photo shapes. Turn on end to form a diamond; determine the sequence of order to link together. Or enlarge and photocopy the diamond photo tile patterns on page 250 to fit photo subject, noting that the cut lines on each pattern is different. Trace diamonds atop desired photos with a wax pencil; cut out to create photo tiles. Use a craft knife and a metal straightedge ruler to slice the photo tiles for locking them together. Interlock photo tiles as shown in the diagram above.

Fold out a gallery of punched photos

A collection of punched photos from a memorable vacation is neatly packaged in a mini fold-out album. Heidi Schueller's (Waukesha, Wisconsin) European photo gallery is made up of punched photos mounted on cardstock squares and linked together with ribbon. To create a fold-out photo gallery, cut twelve 3 x 3" squares of cardstock and ten 1" strips of ribbon for connectors. Apply double-sided adhesive to both sides of ribbons and sandwich ribbons between pairs of cardstock squares to form fold-out; mount fold-out on page. Use a jumbo circle punch to crop photos and journaling blocks; adhere to both sides of fold-out if desired.

Randomly punch positive/negative shapes

Julie Mullison (Superior, Colorado) builds on a bubbly theme with randomly punched circles placed along her photo's edge. Punch large circles first and work down to smallest punch for an overall balanced look. Flip punch over to ensure desired placement. Mount punched shapes just outside of negative punched space for an interesting effect.

Punch a contemporary edge

Kelly Angard (Highlands Ranch, Colorado) punches a little geometric fun into a futuristically themed photo, shaping a unique and eye-catching edge. Randomly punch circle shapes in a variety of sizes along the outside of a photo. Mount punched shapes along the edge to extend the photo's border as shown. This takes some time and patience, but the results are well worth it!

Punch a family tree

Documenting a family's birth line doesn't have to be a complicated project as demonstrated by Kim Rudd's (Idledale, Colorado) simple punched vignettes. Turn circle punch over to center faces before punching. Use a singular shape for consistency, or a different shape to differentiate matriarchal and patriarchal families.

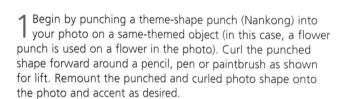

Punch dimensional shape into a photo

Colorful punched poinsettias blossom from JoAnn Colledge's (North Ogden, Utah) photos with realistic dimension and sparkling details. Follow the instructions below to create photo blossoms. Detail flower centers with glitter glue. This technique works well to enhance and embellish a variety of related photos and punches.

1 Begin by punching a theme-shape punch (Nankong) into your photo on a same-themed object (in this case, a flower punch is used on a flower in the photo). Curl the punched shape forward around a pencil, pen or paintbrush as shown for lift. Remount the punched and curled photo shape onto the photo and accent as desired.

Punch a delicate corner design

Decorative corner punches add a hint of color and design to the corners of Kelly Angard's (Highlands Ranch, Colorado) black-and-white portraits. Punch corners of cropped photo; layer on colored paper. Detail photo mat with designs punched from colored paper. You can also experiment with punching a decorative border across the top, bottom or sides of a photo by removing corner punch guides. Flip the punch over and insert photo edge; repeat as needed across the photo.

Punch a decorative edge

Torrey Miller (Thornton, Colorado) adds a unique edge to a photo with a decorative border punch. Line up the repetitive design using the guideline marks on the punch (Border Punch by Fiskars) or flip the punch over to ensure proper spacing of a continuous design. Photo Jodi Amidei (Memory Makers)

Flip a positive shape to reveal negative space

MaryJo Regier (Memory Makers) emphasizes the destructive force of nature with related shapes punched into her photos and achieves interesting positive/negative effects at the same time. Flip over rectangle and fern punches (Family Treasures, Martha Stewart respectively) to capture desired image; mount punched shape upside down, giving a reflective look to the finished artwork.

Embellish and dangle punched photo shapes

Punched leaves dangle in the negative space of a large punched shape as a decorative background element on MaryJo Regier's (Memory Makers) fall photo. Punch two mega birch leaves into the background of an enlarged photo. Repunch resulting mega birch leaves with a large birch punch. Attach eyelets to photo above punched negative space. Punch 1/16" hole in large birch leaves. Dangle large birch leaves from spiraled and beaded wire through eyelet. Secure wire to back of photo with artist's tape. Punch 1/16" holes in mega birch leaves. String together with a twist of beaded wire for an accent.

Punch a shadowbox border

Jodi Amidei (Memory Makers) adds sweet details to a portrait with a punched shadowbox border. Punch squares down the left side of a photo; flip punch over for even placement. Adhere foam tape to the back of the punched photo before matting for shadowbox effect. Punch small shapes from leftover photo scraps; mount in windows with self-adhesive foam spacers. Photo Bruce Aldridge (Broomfield, Colorado)

A dream is a path to the future
A quiet belief in the heart
A small secret wish nurtured deep in a spirit
where all great accomplishments start.

A dream is an endless horizon
That only a dreamer can see.
A dream is a challenge...
A promise of all you can be.

Stitch together a suspended border

Kelly Angard's (Highlands Ranch, Colorado) punched and re-punched seaside photos are carefully stitched together to form a suspended photo border. Crop photos into squares. Flip large circle punch over and center square before punching. Re-punch resulting circles with sun, sailboat and clamshell punches (Emagination Crafts, Nankong), again turning the punches over to center each image. Mount punched and re-punched shapes on patterned paper square and mat on torn cardstock squares. Pierce holes with paper-piercing tool or sewing needle before stitching together with embroidery thread.

"You can't depend on your eyes if your imagination is out of focus."

–Mark Twain

artistic cropping

Now you are ready to unleash your basic and shape-cropping finesse on these simple yet artistic photo-cropping techniques. These crisp ideas will have you transforming your photos into uniquely clever art with little to no effort at all. Turn the pages to find ways to:

- Top a woven background with a silhouette-cropped photo

- Weave an interlocking heart

- Weave photo corners to form a frame

- Freehand cut a woven loom photo

- Weave photos with a graduated template

- Freehand cut a random mosaic

- Make a partial mosaic border

- Crop a silhouette-embedded mosaic

- Float a double-sided mosaic

- Crop a diamond mosaic

- Piece together a 3-D mosaic

- Cut and assemble abstract linear, circle, lifetime, quilt, shapely, mind-blowing and "handy" photo collages

- Create a breezy photo pinwheel

- Slice hinged doors and peek-a-boo panels

- Make bobblehead and animal cut-outs

- Crop movement into photos with wire, slide pulls and wheels

Artistic photo cropping techniques shine with the tasteful, aesthetic flair that will teach you how to become a photo-cropping virtuoso. You'll never look at your photos and scrapbook supplies quite the same again!

weaving

Photo weaving has gained immensely in popularity, and these fresh new twists on the art are sure to get you inspired to experiment. With a few slices here and a few weaves there, photos take on texture without added bulk.

Vancouver Island in B.C. is one of the most beautiful places to live and all along its coast are smaller islands with equally breathtaking views. One of my favorites is

Newcastle Island

Newcastle Island is a tiny island that is about a 10 minute ferry ride just off the coast of Nanaimo. Long ago, people actually lived on it as they were mining coal. That's hard to believe as now its only visitors are day trippers and campers who want to stay at it's campgrounds. When you step off the ferry, the first thing you see is this impressive totem pole that looks as if it's guarding the Island. My favorite part of the Island though, is the incredible sand stone beaches. They are like nothing I've ever seen before and it was on these beaches that I collected the sand dollars that are included on this layout. July 2002

Weave a photo background

A woven photo becomes a textured and mosaic-like background for Trudy Sigurdson's (Victoria, British Columbia, Canada) silhouette-cropped totem pole. Enhance the focal point of any photo using this technique by starting with three copies of the same photo. Refer to the step shots on the following page to create the photo art. This weaving technique will work well with any photo that has a fairly large subject at the center of the photo.

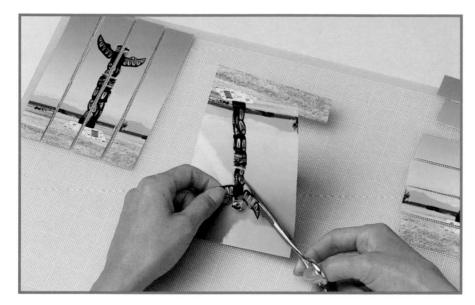

1 Use a craft knife and metal straight-edge ruler to slice the first duplicate photo into four 1" wide vertical strips. Slice the second duplicate photo into six 1" wide horizontal strips. If desired, letter or number the back of all photo strips to keep them in consecutive order for weaving. Use small, sharp scissors to silhouette crop subject from the third duplicate photo, being careful to stay true to the subject's outline and not lob off any necessary parts.

2 Weaving begins in the center, starting with two vertical photo strips and two horizontal strips. Weave all strips together, matching photo features to re-create original photo. Secure loose ends with adhesive.

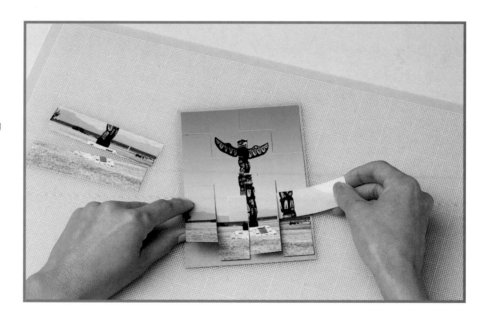

3 Apply self-adhesive foam spacers, cutting as needed to fit, to back of silhouette-cropped photo. Mount in its proper position atop woven photo background.

Weave an interlocking heart

The blending of two lives is symbolically woven together into Jodi Amidei's (Memory Makers) interlocking photo heart. A black-and-white and sepia-toned photo are partially sliced into strips and then woven together to create a dual-toned image. Enlarge the pattern on page 250 and follow the step shots below to weave a shaped image. Photo Lydia Rueger (Memory Makers)

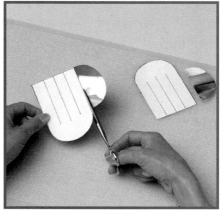

1 Start with a black-and-white and a sepia-toned duplicate of the same photo. Layer photos and hold together with temporary adhesive. Enlarge and photocopy the pattern on page 250 twice; cut patterns out. Join the two pattern pieces together to form a heart; tape together with a temporary adhesive. Position heart pattern atop layered photos; cut around outer edges with scissors. This will result in one black-and-white photo heart and one sepia-toned photo heart. Cutting at the same time is important so that the cuts are exact on both photos.

2 Place the second pattern piece atop the left side of the sepia-toned, heart-shaped photo; trim off remaining photo edge on right side. Place the pattern piece atop the right side of the black-and-white, heart-shaped photo; trim off remaining photo edge on left side. Use a craft knife and metal straightedge ruler to slice the three cutting lines on both photos.

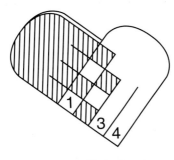

3 Follow the diagram to weave the black-and-white and sepia-toned photo halves together, weaving over and under as you go. Secure loose ends with adhesive.

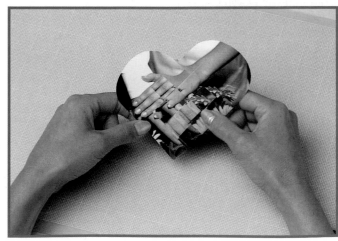

Weave a self-framing photo

Sliced photo strips woven at the corners become a complementary framing variation that doesn't detract from Valerie Barton's (Flowood, Mississippi) photo. Horizontally slice two ¼" strips from the top and two ¼" strips from the bottom of a duplicate photo. Slice two ¼" strips from the left and right sides of the original photo. Crop ½" off the top and bottom of the original photo; mount cropped photo at center of background cardstock. Mount horizontal strips above and below cropped photo, leaving a small amount of space between strips. Leave the ends of strips loose; adhere only the center of the strips. Weave vertical strips on left side of photo in an under/over fashion at ends, starting with the strip closest to the cropped photo. Repeat process with strips on the right side. Secure all ends with adhesive.

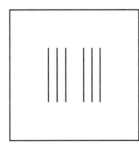
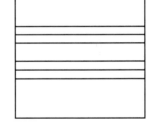

Pattern A   Pattern B

Weave photo strips into sliced slots

Sliced strips are woven into slots, framing the focal point of Brandi Ginn's (Lafayette, Colorado) floral photo. Refer to the step below to create the photo art. Try this framing technique with any photo that has the focal point at the photo's center.

1 Start with two copies of the same photo. Enlarge and photocopy woven panel patterns A & B on pages 250 and 251. Trim photo to same size as patterns. Hold pattern A atop one photo with removable artist's tape; use craft knife and metal straightedge ruler to slice through the six cutting lines on pattern to form slots. Hold pattern B atop second photo with removable artist's tape; use a craft knife and metal straightedge ruler to slice through the photo on the cutting lines. Weave the four resulting thin slices into the photo frame slots lining up to match original image as shown; discard the remaining three thick slices.

How I love the spring time
when the flowers start to grow,
and the lovely little tulips,
poke their heads up through the snow.

Daffodils and violets,
their finest colors wear,
mother nature puts her perfume on,
and decorates her hair.

The valleys blaze in splendor,
the meadows and the streams;
are a riot of all the colors,
seen in psychedelic dreams.

- Robert E. Cuer

BLOOMS

Freehand cut a weaving loom

A freehand-cut loom, sliced into a color photo, provides a framework for weaving in black-and-white photo strips. Kelly Angard (Highlands Ranch, Colorado) integrates black-and-white photo strips into a duplicate color photo sliced into a loom using a traditional under- and over-weaving technique. Follow the step shots on the next page to weave a dramatic and contrasting work of art. Photos Erica Pierovich (Longmont, Colorado)

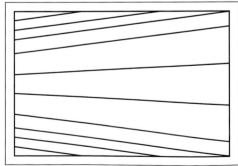

1 Enlarge and photocopy photo loom pattern on page 251 to fit a color 5 x 7" photo, either horizontal or vertical. Mount pattern on the back of your photo with temporary adhesive. Use a metal straightedge ruler and craft knife to slice through cutting lines as shown to create the "loom," being careful not to cut all the way through to photo's edges. Discard the used pattern.

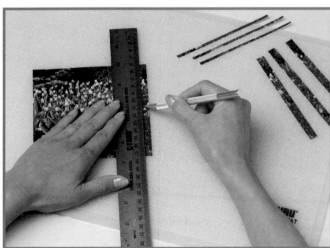

2 For a horizontal color 5 x 7" photo, slice black-and-white photo into ¹⁄₁₀" and ³⁄₁₀" strips alternately. Discard the smaller slices.

3 Weave the remaining larger slices back into the color photo, moving them into their proper position in the original image. Secure any loose ends with adhesive.

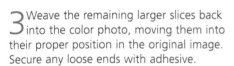

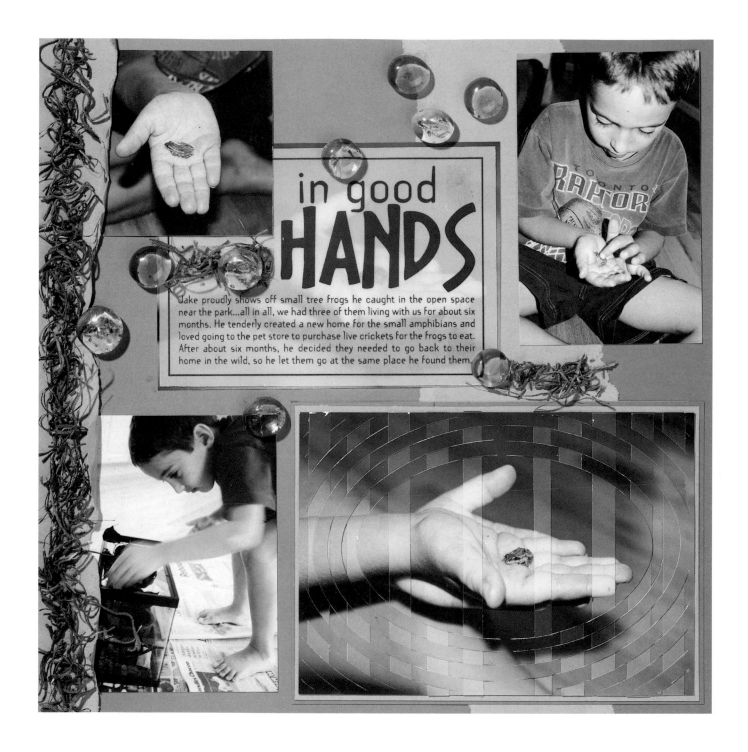

Jake proudly shows off small tree frogs he caught in the open space near the park...all in all, we had three of them living with us for about six months. He tenderly created a new home for the small amphibians and loved going to the pet store to purchase live crickets for the frogs to eat. After about six months, he decided they needed to go back to their home in the wild, so he let them go at the same place he found them.

Make a graduated template loom

An oval-cutting graduated template makes it easy to create an oval loom for photo weaving. Kelly Angard's (Highlands Ranch, Colorado) woven design gives a strong sense of focus when the photo subject is at the center of the design. Try other shapes of graduated templates to make a varied loom. To re-create this look, start with one 5 x 7" color photo and one 5 x 7" black-and-white duplicate. Create the photo loom by following the steps on the facing page.

1 Place the nested oval template (Coluzzle® by Provo Craft) over color photo on a plastic foam cutting mat. Insert the swivel knife into a template-cutting channel and make the cut. Repeat until all desired template channels are cut, being careful to stop the cuts before you reach the outer edges of the photo to keep the rings of the loom intact and connected to the cropped photo.

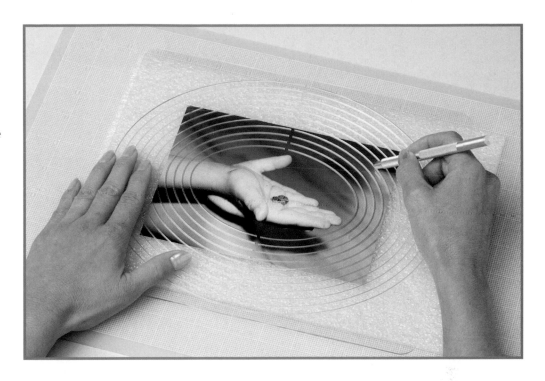

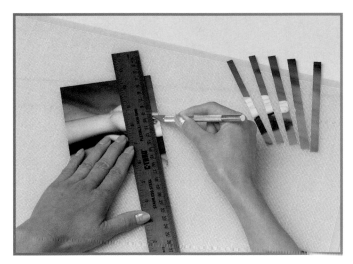

2 Use a metal straightedge ruler and craft knife to slice the black and-white photo into ¼" and ⅜" vertical strips. Only nine strips will be woven back into the color photo loom; the rest will be discarded.

3 Weave select strips vertically into the oval loom, alternating between the two strip sizes as desired and lining up images in their original position in the color photo. Repeat as needed, pulling photo strips over and under the oval-cropped rings until a total of nine strips are woven back into the photo.

mosaics

Just when you thought you'd seen all of the techniques possible for photo mosaics, along comes a new generation of photo mosaic art. You'll fall in love with these fresh embedding, floating, diamond and three-dimensional "tiling" techniques.

Design a freehand-cut mosaic

Jodi Amidei (Memory Makers) fools the eye with two techniques that give a similar free-form mosaic effect. Graceful wavy lines are cut into the first photo (on the left) and reassembled, leaving space between each piece to form the mosaic. The same effect is achieved on the photo on the right, only instead of cutting the photo apart, Jodi scratched the surface emulsion into wavy lines with a piercing tool or sewing needle. Utilize the free-form element showing that the beauty of this type of mosaic is in the imperfections. Photo Kelli Noto (Centennial, Colorado)

Crop a mosaic border

Crop and reassemble segments of a photo into a partial mosaic border for an eclectic variation of mosaic photo art. Heather Parnau (Sussex, Wisconsin) cropped 1" squares from corners of one photo, and a succession of squares along the left side of another photo. Reassemble cropped squares and mount on matting with eyelets as shown here, or implement decorative brad fasteners for a little extra fun.

Crop a mini mosaic within a photo

A mini mosaic, cropped into Kathleen Fritz's (St. Charles, Missouri) photo provides eye-catching relief to a large background while it mimics the ship's netting design. Using a craft knife and metal straightedge ruler, slice a square out of an enlarged photo. Punch or cut small squares from photo square. Reassemble and mount leaving a small amount of space between each piece. Challenge your creativity by inserting a mini mosaic of another photo into the cut out negative space.

Surround silhouette-cut image with mosaic tiles

Valerie Barton's (Flowood, Mississippi) silhouette-cropped rose is lifted from a mosaic-cut background giving dimension to its blooming elements. Follow the step shots below to add artistic effects to a silhouette-cropped photo. Try this technique with any photos that have a focal point that can be easily silhouette-cropped and have an uncomplicated background conducive to cutting into mosaic tiles.

1 Silhouette crop photo subject from photo with a craft knife or small, sharp scissors—being careful not to cut through any of the edges of the photo; set aside. The idea is to remove a chunk of the center of the photo, leaving the photo edges intact.

2 Tape the remainder of the photo to cutting mat with temporary adhesive. Use a craft knife and metal straightedge ruler to cut the remainder of the photo into 1" strips vertically, then repeat horizontally, resulting in 1" square photo tiles. Reassemble mosaic, adding silhouette-cropped photo at center.

Embed small photos into a large mosaic

Kelli Noto (Centennial, Colorado) intersperses small action images and details of the game into a large mosaic. Follow the step shots below to cut and reassemble a mosaic made of 1" squares. Use this mosaic technique with an enlarged photo that has a background conducive to replacing some of its tiles with small themed photos.

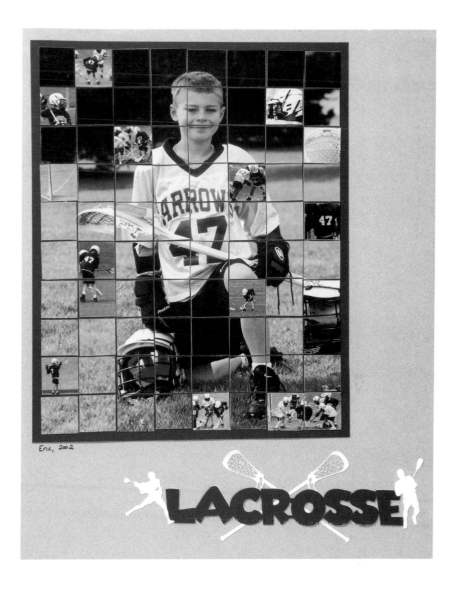

1 Make a grid pattern across the back of your photo with temporary adhesive to hold it firmly to cutting mat as you crop. Use a craft knife and metal straightedge ruler to cut vertical slices at 1" intervals down the length of the photo. Then cut horizontally across the vertical slices at 1" intervals to create mosaic photo tiles.

2 Reassemble large mosaic onto cardstock background of choice. Then strategically remove photo tiles "here and there" without disrupting too much of the original mosaic. Replace removed photo tiles with 1" photo tiles cut from smaller theme- or subject-related photos.

Float a double-sided photo mosaic

Trudy Sigurdson (Victoria, British Columbia, Canada) takes cutting and reassembling a photo mosaic a step further by mounting the cropped pieces back to back on a page protector. The see-through element of the page protector gives the illusion that the photos are "floating" on the page. Follow the step shots below to create your own floating mosaic image. Remember to design the next page that follows in a way that complements the see-through element.

1 Start with two different, yet same-size, photos. Attach strips of temporary adhesive to the back of both photos; adhere back to back to prevent slipping while cropping. Use a craft knife and metal straightedge ruler to slice photos into 1" wide vertical strips. Then slice the strips horizontally to create 1" photo tiles. Keep tiles in proper order as you crop to make reassembly easier.

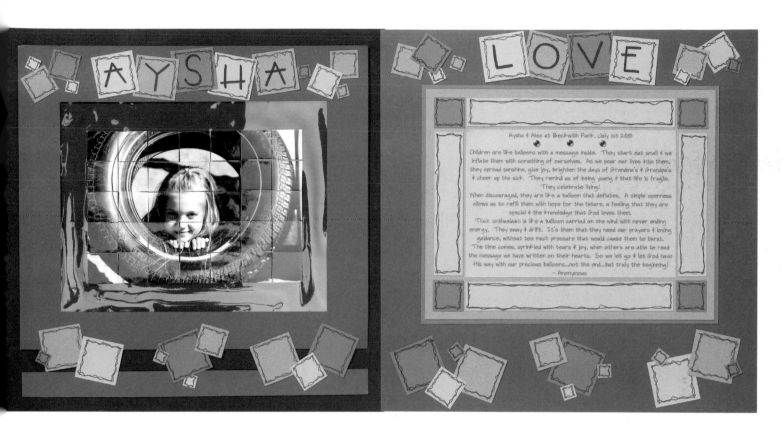

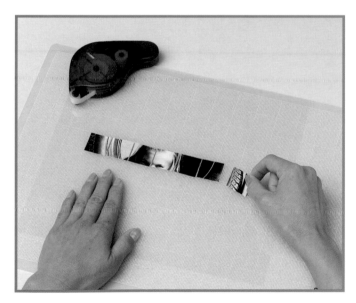

2 Cut apart one page protector to create a single sheet. Begin assembling one photo mosaic on the first side of the page protector, beginning in the center and working outward until center row is complete. Flip the page protector over. Begin assembling the second photo mosaic on the second side of the page protector, beginning in the center and working outward until center row is complete.

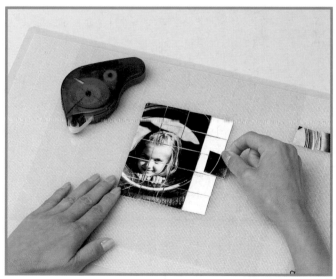

3 Adhere remaining photo tiles row by row, flipping page over as you go, until double mosaic is complete.

Mat a removable mosaic puzzle

How do you tie an element of fun into a photo mosaic? Make it into a removable puzzle as Cindy Wallach (Randolph, New Jersey) did with an enlarged photo of her son. Follow the step shots below to turn a layout into an interactive challenge! Make sure to hide a small intact photo somewhere on the page in case the puzzle needs a little help to be solved.

1 Begin with a matted 8 x 8" photo. Use a wax pencil and graphing ruler to mark three vertical cutting lines 2" apart. Then mark three horizontal cutting lines 2" apart. Finally, draw a diagonal cutting line from corner to corner in each square, all going the same diagonal direction.

2 Hold matted and marked photo on cutting mat with a grid pattern of temporary adhesive to prevent slipping while cropping. Use a craft knife and metal straightedge ruler to cut on all cutting lines. After cuts are made, use a soft cloth to remove any wax pencil residue.

3 Remove mosaic puzzle from cutting mat and place on page in proper order with temporary adhesive to complete. A temporary adhesive will make repeated disassembly and re-assembly of the puzzle easier.

Slice a diamond mosaic

Kelly Angard (Highlands Ranch, Colorado) turned an enlarged photo into an intricately cut geometric mosaic in no time at all with the help of a mosaic template. Follow the step shot below to horizontally slice a photo into diamond shapes and then reassemble. Use the template on a single photo, or combine several photos for even more visual interest.

1 Adhere a temporary adhesive to back of photo. Place photo on plastic foam cutting mat. Layer diamond mosaic template (EZ2Cut Shapemakers by EZ2Cut/Accu-Cut) on top of photo and position template using template's placement guidelines. Holding cutting mat, photo and template firmly in place, slice through template's channels to create diagonal slices. Flip template over. Line up the photo and position template using template's placement guidelines. Slice through template's channels to create diagonal slices in the opposite direction. Reassemble on cardstock.

Piece scraps to form a mosaic scene

Tracy Wynn (Truro, Nova Scotia, Canada) was inspired by a Beatle's album cover which featured a large photo made up of many very small photos to create her own unique work of art. Cut photo scraps into ¼" squares and mount on cardstock into a free-form design. If you prefer, lightly pencil desired design onto background to use as a guideline. Run photo scraps through a Xyron™ and use tweezers for easier assembly.

Create an abstract mosaic

An intricate page full of photo "shards" is creatively assembled together in Kelly Angard's (Highlands Ranch, Colorado) monochromatic mosaic. Using a craft knife and metal straight-edge ruler, cut out large diamond shapes from three enlarged photos that contain focal points for your layout. Mount on background. Randomly cut background pieces into shards in a variety of sizes from photo scraps. Mount pieces in place on your page, leaving a small amount of space between pieces. Run photos through a Xyron™ machine to ease the mounting process and use tweezers for handling small pieces.

Variation 1

Piece together a 3-D mosaic

Kim Rudd (Idledale, Colorado) uses a graduating shape template to create dimensional variations of a photo mosaic. One photo is cut into slices and segments and then reassembled leaving a small amount of space between each piece (variation 1 upper left). The second photo is cut into "L" shapes using the same template (variation 2 below). Reassembly takes a different route by alternately mounting segments with self-adhesive foam spacers for a multidimensional look. Follow the step shots below to create two variations of a dimensional mosaic.

Variation 2

1 For variation 1, adhere a temporary adhesive to back of photo. Place photo on plastic foam cutting mat. Layer nested template (Coluzzle by Provo Craft) on top of photo and center. Holding cutting mat, photo and template firmly in place, use a craft knife to slice through the desired channels on the template. Remove template and use a metal straightedge ruler and craft knife to slice diagonally from center to outer corners as shown in the following picture.

1 For variation 2, follow the first and second steps for variation 1, except make no diagonal cuts. Reassemble sliced mosaic beginning at the center and working outward toward the edges. Use self-adhesive foam spacers to adhere specially selected photo slices for dimension.

2 Reassemble mosaic slices onto cardstock, being careful to keep photo slices in proper order and with even spaces between the slices. Use self-adhesive foam spacers to adhere specially selected photo slices for dimension. Cover corner slices with a piece of cut cardstock if desired.

montage & collage

Try these fun new takes on photomontage (a collage that is just photos) or a photo collage (a collage that incorporates photos with other items). Photo themes as broad as the spectrum of our lives are the perfect medium to use in these techniques.

Integrate color duplicates to form a single montage

Using four copies of the same photo in different tones (two in color, one in sepia and one in black-and-white), Julie Mullison (Superior, Colorado) gives colored variation to a single image with freehand-cut segments reassembled atop one another. Set aside one of the colored photos as the background for this design. Using a craft knife, cut the focal point from a duplicate color photo in a freehand shape and set aside. Cut two more freehand shapes from the sepia and black-and-white photos. Layer freehand-cut shapes atop one another and then on colored background photo varying colored tones with each layer. Make sure to line up layers over original images to provide a multicolored single image.

Assemble an abstract montage

Geometric shaped photo scraps are layered together by Jodi Amidei (Memory Makers) as a free-form background design with visual impact. Geometric photo shapes can be randomly freehand cut, or can be cut to follow a pre-drawn design on background cardstock before layering together. For best results, select thematic photo scraps that provide high contrast when montaged. Photos Kelli Noto (Centennial, Colorado)

Crop a photomontage into a circle

A number of happy faces are silhouette cut and layered in Pamela Frye Hauer's (Denver, Colorado) circle montage. Layer cropped and silhouette-cut photos together on background paper. Cut into circle using a template or plate as a guide. This technique can provide thematic symbolism by cutting into a shape that relates to the photos. Photos Cynthia Anning (Virginia Beach, Virginia)

Assemble a lifetime collage

Valerie Barton's (Flowood, Mississippi)'s oval-cropped photo collage is a fun and successful way to document "then and now" photos in a showcase of lifetime achievements. First, silhouette crop subjects from selected photos. Assemble photos collage-style atop background paper of choice, filling as much space as the size of your oval-shaped template or cutter requires. Adhere photos in place when satisfied with the arrangement. Use oval-shaped template or cutter to cut collage into an oval; mat with cardstock. Accent collage on the left and right with smaller, matted photos of the subject as shown.

Piece together a quilt montage

MaryJo Regier (Memory Makers) pieces together a comforting and symbolic quilt full of peaceful images which reflects the comfort she finds in being a free American. Collect a group of themed photos to crop into shapes. Lightly draw wavy guidelines onto background cardstock; freehand cut photos to fit between drawn guidelines. Make sure to leave a small amount of space between cropped photos when mounting.

Victorian

BEAUTIES

Anne Estelle & Mary Katherine

POST CARD

1904

Form a shapely collage

Pamela Frye Hauer (Denver, Colorado) gives feminine shape to a layered collage of heritage photos. Size and cut out torso pattern on page 251. Layer cropped and silhouette-cut photos over torso shape. Turn over layered shape and trim off photo edges around torso. Embellish with stickers, fabric and jewels as desired.

Create a "handy" collage

We've got to hand it to Holle Wiktorek (Clarksville, Tennessee) for assembling a unique collage symbol that encompasses a rewarding teaching career. Size and silhouette-cut the pattern on page 251 to work with your page. Lay silhouette-cut pattern and photos on a light box to determine desired placement. Mount photo pieces over pattern in a collage-like fashion; trim off edges along pattern. Collect a handful of themed photos to layer into an interesting collage variation.

Silhouette crop an imaginative montage

MaryJo Regier (Memory Makers) captures the many things on her husband's mind with an artistic and imaginative photomontage. Silhouette crop a myriad of images in a variety of sizes and arrange in an eye-pleasing fashion. Leave open space on the page so that the eye will fall on collected images. Use a photo scrap to create a journaling mat for a perfect match. Have fun with this technique and open your mind to its unlimited possibilities!

Louis Edward Fitzner

1903-1993

Beloved father, brother, husband, most of all one special grandfather.

Crop a triptych for a montage's focal point

Jill Tennyson (Lafayette, Colorado) pieces together a meaningful tribute with a biographical montage of cropped photos set off by a three-panel "triptych" at the montage's center. Enlarge the pattern on page 251 to fit your page. Silhouette cut pieces to serve as a pattern for your photos. Trace shapes over photos, silhouette cut and assemble as shown.

Cut free-form shapes into travel montage

Julie Mullison (Superior, Colorado) adds an imaginative accent to her travel montage by cutting free-form bird shapes into a handful of layered photos. Slicing shapes into photos breaks up the montage enough to keep the eye from being overwhelmed with layered images. Follow the step shots below to add visual interest to your photos with negative shapes.

1 Assemble and adhere photomontage on cardstock of choice, trimming away any overlap of photos at cardstock edges. If desired, use a wax pencil to freehand draw birds in flight before cutting or use a craft knife to cut them freehand from the photos—cutting through photos and cardstock. Discard negative bird pieces or use them as a page embellishment.

movables

What could be more fun than "moving" photos? From spinning and hinged-door photos to photo bobbleheads, animal cut-outs, slides, wheels and dissolving scenes, these animated cropping techniques are sure to propel your scissors into full motion!

Twirl a pinwheel

Jodi Amidei (Memory Makers) crafts a fanciful pinwheel that is easier to make than it looks. Photocopy pattern on page 251, enlarging until pattern is 4" square. Follow the step shots below to slice and fold your own photo pinwheel. Use colorful photos with complementary-colored cardstock or black-and-white photos with colored cardstock for eye-catching contrast.

1 Apply adhesive to back of photo; mount atop lightweight cardstock. Transfer pattern to photo or crop photo into a 4" square. Use a graphing ruler to draw 1½" cutting lines perpendicular to square corners as shown; cut on lines to form pinwheel "blades." Punch a ⅛" hole in the center of square.

2 One at a time, fold or curl pinwheel blades in toward center of the pinwheel, secure in place with glue dot adhesive. When all blades are securely in place, add brad fastener at the center of the pinwheel.

Assemble a hinged door

Hinged photo "doors" open up to reveal Kelly Angard's (Highlands Ranch, Colorado) breathtaking view from the top of one of Colorado's 14,000-foot mountains. Photo "doors" are created from an enlarged double matted photo sliced vertically down the middle. Mount hinges on each photo door and to the page with brad fasteners for a secure hold. Place hinge on one side of photo door and mark holes with a pencil; set hinge aside. Pierce holes with paper piercer or craft knife; secure hinge to photo door with brad. Lay photo door with attached hinge on page; follow the above steps to secure doors to page.

Add hardware hinges to a photo window

Matted photo doors secured with hardware hinges open to reveal one of Brandi Ginn's (Lafayette, Colorado) favorite family portraits. Follow the step shots below to assemble peek-a-boo photo panels. Landscape or textile photos are a good choice to use as framing images for photo panels.

Adam was so excited when you were born because you share the same birthday! You are exactly 17 years apart. For the past two years of your life he's been in Uruguay so he's missed getting to share birthdays when you were old enough to understand what that meant. Even during our visit when we tried to explain it you asked him "did you had a Mini Mouse Cake too?"

1 Use an oval shape cutter (Shaping Memories) to crop oval "peek-a-boo door" into top photo. Place cutter directly on photo at center and adjust to the desired size following manufacturer's instructions. Hold photo and cutter firmly to ensure precision cutting. To cut with a template, position template atop photo at center. Trace oval outline with a wax pencil. Cut a slit in center of oval with a craft knife; insert scissors to cut out oval. Discard resulting oval; slice oval frame vertically down center to create door panels.

2 Mat door panels with cardstock. Mount "peek-a-boo photo" on cardstock trimmed to the same length and width as the matted door panels. Mount hinges using Terrifically Tacky Tape (Art Accents) or glue dots, tucking adhesive-laden hinge behind cardstock so it won't show.

Create a photo bobblehead

Kelly Angard (Highlands Ranch, Colorado) adds "character" to photo characters with a movable, silhouette-cut bobblehead. Follow the step shots below to add interactive fun to your own cast of characters with a little bit of coiled wire. Try this easy technique with photos of animals or favorite family members with a good sense of humor!

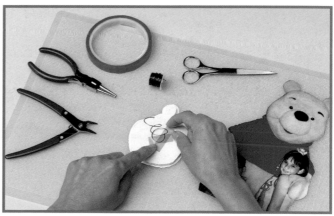

1 Start with two same-sized photo enlargements. Silhouette-crop subject (in this case, Pooh and children) from first photo; set aside. Silhouette-crop photo subject that you wish to "bobble" (in this case, Pooh's head) from second photo. Trace head onto foam core board and cut out with a craft knife, cutting ⅛" inside your traced lines. Mount cropped photo on cropped foam core.

2 To create bobblehead, attach a 2½" coil of heavy-gauge wire to back of foam core using Terrifically Tacky Tape (Art Accents). In the same manner, mount bobblehead atop first photo, placing atop its position in the original photo.

Give movement to animal silhouettes

Looking for a new idea for zoo photos? MaryJo Regier (Memory Makers) transforms sil-houette-cut animal photos into movable elements by reassembling body parts with small brads. Start with one photo and a duplicate; silhouette cut body from one photo, and legs, tail and head from the other photo. Follow the step shot below to reassemble silhouette-cut body parts.

1 To reattach silhouette-cropped legs and head to body, hold the limbs in place atop the body, lining up all markings to get limbs in their original positions. Punch through both photo layers at the same time with a ¹⁄₁₆" round hand punch. Insert a brad fastener in hole, flip photo art over and flatten brad legs. Repeat as needed until all limbs are reattached.

Add a spring-action surprise element

Kelli Noto (Centennial, Colorado) puts a little spring into her page with a springy wire attachment. A simple addition of wire attached to a grounded silhouette cut shape brings an element of action and fun to photo cropping. Follow the step shot below to add kinetic movement to your page.

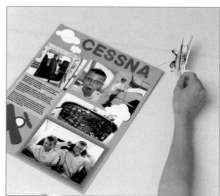

1 Silhouette-crop photo subject (in this case, an airplane) and adhere to one end of Kinetic Wire™ (Kinetic Scrapbooking). Freehand cut a cloud from craft foam and adhere to other end of wire. Leave backing on plane end. Remove backing from cloud end of wire and mount in proper place on page layout. Tuck airplane under another page element when storing.

Integrate slide pulls into photo

Kim Rudd (Idledale, Colorado) integrates movement into her action photos with a crafty slide-pull mechanism. The surfing photo slide pull simulates riding a wave with horizontal movement. Follow the step shots below to add an interactive element to sports or movement-oriented photos.

1 Start with one photo and a duplicate. Freehand draw the slide pull slot on first photo with wax pencil; cut out with craft knife. Slot can be wavy or straight, horizontal or vertical, depending on the photo subject and the movement you wish to create. Use small, sharp scissors to silhouette crop photo subject from second photo (in this case, the surfer).

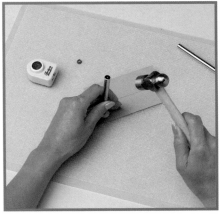

2 To create the pull-tab slide, cut a 2½ x 4½" rectangle from cardstock. Score rectangle and fold in half. Punch a ¾" circle (Family Treasures) from white cardstock; place atop unfolded rectangle and punch a ⅛" hole through both layers as shown. Insert eyelet through opening in circle and rectangle cardstock; set eyelet (see page 165). Fold rectangle in half and adhere together with eyelet circle on outside.

3 To assemble sliding mechanism, insert white cardstock circle with eyelet into cut slot, leaving cardstock rectangle behind first photo. Sandwich first photo and second photo together and adhere around sides, keeping area near slide-tab pull adhesive free. Mount silhouette-cropped photo subject (the surfer) atop eyelet to complete.

Assemble a photo turning wheel

A photo wheel that showcases eight photos in the space of one is assembled by Jeanne Norman Sarna of Page Additions. A circle-cut window provides the viewing area for changing images with an easy-to-assemble turning wheel. Follow the step shots below to craft a multi-photo turning wheel on your scrapbook page.

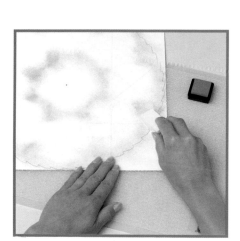

1 If desired, add color to Spin-N-Wheel™ (Page Additions) by blotting stamping ink with a makeup sponge on the spinning wheel's outer edges and inner circle. Use an ink color that is complementary to the photos you will mount on the wheel. Allow drying time. Remove perforated corners of page that hold the wheel; discard.

2 Use the template provided to crop eight photos into circles. Trace template onto each individual photo in desired position; cut out with scissors. Wipe any wax residue from photos with soft cloth.

3 Mount and adhere cropped photos to wheel, using the wheel's preprinted arrows for proper placement and overlapping photos as needed, all going in the same direction. This will prevent the wheel from "catching" on the photos when it is turned. Use a brad fastener to attach wheel to background page provided in kit. Remove adhesive backing from corners of background page and mount cover page. Embellish and accent cover as desired with wheel turn at bottom of page.

Slice a dissolving scene

Jeanne Norman Sarna for Page Additions highlights a "moving" way to transition from one photo image to another with a sliding photo element. A moving, louvered-like window is created using Slide-n-See™ pre-made tabs and sliding wheel which changes a photo image right before your eyes. Follow the step shots on the next page and manufacturer's instructions to add hidden photo images to your scrapbook pages.

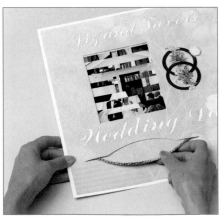

Photo 1

Photo 2

1 Start with one duplicate each of two different photos (total of four photos). Use a craft knife and a metal straightedge ruler to crop the four photos into slices, following the diagram and the diagram below. Keep pictures in order. The photo slices that are turned upside down will be discarded.

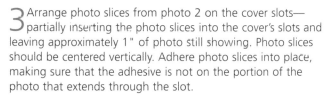

2 Arrange Slide-N-See™ tabs provided in front of you, marked side down, in the order shown at left. Mount and adhere the photo slices from both photo 1s onto the tabs following manufaturer's instructions, making sure to adhere the photo corners well to prevent "catching" when the slide is pulled.

3 Arrange photo slices from photo 2 on the cover slots— partially inserting the photo slices into the cover's slots and leaving approximately 1" of photo still showing. Photo slices should be centered vertically. Adhere photo slices into place, making sure that the adhesive is not on the portion of the photo that extends through the slot.

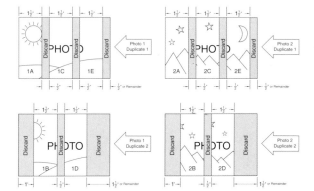

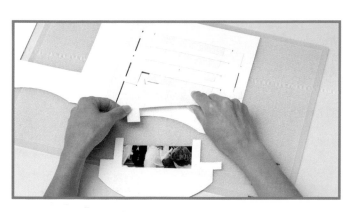

4 Working from the back side of the cover, insert photo tabs photo side down under photo slices—pushing tabs all the way in and then laying them flat against the cover. Each new tab overlaps the previous tab in two places; you will finish with the pull tab. Adhere the overlapping sections in the boxes marked by an X symbol. Adhesive should not overhang the boxes; it may inhibit movement of the sliding mechanism.

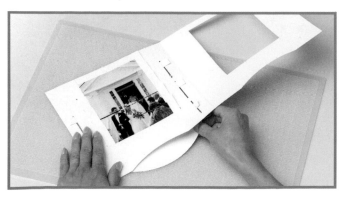

5 Flip cover back over and gently bend each of the five "motion limiting" tabs and insert them through the corresponding slot in the cover. Gently push and pull the pull-tab to test the sliding mechanism. Follow manufacturer's instructions to properly mount the Slide-N-See photo art on a scrapbook page.

additional instructions

Add dimension with well-placed slices (Bookplate)

Trudy Sigurdson (Victoria, British Columbia, Canada) gives you the feeling you are really walking out onto this pier. First, start with two duplicates of the same photo. Use a craft knife and a metal straightedge ruler to slice along the lines of the pier on one photo and crop out the horizon from the second photo. On the second photo, slice just below the horizon. Triple mat the second photo. Mount first photo over the top of the original. Use ¼" self-adhesive foam spacers beneath the sliced pier for lift. Use ⅛" self-adhesive foam spacers beneath the sliced horizon line for lift.

Slice and stair-step tri-colored photos (Introduction)

A great way to give your photos visual appeal is to "stair step" them while relining up the original image. Add a second twist—each photo slice is a different color! Begin with three 5 x 7" enlargements of the same photo: one in color, one sepia-toned and one black-and-white. Slice each picture into three equal segments with a craft knife and metal straightedge ruler. Choose one cropped photo segment from each of the three photo colors. Cut ½" from bottom of left-side photo. Cut ¼" from top and bottom of center photo. Cut ½" from top of right-side photo. Assemble photos together & mat segments permanently, lining up photo segments to recreate original image. Michele Gerbrandt (Memory Makers)

Photo Credits

Aldridge, Bruce & Leslie
(Broomfield, Colorado) 153, 161, 182, 209

Amidei, Jodi
(Memory Makers) 137, 198, 207

Anning, Cynthia
(Virginia Beach, Virginia) 232

Cummings, Brian
(Aliso Creek, California) 145

De St. Croix, Sandra
(St. Albert, Alberta, Canada) 195

Dischner, Lora Lee
(Denver, Colorado) 195

Gerbrandt, Michele
(Memory Makers) 134, 184

Hauer, Pamela Frye
(Denver, Colorado) 195

Klassen, Pam
(Reedley, California) 171

Martinez, Brenda
(Lakewood, Colorado) 197

Miller, Torrey
(Thornton, Colorado;
2002/2003 Memory Makers Master) 174

Mock, Debbie
(Memory Makers) 195

Neal, Jeff
(Huntington Beach, California) 144

Noto, Kelli
(Centennial, Colorado; 2002/2003
Memory Makers Master) 143, 220, 231

Payne, Mona
(Henderson, Nevada) 163, 164, 175

Perkins, Kris
(Northglenn, Colorado) 192

Petersen, JoAnn
(Parker, Colorado) 183

Pierovich, Erica
(Longmont, Colorado) 146, 185, 216

Regier, MaryJo
(Memory Makers) 137, 155

Rueger, Lydia
(Memory Makers) 214

Stutzman, Pennie
(Broomfield, Colorado) 150

Tepe, Chrissie
(Lancaster, California) 137, 169, 171

Trujillo, Ken
(Memory Makers) 137

Yanisko, Sandra
(Barto, Pennsylvania) 170

Artist's Index

Amidei, Jodi (Memory Makers)

Angard, Kelly
(Highlands Ranch, Colorado)

Anning, Cynthia
(Virginia Beach, Virginia)

Barton, Valerie (Flowood, Mississippi;
2002/2003 Memory Makers Master)

Childers, Kathleen
(Christiana, Tennessee)

Ciolli, Jeanne (Dove Canyon, California)

Colledge, JoAnn (North Ogden, Utah)

Fischer, Melanie (Centennial, Colorado)

Fritz, Kathleen (St. Charles, Missouri)

Ginn, Brandi (Lafayette, Colorado;
2002/2003 Memory Makers Master)

Grabowski, Ruthann (Yorktown, Virginia)

Graham, Kathy (Miamisburg, Ohio)

Hauer, Pamela Frye (Denver, Colorado

Hudson, Diana (Bakersfield, California;

2002/2003 Memory Makers Master)

Klassen, Pam (Reedley, California)

Kuhn, Pam (Bryan, Ohio)

Lindsay, Alison (Edinburgh, Scotland)

McCloskey, Monique
(Oceanside, California)

Miller, Torrey (Thornton, Colorado;
2002/2003 Memory Makers Master)

Mullison, Julie (Superior, Colorado)

Noto, Kelli (Centennial, Colorado;
2002/2003 Memory Makers Master)

Nunamaker, Sue (Villa Park, Illinois)

Parnau, Heather (Sussex, Wisconsin)

Regier, MaryJo (Memory Makers)

Rudd, Kim (Idledale, Colorado)

Sarna, Jeanne Norman

(Page Additions, Inc.)

Schueller, Heidi (Waukesha, Wisconsin;
2002/2003 Memory Makers Master)

Sharp, Terri (Hillsborough, New York)

Sigurdson, Trudy (Victoria, British
Columbia, Canada; 2002/2003 Memory
Makers Master)

Sizemore, Beverly (Sulligent, Alabama)

Tennyson, Jill (Lafayette, Colorado)

Wallach, Cindy (Randolph, New Jersey)

Whitten, Jennifer (Stephenville, Texas)

Wiktorek, Holle (Clarksville, Tennessee;
2002/2003 Memory Makers Master)

Wilson-Bonnar, Karen
(Pleasanton, California)

Wynn, Tracy (Truro,
Nova Scotia, Canada)

patterns

Use these helpful patterns to complete photo-cropping projects featured in this book. Use a photocopier or scanner to enlarge the patterns as needed to fit your photographs, then reproduce the patterns.

International female symbol, page 196

Tags, page 180

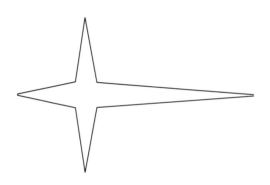

Cross, page 197

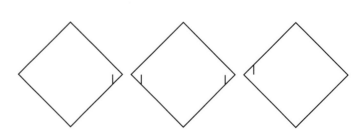

Interlocking photo tiles,
page 202

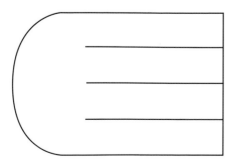

Woven heart, page 214

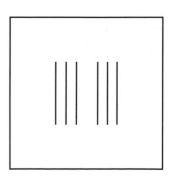

Woven panel A, page 215

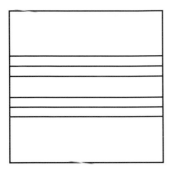

Woven panel B, page 215

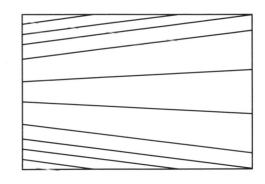

Photo loom, page 216

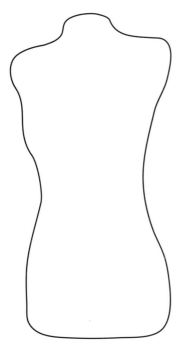

Collage torso, page 234

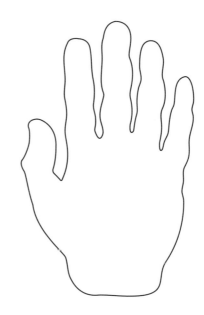

Collage hand, page 235

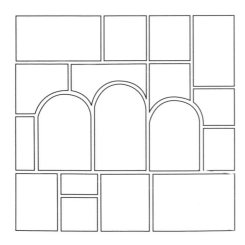

Triptych, page 236

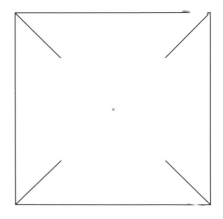

Pinwheel, page 238

glossary of techniques

3-D Photos

Using foam spacers between layers of photos to add depth and dimension can create 3-D photo art.

Borders

Photo borders put all of those leftover photo trimmings and snippets to use. Or, make great use of extra people shots, mini studio portrait shots and extra travel photos by creating interesting photo page borders.

Collage

Collage is a collection of different photographs adhered together on a page and usually includes other embellishments or craft supplies. The elements may or may not overlap.

Cropping

Traditionally, cropping means cutting or trimming a photo to keep only the most important parts of the image. This book gives creative cropping a whole new meaning, however, with a multitude of ideas, tips and techniques for using every bit of a cropped photo.

Digital

A computer-related term for the process of using numerical digits to create uniform photographic images as shot with a digital camera or scanned into a computer with a scanner and saved on and retrieved from a CD-ROM.

Frames

Cropping frames into photos is an easy way to add class to your photos without taking attention away from the photo's subject, and the framing variations are many.

Illusions

Creating photo illusions through creative photo cropping extends the imagery of a conventional photograph. The trickery of photo illusions can exaggerate size and scale, pair unlikely photo subjects for interesting, comical effects or play upon dimension and light.

Interlocking

Interlocking is a cropping technique used to tuck slices of a photo into itself or to join different photos together.

Letters, Numbers & Symbols

Another fun variation of shape cropping is cutting your photos into letters, numbers and widely recognized symbols. Many templates are available for this use. We've provided examples of freehand-cut designs to inspire you as well.

Mats

This cropping technique accents the photo layered beneath the mat and makes a great use of photos that might otherwise go unused.

Mosaics

Pieced photo mosaics are a captivating way to display photos, whether you are cropping and reassembling a single photo or combining several photos. Photo mosaics are as diverse as the photos you use, each lending its own fresh originality to the finished design.

Movables

What could be more fun than "moving" photos? From spinning and hinged-door photos to movable bobble-heads, slides, wheels and dissolving scenes, these animated cropping techniques are easier than they look!

Photomontage

Montage is similar to collage, but the pictures or parts of pictures are superimposed or overlapped so that they form a blended whole. Photomontages are made of strictly photos, with no other scrapbook embellishments.

Punches

Discover the versatility and ease of using punches to crop photos. With so many different punches on the market today, photo-cropping possibilities are as limitless as your imagination.

Reverse-Image

Reverse-image photos are useful when a mirrored photo effect is desired. To obtain a reverse-image reprint of your original photo, the photo print operator should flip the negative so that the emulsion side is opposite of the correct printing method normally used. Request that the original image and the reversed image are an exact match.

Shapes

Whether freehand cut or cropped with the use of a template, shape cropping adds simple style to scrapbook theme pages while narrowing the focus of the photo's subject.

Silhouettes

One of the most popular cropping techniques, silhouette cropping requires you to trim around the contours of the figures in your photos. For added interest, experiment with partial silhouetting to add a whole new dimension to page design.

Slicing

Slicing usually involves cropping a photo into slices or segments either freehand or using a craft knife and metal straightedge ruler. Slicing can be horizontal, vertical, straight, wavy or random.

Tearing

Tearing is fairly new to the photo cropping scene. It's a great way to add drama or soften photos. Remove the clear plastic backing from a photo to make tearing easier. Tear slowly to stay in control of the tear's direction.

Weaving

Cropping and weaving two copies of the same photo together, one in color and one in black-and-white, is a unique and highly visual technique that works great with any photo subject and any photo size.

sources

The following companies manufacture products featured in this book. Please check your local retailers to find these materials. In addition, we have made every attempt to properly credit the items mentioned in this book. We apologize to any company that we have listed incorrectly or the sources were unknown, and we would appreciate hearing from you.

3L Corp.
(800) 828-3130

3M Stationary
(800) 364-3577
www.3m.com

AccuCut®
(800) 288-1670
www.accucut.com

American Tombow, Inc.
(800) 835-3232
www.tombowusa.com

Art Accents - See Provo Craft

Carl Mfg. USA, Inc. (wholesale only)
(847) 956-0801
www.carl-products.com

C-Thru® Ruler Company, The
    (wholesale only)
(800) 243-8419
www.cthruruler.com

Eastman Kodak Company
www.kodak.com

Ecstasy Crafts
(888) 288-7131
www.ecstasycrafts.com

EK Success™ Ltd. (wholesale only)
(800) 524-1349
www.eksuccess.com

Emagination Crafts, Inc.
(866) 238-9770
www.emaginationcrafts.com

Epson America, Inc.
www.epson.com

Excel Hobby Blade Corporation
(800) 845-2770
www.exceltools.net

EZ2Cut Templates - See AccuCut

Family Treasures
(949) 457-2258
www.familytreasures.com

Fiskars, Inc.
(800) 500-4849
www.fiskars.com

Fredrix Artist Canvas
(770) 963-5256
www.fredrixartistcanvas.com

Glue Dots® International (wholesale only)
(888) 688-7131
www.gluedots.com

Highsmith®
(800) 558-2110
www.highsmith.com

Hot Off The Press, Inc.
(888) 300-3406
www.craftpizazz.com

Hoyle Products, Inc.
(800) 345-1950
www.hoylegrips.com

Kinetic Scrapbooking
(800) 893-0639
www.kineticscrapbooking.com

Martha Stewart
(800) 950-7130
www.marthastewart.com

Nankong Enterprises, Inc.
(302) 426-9208
www.nankong.com

Page Additions™
(248) 813-8888
www.pageadditions.com

Photographic Solutions, Inc.
(800) 637-3212
www.photographicsolutions.com

Pioneer Photo Albums®, Inc.
(800) 366-3686
www.pioneerphotoalbums.com

Provo Craft® (wholesale only)
(800) 937-7686
www.provocraft.com

Ranger Industries, Inc.
(800) 244-2211
www.rangerink.com

Scrapbook Magic
(763) 424-6627
www.scrapbookmagic.net

Shaping Memories - See Fiskars, Inc.

Speedball Art Products Company
(800) 898-7224
www.speedballart.com

Stamping Station Inc.
(801) 444-3828
www.stampingstation.com

Stamporium
(800) 398-6260 (orders only)
www.stamporium.com

Un-du® Products, Inc.
(888) 289-8638
www.un-du.com

U.S. Shell, Inc.
(956) 554-4500
www.usshell.com

Xyron™, Inc.
(800) 793-3523
www.xyron.com

Mackenzie

18 Months

Weight: 25 lbs 6oz
Height: 33 inches
Favorite food: lasagna, cheese, pasta + fru...
Favorite things to do: going down the big sli...
the park, coloring, looking at books, pla...
with blocks, playing with dolls, playing i...
the sandbox, dancing, playing with the
train set.
Accomplishments: Knows 100+ words, can feed herself
with a spoon or fork, can throw and
catch a ball, pretends to brush and floss her
teeth, pretends to go potty, tells us when she
wants to go to bed, GIVES THE BEST HUGS!

Toddler Scrapbooks

Ideas, Tips & Techniques
for Scrapbooking
the Early Years

COLIN, 3 YRS.

MEMORY
MAKERS
BOOKS

DENVER, COLORADO

Contents

Blanketed in...

DANIEL. 1½ YRS.

SASHA 2 YRS.

ANNA 2½ YRS.

...Love

MY CHILDREN QUICKLY BECAME
ATTACHED TO THE SOFT BLANKETS
AUNT PAM HANDMADE FOR THEM
WHEN THEY WERE BORN.

Introduction

Run! Climb! Eat! Play! No! Mine! Nap! Read! These words ruled our everyday lives during toddlerhood. With all three of my kids now entering new phases of development, I look back at these years with a blur. Energy, joy and surprises blessed our days, as they continue to do so, and I'm so grateful for the photos and memories captured during this time.

Between the ages of one and five are the whirlwind years of accomplishments. Learning to walk, communicate, explore, and much more. These years revealed my kids' personalities and defined their characteristics. Scrapbooking these special moments and milestones imprints a memory and creates a foundation of confidence and love.

For this book we had over 2,000 page ideas to sort through. What helped our selection process was to ask the question "Is this page unique to the life of a toddler or is it a great page that happens to have a picture of a toddler on it?" There were so many amazing pages, and in the end, it was very difficult to narrow it down to what would fit on these pages.

We have featured many unique page ideas for recording everything—from your child's daily rituals, playtime, and best friends to potty training, trips, and social activities. In addition, we have included the stories behind the pages, as well as ideas for recording growth and those all-important milestones and "firsts." Lastly, we offer how-to steps for special techniques—such as paper piecing and color blocking—as well as numerous theme album ideas, patterns and reproducible art to help you get started.

One thing I've realized though, through raising kids, is that it sure helps to approach the toddler and preschool years with a sense of humor. As you glean ideas from this book and reminisce, I hope you find a smile on your face and your wheels start turning about the pages you want to create or the pictures yet to take.

Michele

BLANKETED IN...LOVE
MY KIDS THEN & NOW

MICHELE GERBRANDT
FOUNDER OF *MEMORY MAKERS*® MAGAZINE

1 Getting Started

Early childhood years are energetic times, filled with humorous explorations, innocent chaos, and ever-changing contradictions. With young children, you may feel too busy to create a scrapbook album that captures the essence of toddler and preschool life, but a little organization and inspiration will help you stay on the right path despite the detours that young children bring. Here, we will show you how to get started on building those first pages in five easy steps.

3 CREATE CATEGORIES
Write categories for your photos and memorabilia on sticky notes. Categories can be in chronological order or even modeled after the chapters in this book. See the photos and memorabilia checklists on page 267 for ideas. You can add or remove categories as you go.

4 ORGANIZE PHOTOS & MEMORABILIA
Sort photos and memorabilia into your categories. As you work, jot down memories that the photos inspire on sticky notes or on the back of the photos with a photo-safe wax pencil to help with journaling. After sorting photos into your chosen categories, put each category into chronological order.

5 STORE PHOTOS & NEGATIVES
Store sorted photos and negatives in a safe environment while you work on your album. Use only 100% acid-, lignin-, and PVC-free negative sleeves, storage binders, and photo boxes.

1 SET UP A WORK AREA
Set up a well-lit work surface stocked with sticky notes, a pen, your photos, and an acid-free photo box.

2 DECIDE ON A THEME
Decide if your album will be an ongoing, continuous "life" album or a theme album that tells the story of specific events from early childhood.

ALBUMS
Albums come in three-ring binder, post-bound or strap-style, allowing you to remove, add, or rearrange pages as needed. Spiral-bound albums make great theme albums for children or as a gift. The quantity and physical size of your photos and memorabilia will help determine the size of album you need.

SCISSORS &
PAPER TRIMMER
Keep a pair of sharp, straight-edge scissors and a paper trimmer at hand. Also, use decorative scissors for creative edges on photos and mats. Turn decorative scissors over to achieve a varied cutting pattern.

2 Basic Tools & Supplies

Once you've chosen a theme and
organized your photos and memorabilia,
you're almost ready to create your first
page. But first, gather the following tools:

ADHESIVES

*Use scrapbooking adhesives, such as glues, tapes, and
mounting corners, that are labeled "acid-free" and "photo-
safe." Rubber cement, white school glue, and cellophane tape contain chemicals that can harm photos over time.*

PAPERS

*Acid- and lignin-free decorative
papers are available in countless
colors and patterns. Use these versatile papers for a background, an
accent, or to mat or frame photos.*

DESIGN ADDITIONS

*Unique design additions can give a
page theme continuity. These can
include stickers, die cuts, memorabilia
pockets, photo corners, and more.
Shop with a list of needed supplies
and some photos to match colors
and avoid any unnecessary
spending.*

PENCILS, PENS & MARKERS

*Journaling adds the voice and pertinent facts to
your scrapbook. A rainbow of journaling pens
and markers, with a variety of pen tips, make
fancy penmanship a snap. Pigment ink pens
are best because of their permanence.
Photo-safe pencils and wax pencils can
be used for writing on the back and
front of photos.*

RULERS & TEMPLATES

*Use rulers and templates to crop
photos or trace shapes onto paper, to
cut decorative photo mats, or to create
your own die cuts.*

3 Create a Layout

FOCAL POINT

Choose an enlarged, matted, unique, or exceptional photo for a focal point on the page to help determine an eye-pleasing layout. This is where the eye will look first. Other photos on the page should support this image.

BALANCE

Place your photos on a one- or two-page spread. Large, bright, or busy photos can feel "heavier" than others so move the photos around until the page no longer feels weighted or lopsided while leaving enough space for journaling.

COLOR

Choose background and photo mat papers and design additions that complement the photos, making them stand out, rather than compete for attention. Sometimes less is more. Too much color can be distracting.

Crop-n-Assemble

4

CROPPING

Photo cropping can add style, emphasize a subject, or remove a busy background. See Memory Makers Creative Photo Cropping for Scrapbooks for hundreds of cropping ideas.

MATTING

Single or layered paper photo mats focus attention and add balance to a page. Use a paper trimmer, decorative scissors, a template, or freehand cut a mat, leaving a border around the photo.

MOUNTING

Mount photos on your page with double-sided tape or liquid adhesives for a permanent bond. Paper or plastic photo corner triangles allow for easy removal of photos, if needed.

5 Journaling

The stories behind the photos are details that can be lost forever if they're not included on your page. Start with one, or a combination, of the simple journaling styles shown below:

JOURNALING TIPS

◆ *Write freehand in light pencil first, then trace with ink.*

◆ *Journal on a separate piece of paper, cut it out, and mount it on the page.*

◆ *Use pencil to trace a lettering or journaling template on the page, then trace with ink.*

◆ *Print journaling on your computer. Crop, mat, and mount journaling or trace the journaling onto your page using a light box.*

◆ *Journal onto die cuts or mats, write around your photos in curved lines, or turn paragraphs into shapes.*

◆ *Photocopy and color the lettering patterns on pages 372-373 for quick page titles.*

◆ *Use the journaling checklist on page 267 to help bring your photographic story to life.*

STORYTELLING

Give details about those in the photo at the time the photo was taken. Include everything from clothing, background items, mood, and conversation—perhaps even the weather!

BULLETS

Start with the basics of who, what, when, and where in bullet form.

QUOTES, POEMS & SAYINGS

Search for your subject on quotation-related Web sites, in poetry books, in the Bible, even on T-shirts!

CAPTIONS

Expand on bulleted information with complete sentences, allowing for more creative expression.

• Christian

• Age 3

• March 1997

• Playing peek-a-boo

I See You!
Sweet Christian
Age 3
Playing peek-a-boo
In his tunnel of
puzzle blocks on a
cold snowy day
March 1997

Do I See You!

Yes, Christian
Just came into view!

Oops, gone again,
But wait and see,

I'll bet his smile
comes back for Me!

Age 3
March 1997

The Complete Page

It's easy to get caught up in the avalanche of scrapbooking products available, but it's important to stay focused on the purpose of scrapbooking when completing a page— to preserve your youngster's memories. With that in mind, make sure your page has the five basic elements of a great scrapbook page: photos, journaling, complementary color, effective design, and long-lasting construction.

Peek-A-Boo!

BOO

I See You! The cold and snow kept Christian inside this March day. But it didn't stop him from having fun. He used his puzzle blocks to build a tunnel, then had fun peeking out to pose for these photos. At 3, he is such a sweet, fun-loving little boy. 1997

CHRISTIAN, 3 YRS.
Photos Cheryl Rooney, Lakewood, Colorado

Checklists

As your child quickly maneuvers through the toddler and preschool years, you will have lots of photos, memorabilia, and stories to record. Use these lists as a basic framework for organizing your keepsakes.

- [ ] Being a "little helper"
- [ ] Being "artistic"
- [ ] Daily routines:
  - Bath time
  - Brushing teeth
  - Grooming
  - Mealtime
  - Reading
  - Sleeping
  - Waking up
- [ ] Favorite things (see page 123)

- [ ] Funny faces
- [ ] Growth
- [ ] Holidays
- [ ] Illnesses and boo-boos
- [ ] Messes
- [ ] Milestones and firsts
- [ ] Organized activities
- [ ] Personality traits
- [ ] Playtime, dress-up and pretend play
- [ ] Potty training
- [ ] Preschool, nursery, and Sunday school

- [ ] Professional portraits
- [ ] Travel and outings
- [ ] Visits to doctor and dentist
- [ ] Your child with:
  - Family and siblings
  - Family pets
  - Favorite people
  - Friends and playmates
  - Teachers, coaches, and caregivers
  - Visitors to home

MEMORABILIA

Keep your child's most interesting and important memorabilia, as well as those your child cherishes the most. Consider photographing an overabundance of memorabilia for your album, if necessary. See page 347 for tips on de-acidifying memorabilia.

- [ ] Artwork
- [ ] Birthday invitations, cards, decorations, wrapping paper samples
- [ ] Certificates, ribbons, and awards from organized activities
- [ ] Color-copied favorite book covers
- [ ] Color-copied wallpaper and fabric swatches from bedroom
- [ ] Copy of doctor and dentist notes
- [ ] Early childhood heritage photos of relatives for family tree (see page 376)
- [ ] Growth and development records
- [ ] Hair clippings
- [ ] Hand and foot prints
- [ ] Labels from favorite foods
- [ ] Letters to child from family and friends
- [ ] List of gifts
- [ ] Preschool, nursery, and Sunday school mementos
- [ ] Souvenirs from travel and outings
- [ ] Time capsule souvenirs

JOURNALING

Keeping a daily journal can be demanding with a toddler in the house. Instead, jot tiny notes on a calendar to add to the scrapbook later. Some things you might wish to record:

- [ ] Beloved books, rhymes, songs and games
- [ ] Family tree information
- [ ] Favorite things at a given age
- [ ] Funny things your child says and does
- [ ] Height and weight for growth chart
- [ ] Milestones and firsts
- [ ] Growth and loss of baby teeth
- [ ] Personality and character traits
- [ ] What you like about your child and why
- [ ] Assign an adjective to each letter of your child's name

A Day in the Life...

Everyday with Christine and Lauren is filled with constant entertainment

of our Toddler

A Day in the Life

IT ISN'T THE GREAT BIG PLEASURES THAT COUNT THE MOST; IT'S MAKING A GREAT DEAL OUT OF THE LITTLE ONES.

—JEAN WEBSTER

Her eyes fly open in the morning and flutter begrudgingly shut at night. In between, a toddler is a force of nature, a swirling mass of energy and emotion. She is a baby still, but empowered with walking and words; she wants to know more. Are hot dog bits more fun to eat or throw? Why walk when you can run, run, run! Establishing predictable routines—from warm bubble baths to cozy times reading together to regularly scheduled meals around the family dinner table—helps your toddler focus her enthusiasm and settle down when she needs to. And you get a chance to catch your breath. In the meantime, try to keep your camera loaded with film at all times and your scrapbooking supplies handy!

A DAY IN THE LIFE...
CHERI O'DONNELL, ORANGE, CALIFORNIA

ADAM, 2 YRS.

A Typical Day

PHOTOJOURNAL A BUSY DAY

Debbie decided to document "one of those crazy days" of running after her busy toddler. Document a day by first cropping photos with decorative scissors or into silhouette shapes. Cut paper strips; trim with decorative scissors or round corners. Layer photos and strips on page with conversation "bubble" stickers (Mrs. Grossman's). Add journaling and humorous toddler thoughts. Complete with freehand-drawn title and arrows leading a path around the page.

Debbie Lucero, Colorado Springs, Colorado

Geometry Lesson

SHAPE A COLORFUL BORDER

Janie's page design is both easy to make and educational. To create a page full of simple shapes, adhere geometric stickers (Mrs. Grossman's) around page to create border. Crop photos into basic shapes; mat on colored paper. Freehand journal title and captions.

Janie Thomas, Blakely, Georgia

Michael is Learning Skills Needed for School!

Reading

Writing

Sharing

Building

and of course, Problem Solving!

Michael Is Learning Skills...
ILLUSTRATE EARLY LIFE-SKILLS

Dawn shows how everyday tasks are learning experiences for toddlers, preparing them for the years that lie ahead. Begin by cropping photos; double mat, cutting first mat with decorative scissors. Layer on page and adhere. Add title and photo captions to complete layout.

Dawn Scott, Midlothian, Texas

A Day in the Life
RECORD ONE DAY ANNUALLY

Once a year, Mary Ellen photographs the events of a single day—usually the same Tuesday each November—to show how routines change as her two sets of twins grow. This day is actually six page spreads, ending with Mary Ellen collapsed on the couch at 6:41 p.m. before she heads off for a meeting. Start with a title page in white ink; embellish with various punched flowers. Assemble photos in chronological order; mat, trim with decorative scissors (Family Treasures) and adhere. Add journaling in chronological order; embellish pages with assorted punched and layered flowers.

Mary Ellen Scullin, Lansdale, Pennsylvania

1. Help Dad fill the bathtub + pick out bath toys!

2. Play a lot in the water!

6. Check + make sure Dad did a good job!

7. Bounce on Mom and Dad's bed!

8. Turn Dad's radio on + off many times!

3. Have Dad get the cleaning over with quickly!

4. Chew on turtle (or other available bath toy!)

5. Stand still long enough to dry off a bit!

9. Pose with Mom for a cute picture!

10. Put on pajama bottoms then chew on toothpaste tube!

11. Use blowdryer like a microphone + chew on brush!

Aidan's Bath-time Routine

FOLLOW STEPS TO BATH-TIME FUN

Photojournaled steps of Ellen's busy boy tell the story of his bath-time routine. Start with a solid background. Crop photos and mats; round corners and assemble. Create rounded caption and title blocks from yellow paper. Mount photos, caption, and title blocks on green paper; trim edges with decorative scissors (Fiskars). Add number stickers (source unknown) and journaling.

Ellen Underhill, Seattle, Washington

MORGAN, 2 YRS.

THE SERIOUS LITTLE SHAVER

Shaving is serious business for Dianne Miller's (Medinah, Illinois) son, shown here in deep concentration on the task at hand with his new toy razor. It makes one wonder if Dad is a serious shaver too!

JOSHUA, 3½ YRS.

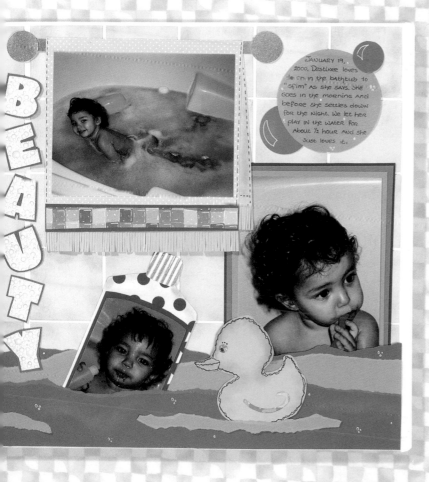

Bathing Beauty

LAYER A SPLASHY BATHTUB SCENE

Nicole was challenged to come up with a new layout for bath-time photos, so she layered a creative bathtub scene. Cut 2" "tiles" from colored paper for background; chalk around edges to add depth and mount on page, leaving space to look like grout. Tear blue paper strips for water. Cut shampoo bottle using patterned paper (The Paper Patch); crop photo to fit and layer in between water strips. Freehand cut towel and bar; detail towel with patterned paper (Colors by Design) and paper sliced at ¹⁄₁₆" intervals for "fringe." Cut towel bar from silver paper. Crop photos; double mat on solid paper. Embellish die cut duck (Creative Memories) with pen and patterned paper. Circle cut photos and mats for "bubbles." Journal on blank bubbles. Cut title using template (Frances Meyer) on bubble patterned paper (Hot Off The Press); mat on solid paper before mounting on page.

Nicole Ramsaroop, Horst, Netherlands

Scrambled Z's!

Apparently Jimmy didn't get enough sleep one night. Mom caught him falling asleep right in the middle of his cheese omelette one morning. Who says there's never a camera around when you need one. Is he adorable — or what!

January 1995

Going Going Going

Gone!

Shhh!

Christine & Kevin O'Donnell (1994)

Scrambled Z's!

SHOW A SERIES OF SLEEPY SNAPSHOTS

Lisa caught her son snoozing in the middle of breakfast and grabbed her camera just in time to show how he literally ended up with egg on his face! Create a layout with a series of photos by matting cropped photos on white paper trimmed with decorative scissors (Family Treasures). Mount on black triangles at corners, cut diagonally from 1" squares. Layer photos over strip of black paper trimmed with decorative scissors. Add title, journaling, and captions to complete the page.

Lisa Dixon, East Brunswick, New Jersey

Shhh!

UNITE PHOTOS WITH A THEME

Toddlers can "zonk out" just about any time, anywhere. Cheri discovered a great way to combine many unrelated photos of her daughter's angelic sleeping face by creating a theme page. Begin by rounding photo corners and floating the photos on a softly colored background of cloud paper (Design Originals). A caption die cut (source unknown) provides the title for the page.

Cheri O'Donnell, Orange, California

Night Night, Zoryana

PHOTO CROP A SNUGGLY BED

Oksanna tucked photos of her daughter into a
cozy, photo-cropped bed floating on a nighttime
sky (Making Memories). Photocopy and size
pattern (see page 374) to fit page and photos.
Crop photos and paper to fit pattern shapes.
Craft bedding from yellow paper; detail with
blue pen. Cut large pillows from gingham paper
(The Paper Patch); mat on blue paper trimmed
with decorative scissors (Fiskars). Cut small
pillows and caption; trim with decorative
scissors and mat. Add punched small bow
(All Night Media) and white pen details. Punch
small hearts around title block before matting;
add punched bunnies (Family Treasures) with
feet removed to form slippers. Print title
(*Curlz* by Microsoft) and add journaling.

Oksanna Pope, Los Gatos, California

Bedtime

DOCUMENT A DAY'S END

Chris shows the steps that make up her son's
nighttime routine. Begin by cropping photos
and matting on patterned paper (Keeping
Memories Alive) trimmed with decorative
scissors (Fiskars). Mount on dark patterned
paper (Keeping Memories Alive). Color copy
and reduce covers of favorite books; silhouette
and layer on page. Add moon die cut (Ellison);
draw dash detail with pen. Adhere title letters
(Making Memories), star (Mrs. Grossman's)
and bedtime stickers (Hallmark, mc & my
BIG ideas, Michel & Co., Mrs. Grossman's).
Complete the page with journaling.

Chris Peters, Hasbrouck Heights, New Jersey

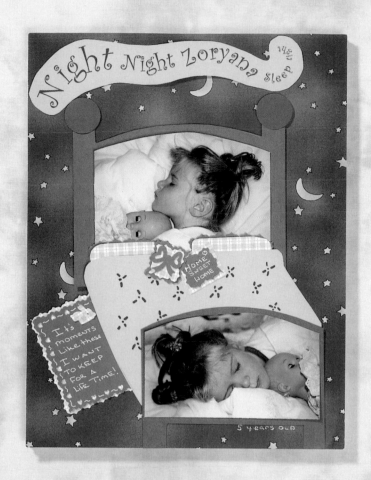

Books Are Friends
RECORD AN EARLY LOVE OF LEARNING

The big book background provides a perfect setting for Kristi-Ann's photos of her daughter "reading." Freehand cut book background from colored paper to fit page. Make "spine" by cutting two 1" strips; mount at inside edges of spread. Cut two "pages" from large piece of tan paper, arching up at the top and bottom, keep sides straight. Mat "page" on colored paper as spine; mount on scrapbook page. Crop photos and round corners. Silhouette crop photos of favorite books. Cut title from template (Frances Meyer); outline with black pen.

Kristi-Ann Watrin, Sparwood, British Columbia, Canada

Storytime
CREATE A LIBRARY OF FAVORITES

To make "books," Betsy cut various-sized squares and used a corner rounder on two left corners. Make a small diagonal cut on bottom right corner and freehand draw lines for "pages" and "binding." Journal book titles with pens. Layer over silhouette-cropped photo.

Betsy Campbell, Slidell, Louisiana

EMILY, 4 YRS.; BETSY; ANDREW 2½ YRS.

TODAY'S TOP TEN BEST-LOVED TODDLER BOOKS

Reading to young children helps them increase their vocabulary and they love to hear the same stories over and over again. Check out some of these tried and trusted favorites:

Alexander & the Terrible, Horrible, No Good, Very Bad Day —Judith Viorst

The Adventures of Curious George —H. A. Rey

Brown Bear, Brown Bear, What Do You See? —Bill Martin/Eric Carle

Cloudy With a Chance of Meatballs —Judith Barrett

Goodnight Moon—Margaret Wise Brown

Harold and the Purple Crayon —Crockett Johnson

If You Take a Mouse to the Movies —Laura Numeroff

Pat the Bunny —Dorothy Kunhardt

The Tale of Peter Rabbit —Beatrix Potter

Where the Wild Things Are —Maurice Sendak

MARISSA, 2½ YRS.

I Love Books

PAPER TEAR FAVORITE BOOK CHARACTERS

Missy highlights her son's love of literature with paper torn characters from favorite books. Begin by tearing colored letters for paper title. Draw thick dashed lines and yellow hearts along edges of page. Silhouette and crop photos; round corners. Tear and layer paper shapes to represent favorite books. Journal book titles and photo captions with colored pens.

Missy Rice, Whittier, California

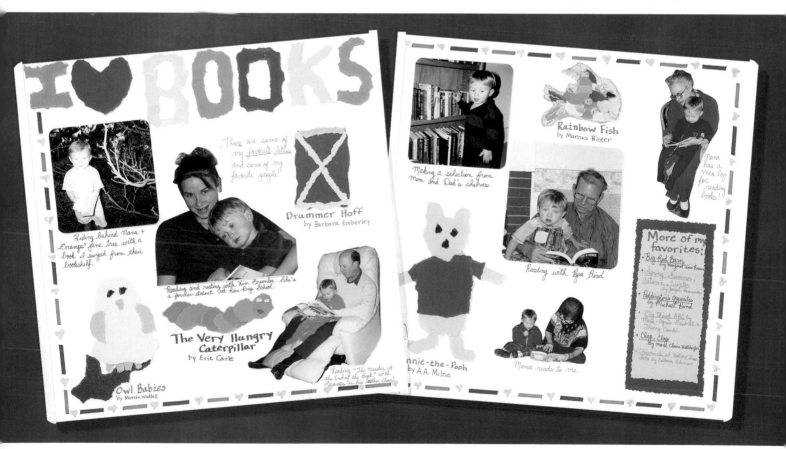

Master of Chopstix

CREATE A COLLAGE FROM SCRAPS

(UPPER RIGHT) Leslie knew her paper scraps would come in handy one day, she just needed to wait for the right photos! Her son's first experience with chopsticks presented the perfect opportunity. To create a colorful collage, begin with a solid colored background. Layer and mount scraps and strips randomly on page. Partially silhouette photos; double mat, first on solid paper, then on striped paper (Hot Off The Press). Freehand cut chopsticks from gold cardstock (Hot Off The Press). Freehand cut bowl; fill with paper scrap "veggies."

Leslie Paskus Amador, Silverado Canyon, California

3 Easy Steps to Eating Spaghetti

DOCUMENT EATING HABITS

(FAR UPPER RIGHT) The art of eating spaghetti without using utensils is illustrated and explained by Tammy and her son in an easy, three-step method. Begin by cropping photos and rounding corners. Use leftover number outlines from die cuts (Ellison); round corners. Complete page with title and journaling.

Tammy Watson, Maple Ridge, British Columbia, Canada

Robertazzi Ziti

PACKAGE CHILD'S NOODLE FUN

(LOWER RIGHT) Maureen cleverly framed funny photos of her daughter eating pasta with a handmade duplication of a pasta box. Start with solid background layered with red zigzag border. Add freehand cut triangles; mount to fit red border. Adhere sticker strips (Mrs. Grossman's) around page, leaving room for box information at bottom. Crop photos and mount together as shown. Adhere sticker letters (Making Memories); freehand cut fancy "R." Outline stickers with yellow brush pen. Journal box information. Complete page with handmade or color-copied box label; silhouette to size and mount.

Maureen Robertazzi, East Hanover, New Jersey

I Love to Eat

SHOWCASE FAVORITE FOODS

(FAR LOWER RIGHT) Funny-faced foods and photos of Jennifer's son frame a poem about his favorite things to eat. Photocopy and size patterns (see page 374); transfer to colored papers of choice and cut out. Silhouette crop photos. Write poem in decorative lettering with different colored pens. Layer photos and food around poem over patterned paper (Hot Off The Press).

Jennifer Gould, Costa Mesa, California

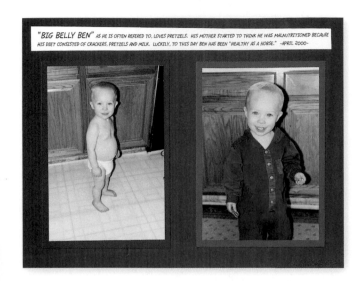

"BIG BELLY BEN" AS HE IS OFTEN REFERED TO, LOVES PRETZELS. HIS MOTHER STARTED TO THINK HE WAS MALNUTRITIONED BECAUSE HIS DIET CONSISTED OF CRACKERS, PRETZELS AND MILK. LUCKILY, TO THIS DAY BEN HAS BEEN "HEALTHY AS A HORSE." -APRIL 2000-

Big Belly Ben

FEATURE A SATIRICAL "SUCCESS STORY"

Kim wasn't quite sure what to do with photos of her son's physique, so she decided to play on the humor of "before" and "after" weight-loss ad photos. Print title and journaling in your favorite computer font or handwriting to finish.

Kim Jones Shafer, Moab, Utah

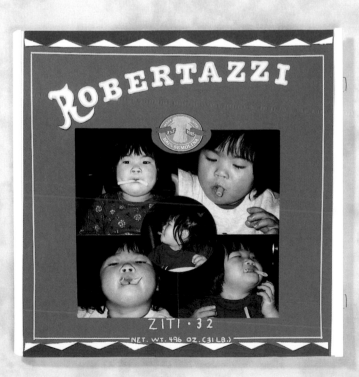

3 Easy Steps to eating Spaghetti ~
from a toddler's point of view!

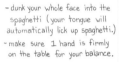

step 1
- get comfortable in a chair, (but make sure your chair is pulled in close to the table.)
- put face over bowl and stick your tongue out.

- dunk your whole face into the spaghetti (your tongue will automatically lick up spaghetti.)
- make sure 1 hand is firmly on the table for your balance.

2

step 3
- chew spaghetti well, then swallow.
- feel proud of your accomplishment, (but be prepared for a bath!)
- if you didn't eat all your spaghetti in 1 dunking, repeat step 1-3 until gone or your tummy is full!

i love to eat
grapes and bananas
watermelon too
corn and carrots
are good for you
raisins and peas
are okay...
but i'll take
cookies and cake
anyday!

Miniature Mayhem

Toddlers follow their insatiable curiosity on the road from triumph to "trouble" in two seconds flat. But consider that one person's mess may be a youngster's masterpiece. Even cuts and scrapes are lessons in the school of life, and chronicling them reminds us of the humor and compassion we all deserve.

SERENA, 14 MOS.

UH O'S

Caroline LeBel of Toronto, Ontario, Canada says she's still finding "those little 'O's" in the strangest of places after her daughter dumped a box of Cheerios® on the floor. Title letters were cut freehand from photos of the mess on the floor.

Home Wrecker

FEATURE PINT-SIZED DESTRUCTION

Kim is constantly amazed at the amount of destruction her son is capable of the second her back is turned. She cleverly constructed a wrecking ball for the background and penned a graphic border with a template (Provo Craft). Crop photos into ovals and squares; round corners. Mat ovals and trim with decorative scissors. Cut die cut letters into fragments; mount in "topsy-turvy" fashion. Add journaling.

Kim Penrod, Overland Park, Kansas

A Little Dirt Never Hurt

DOCUMENT MESSY MOMENTS

The saying she found couldn't be more appropriate for Maureen's photos of her dirt-lovin' daughter. Brown speckled paper (Westrim), layered over black paper, is smudged with chalks to create "dirty" background. Silhouette and crop photos; mat on patterned paper (Provo Craft). Cut title block, smudge with chalks, and mat. Trace computer font (*Andy* by Monotype) lettering. Mount pig die cut (The Beary Patch) over freehand-cut mud puddle. Print saying; crop and mat. Complete page with journaling.

Maureen Spell, Carlsbad, New Mexico

A Little Dirt Never Hurt

oink

What a mess! April 22, 2000 Dog Canyon.

When you're close to the ground, There's more dirt to be found!

CHERYL'S STORY

With all of the cute pictures vying for a spot in your scrapbook, it's sometimes easy to forget to take time to record the stories behind the photos. Cheryl deliberately created an album page with fewer visual elements to highlight the hilarious-in-hindsight story of her sons, Jeremy and Josh.

"I wanted to preserve these memories for their future wives who may need some help to understand why their children are so mischievous," says Cheryl of her boys' mischievous exploits.

At the ages of four and two, Cheryl's sons became true "Partners in Crime." Their escapades included tracking wet ashes through the house after playing in the burnt trash pile, and splashing in the bathtub like Shamu until the water soaked through the carpet and dribbled into the basement.

Even activities with the best of intentions somehow turned out wrong. Jeremy and Josh plucked wildflowers one day with their dad to surprise Cheryl. While this sent her heart soaring, she was not so thrilled when the boys later picked all of the blooms off of her favorite peony bush. Asked for an explanation of their actions, the boys said it was "to surprise Mamma."

"I can laugh when I read the journaling now," says Cheryl. "But it wasn't funny back then!"

Cheryl Miller, Quaker City, Ohio

Partners in Crime...

In March '98 Josh had surgery for chronic nosebleeds. The very next day you boys were outside riding bikes down the "hill" in the back yard.

This was a rainy day. You & Josh played in the trash pile and got wet ashes all over yourselves. Then you tracked wet ashes through the garage, for an unknown reason. Next you played in the mud puddles in the driveway. At that point, I gave up and decided boys will be boys. You guys were soaked to the skin and so filthy till you decided you were finished that I had to take a picture as a reminder how bad it was. I should have taken the picture while you still had your shirt on because you were every bit as dirty as Josh looks.

Messes Are My Specialty

MAKE A TORN PAPER COLLAGE

Amy brought the messes her little one makes to life with a torn paper collage. Begin by cropping photos and matting on color copied magazine pages, torn on all sides. Tear out characters and title strips. Layer with photos on page and mount on solid background paper. Add title lettering to finish the page.

Amy Rognlie, Littleton, Colorado

DAVID, 3 YRS.

No, No, No

DOCUMENT THE MISCHIEF

(ABOVE) A toddler's innate curiosity not only keeps parents on their toes, it keeps them constantly saying "No!" Chris can't count the times she's said it to her son, so she documented his mischief on a page. Start with a red patterned background (Memories by Design) layered with strips of yellow patterned paper (MPR Assoc.) trimmed with decorative scissors. Crop photos and mats in circles or ovals; trim both with decorative scissors. Freehand cut letters for title. Add die cut stars (Ellison) to complete page.

Chris Peters, Hasbrouck Heights, New Jersey

Marker Madness

RECORD COLORING CHAOS

(UPPER RIGHT) Caroline's daughter expresses her artistic personality by seeing everything as a canvas to be colored. Begin with patterned background paper (Design Originals). Crop photos, round corners, and mat on solid paper. Print title and journaling; mat on solid paper. Adhere crayon stickers (Frances Meyer).

Caroline LeBel, Toronto, Ontario, Canada

What an Angel!

SHOW A TODDLER'S TWO SIDES

(LEFT) Suzi shows both sides of her daughter: the sweet, innocent side and the mischievous toddler who broke a window! Use heart template (Creative Memories) to cut angel wings; layer behind silhouette-cropped photos. Freehand draw clouds, double mat and layer with "angels." Adhere letter stickers (Creative Memories). Add halos, gold pen details and journaling.

Suzi Leverington, Narre Warren, Victoria, Australia

Time for a Makeover

CAPTURE A COLORFUL CRIME SCENE

(BELOW) Amy's page was in the making when she caught her kids covered in makeup. Stamp and emboss lips (Stampendous!) on solid background. Crop and mat photos on patterned papers (The Paper Patch); mount with foam spacers. Print font title and mat. Add custom paper dolls (Scrapable Scribbles), stickers (Mrs. Grossman's) and journaled photo captions.

Amy Curtis, Carmel, Indiana

a pox upon our house

Ally got chicken pox on Father's Day of 1998. We kept waiting for Karly to break out but she never did, so we took her to a July 4th party at the Howard's. Two days later she broke out! It had been over 2 weeks since Ally broke out.

Everytime Karly sits on the potty Ally gets on (like it's a motorcycle)

Karly was a good pox-girl. She hardly ever scratched. She wore panties a few days so the pox on the "private parts" would heal faster. (still not potty trained, though!)

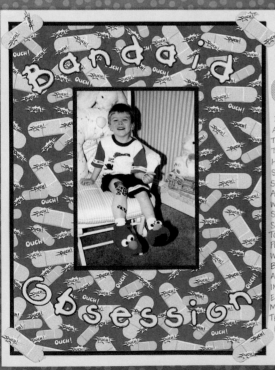

Banda'id Obsession

SPENCER (4) AND A BOX OF STAR WARS BANDAIDS

June '99

IT ALL STARTED AFTER SPENCER TOOK A SPILL ON HIS TRIKE AND SCRAPED HIS ARM. IT WAS THE SIGHT OF BLOOD THAT SET HIM OFF. AS SOON AS WE COVERED IT WITH A BANDAID, IT SEEMED TO BE "OUT OF SIGHT, OUT OF MIND." TOP THAT OFF WITH A POPSICLE AND ALL WAS WELL AGAIN. HE BEGAN TO PUT BAND AIDS ON EVERYTHING, INCLUDING HIS STUFFED ANIMALS! IT WAS MY MISTAKE KEEPING THEM IN HIS BATHROOM DRAWER!

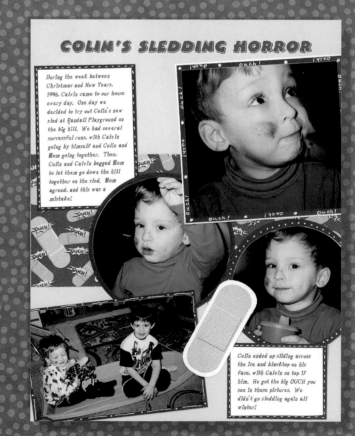

COLIN'S SLEDDING HORROR

During the week between Christmas and New Years, 1996, Calvin came to our house every day. One day we decided to try out Colin's new sled at Randall Playground on the big hill. We had several successful runs, with Calvin going by himself and Colin and Mom going together. Then, Colin and Calvin begged Mom to let them go down the hill together on the sled. Mom agreed, and this was a mistake!

Colin ended up sliding across the ice and blacktop on his face, with Calvin on top of him. He got the big OUCH you see in these pictures. We didn't go sledding again all winter!

A Pox Upon Our House
CHRONICLE QUARANTINED DAYS

(UPPER LEFT) Chicken pox descended upon the Hazelrigg house with a vengeance, casting spots on both of Kristi's daughters. She chronicled their five weeks of quarantine with humor on patterned "baby chick" paper (Colors by Design). Trim ½" orange strips with decorative scissors (Fiskars) for top border. Crop photos, round corners, and mat with orange paper. Create title from sticker letters (Making Memories) and die cut letters cut from patterned paper (The Paper Patch); mat on yellow and outline with black pen. Complete with journaling.

Kristi Hazelrigg, Sand Springs, Oklahoma

Band-Aid® Obsession
PICK THE PERFECT PATTERNED PAPER

(LOWER LEFT) Shauna's son went berserk with bandages ages after falling off his tricycle, sticking them not only on his boo-boo, but all over his body, his toys, and his stuffed animals. Begin with a solid yellow background. Mat photo on black paper, then again on bandage paper (Hot Off The Press), leaving a 2" matting border. Mat a third time on black paper. Silhouette crop four bandages from patterned paper; mount over photo mat corners. Cut title from template (Provo Craft), mount on matting, and outline with black pen. Add bandage punch out (Hot Off The Press) and journaling.

Shauna Immel, Beaverton, Oregon

Colin's Sledding Horror
DOCUMENT THE IMPACT OF AN INJURY

(LOWER RIGHT) Laura tells the story of her son's sledding accident with vivid images and great journaling. Start with computer font title (*Creative Scrapbooks Deluxe* by Palladium Interactive) printed on yellow background paper. Layer patterned bandage paper (Hot Off The Press) across center page. Crop and mat photos. Add matted journaling, decorative white pen work, and bandage punch-out (Hot Off The Press) to complete design.

Laura Friedrichs, Madison, Wisconsin

X is for...
ASSEMBLE AN ARTFUL BODY

Laura shows her daughter is the picture of perfect health on a page out of an ABC album she made. Freehand cut "bones" and assemble into a skeleton on black paper, matted with red. Silhouette-crop photo; add to top of "x-ray." Finish design with a heart sticker (Mrs. Grossman's).

Laura Woop, Branchville, New Jersey

JUST FOR FUN

Toddlers thrive in a world of chaos. And so must you! Just find the eye of the storm and brace yourself with humor as your toddler tries on new moods for size. Accept and record your child's many facets; it shows you love them all.

A little girl is... innocence playing in the mud, beauty standing on its head, and motherhood dragging a doll by the foot.

JENNA, 18 MOS.

Irresistible Faces!

PRESERVE A CHILD'S PERSONALITY

Her son often charms Danine, even though she knows that his angelic smile is usually a disguise for a devilish grin! Begin with patterned paper (Provo Craft) for background. Crop photos and print poem; double mat on solid paper. Freehand letter and color title and journal with black pen; mat on solid paper.

Danine Curtis, Naugatcuck, Connecticut

Acting Faces!

SHOWCASE PRICELESS EXPRESSIONS

Kristi usually creates scrapbook pages around her photos; however, she took these photos specifically to fit the idea of a layout she had in mind! Begin with a patterned background (source unknown). Crop photos, mat some on yellow paper (Everafter) and trim with decorative scissors (Fiskars). Add matted letter stickers (Making Memories) and journal captions to finish.

Kristi Hazelrigg, Sand Springs, Oklahoma

Silly

SET THE STAGE FOR SERIOUS SILLINESS

Chris sets a whimsical tone for silly photos of her son. Start with layering freehand letters cut from patterned paper (Colors by Design) and matted on yellow paper. Crop and mat photos; mount along with letters on page in "topsy-turvy" fashion. Add punched swirls, journaling and pen embellishments to complete.

Chris Peters, Hasbrouck Heights, New Jersey

RECORDING PERSONALITY & CHARACTER TRAITS

Your child's personality and character are derived partly from heredity and partly from her environment. All of your child's preferences, the things that make her laugh or cry and everything in between, come together to create her unique personality. Through photos and journaling, try to capture her rapidly evolving personality and character traits. Watch for things that make your child:

Alert	Frightened	Insecure
Amused	Frustrated	Nervous
Angry	Gleeful	Sad
Bored	Grumpy	Scared
Calm	Happy	Sleepy
Confident	Hysterical	Surprised
Excited	Inattentive	Thoughtful

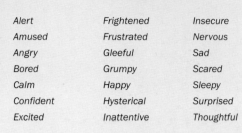

MERCEDES, 2 YRS.

Cayra of So Many Colours

REFLECT ON HER MANY MOODS

Diedre was unable to decide on a single color to mat these adorable candid photos, so she used four, giving her the idea for a title and page theme. To begin, cut two 5" squares of patterned paper (Hallmark) into triangles; mount in corners. Double mat photos, trimming with decorative scissors (Fiskars). Freehand cut leaves; draw green veins. Journal with colored pens.

Deidre Tansy, Smithers, British Columbia, Canada

THE THINKER

LE PENSEUR by Rodin

Ashton had been playing "in" (and we do mean "in") the dirt. Dennis took his clothes off outside to shake out the dirt before he would let him come in the house.
Ashton went over and sat down on the railroad tie waiting patiently for Grandpa to shake the dirt out of everything. He looked so cute Dennis had us all come outside to see him and to take this picture.
Jordan came out and wanted his picture taken too. Dennis was trying to get Ashton to move over next to Jordan - so Ashton started to slide down the rough, slivery railroad tie. Everybody started to yell "No, don't slide, get up and walk over by Jordan". Ashton just looked at us and started to slide down the rough railroad tie again. Someone ran over and got him up to walk over next to Jordan. He survived the incident without getting any slivers in his tender little bottom. (July 1997)

The Thinker

RECORD LIFE IMITATING ART

Serious thoughts weighed heavy on the mind of Jeri's grandson, reminding her of the famous Rodin sculpture, *Le Penseur* or "The Thinker." Jeri enlarged the original Polaroid photo to size on a digital photo machine. Images and journaling are all matted on green paper trimmed with decorative scissors (McGill). Sticker letters (Creative Memories) title the page.

Jeri McBride, Pingree, Idaho

Head, Shoulders, Knees & Toes...

TITLE A FAVORITE SONG

Kellene captured some of the silly ways her son makes her laugh and paired the photos with words to a classic children's song. Begin with green paper cut to fit inside lines of patterned background paper (me & my BIG ideas).
Crop photos and round corners. Adhere sticker letters (Frances Meyer, Making Memories, Provo Craft) in various colors.
Complete page with journaling.

Kellene Truby,
Wichita, Kansas

DEREK, 3 YRS.

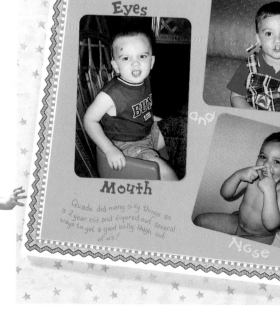

Head, Shoulders, Knees & Toes...
Eyes
and
Ears
Mouth
Nose
Quade did many silly things as a 2 year old and figured out several ways to get a good belly laugh out of us!

Paper Piecing

Paper piecing is a simple technique used to construct cut paper designs from various sources, such as freehand shapes, punches, or template designs. Many companies offer paper piecing patterns, but you can easily create your own paper-pieced designs for a personal touch.

When the Mommy Cat's Away, the Mice Will Play

PAPER PIECE AN ORIGINAL DESIGN

Donna's original paper-pieced design is the perfect showcase for featuring her active and mischievous twin toddlers. To make Donna's cheese and mouse designs, begin with patterned paper (MPR Assoc.) for a background. Photocopy and size the cheese patterns (see page 374), then follow the instructions below to complete the page.

Donna Pittard, Kingwood, Texas

CHEESE

1 *Photocopy large and small cheese patterns, enlarging or reducing to fit page and photo size. Transfer the patterns twice, once onto orange cardstock for front of cheese wedges, and again onto a lighter orange or yellow cardstock for back of cheese wedges. Do this by either photocopying patterns directly onto the cardstock or by using transfer paper to trace over the lines onto cardstock. Cut out pattern pieces (Figure 1).*

2 *Use various-sized circle punches to randomly punch holes on outer edges of front cheese "wedges" (Figure 2).*

3 *Apply orange color accents to front cheese wedges by shading lightly with chalk or colored pencils (Figure 3). Layer front cheese wedges over back cheese wedges; adhere and set aside.*

MOUSE

4 *Cut three circles, sized in proper proportion to the cheese (ours measure 4¾"), from gray cardstock, with a circle cutter or a circle template (Figure 4).*

5 *Apply gray color accents to outer edges of circles by shading lightly with chalk or colored pencils (Figure 5).*

ASSEMBLY

6 *Crop and adhere photos to cheese and mouse ears, as shown. Place cheese and mouse elements on page, moving around for proper placement, then adhere. Punch two small black ovals for eyes, one large pink heart for nose, and freehand cut strips of black paper for whiskers; adhere to mouse to complete face (Figure 6). Journal.*

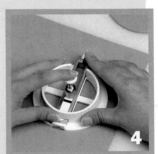

The Naked Sportsman
SHOWCASE AN ALL-AROUND ATHLETE

Active little boys can be multitalented, so Kelly shows nonstop action with multiple photos of a similar theme. To begin, layer patterned paper (NRN Designs) over solid background paper, leaving ¼" border. Single and double mat photos; layer on background paper. Mount die cut letters (AccuCut) and adhere ball stickers (Stickopotamus) over "privates."

Kelly Angard, Highlands Ranch, Colorado

This Little Piggy
USE CHILDHOOD RHYME TO TELL STORY

Linda combined photos of her son at his messiest to illustrate a classic *Mother Goose* nursery rhyme. Paper torn "piggies," outlined with black fine tip pen, are randomly layered with photos matted on white paper, keeping the "messy" theme of the page. Freehand drawn border, creative journaling and title complete the page.

Linda Strauss, Provo, Utah

Daniel's Guardian Angel
FIND INSPIRATION IN THE FUNNY PAGES

Lisa takes inspiration straight from the funny pages after clipping this *The Family Circus®* cartoon, which shows an active child who wears out his guardian angel. Build on a theme for a quick and easy page by silhouette cropping photos and layering them around de-acidified (Archival Mist™ by Preservation Technologies) cartoon matted on patterned paper. Add pen detail and captions with black pen.

Lisa Laird, Orange City, Iowa

Humor Album

CHERI O'DONNELL, ORANGE, CALIFORNIA

When you have spirited toddlers like Cheri's in the house, finding humor in daily life becomes therapeutic—even a necessity. Their curious, fast-paced world provides an abundance of comical moments to capture on film. And even if you miss those comical moments on film, just about any photo, when combined with clever captioning, quickly becomes part of a humorous page.

TODDLER THEME ALBUMS

Toddler theme albums are scrapbook albums that contain photos, memorabilia and journaling about a specific theme or topic. Theme albums are a fun alternative to chronological albums and they make great gifts. Best of all, they're quick and easy to make.

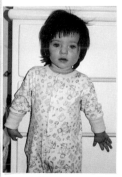

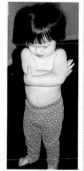

Photos that successfully capture personality and character traits (see page 288) are often the hallmark of great humor pages. As you can see, humor pages don't need a lot of embellishment; the photos speak for themselves!

I am a child at play

...who dances like a bouyant kite
caught up by a mischievous breeze.
I dart and drift and glide and soar.
Then I stop sometimes abruptly,
motionless a moment,
delighting in the heady atmosphere...
Savoring the peaceful view
spreading out before me at
these heights of freedom.

Child's Play

Toddlers don't need power suits or briefcases to get ahead in their careers. They play for a living! Yet every form of play serves an educational purpose. The lesson might be theoretical physics, say, building block towers vs. gravity. Or it might be role-playing: today a firefighter, tomorrow a ballerina. Preschool artwork, done in vibrant paint and crayons, shows how they see the world. Toddlerhood favorites give insights into emerging personalities, while ride-on toys encourage developing motor skills. Join right in on healthy games of imaginary play to let your child know that you know it's only a game and that you enjoy it too. Devote many pages to your youngster's world of play to serve as a rewarding reminder of his or her creative young mind.

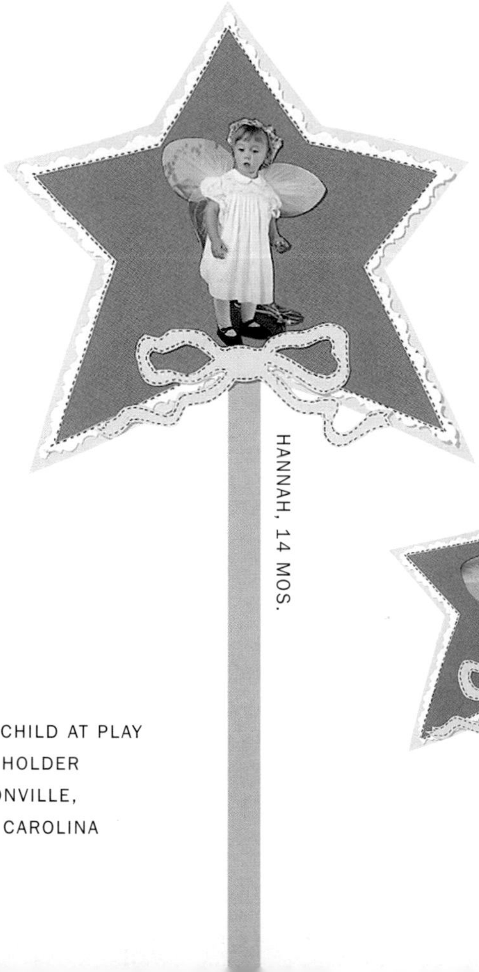

HANNAH, 14 MOS.

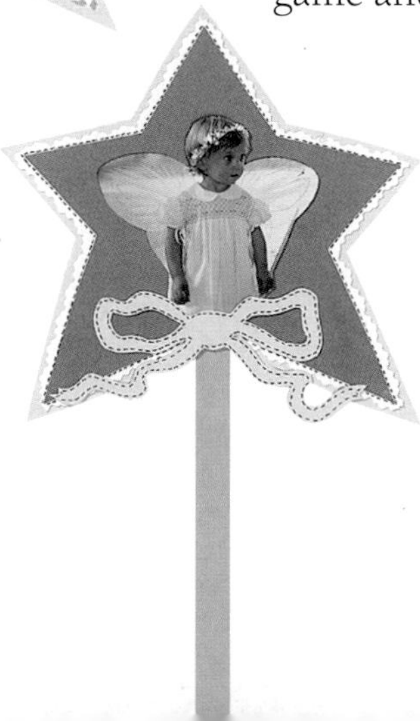

I AM A CHILD AT PLAY
KAREN HOLDER
JACKSONVILLE,
NORTH CAROLINA

Playtime

MAKE TOY-SHAPED PHOTO MATS

Nancy ties together various photos of her daughter playing by framing the photos in toy shapes. Photocopy and size telephone and stacking ring toy patterns (see page 374) to serve as a photo template. Crop photos to fit and mat. Silhouette crop toys from photo scraps and layer in bottom corner. Title and journal with red pen.

Nancy Chearno-Stershic, Bel Air, Maryland

Playtime

STACK UP PLAYFUL PICTURES

The random placement of the rings on Trish's page mimics the rambunctious activity of her children at play. First, crop photos and mat on bright colored paper; round corners of photos and mats. Photocopy and enlarge ring toy and ring patterns (see page 374); transfer to colored paper and cut out. Layer photos; slide ring shapes over corners of photos and mount. Adhere title letters (Creative Memories) and colored dot stickers (Mrs. Grossman's). Complete page by outlining photos, detailing toy and journaling with black pen.

Trish Tilden, Westmont, Illinois

REAGAN, 3 YRS.

MITCHELL, 3½ YRS.;
SPENCER, 2 YRS.

Sticky fingers,
dirty face
Rugs and pillows
out of place.
Cars and tractors
here and there,
blocks and boats
everywhere.
Gold and Silver
have I none,
but worth a million
are my sons.

--Ruth Joy

I dropped my dolly
in the dirt.
I asked my dolly
if it hurt
and all my dolly said is
wa-ah, wa-ah, wa-ah

BRITTANY, 18 MOS.

Hannah, An Object in Motion...

CAPTURE THE WHIRL OF ACTIVITY

Photos of Brenda's daughter in nonstop action are
shaped into a colorful, geometric design that illustrates
Sir Isaac Newton's law of motion. Start by cropping the
center photo freehand or with a template. Crop surround-
ing photos into geometric shapes, matching one side of
each photo to the center photo. Triple mat on colored
paper. Mount center photo with foam spacers between
matting to add dimension. Freehand crop directional triangles and mount around photos. Trace and crop font
title and lettering, mount on page.

Idea and Photos Brenda Gottsabend, Canton, Ohio

Future Farmers

CAPTURE A TIMELESS MOMENT

Vicky caught a glimpse of her two boys'
future one afternoon when she snapped these
beautiful photos. Complementary paper colors
for the background and matting enhance the
natural setting of the photos. Freehand draw
title letters, mat and trim with decorative
scissors (Fiskars).

Vicky Clayton,
Maymont, Saskatchewan, Canada

Alt Computer Whiz

PROGRAM KEY-PUNCHING FUN

Jana's son, a true 21st-century kid, was introduced to the computer at an early age, and has
loved it ever since. Complement photos with
keyboard paper (Hot Off The Press) for the
background. Cut a 2½" border strip from brown
paper; adhere title letters (Creative Memories).
Mat photos; trim with decorative scissors
(Family Treasures).

Jana Tafelski, Grand Haven, Michigan

FUTURE BUILDER

Constructing a page around this photo of
Amanda Bott's (Hendersonville, Tennessee)
architect-in-training began as her son's love
for building blocks grew. It's fun to imagine
your child's future career, based upon the
types of toys and activities he favors most,
and then build a page around that "career."
Twenty years from now, your scrapbook page
may prove to have been a prediction!

CHRISTIAN, 3 YRS.

Paging Dr. Bozeman
REMEMBER ROLE-PLAYING FUN

Pretend play is an entertaining and cru-
cial part of toddler development. Debbie
recorded her son, the budding doctor,
attending to his first patient. Start the
page with a patterned paper background
(Keeping Memories Alive) and mat
cropped photos with darker patterned
paper (Keeping Memories Alive), leaving
space for journaling. Finish with a custom-made paper doll (Barbra's Dolls)
and sticker letters (Provo Craft).

Debbie Bozeman, Rochester Hills, Michigan

Jammin

HIGHLIGHT A CLASSIC TODDLER ACTIVITY

Yvonne silhouette-cropped her daughter's classic "banging on the pots and pans" photos for this
groovy page design. Circle cut graduated paper rings in three different colors; mount as shown.
Mat silhouette-cropped photos on paper circles; mount as shown.
Add punched flowers (Family Treasures), letter stickers (Making Memories),
journaling and ink dots around letters to finish.

Yvonne Nickerson, Mashpee, Massachusetts

Jared's First Painting
FRAME PHOTOS WITH FLAIR

Jennifer framed photos of her little artist creating his first masterpiece with artistic flair. Create your own "gallery" by cropping photos and mounting on page. Frame with colorful paper scraps or hand drawn designs. Freehand cut paper-pieced artist from paper scraps. Adhere crayon and paint-related stickers (source unknown). Complete page with photo captions and title.

Jennifer Gould, Costa Mesa, California

Artist at Work
CREATE A SCRAP MASTERPIECE

While capturing her son's creative efforts, Jolene puts her cropping leftovers to use. She calls her finished product, "The Frugal Format: Pages for Pennies." Leftover patterned paper strips line the bottom of the page and provide a background for the title. Title blocks, which are actually the sticky paper leftovers from sticker letters, are adhered to square decorative paper scraps. Paint splats are crafted from leftover pieces of maple and oak leaf die cuts (Ellison).

Jolene Wong, Walnut Creek, California

Mommy's Little Artist
PRESERVE THE CREATIVE PROCESS

Splashes of color enliven Donna's daughter's first paintings. To feature the artwork of your budding artist, layer red paper over gingham paper (Frances Meyer). Freehand cut palette and brush. Freehand crop large photo and circle cut two smaller photos; mat with freehand "color splotch" shapes. Adhere artist stickers (Stickopotamus). Add title and journaling with black pen.

Donna Pittard, Kingwood, Texas

Busy Little Hands
FEATURE CLAY CREATIONS

Playing with Play-doh® is a favorite activity for Caroline's daughter and husband! Begin by backing photos with single and double mats layered on a yellow speckled background (Westrim) trimmed with border sticker strips (me & my BIG ideas). Layer double matted title lettering (Cock-A-Doodle Designs) partially over photo. Complete page with journaling using template (EK Success) to make wavy lines.

Caroline Lebel, Toronto, Ontario, Canada

Color My World
CROP A CRAYON BACKGROUND

Larger-than-life crayons make a colorful background for photos of Diane's little artisans. To make crayons, cut an 8½ x 1⅞" strip of colored paper and a 11⅞ x 1⅞" strip of darker paper in the same color family. Cut one end of the darker strip into a 2¼" point to form tip. Mount light strip atop darker, pointed strip. Make five more crayons. Crop photos; mount on crayon background. Add sticker letters (Frances Meyer) and journaling.

Diane Bottolfson, Sioux Falls, South Dakota

ELISE, 3 YRS.

Hot Wheels

RECORD CREATIVE CAR COLLECTION

Melissa's mind raced into action when her son
was looking for a way to beat the boredom blues.
Together, they outlined Alex's body with his car
collection, making a "Car Alex." Blue cardstock
provides the background for silhouette-cropped
car outline and cropped photos matted on red or
white paper. Auto stickers (Current) matted on
white paper build on the page's theme. Print title
lettering, journaling and mat.

Melissa Abbe, Vancouver, Washington

Love My Blocks

BUILD ON CONSTRUCTIVENESS

Mitzi was so inspired by her son's elaborate block
designs, she decided to craft her own. Creatively
shaping scraps into geometric shapes can reflect a
child's creative designs and add playful fun to your
pages. Small title letters (Provo Craft) keep the focus
on the design element and photos.

Mitzi Stuart, Paducah, Kentucky

TV Time

SPOTLIGHT YOUR STAR

Andrea displays her favorite "couch potatoes" on their own TV screen! To make a television, cut a 10¼ x 8" rectangle from taupe cardstock. Cut a gray 8 x 6¾" rectangle for TV screen; round corners. To make dials, punch large black circles and mat with jumbo punched gray circles; adhere. Mat a gray rectangle with rounded corners to black rectangle for speaker; adhere. Draw details with silver ink and add journaling.

Andrea Wheatcraft, Frankfort, Kentucky

ELIJAH, 4 YRS.; CHLOE, 12 MOS.

Little Dolls

DOCUMENT CHERISHED DOLLS

Angi created an appropriately titled layout with photos of her twins and their favorite dolls. Begin with pink and blue paper over gingham paper (The Paper Patch), leaving a 1" border for the background. Mount photos with white photo corners (Boston International) over layered mats. Circle cut and partially silhouette crop photo; mat on solid paper. Cut title letters from template (EK Success) on polka dot paper (The Paper Patch); double mat on colored paper. Freehand craft doll head and hair for letter "O"; punch bows (McGill). Punch flower bouquets: daisy, circle and birch leaf (Family Treasures), large flower (All Night Media), teardrop (EK Success), mini sun (Marvy Uchida) and small daisy (Carl). Layer to create bouquet; mount. Print journaling, mat on solid paper and add pink triangles at two corners.

Angi Holt, St. George, Utah

pickles · pull toys · cheese ·
trains · raisins · horses ·
whales · pickles · juice ·
race track · horses · crackers
little wooden toys · pickles
animals · juice · dogs · cheese
trains · cereal · pickles ·
whales · juice

All of My Favorite Things

SHOWCASE FAVORITE TOYS AND FOODS

To help remember the details of her toddler's favorite things, Michele
photographed them. To create this page, start with patterned paper
(Gussie's Greetings) for the background and add double-matted photos,
cropped in ovals and squares. Create page title with ⅝" wide
strip with matted oval centered; journal with black pen.

Michele Fischer, Aberdeen, Washington

JESSICA, 2 YRS.

Going Places in My Car

(BELOW) Catherine's son takes to the road on this two-page spread. To create your own road, start with blue background paper. Use template (AccuCut) to cut road, photos and journaling block; shade top of road with gray chalk. Double mat large photo. Use template (AccuCut) for title and mat. Cut car and decorations from template (AccuCut); assemble. Punch 38 black small squares; mount on white cardstock for banner and flags. Cut doll and clothing from template (AccuCut); assemble. Adhere doll to car, placing vellum behind windows and doll. Mount on page. Finish spread with journaling.

Catherine Schulthies for Accu-Cut, Fremont, Nebraska

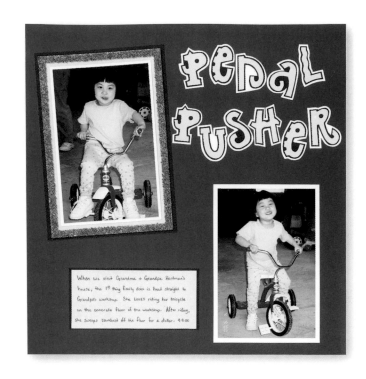

ZACH, 11 MOS.

306

Pedal Pusher
FEATURE A FAVORITE PASTIME

(FAR UPPER LEFT) Lois captures her daughter's spirit soaring while riding her favorite tricycle in Grandpa's workshop. Start with the title using a lettering template (EK Success); double mat on black and white paper. Single mat one photo and triple mat another. Add Beedz™ (Art Accents) for texture on the triple mat. Complete page with journaling.

Lois Rodgers, Lowell, Arizona

Get Ready, Get Set, Go!
SILHOUETTE TODDLER TRANSPORTATION

(UPPER LEFT) Mary gathered photos of her little one on the go, showing some of the ways he takes to the road. To begin, freehand cut "road" with decorative scissors (Fiskars); draw white dashed line. Silhouette crop photos; layer on road. Adhere character (Suzy's Zoo), transportation and road sign (both Mrs. Grossman's) stickers. Stamp grass background (Posh Impressions). Add title sign and journaling.

Mary Ellefson, Freeport, Illinois

Caution, Future Driver
POST SIGNS OF THE TIME

(UPPER RIGHT) When Jeanette's son got behind the wheel with his "cell phone," she saw warning signs all over the place! Freehand cut street signs and mount atop strips of black paper for sign posts. Double mat photos. Freehand title and letter street signs.

Jeanette Goyke, China Township, Michigan

Creating Shadows

From hand-puppet animal shadows cast upon walls to the long end-of-summer shadows cast by bridges and trees, shadows intrigue all of those who are young at heart. If you have photos with great shadows, you can easily re-create the shadows as one-of-a-kind page embellishments. Simply make a paper-pieced version of the object in your photo that casts a shadow, then trace around it on black paper to create the shadow. To achieve the most realistic shadow based on the direction of the implied light source, experiment with proper placement of the shadow on the page beneath its paper-pieced counterpart before adhering to page.

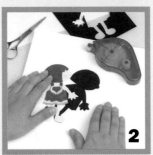

Me and My Shadow

EXPAND ON A PHOTO ELEMENT

Judy loved the shadows of her daughter at play, so she carried the look onto her scrapbook page. To create this look, double mat photos, offsetting the second mat. Freehand draw a hopscotch grid. "Dress" a paper doll (Stamping Station) with paper-pieced hair and clothing to match your child's. Follow the steps to the right to make the doll shadow and shadowed title letters traced and cut from a lettering template (Provo Craft).

Judy Diehm, San Antonio, Texas

DOLL SHADOW

1 *Trace around paper doll onto black paper; cut out (Figure 1).*
2 *Layer "shadow" doll at an angle beneath paper doll (Figure 2), using the light source direction of the shadow in your photo(s) as a guide for proper doll shadow placement, and adhere.*

SHADOWED LETTERS

3 *Adhere black "shadow" letters on page first, then layer red letters atop, slightly lower and to the left (Figure 3). In this manner, the black shadow letters will fall in the same direction as the black doll shadow, staying true to the direction of the implied light source.*

Me and My Shadow
RE-CREATE SHADOW PLAY

Chris created a clever page depicting her son's fascination with his shadow as light streamed through a window. Start with an orange background. Create window by layering the scene from the background out, beginning with blue paper for sky. Add hill, tree, cloud and butterfly stickers (Mrs. Grossman's) and sun die cut (Dayco). Freehand cut window frame and sill out of yellow patterned paper (source unknown); add cat sticker (Mrs. Grossman's). Freehand cut large sunray out of rainbow paper (Paper Adventures) and craft paper doll (Accu-Cut) with shadow; adhere. Crop photos, mat on black paper, and trim corners as shown to achieve shadow effect. Finish pages with title letter squares, matted the same as photos; adhere sticker letters (Provo Craft) and hand draw the rest of title.

Chris Peters, Hasbrouck Heights, New Jersey

It's Fun to Imagine That...
BUILD ON AN ACTIVE IMAGINATION

Michelle was inspired to create an imaginative page with photos of her daughter playing in a box. Begin with pink background. Create the foursquare look by adding two green rectangles to background, as shown. Silhouette crop photos. Freehand cut title block. Cut journaling blocks with decorative scissors (Fiskars). Title and journal with black pen. Complete page with transportation stickers (Mrs. Grossman's); punch "thought dots" with circle hand punch.

Michelle Siegel, Lake Worth, Florida

MITCHELL, 21 MOS.

All in a Day's Work

Toddlers mimic Mommy and Daddy in pure "monkey see, monkey do" fashion. But work doesn't always have to be, well, work. Folding clothes can easily become an impromptu fashion show or dress-up play. Early chores and working together set a productive pattern for life. Just set reasonable goals and be there to capture your damsel in distress or your courageous little superhero.

Penny, nickel, quarter, dime....Penny, nickel, quarter, dime, I just earned an allowance for the very first time!

COLIN, 4 YRS.

CHORE LIST

✓ Fold kitchen towels
✓ Pick up toys
✓ Dirty clothes to laundry

Mommy's Little Helper
SHOW OFF HOUSEKEEPING SKILLS

Cleaning the house is no chore for Michelle's daughter, and helps take the load off of Mom! Start by creating a border with descriptive words scalloped across top of page using a decorative ruler (Creative Memories) for guidance. Layer furniture clutter and object stickers (Mrs. Grossman's) across bottom of page. Draw thick lines down sides of page with pen. Crop photos; round corners and mount. Create title block with solid paper matted and trimmed with decorative scissors. Complete page with title lettering and photo captions.

Michelle Siegel, Lake Worth, Florida

Mommy's Helper

PRESERVE A TIMELESS TRADITION

Cara shares the baking of cookies with her daughter, and has captured a timeless feel with
hand-tinted black-and-white photos. Mat and mount photos on solid paper trimmed with
decorative scissors (Fiskars) over patterned background paper (The Paper Company).
Craft paper dolls (Stamping Station); freehand draw clothes and baking accessories out
of patterned (Everafter), solid and specialty (Paperwood by Lenderink) papers. Punch
title squares (Family Treasures); outline with metallic pen and adhere sticker letters
(Paper Adventures). Create journaling block with stamp (Colorbōk) on gingham paper
(Keeping Memories Alive); mat and trim with decorative scissors.

Cara Wolf-Vaughn, Carversville, Pennsylvania

Mommy's Helper

ADD PAPER-PIECED DETAIL

Melissa's daughter is a great help around the house, especially when she's willing to do the dirty work! Begin with soft-colored patterned paper (The Paper Patch) for background. Crop photos; single and double mat on solid and patterned (Keeping Memories Alive) paper. Craft paper-pieced vacuum from pattern (*Paperkuts*); adhere sticker letters (Provo Craft). Print title (*Lettering Delights CD* by Inspire Graphics); double mat. Print decorative corners; trim to size and mount.

Melissa Abbe, Vancouver, Washington

JAMI'S STORY

Sometimes the best part of parenting comes when you see the world anew through your child's eyes. Jami experienced this joy with her 15-month-old son, Travis, as their family was preparing to move into a new home. The house needed lots of work, including a fresh coat of paint inside and out. Travis soon became best buddies with the painting company owner, Todd, as he painted the house's interior a sunny yellow.

One fall evening following move-in, Jami took Travis out into their backyard to enjoy the view of a full harvest moon. As they watched the golden orb sitting low in the sky, Travis suddenly blurted out, "Todd paint a moon!" Jami was amazed that her son could connect their wall color with the moon, remember the painter, and that he could even articulate the thought.

"I am so grateful to have this bright, creative spirit by my side to help me discover the world again," says Jami. "I look forward to many more months and years to come of painted moons, animal clouds, lemonade rain and wishing stars."

Jami McCormick, Louisville, Colorado

THEO, 2 YRS.

"Mom, I Ate the Bills"

HIGHLIGHT LITTLE HELPER'S MISCHIFF

Lisa's daughter thought it would be better to eat the bills, rather than pay them! To capture your little helper's mischief, double and triple mat photos and layer on background paper. Create title letters using template (Cut-It-Up) on specialty paper (Sandylion). Punch flowers (All Night Media, Family Treasures). Adhere postmark stickers (Stickopotamus) and bill memorabilia. Finish page with journaling.

Lisa Shupe, Ben Lomond, California

Men at Work

GROW A GRASSY BORDER

Little boys love to work with Dad, especially when they have their own tools. Begin with a blue patterned paper (Provo Craft) background, layered with a 2½" grass paper (Hot Off the Press) border sliced every ⅛". Silhouette crop photos; layer over grass. Crop additional photos; mat on red paper. Freehand cut sign for title; layer over brown paper strip for post and detail with black pen. Add silhouette-cropped bugs from paper (Current). Complete with title, journaling, and pen details.

Idea Cara Stroud, Midland, Texas
Photos Pennie Stutzman, Broomfield, Colorado

Pretty in Pink

THEME TOGETHER COLORFUL CLOTHES

A collection of colorful outfits comes together for Allie to feature her daughter all dressed up.
To begin, crop photos; mat on a variety of patterned papers (Close To My Heart, The Paper
Patch) and round corners of photos and mats. Adhere appropriately colored stickers
(Frances Meyer, Mrs. Grossman's) and sticker letters (Making Memories) around photos.

Allie Littell, Mebane, North Carolina

Brittany Anne

SHOW OFF YOUR LITTLE DOLL

So many clothes, so little time for Charla's darling paper doll daughter. To make a quick-
and-easy page, silhouette crop photos of "doll" and clothes. Add small white paper clothes
"tabs" outlined in black ink. Display on page as desired.

Charla Campbell, Springfield, Missouri

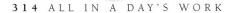

Disney® Prêt-à-porter

CATALOG FAVORITE CLOTHES

Cindy collected various photos left over from previous layouts and found a common thread...all had her daughter dressed up in Disney "ready-to-wear" fashions. Create a catalog-themed layout by cropping photos and matting on paper. Create "mouse ear" decoration with large circle punch mounted over freehand cut "ears;" detail with pen. Freehand cut sewing accessories; detail with black pen. Freehand draw title from logo; journal with black pen.

Cindy Kitchin, Naslemoore, California

Poor Girl

PRESERVE TODDLER WARDROBE

Cheri's quick-and-easy page serves a dual purpose—it effectively ties together several unrelated photos of her daughter while successfully documenting the youngster's wardrobe. First, adhere one uncropped photo directly on page to serve as a focal point. Add freehand cut hangers with title and journaling, as shown. Silhouette crop remaining photos; place randomly on page. Finish with stamped swirl (Biblical Impressions) designs.

Cheri O'Donnell, Orange, California

Hats!

FEATURE COLLECTION WITH STYLE

Candid photos caught Emily's kids raiding her closet and trying on all of her hats. Begin with yellow and blue papers, cut into geometric shapes, layered over a soft-colored background. Silhouette and square crop photos. Create title and journaling blocks in geometric shapes on ivory paper; lightly dust around edges with pink chalk (Craf-T Products). Freehand creative lettering; detail with pens and color with chalks. Add journaling.

Emily Tucker, Matthews, North Carolina

Fashion Footwear

SHOW OFF FASHION FLAIR

There's no such thing as a fashion faux pas in the eyes of a toddler, as shown in Tamara's comical fashion layout. To create your own stylish page, crop photos; mat on white paper. Freehand draw photo corner details and outline mat with black pen. Highlight fashionable photo details with silhouette cropping. Layer photos and title blocks on page. Adhere camera die cut, photography-related stickers and photo corner stickers (Creative Memories) to complete the design.

Tamara Ruby, McKinney, Texas

Color Blocking

Use blocks of color to add a dynamic dimension to your page. The clean lines of color blocking add just the right splash of color, which is a great substitute for pattern and texture. Experiment with tried-and-true, as well as uncommon, color combinations for a truly contemporary effect.

See Jack Go

CRAFT A CONTEMPORARY DESIGN

As you can see from our cover art, bold colors, combined with silhouette-cropped photos of busy Jack, work together to form an energetic color-block design. To make a similar 8½ x 11" scrapbook page spread, begin with white paper for background. Then follow the steps below to create the pages.

1 *Freehand cut six 4" squares, six 4 x 4¾" rectangles, and five ½" wide strips from colored and patterned papers; trim to fit pages. Use bold-colored markers to shade some of the squares and strips (Figure 1) and set aside.*

2 *Carefully silhouette crop 7 or 8 selected photos with scissors (Figure 2). Cut slowly, following the child's outline, and be careful around hair and facial features. Random photos of hands, feet, even a child's mouth will lend a more abstract touch to the layouts.*

3 *Assemble color block shapes in a pleasing scheme and layer with silhouette-cropped photos. Apply an adhesive (Figure 3) that is flexible enough to use on tiny areas of silhouetted photos to ensure adherence prior to mounting on color blocks. Finish pages by adhering hand-cut, slightly uneven paper strips atop color block seams and adding bold-colored journaling. Note: For a 12 x 12" scrapbook spread, cut six 4" squares and six 4 x 7½" rectangles with ½" strips in between or six 4" squares and six 4 x 6" rectangles with 2" strips in between.*

Two Little Shoes

PRESERVE A SPECIAL PAIR OF SHOES

Lynn cherished how proud her son was of his favorite pair of shoes, so she made an ink impression of one. The page was highlighted with a shoe-related poem (author unknown) and two cropped and matted photos trimmed with decorative scissors. A small star punch was used to embellish the page.

Lynn Butler, Palm Bay, Florida

Superboy

SPOTLIGHT A SUPER-TODDLER

Linda captures her son in superhero style as he flew in and out of different outfits, dressing up in the flash of an eye. Spotlight your superhero on a red background surrounded by bold colors. Crop photos, mat on yellow paper. Freehand cut star burst, arch, and zigzag matting for silhouette-cropped photo. Create title and captions in shadowed letter style with colored pens. Complete page with journaling in blue pen.

Linda Wright, Hartford, Connecticut

I spy Hew in a flannel shirt,
a hard hat,
a hammer,
a pile of dirt!

I spy Hew trying to hide,
a soccer ball,
a bouncing frog,
a yellow slide!

Now that you have
looked at Hew,
Go back and find
something new!

sun
star
ball
triceratops
arrow
mail
gloves
lotion
hat

"I Spy" Album

Children love looking for hidden objects and solving riddles, as seen in the popularity of Scholastic & Cartwheel Books® "I Spy" book series. Tracy's "I Spy Hew" album is a homemade, toddler-themed version with personalized rhyming text that leads her son to find objects hidden on the scrapbook pages.

"Hew just loves it!" says Tracy. An added bonus— the very nature of an "I Spy" album allowed Tracy to use many leftover and extra photos and paper scraps that might have otherwise gone unused. In addition, a wide array of colorful stickers allowed her to illustrate the rhymes with ease.

Tracy Haynes, Boynton Beach, Florida

"I SPY" VARIATIONS

Photograph numerous still-life collages composed of a hodgepodge of your child's favorite things (see page 377 for ideas), create photo collages of cropped and silhouetted photos of family and friends, or create a photo collage of animal pictures from the zoo. Then write text that leads your child to find certain objects, people or animals.

1997

A year of family, friends, and fun!

Left page: Tony comes to visit • Jake starts preschool • Rachel & Daddy go for a swim • Sydney Bidney • Rachel says goodbye to Brynn • Fourth of July fun at the Aberbook's • Crazy Uncle Richie • Rachel makes her favorite sandwich (peanut butter) all by herself! • Sydney gives Jake a kiss.

This page: Hangin' out at the Gambi's • Kindergarten friends come over to play with Rachel • Playing at the park with baby Talia • Swingin' in the backyard • Jake's tries to catch flying money at a spring carnival • Mommy turns 35 • Lauren and Jake splash splash in the bath • Rachel holds baby Talia for the first time • Alex gives Jake some basketball pointers • Mommy and Jake have some photo fun!

Family & Friends

The world of our toddlers starts in the hearts of family and friends. They're the people who love our little ones simply because they are. Starting with Mom and Dad, then radiating out to relatives and friends, a toddler's ties spread to all who will play and cuddle and tussle a bit. A toddler has other connections too, to those who came before and those who will follow. It's never too early to start "family tree" pages for your toddler, showing not just family but friends, also. Photos and journaling are especially vital here to ensure that memories of faces and good times will last forever.

1999:
A YEAR OF FAMILY,
FRIENDS & FUN!
KELLY ANGARD
HIGHLANDS RANCH,
COLORADO

There Are Little Eyes Upon You

HIGHLIGHT A SPECIAL RELATIONSHIP

Photos of a special father-son relationship are accompanied by a meaningful poem (author unknown) to create a page that brings tears to Tammy's eyes. Begin with black cardstock background. Crop photos with decorative scissors (Family Treasures) or oval template (Family Treasures) before matting on red paper. Print poem on tan paper, then crop with scalloped heart template (Family Treasures) and mat on red paper. A punched train (Family Treasures) is the final embellishment.

Tammy Layman, Sterling Heights, Michigan

Once Upon a Time

JOURNAL A MAGICAL MOMENT

Kelly captures her daughter's dress-up play with Daddy in fairy tale fashion using storybook journaling. First, crop photos and mat on solid paper trimmed with decorative scissors. To help carry out the theme, add a color-copied scene from an actual storybook, if desired. Mount photos and art on page. Finish with title, journaling and pen work in black ink.

Kelly Angard, Highlands Ranch, Colorado

2 of a Kind

RECORD DRESS-ALIKES

Laura's page illustrates the day she and her daughter dressed alike. Create this colorful border using a filmstrip border punch (Family Treasures) around edges of colored background paper and weave ¼" red paper strip through holes. Adhere background paper to page. Cut ½" strips of polka dot paper for inside border; adhere to background paper. Double mat larger photos with red and polka dot paper and trim with decorative scissors. Frame single photo with heart die cut (Creative Memories). Layer polka dot and solid color sticker letters (Making Memories) to add dimension to title. Add heart stickers (Mrs. Grossman's) and journaling to complete the page.

Laura Elliott, Seaford, New York

Look-Dad, I'm wearing your shoes!

LOOK, DAD!

For the little boy who dreams of growing up to be like Daddy, slipping on the shoes is the easy part! Elizabeth Barnes of South Federal Way, Washington, captured her son standing tall in his dad's boots.

JOHNNY, 3 YRS.

BEN, 1½ YRS.

Get Down and Get Dirty

UNITE TWO GENERATIONS

Color and black-and-white photos unite two generations of
Linda's family playing in the mud! To begin, cut 1⅛" strips of
plaid paper (Hot Off The Press); mount on outer page edges.
Mount black-and-white photos; add photo corners cut from
plaid paper. Crop color photos; double mat with solid paper.
Freehand draw title letters; mount on paper squares. Tear brown
paper pieces for journaling to complete title. Add dot detail
around title letters and journaling with black fine tip pen. Cut
mud splats from template (Provo Craft); mount on page.

Linda Cooper, Haines City, Florida

Grandma and Kylen

FRAME A TENDER MOMENT

Rhonda framed a sweet moment between grandma and grandson,
knowing that even though the peaceful memory won't stay with
her son, the photo will. Create a frame by cutting strips of patterned (The Paper Patch) and solid paper with a wavy ruler
(Creative Memories). Print title and journaling on background
paper before layering wavy strips around sides of page. Crop
photo and round corners; mat and trim with decorative scissors.
Adhere flower stickers (Frances Meyer).

Rhonda Thompson, Layton, Utah

In His Sunday Best

Pamela highlights heritage photos of her husband's family dressed in their Sunday best. Black paper provides a striking background for red and white diamonds, matted, layered, and crossed with silver metallic stickers strips (Mrs. Grossman's). Crop photos with decorative scissors (Family Treasures); mount with embossed photo corners. Paper doll (Accu-Cut), custom "dressed" in outfit to match photos, stands on cobblestone and grass sticker strips (Mrs. Grossman's). Make custom clothes by tracing paper doll outfit pieces on your own paper. Complete page with printed title and journaling, matted over two red rectangles at corners.

Pamela James, Ventura, California

LISA'S STORY

The newborn calf appeared suddenly one morning at Lisa's father's home. Still trailing the umbilical cord, the cow resisted repeated attempts to shoo it back to its mother. The following day, Lisa's dad fed the cow, dubbed Bob (short for "Shish K. Bob"), milk from a baby bottle. Thereafter, Bob circumnavigated the yard as he followed her dad's voice.

Just a few days after Bob's arrival, Lisa's grandfather died. Bob unexpectedly began to kick and bounce around the front yard as the mourners left for the funeral. The cow's unusual behavior reminded Lisa's dad of how his mother Elise, who is also deceased, would bounce around when she was excited. "Bob brought a lighthearted feeling of wonderment and comfort to my father's home during our time of mourning," remembers Lisa gratefully.

About a week after the funeral, the cow disappeared as quickly as he had arrived. Lisa's dad sadly looked for his new companion and later learned a nearby farmer had reunited the calf with his herd. Perhaps Bob knew he had fulfilled his purpose in bringing Lisa's family a hint of joy in their time of need, and so returned to his own family.

Lisa Horst, Sacramento, California

TEN GREAT WAYS TO HELP YOUR GRANDCHILDREN REMEMBER YOU

1 Tell them about your family's history. Make tape recordings of these moments of sharing together.

2 Create something together: build a doghouse, sew doll clothes, or start a scrapbook.

3 Open a savings account and make a tradition of going to the bank and adding to it.

4 Be open to the nicknames your grandchildren choose for you and find a nickname for each of them.

5 Teach a grandchild about the constellations; he'll remember you every time he looks up at the stars.

6 Share your hobbies with them, and help them start hobbies of their own.

7 Read with them, read to them, read together.

8 Plant a garden together. You'll be planting seeds in the present and the future.

9 Let your grandchildren share secrets with you. Be sure to keep them.

10 Write letters, even in this age of e-mail. Your grandchild will treasure them.

GRANDPA JOHNSON
AND DEREK, 3 YRS.

Boys in Blue

CAPTURE RESEMBLANCES

Cathryn created a striking monochromatic layout with special photos of her son and his grandpa. A solid blue background, layered with patterned paper (Hallmark) provides striped matting for photos. Freehand draw and color lettering and journaling; mount on paper squares to enhance the monochromatic mood of the page.

Cathryn Wooton, Richmond, Virginia

Jansen really resembles his Grandpa Wooton with his solid build, blue eyes, his nice hands & his BIG head !

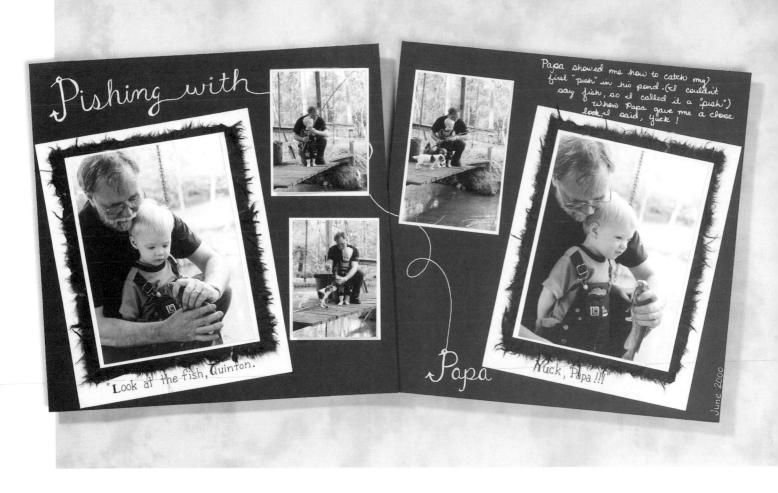

Pishing with ... Papa

"Look at the fish, Quinton."

Papa showed me how to catch my first "pish" in his pond. (I couldn't say fish, so I called it a "pish.") When Papa gave me a close look, I said, yuck!

Yuck, Papa!!!

June 2000

Making Biscuits

Granny shows Lexie how it's done.

Lexie helps shape the biscuit dough.

Granny is an excellent cook and biscuits are one of her specialties. She keeps her flour in a big tupperware bowl. When it's time to make biscuits, she grabs a handful of shortening and squishes it into the flour. Then she pours in just the right amount of buttermilk. Then she shapes them and puts them on the tray and "washes" them before baking. Lexie loves to help make biscuits with her Granny.

Pishing with Papa

DRAMATIZE A NEW EXPERIENCE

Dramatic black-and-white photos of a first-time fishing trip tell of a precious day with Grandpa. Patricia kept the layout simple with matted photos on a black background. Enlarged photos are featured with torn mulberry paper, layered between white matting. Freehand title and journaling completes the page.

Patricia Johnson, Cowpens, South Carolina

Making Biscuits

BAKE UP A BONDING TRADITION

Karen passes on the art of making the perfect biscuit by documenting the special grandmother-granddaughter bonding and baking time, complete with a recipe to remember. Create page title by cropping various sized rectangles to fit mat size. Add letters (Frances Meyer), stickers (Mrs. Grossman's) and stitching lines with pen. Double mat photos and journaling with patterned and solid paper.

Karen Holder, Jacksonville, North Carolina

LAUREN, 2½ YRS.; MITCHELL, 2½ YRS.; MEGAN, 4 YRS.

Sisters

GROW A MEMORY GARDEN

Evangelynn crafted a multi-dimensional garden from photo memories of herself and her sister as youngsters. To begin, freehand cut white strips and assemble picket fence over blue background paper. Jumbo punch (Emagination) photos into flowers; mat on white paper. Freehand cut jumbo daisies from white paper and vellum. Cut daisy center from yellow mulberry paper; layer pieces and mount together at center of flower. Cut green grass paper strips. Freehand cut stems and leaves. Freehand cut ladybugs; detail with black pen. Layer daisies, photo flowers, stems and leaves; mount over fence and under grass strips. To create foldout, jumbo punch additional photos into flowers; tape together on edges and adhere to jumbo flower embellished with jumbo daisy and ribbon tie. Trace printed title (*Curlz* by Microsoft) onto pages; outline in black. Freehand cut dragonfly and bee from solid, metallic (Making Memories) and textured paper (Paper Adventures). Complete page with journaling and pen work.

Evangelynn Lenz, Buckley, Washington

He Ain't Heavy, He's My Brother

PUNCH A RETRO DESIGN

The arrival of another baby boy gave birth to Kenna's retro floral design without looking "girlish." Double and triple mat photos on solid and patterned (The Paper Patch) papers; embellish with mini punched flowers. Punch and layer small and large daisies (Family Treasures), jumbo oval (Emagination Crafts), and $\frac{1}{8}$", $\frac{1}{4}$", $\frac{5}{8}$" and 1" circle punches (Family Treasures) to create random flowers. Freehand cut peace signs. Layer elements on page as shown. Trace title letters (Cock-A-Doodle Designs) onto paper squares; overlap and mat on solid paper. Adhere sticker letters (Making Memories).

Kenna Ewing, Parkside, Pennsylvania

Boy Oh Boy Oh Boy

SHOW OFF BOYISH CHARM

Kathy's husband captured this delightfully boyish photo. Begin with patterned background (Keeping Memories Alive). Crop photo, double mat and trim with decorative scissors. Finish with die cut letters (AccuCut).

Kathy Hartlaub, Williams Bay, Wisconsin

Brother or...Bully

LIGHTEN UP A SIBLING SQUABBLE

Kelly's ruffian toddler sometimes gets the best of his older brother! Punch characters with stencil-drawn faces (Tapestry in Time) to add comedy. Crop "weapon" photo; triple mat. Title the page with small (Making Memories) and large (Provo Craft) sticker letters.

Kelly Starr, Las Vegas, Nevada

Best Friends

PRESERVE YOUNG SILHOUETTES

Jean paired black-and-white photos with the simplicity of paper silhouettes to create a classic look. Start with a solid colored background. Crop photos with decorative scissors (Family Treasures) on side edges. Add photo corners (Canson) and mount to black mats trimmed with decorative scissors. Silhouette-crop silhouette portraits; trace onto black paper and cut out. Mount paper silhouettes on cream paper. Adhere photos and add journaling. Add pen stroke design to finish.

Jean Guernsey, Brookfield, Connecticut

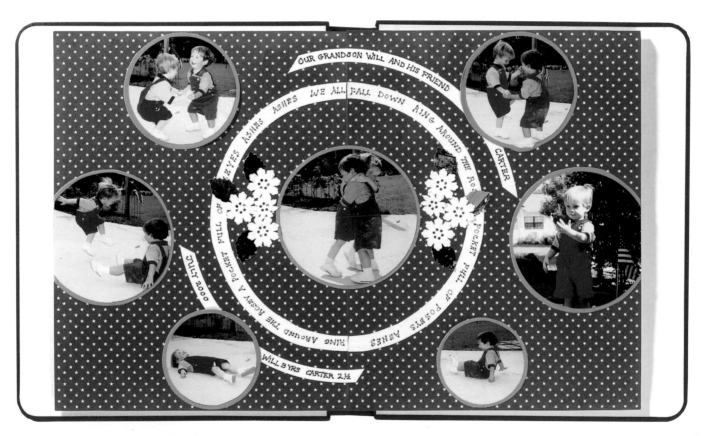

Ring Around the Rosey

ENCIRCLE PHOTOS WITH A SONG

JoAnn expanded on the idea of rings and circles when she photographed her grandson and his best friend playing "Ring Around the Rosey." First crop photos into circles; mat on solid paper. Create "rings" for title and journaling, either with a circle cutter or by tracing around a small plate. Cut one ring apart for outer ring. Layer photos and rings on patterned paper (The Paper Patch). Punch flowers (Family Treasures) from solid paper and leaves from photo scraps. Mount on page and complete with journaling.

JoAnn Petersen, Mukwonago, Wisconsin

Best Friends

PAPER FOLD A FRIENDSHIP QUILT

Jennifer's daughter and best friend are just inseparable! Cut strips of patterned paper (Provo Craft); mount on cardstock border. Paper fold large flower and corner details (see page 380). Mat photos on solid, floral, and patterned (Keeping Memories Alive) papers. Mount photos, filling spaces with papers, journaling, girl die cuts (Hot Off The Press), and paper folded flower. Draw lines. Punch large circles and cut purple flowers from patterned paper; mount as shown.

Jennifer Wellborn, The Memory Tree, Las Vegas, Nevada

Forever Friends

CHALK UP A SPECIAL FRIENDSHIP

A sweet hug between friends is captured by Nicola's freshly chalked layout. Layer patterned paper (Provo Craft) over chambray cardstock (Pebbles in My Pocket) leaving a ¼" border. Double mat photo on solid and patterned (Provo Craft) paper. Freehand cut layered flowers from patterned (Provo Craft), solid, and vellum papers. Add sticker title and bees (Karen Foster). Dust blue chalk around title, photo, and flowers. Finish with pen work and journaling.

Nicola Howard, Pukekohe, New Zealand

"All About Me" Album

Another toddler favorite is an album devoted strictly to him or her, such as Anne's clever "see-through" gift album depicting qualities she loves about her son.

"It made him feel so special after a year of having a new baby brother in the spotlight," says Anne. "It reminds him that he is special and unique."

Anne simply mounted two photos on the inside front and back covers and cropped circles at the same place on each page to create the windows for her son's face to show through. Stephen's outfits (My Mind's Eye), setting, and character traits change with every turn of a page.

Anne Heyen, Glendale, New York

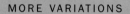

MORE VARIATIONS

Use photos that capture a daily routine, character and personality traits, social activities, important milestones, favorite things, or a month-by-month, calendarlike growth album. Add journaling to tell the story of each photo.

You love to go to the beach. You jump the waves in the ocean and you love to DIG!

You LOVE eating watermelon. You and Daddy always share a bowl full and he takes the pits out for you.

You like the rain because you get to use your umbrella and you LOVE to jump in puddles.

You are very creative! You love to do all crafts – especially with Mommy.

You are Daddy's helper in the Kitchen. You call yourself the Little Chef.

You are our SUNSHINE!

HAPPY BIRTHDAY

KEVIN, 20 MOS.

Going Places

THE REAL VOYAGE OF

DISCOVERY CONSISTS NOT

IN SEEING NEW LAND-

SCAPES, BUT IN

HAVING NEW EYES.

—MARCEL PROUST

Whether it's by plane, train, or automobile, your toddler has places to go and things to do. It might be just an impromptu Saturday jaunt to the neighborhood playground or a once-in-a-lifetime family odyssey to Disneyland. Getting there is part of the story, so look for opportunities to hike or bike or ride horses, too. Memories of travel will whet your little one's appetite for seeing the world and remind him that there is no place like home. When photographing your adventures, be sure to capture your toddler in the frame and remember it's not just the zoo elephant that's important—it's your little one marveling at the elephant.

BRANDON, 18 MOS.

THE PARK
KELLI NOTO, AURORA, COLORADO

Round 'n Round We Go!

LIGHT A FERRIS WHEEL

Create a carnival atmosphere with an "illuminated" Ferris wheel. Start with yellow patterned paper (The Crafter's Workshop). Punch jumbo blue circle and freehand cut paper strip for wheel base. Crop photos into ovals; layer to form a circle. Hole punch about 275 colored circles for "lights" after running paper through Xyron™ adhesive machine for easy mounting; adhere from center circle out toward photos for wheel arms. Adhere remaining "lights" around photos. Freehand draw and cut title letters; mount.

Idea Caroline Van Dorp,
Edmonton, Alberta, Canada

Photos Pam Klassen, Westminster, Colorado

Brookfield Zoo

FEATURE ANIMAL PAPER ART

Darla's daughter will remember her first trip to the zoo with a creative multipage layout featuring punched and paper-pieced animals. Begin with freehand cut and colored rock and water formations on backgrounds. Mat and adhere photos. GIRAFFE Freehand cut, piece, and layer with trimmed medium white heart for snout. PALM TREES Freehand cut leaves; layer over trunk trimmed with scissors. TIGER Freehand cut, piece, and layer with hand-drawn facial features. PARROTS Freehand cut, piece, and layer from colored paper. PENGUINS Punch medium heart for body, small heart for head, mini hearts for feet and nose; trim white medium heart for belly; freehand cut arms; hand-draw eyes. BEARS Punch and trim jumbo, large, and medium circles; small hearts for paws; freehand cut ears; draw eyes and noses.

Darla Stavros, Wheeling, Illinois

SHERRY'S STORY

Almost nothing in the life of a scrapbooker is more disappointing than picking up your photos from the photo lab only to discover a major disaster such as double-exposed shots. Sherry turned the tragedy of her Christmas pictures overlaying her July vacation photos into a unique page idea.

"I didn't want to discard the pictures," remembers Sherry. While flipping through the photos, her daughter Lindsay noticed a river shot with the superimposed mascot of their elementary school, a cougar. Since Sherry's son Ryan's favorite books at the time were the *I-Spy* and *Where's Waldo* series, her solution was to create a page featuring the same hide-and-seek concept.

Sherry thinks some of the pictures actually provided a hidden commentary on their life, such as a summer picture of her kids at the Royal Gorge overlapping a holiday picture of their great-grandma.

"Grandma will go sit by herself and finish her meal while we clean up because she's a little slow," says Sherry. "It's funny because I wouldn't be surprised if she was still eating when we were in Colorado!"

Sherry Baker, Florissant, Missouri

Photo Mosaics

Pieced photo mosaics are a captivating way to display just one or many related photos together on one page. The concept of photo mosaics is simple—cut your pictures into square "tiles" and arrange them as desired. The outer edges of your finished mosaic can be left intact or trimmed into a shape, such as the hamburger at left.

Playland Mosaic

Marsha's handmade hamburger fixings are the perfect showcase for a mosaic that features photos of her grandson playing at a McDonald's® Playland. To make your own mosaic hamburger to fit a 12 x 12" scrapbook page, begin by freehand cutting "veggies" and "cheese" from colored papers; trim with decorative scissors and layer onto background. Cut a 10¼" brown paper "bun" to serve as background for actual mosaic. For larger or smaller scrapbook page sizes, simply cut hamburger "fixings" larger or smaller. Then follow the steps below to create the mosaic.

Marsha Davis, Peetz, Colorado

CREATING A PHOTO MOSAIC

1 *Select photos and lay them out on paper "bun" circle, in a general format. Use a photo-safe wax pencil and a ruler to create a grid of 1" squares on the back of each photo (Figure 1), holding photo against a light source to ensure that your lines will not cut through facial features. Adjust where you draw the grid lines as necessary.*

2 *Number each square on the back of photos by row (Figure 2), numbering backward to maintain proper order when photos are flipped over.*

3 *Cut photos into 1" squares (Figure 3) and put individual photos in sandwich bags or envelopes to keep them separate.*

4 *Begin with the photo squares that feature faces, placing them in the center and working outward as desired (Figure 4), using the most interesting pieces of each photo. Do not adhere tiles yet.*

5 *Fill in the rest of the "bun" with remaining squares until the desired layout is achieved (Figure 5). Straighten squares neatly into mosaic pattern; adhere squares one at a time.*

6 *Flip "bun" over; trim away overlapping photo squares (Figure 6). Mount mosaic atop hamburger "fixings" on scrapbook page.*

1

2

3

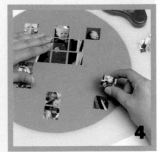

4

5

6

Having a Ball at Playland
CROP CIRCLES TO MIMIC A THEME

Sharon cropped playtime photos into circles to replicate the fun her grandkids had playing in a bounty of balls. Begin with red and green background. Crop photos into circles; mat some on colored paper trimmed with decorative scissors (Fiskars). Cut title banner and caption circles from yellow paper. Mat captions on layers of colored paper; trim all with decorative scissors. Draw title and lettering. Add decorative dots and dashes in black ink.

Sharon LaCroix, Orem, Utah

Rest Area

EXPAND ON ELEMENT FROM PAPER

Shauna chose an ideal sign to mat a photo of her son snoozing in the car. First, mat and trim patterned paper (Hot Off The Press) with decorative scissors (Family Treasures); layer on yellow background. Triple mat photo, leaving wide border for lettering. Freehand draw sign letters and arrow in white. Cut letters from template (Provo Craft) from patterned paper; outline in black ink. Silhouette crop road signs from paper; mount on page.

Shauna Immel, Beaverton, Oregon

5 Alarm Kid

SHOWCASE A SPECIAL VISIT

Jennifer's son's fascination with firetrucks lands him in the driver's seat at a local fire station. Begin with plaid paper (Creative Memories) background. Cut two 11" and two 4" yellow paper strips for ladder; crop photos to fit and assemble. Freehand draw alarm; mat alarm and large photo on yellow paper. Jennifer enlarged dog sticker (Creative Imaginations) to layer behind photo. Freehand draw, cut, and assemble hose and spray; crop photo to fit. Freehand draw title letters; add flame detail. Journal on yellow paper.

Jennifer Guyor-Jowett, Saranac, Michigan

Preschool Circus

SPOTLIGHT A GREAT PERFORMANCE

Liza's choice of bright colors and friendly circus animals reflects the festive atmosphere of her son's preschool circus. Begin by layering yellow and red patterned papers (Close To My Heart) for background. Freehand draw a semicircle at page top, layer freehand cut triangles for flag banner. Silhouette crop animals from stationery (Amscan); layer with photos trimmed with corner rounder. Use performance program for title. Add silhouette-cropped photo at top and finish with journaling.

Liza Wasinger, Fairfax, Virginia

Dear Noah,

We have always enjoyed traveling to see our family, friends, and to visit new places. Mommy and Daddy went to England for our honeymoon. One day, we hope to take you there. When you were born, we decided to make you a traveler from the beginning. Your first road trip was when you where just a two months old. We went to Tennessee to visit Grandma & Grandpa Myer. A few weeks later, you had your first stay in a hotel when we went to Charleston, South Carolina for the weekend. One day, we were curious about how many miles you had traveled. We were so surprised when we discovered that you had ridden over 20,000 miles in your car seat. Some years we've gone more places than others. We thought it would be great fun to start documenting the states that you had traveled to or through. Our hope is that this travel journal will remind you of all the places you have been and the memories of getting there. One day, it will be up to you to complete the journey. We hope you that your enjoy the trip!!

Happy Trails!

Love,

Mommy
10/00

TRAVEL VARIATION

Travel can be as simple as a walk around the neighborhood or a day of running errands with Mom, with photos and journaling of what your child does, says, and sees. Or put a reverse spin on travel, by photographing and journaling about the visitors who come to see your child at home.

Travel Album

Toddlers live to go "bye-bye," whether it's across the city or across the country. Their memories of travel are often shorter than the trips themselves, which is why Monica made an album with each page representing a different state. As her family visits each state, she adds to the page. The album also incorporates postcards, memorabilia, hand-journaled state trivia, and travel photos.

"We were so surprised to discover that Noah had ridden over 20,000 miles in his car seat," writes Monica. "One day, it will be up to Noah to complete the journey. Happy trails!"

Monica Sautter, Greenwood, South Carolina

My Trip
DOCUMENT A COCKPIT TOUR

Kelly and her daughter get a close look at how to fly the friendly skies. Background cloud paper (me & my BIG ideas) provides the border. Cut decorative photo frames from patterned paper (me & my BIG ideas); crop photos to fit. Double mat remaining photos; layer on page. Double mat printed journaling. Mount airplane die cut (Ellison) and small, freehand-cut airplanes. Add title sticker letters (Provo Craft) and journal with black pen.

Kelly Angard, Highlands Ranch, Colorado

What a Character!
ADD CHARM TO THEME PHOTOS

A picture-perfect day at Disneyland resulted in magical photos of Kelly's family with colorful characters. Vibrant colors jump off of a black background bordered with cropped, colored rectangles. Crop photos into shapes and mat on solid colored paper. Feature a favorite photo over freehand cut mouse ears; mat on white paper. Silhouette crop Disney character from patterned paper (Hot Off The Press). Adhere sticker letters (Provo Craft) on title block and paper squares; detail with black pen. Mat title block on patterned paper (Hot Off The Press).

Kelly Angard, Highlands Ranch, Colorado

At the Beach
CAPTURE SANDY TEXTURE

Heather adds simple style with texture on a layout of her daughter enjoying a quiet day on a shell-filled beach. Photos are matted on complementary colors, keeping the focus on the beauty of the landscape. The star, cut from sandpaper using a template (Frances Meyer), adds a textural element. Cut title from beach photos using a template (Provo Craft); adhere onto matted paper squares. Complete page with journaling and gold ink details.

Heather Ho, Milwaukee, Wisconsin

Magical Moments
RECAPTURE SIMPLE PLEASURES

With so much going on at the Magic Kingdom®, Tina found it hard to remember every moment; so she recorded a few of her favorites on a clean, two-page spread. Begin with patterned paper backgrounds with a yellow patterned side border matted with purple patterned paper (Everafter). Freehand cut mouse ears and Mickey; mount on side border. Crop photos; mat on patterned papers. Cut title letters from patterned paper using template (Pebbles In My Pocket); mount on matted paper squares; adhere. Punch small stars and small Mickey® (All Night Media); mount at bottom of printed journaling and dot "I" in the title.

Tina Burton, Mounds, Oklahoma

Preschool & Social Activities

Everything we need to know in life, we begin to learn in preschool and other social settings. How to wait our turn. How to play well with others. When to stand up for ourselves. With the lessons come a wealth of mementos for scrapbooking: nametags, early drawings, experimental writing, and photos—lots of photos.

At Lamb's Gate Preschool
PRESERVE MEMORIES AND HANDWRITING

Memorabilia and creative journaling help Laurie capture the essence of her son's preschool days and his first attempts at writing his own name. Cut 1½" wide strips of different colored papers to fit page; adhere to top, bottom and sides of pages. Crop photos; mount. Add journaling, leaving room for memorabilia and stickers (Mrs. Grossman's).

Laurie Connolly, Mukilteo, Washington

The First Day of School
CREATE A PORTRAIT BLACKBOARD

A blackboard kit (source unknown) sets the perfect stage for Janie's son's preschool photos. Silhouette-crop child and teacher; mount at bottom corner. Mat portrait on yellow paper; attach photo corners. Add pencil (Carson-Dellosa Publishing), apple (Ellison) and title die cuts and journaling.

Janie Thomas, Blakely, Georgia

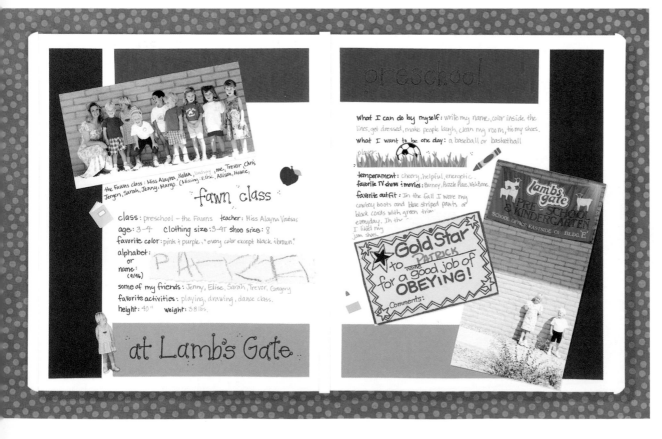

A, B, C, D, E, F, G...

SAVE CHILD'S FIRST WRITING

Debbie combined a school year's worth of work in one layout by taking photos of her son's alphabet artwork each week as he learned the letters. The child's own writing provides the title atop a sticker strip (Mrs. Grossman's), while circle-cut photos, matted on colored paper, frame the page. Journaling about a favorite letter completes the page.

Debbie Kelly, Carl Junction, Missouri

Preschool

CROP ELEMENTARY SHAPES

Catherine cropped photos in simple geometric shapes to boldly highlight her son's first friends and special preschool teachers. Top and bottom borders (EK Success) layered over background paper frame matted photos cropped in geometric shapes.

Catherine Wooton, Richmond, Virginia

The Bible

PRESERVE PRECIOUS MEMORABILIA

Sarah created a unique way to preserve the memory of her daughter's favorite book. Color copies were made of the Bible's cover and special inside pages, cut to size, and then "bound" back to back with adhesive. Gingham bordered paper with praying children (Hiller Industries) provides the perfect background for a favorite matted photo and text block. Stamped title (Stampin' Up!) completes the layout.

Sarah Swanson, Maplewood, Minnesota

My 1st Day of Sunday School

CELEBRATE AN IMPORTANT BEGINNING

Jacqueline wanted to incorporate the importance of faith in daily life in her daughter's scrapbook. First, crop photos, round corners and mat on patterned (source unknown) or plain paper. Mat class schedule; trim with decorative scissors (Fiskars). Freehand cut Bible for journaling; layer over photo. Craft paper doll (Scrapable Scribbles); mount under die cut grass border (Crafty Cutter). Adhere sticker letters (Frances Meyer) and school theme stickers (Mrs. Grossman's). Finish page with decorative pen work and journaling.

Jacqueline O'Beirne, Lake Barrington, Illinois

DOCUMENTING SOCIAL ACTIVITIES

Today's toddlers have many options for participating in activities that stimulate the mind, strengthen the body, and help develop social skills. Keep a camera and journal handy while you're busy running from games to recitals to lessons, and use these handy checklists to help you capture every detail.

PHOTOS

- [ ] Action and candid shots
- [ ] Art exhibitions
- [ ] Child with teacher, coach, or instructor
- [ ] Close-up of footwear (also documents growth)
- [ ] Close-ups of trophies or awards
- [ ] Costumes, uniforms, and equipment
- [ ] Getting ready for activity and practice
- [ ] Group or team mascot, emblem, or logo
- [ ] Individual and group or team portraits
- [ ] Still life of memorabilia associated with activity
- [ ] The joy of victory, the agony of defeat

JOURNALING

- [ ] Activity-related poems, quotes, and sayings
- [ ] Games played and lessons learned in preschool
- [ ] Group or teammate signatures
- [ ] In child's own words:
    Goals for next season
    Likes and dislikes about activity
    Memorable, embarrassing, and fun moments
    Opinions about teacher, coach, or instructor
- [ ] Letter to child from parent about accomplishments
- [ ] Team spirit cheers and mottoes

PAIGE, 5 YRS.

PATRICK, 5 YRS.

MEMORABILIA

Assume memorabilia is acidic; don't let memorabilia and photos touch. De-acidify newspaper clippings and announcements with Archival Mist™ (Preservation Technologies) or use PVC-free memorabilia protectors to encapsulate memorabilia before mounting on page.

- [ ] Artwork
- [ ] Certificates of participation
- [ ] Hand prints
- [ ] Newspaper clippings or announcements
- [ ] Programs
- [ ] Receipts
- [ ] Ribbons
- [ ] Rosters
- [ ] Schedules
- [ ] Teacher, coach, or instructor letters to child

JAKE, 4 YRS.

MADISON, 15 MOS.

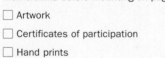

LARISA, 3½ YRS.

JORDAN, 5 YRS.

MacKenzie

18 Months

Weight: 25 lbs. 6oz
Height: 33 inches
Favorite food: lasagna, cheese, pasta + fruit
Favorite things to do: going down the big slide
at the park, coloring, looking at books, playing
with blocks, playing with dolls, playing in
the sandbox, dancing, playing with the
train set.

Accomplishments: knows 100+ words, can feed herself
with a spoon or fork, can throw and
catch a ball, pretends to go brush and floss her
teeth, pretends to go potty, tells us when she
wants to go to bed, GIVES THE BEST HUGS!

Recording Growth

THE EVENTS OF CHILD-
HOOD DO NOT PASS BUT
REPEAT THEMSELVES LIKE
SEASONS OF THE YEAR.

—FLEANOR FARJEON

MACKENZIE, 18 MONTHS
KAREN DAHLGREN
PORT COQUITLAM,
BRITISH COLUMBIA, CANADA

Early childhood can go by so quickly! To cherish each moment, keep track of how your little one is growing on the outside and on the inside. To measure physical changes, nothing can replace the precision of growth charts. One day, perhaps, your child will be a parent, comparing her inches and pounds to those of her own offspring. To measure your toddler's more subtle developmental achievements, track her success with practical, everyday tasks in simple language, not clinical terms. To bring it all together, stage formal or semiformal portraits. There's nothing better to catch a fleeting glimpse of a beautiful soul.

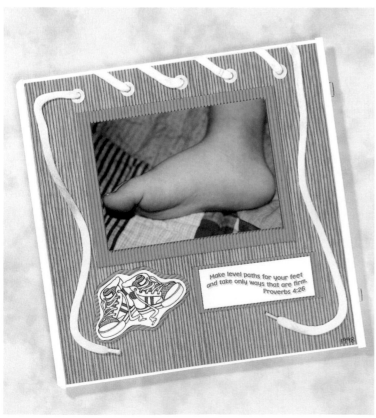

Amanda Can...

RECORD DETAILS OF DEVELOPMENT

Descriptive journaling and a collage of photos detail the development of Shelly's daughter. First, crop photos and mat on colored paper. Layer and mount on patterned (Keeping Memories Alive) paper. Title and journal in framed area with colored pens.

Shelly Claywell, Kirkwood, Missouri

Make Level Paths...

DOCUMENT A MOMENT IN TIME

Linda's laced-up page features a photo taken by accident of her son's foot; she'd always wanted to remember how little his feet once were. Before adhering paper to page, punch holes ¾" from top of patterned paper (Keeping Memories Alive) using a ¼" round hand punch. Adhere circle reinforcements. Lace shoelace through holes; adhere lace ends to paper and mount paper to page. Mat photo, die cut (My Mind's Eye) and printed journaling on blue corrugated paper (DMD Industries).

Linda Smith, Deerfield Beach, Florida

Hear Me Spell Jake

CAPTURE LITTLE VOICES

When Sandy's son learned how to spell his name, she found a way to capture the sights and sounds of the moment. Frame photo with embossed paper frame (Current). Print journaling, crop, and mat. Record voice on memory button (Ellison); slip into memorabilia pocket (3L Corp.) and mount on page. Adhere letter stickers (Frances Meyer) on envelope and sides of photo.

Sandy Mudrick, Gaithersburg, Maryland

When You Were 2 Years...

JOURNAL ABOUT PERSONAL FAVORITES

Every year Bethany charts her daughter's personality and growth by journaling about favorite activities, books, foods, etc. Print journaling on white paper; mount over pink background with photo and hand print. Complete page with decorative pen details.

Bethany Triplett, Guilford, Connecticut

Fredrick's 2

FORM PHOTOS INTO NUMBER

Ruth links twelve unrelated photos of her son, taken throughout the year, to document his amazing growth. Begin by cropping photos with a circle cutter or graduated circle template in various sizes. Mat, assemble in chronological order, and mount on page to form numeral that represents child's age.

Ruth Weaver, Gastonia, North Carolina

Adrienne Joy Lowry
3 years old ♥

Adrienne Joy Lowry

PHOTOCOPY PORTRAIT FABRIC

Jacqueline added a personal touch to her daughter's portrait by photocopying the fabric of her favorite dress. To create this look, mat photo on black paper trimmed with decorative scissors (Family Treasures) prior to mounting on photocopied background. Freehand lettering on black paper, trimmed with decorative scissors, completes the layout.

Jacqueline A. Lowry, Clear Lake, Iowa

EMILY, 2½ YRS.

EXPERIMENT WITH AVAILABLE LIGHT FOR GREAT PORTRAITS

Create beautiful, soft highlights and shadows in do-it-yourself portraits with these time-proven photo tips:

◆ Use fast, 400- or 800-speed film and turn off flash.

◆ Indoors:

   Shoot near a north-facing window with indirect light.

   Try a west-facing window in the morning.

   Try an east-facing window in the afternoon.

◆ Outdoors:

   Shoot in open shade (any area exposed to a lot of sky with no direct sunlight).

   Shoot in late afternoon light.

◆ Back lighting will silhouette child or highlight her hair.

◆ Side lighting will illuminate child's profile.

◆ Get in close to eliminate busy backgrounds and capture the innocence of the eyes.

◆ Take both horizontal and vertical photos, framing child off-center.

◆ Shoot at child's eye level to record perspective.

◆ Encourage interaction with toys, props, even clothing.

◆ Snap more than posed smiles; semi-posed and candid shots capture personality.

◆ Try black-and-white film for a softer touch.

MERCEDES, 2½ YRS.

BIG USES FOR TINY PORTRAITS

Try these nifty uses for those tiny photos that come in professional portrait packages:

◆ Add to a growth "time line."

◆ Add to mini "filmstrip" made with paper and filmstrip border punch.

◆ Create a shaped photomontage, like the cowboy hat shown below.

   Idea Sherry Harrison, Henderson, Nevada

◆ Frame a large portrait with them.

◆ Make personalized greeting cards with them.

◆ Place in windows of paper-pieced houses and family cars.

◆ Punch with a large shape punch; use for a border.

◆ Silhouette crop photos; tuck into paper-pieced designs.

◆ Silhouette crop photos; use for border.

◆ They're the perfect size for creating "family trees."

◆ Trim edges with decorative scissors to make a "postage stamp."

◆ Crop or stack and use to spell out child's name or age.

DAKOTA, 4 YRS.

Avery

WRITE A TOUCHING TRIBUTE

Tanya ends her children's albums by writing a tribute to them. Black-and-white portraits are double matted; first on patterned paper (Hot Off The Press), then on coordinating colored paper. Trim mats with decorative scissors (Fiskars) and add journaling to finish.

Tanya Anderson,
Winnipeg, Manitoba, Canada

MILESTONES & FIRSTS

Life is full of "firsts," but never are there more than in toddlerhood—from first haircuts and that move to a "big kid" bed to potty training and every single birthday before kindergarten. To fully capture these moments, save "first haircut" certificates, party invitations and decorations, even photos of potty training taken from discreet angles.

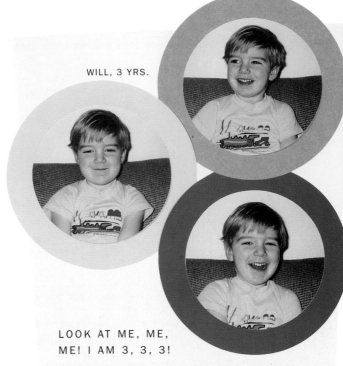

WILL, 3 YRS.

LOOK AT ME, ME, ME! I AM 3, 3, 3!

While her three-year-old son's favorite childhood song titled the theme for beloved photos, Leanne Scott, of Houston, Texas, used simple cropping and matting to keep her son's spirit and personality as the focus of a birthday page.

Mitch's 2nd Birthday

RECORD A COLORFUL MILESTONE

Inspired by a photograph of an album cover, Joy vibrantly colored her son's 2nd birthday celebration. To make colors "pop" off the page, start with a black background. Add freehand, matted title across spread. Double mat cropped photos; mount. Adhere freehand-cut balloons and candles with mini punched stars for flames. Journal and add decorative elements with white pen.

Joy Carey, Visalia, California

How to Have a Happy Birthday

MAKE A LESSON-FILLED FOLDOUT

Her first attempt at a foldout spread resulted in Jamie's fun, unique, and well-journaled progression of her daughter's 2nd birthday. Begin by trimming the binding edges from two blank scrapbook pages, then use artist's tape to tape the pages to the two outer edges of a scrapbook page spread to form the gatefold foldouts, as shown above. Single, double or triple mat photos, printed title blocks, and printed journaling. Arrange invitation (Peaceable Kingdom Press) and elements in chronological order; adhere. Finish with sticker (Stickopotamus) embellishments.

Jamie Carney, Germantown, Tennessee

EARLY CHILDHOOD MILESTONES & "FIRSTS"

Your child's toddler and preschool years will be packed with many milestones and "firsts" unique to this age group. While it may sound like a lot of work to photograph and record these incidents, you will never regret it.

Be on the lookout for any of the following:

Feeds self

Builds things

Uses identifiable words

Puts two words together

Throws and/or catches a ball

Sits in a normal chair

Washes face, brushes teeth

Sleeps in a "big" bed

Rides a tricycle

Names colors

Recites a nursery rhyme

Counts to ten or more

Draws a recognizable figure

Completes a simple puzzle

Dresses self properly

Hops on one foot

Skips

Forms letters

Recites own address

Tells a joke

Writes own name

Swims unaided

Blue Birthday

RE-CREATE PAPER DOLL GUESTS

Kristi made paper doll kids to resemble the guests in the group photo taken at her daughter's 4th birthday party. Begin by layering three solid papers for the background, creating a double border. Freehand cut paper dolls with clothes to match photo; mount dolls on page. Silhouette crop photo of birthday girl. Cut title block from white paper; mat on navy blue paper. Cut white title letters using template (Frances Meyer); stripe with colored pens and double mat. Freehand cut Blue® character; add to title block. Draw remaining title with colored pen; adhere stickers (Frances Meyer, Mrs. Grossman's, Sandylion).

Kristi Hazelrigg, Sand Springs, Oklahoma

Just What I Wanted

PACK A MEMORY POCKET

Shauna's "present" pocket page is a great storage solution for her son's birthday cards. Begin with yellow background. Mount pocket on background with adhesive on sides and bottom, leaving top open to form pocket. Cut various colored paper strips; mount vertically on pocket for "wrapping paper." Top the decorated paper with another strip of paper to form top of present. Crop photos; mat and mount in place. Cut letters with template (Provo Craft) and outline with neon pen. Triple mat letters; adhere. Add bow die cut (Ellison) and "gift tag." Journal to complete.

Shauna Immel, Beaverton, Oregon

Hot Dog Birthday Lunch

SERVE UP A PAPER-PIECED BORDER

Deleise's son celebrated his 3rd birthday with friends and his favorite food. A clever, paper-pieced mustard border, freehand cut from wavy strips, was mounted around the page, creating a frame for corner-rounded photos. Freehand cut mustard bottle top and hot dog from colored paper. Add texture to hot dog with paper crimper. Adhere title stickers (Provo Craft) to hot dog bun and add journaling.

Deleise Klaassen, Edmond, Oklahoma

Big Boy Bed

TELL ABOUT A TRANSITION

One of the many steps to becoming a big kid is moving from a crib to a "big kid bed." Lynn's son had an easier time with the change than she did! Start with blue paper layered over red for background. Crop photos in shapes and round corners. Draw title with template (Delta Magic) and journal with black pen. Punch and layer small and large stars; mount on page.

Lynn Butler, Palm Bay, Florida

Goodbye Crib...

PAY TRIBUTE TO A ROUGH TRANSITION

The time came for Linda's daughter to say "goodbye crib" and "hello bed"... or so she thought! Linda humorously documents the story of her daughter's rough transition from crib to bed and back again. Begin with polka dot background (The Paper Patch). Crop and silhouette photos; mat. Layer with computer clip art "waving hands" (*Masterclip* by IMSI) on page, saving room for journaling. Title on hands and add journaling.

Linda Fiore, Knoxville, Tennessee

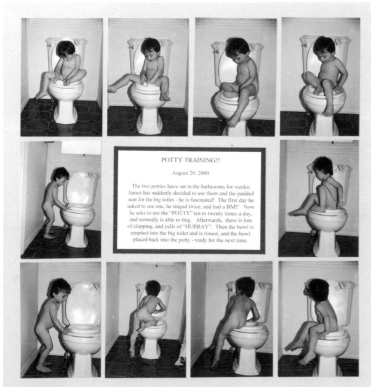

Bye Bye Binkey

HIGHLIGHT AN ACCOMPLISHMENT

When Kathy's daughter said goodbye to her constant
companion, Kathy documented the "binkey" love affair in
a quilt-like layout. Create page borders with ⅜" strips of
patterned (Colors by Design) and solid paper; mount yellow
background paper over strips. Crop photos, arrange in
quilt-like fashion. Cut title from template (Frances Meyer);
mat. Double mat photos. Print journaling. Mount pacifier
die cuts (Westrim).

Kathy Mancini, San Jose, California

Potty Training!

SHOW A PROGRESSIVE SERIES

Rachel exercised patience as she sat in the shower stall
to take 36 photos when her son became fascinated with
the potty. Patience paid off with a great series of discreet
photos which documents his training process. Crop photos
the same size; mount on yellow background. Print title and
journaling; mat on black paper and adhere.

Rachel Smith, Vancouver, British Columbia, Canada

Tami struggled to figure out how to motivate her son Isaac to stick with potty training. She finally settled on allowing Isaac to choose a toy, which he would acquire
only upon completion of a toilet training progress chart. His pick—a Tonka®
remote-controlled dump truck.

"It seemed appropriate," says Tami. "Take a dump and get a truck!"

Isaac added a smiley face to the record each time he did his duty. The chart
finally filled up and Isaac got to bring home his reward.

"I choked on the price of the truck at first," Tami says of the $50 toy. "But
I rationalized that it cost less than a couple months worth of diapers."

Once home, Isaac ran to get his
hard hat and took his dump truck
for a test drive. Tami later memori-
alized the experience in Isaac's
scrapbook for posterior posterity.

Tami Comstock, Pocatello, Idaho

Queen Victoria

CROP A REGAL PRIVY PAGE

The royalty in Jennifer's castle stands just a
few feet high and loves taking her place on
the "throne." Create a regal layout for your
king or queen by starting with a red background. Silhouette and crop photos; mount
on page. Freehand draw title on royal blue paper
(of course!) with gold pen. Adhere royalty-related stickers
(Creative Imaginations). Finish with gold ink dotting
around title, stickers, photos, and border of page.

Jennifer Motter, Riverside, California

Potty Training Tips

CREATE A "GLASS" GOODY JAR

Stephanie believes every parent has at least one potty training tip. Here, she illustrates Tip #3—the jellybean jar. Freehand draw wavy border; add jellybean stickers (Mrs. Grossman's). Double mat photos; trim with decorative scissors. Freehand draw jar on cream paper; outline and detail with black pen. Adhere jellybean stickers on lower half of jar. Cut vellum to jar shape; mount. Adhere sticker letters (C-Thru Ruler Co.).

Stephanie Dueck, Whitehall, Montana

Once Upon a Potty

RE-CREATE HELPFUL BOOK

Inspired by artwork from a potty training book, Mena details her son's departure from diapers. Start with patterned paper (Glad Tidings) trimmed with shape cutter (Creative Memories) for title side borders. Add sticker letters (Creative Memories) and punched flowers. Mat photos and printed journaling. Cropped, color-copied book cover finishes the page.

Mena Spodobalski, Reno, Nevada

False Start

"STRETCH" PAPER TO FIT PAGE

Debbie found a terrific way to "stretch" patterned paper (The Paper Patch) that doesn't quite extend to the edges of the page AND create a decorative border at the same time. Begin by cutting 1" border strips at the upper and lower ends of paper with decorative scissors (Fiskars). Mount strips flush with upper and lower page edges; center large piece of paper on page, leaving white space. Embellish borders with punched hearts. Round corners of photos and mats. Create matted title blocks from 1" paper squares; adhere letter stickers (Making Memories), mat and round corners. Print journaling; trim with decorative scissors on two sides.

Debbie Meyer, Elida, Ohio

Austyn Potty Training

CROP SOME "BIG GIRL" PANTIES

Missy cleverly created a page of panties to document the days her daughter tried to master the art of potty training. Photocopy and size pattern (see page 374); crop photos to fit shape and mount on page. Adhere stickers (Frances Meyer). Freehand draw title. Complete page with journaling and decorative dotting in black ink.

Missy Williams, Artesia, New Mexico

Potty Train

DOCUMENT INNOCENT MISUNDERSTANDING

When Silene's train lovin' little boy heard he was going to be "potty trained," he thought if he went potty, he'd get a new train! To begin, crop photos in ovals; double mat and trim with decorative scissors. Adhere train stickers (Mrs. Grossman's). Freehand draw clouds and journal with colored pens.

Silene Walters, Panda Bears, Rochelle, Illinois

Big Boy Pants

HANG A PROUD CLOTHESLINE

Chris wanted to remember her son's transition out of diapers without a photo of him on the potty. To create the clothesline, draw the "line" with black pen over striped background paper (Hallmark) trimmed with a ½" solid border. Freehand draw underwear. Adhere title letter stickers (Provo Craft) to paper squares; outline with blue pen. "Hang" letter squares and "undies" to clothesline with red sticker scraps cut into small pieces. Mount sun and cloud die cut (Stamping Station). Finish with sticker letters (Provo Craft), journaling, and decorative stickers (Frances Meyer).

Chris Peters, Hasbrouck Heights, New Jersey

Photo Encyclopedia Album

Making an ABC theme album can be so addictive that it's often hard to stop at the end of the alphabet. "It was just a blast to make, so I expanded it to include 123s, the seasons, and colors, too!" says Kristi. When her scissors and adhesives were put to rest five days later, she had completed 102 pages of Karly & Ally's Fun Photo Encyclopedia!

Vivid colors, lots of familiar family photos, and a wide array of playful stickers are what make Kristi's theme "encyclopedia" an enduring and irresistible book of knowledge for toddlers. "My daughters love to look through their book and I think it's a great way to help them learn."

Kristi Hazelrigg, Sand Springs, Oklahoma

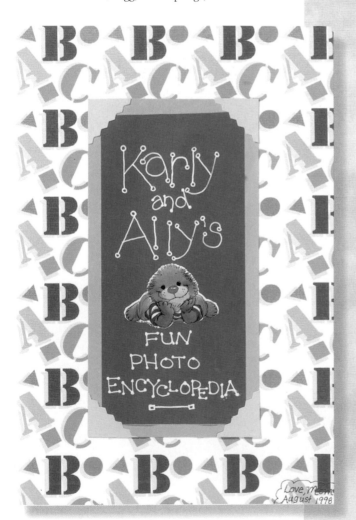

ABC, 123, SEASONS, COLOR VARIATIONS

Just about any topic lends itself well to an ABC album. Some topic ideas include animals, favorite toys, favorite people, favorite places, personality or character traits, childhood memories, accomplishments, and so on. Start by creating an A-Z word list based on your topic. Then gather photos and design additions that help illustrate each word.

Number theme albums can include any people, animals or objects. For example, 1 aunt, 2 grandmas, etc., or 1 turtle, 2 horses, etc.

For the seasons, try showcasing your child dressed for and at play during the various seasons, which can include holiday celebrations. There are a myriad of season-related papers, die cuts, stickers, and punches to help you carry out the theme.

Color theme albums can easily become ABC or 123 albums. For example, A is for aquamarine, B is for brown, etc.; or 1 red apple, 2 yellow bees, etc. To give these types of albums continuity, use the same style and type of letters or numbers, similar page arrangement, or border through the album. Just a little inspiration and imagination is all you need to create your own personalized "book of learning!"

1st Trip to the Dentist

DOCUMENT DENTAL CHECK-UP

Melissa's son was a perfect patient at his first visit to the dentist, and became quite an avid brusher! Crop photos, double mat on solid paper. Print title, journaling, and date; mat on paper. Adhere dental-related stickers (Mrs. Grossman's). Layer photos and title over patterned paper (PrintWorks).

Melissa Caligiuri, Winter Park, Florida

Me, My Brush, and I

ACCENT NEW SKILL

Cindy's photos of her son brushing his teeth for the first time are surrounded by clever, hand-made die cuts, crafted to look like the real thing. Double and triple mat circle-cut photos on solid paper; mount on patterned paper (Provo Craft) background. Freehand draw title, silhouette crop words and mat. Assemble on black paper, trim to shape. Print journaling; crop with decorative scissors and mat.

Cindy Mendiola, Norwalk, California

NICO, 3 YRS.

My First Haircut

FEATURE A TINY TRIM

Nicole's daughter needed just a tiny trim for her first haircut, so Nicole did it herself and documented the process. Start by cropping and circle cutting photos. Mat on solid paper. Craft paper doll heads (Stamping Station); add detail with pens and chalk. Layer freehand-cut bow and thinly sliced paper curled into hair wisps. Print title and journaling, crop and mount. Color copy scissors; silhouette crop and mount. Save small lock of hair tied with ribbon in memorabilia pocket (3L Corp.); mount on page.

Nicole Ramsaroop, Horst, Netherlands

Beauty School Drop-Out

RECORD A SPONTANEOUS SNIP

Nicole's daughter got fed up with her hair falling over her eyes, so she took matters into her own hands and cut it off! Document a self-styled mishap by matting photos with paper and trimming with decorative scissors. Layer scissors die cut (Ellison) on photo. Adhere sticker letters (Creative Memories) for title and decorative stickers (Mrs. Grossman's) around page. Complete with journaling.

Nicole Slager, Frankfort, Illinois

Travis' First Nightmare

JOURNAL ABOUT TODDLER FEARS

Damaged film couldn't erase the memories of Jami's son's first visit to the museum, so she used
brochure clippings and lots of journaling to tell the story of why Travis had his first nightmare.
To begin, layer patterned paper (Masterpiece Studios) over yellow background.
Journal title and story with computer font (*Chiller* by Microsoft Word); crop to fit in clouds.
Crop dinosaurs from brochures; mount. Add captions in brown ink
and die cut stars (Katee's Kut-Ups) to finish.

Jami McCormick, Louisville, Colorado

Josh's Buzz

MAKE PAGE THEME A PLAY ON WORDS

Alison chronicles the story of a haircut gone wrong when Dad tried his hand at being a barber. The page humorously plays on the word "buzz" with bee stickers (Mrs. Grossman's) scattered on the page. A freehand-cut beehive, crafted from tan paper and detailed with brown pen, title stickers (Creative Memories), and journaling complete the page.

Alison List, Jacksonville, North Carolina

First Movie

PAPER PIECE FAVORITE CHARACTERS

Chris spent many hours re-creating characters that stand tall in her son's eyes. Though paper piecing can take time, the spectacular outcome is worth the effort. To create your own paper-pieced movie character, enlarge a coloring book page and cut apart into pattern pieces, or trace over lines with carbon paper onto desired papers, cut apart, and assemble. Top the page with a title banner that combines movie-theme stickers (Frances Meyer) with sticker letters (Provo Craft).

Chris Peters, Hasbrouck Heights, New Jersey

Once upon a time, not so very long ago, my dear, there was a little boy and his name was James Colin Siler.

James was ever such a good little boy and always did what his Mama told him to.... (well almost always)

One night, James's Mama told him his story, listened to his prayers and tucked him up in his ever-so-warm bed. Then she turned out the light and closed the door and James fell fast, fast asleep.

STORYBOOK VARIATIONS

Center a favorite childhood story on your child; perhaps one of the toddler favorites listed on page 23. Simply use the book's illustrations for your own illustrating inspiration and alter the text to fit your child's personality. Or, feature songs—from nursery rhymes to show tune favorites to Sunday school hymns—illustrating each with family photos that match the theme or the mood of the songs. Perhaps let your child make up his own story and help you illustrate it. It'll be the silliest story you've ever heard, and will provide great insight into your child's preschool character years from now!

James and the Moonbeam Bear

by Mommy

1986

James and the Little Red Rabbit

by Mom 1984

Storybook Album

Toddlers love to hear stories when they are featured as the main character. In fairy tale fashion, Lynnette spins many stories—each with its own title page— with her son James as the main character.

"I've always enjoyed making up children's stories and James had special ones he wanted to hear over and over again," says Lynnette. "We even act out the stories and take photos to help illustrate them. It's a fun family activity!"

Lined album pages, cropped photos, stickers, and die cuts help Lynette spin her tales with ease.

Lynnette Siler, Corona, California

Poems & Sayings

You'll have no trouble finding photos to go with these great little sentiments for your child's scrapbook.

Every child is a different kind of little flower, and all together, they make this world a garden. —Author unknown

Children pull on our apron strings for a while, but on our heart strings forever. —Author unknown

Today I am a child.
My work is play!
—Author unknown

A mother's children are portraits of herself. —Author unknown

HOP POP. We like to hop.
We like to hop on top of pop. —Dr. Seuss, Hop on Pop, 1963

The Toddler Creed
If I want it, it's mine.
If I give it to you and change my mind later, it's mine.
If I can take it away from you, it's mine.
If I had it a little while ago, it's mine.
If it's mine, it will never belong to anybody else, no matter what.
If we are building something together, all the pieces are mine.
If it looks just like mine, it is mine. —Author unknown

How will our children know who they are if they don't know where they came from? —Ma in Grapes of Wrath

Our children are the only possessions we can take to heaven.
—Author unknown

There are no seven wonders of the world in the eyes of a child. There are seven million. —Walt Streightift

A truly rich man is one whose children run into his arms when his hands are empty. —Pilar Coolinta

All kids are gifted; some just open their packages earlier than others. —Michael Carr

Children are to be treated gently. They are like snowflakes—unique, but only here for a while. —Don Ward

The only thing worth stealing is a kiss from a sleeping child.
—Joe Hollsworth

Cleaning your house while your kids are still growing is like shoveling the walk before it stops snowing. —Phyllis Diller

My best creation is my children. —Diane von Furstenberg

You can learn many things from your children. How much patience you have, for instance. —Franklin Jones

Turn around and you're two, turn around and you're four, turn around and you're a young girl going out of my door.
—Malvina Collins, Turn Around, 1958

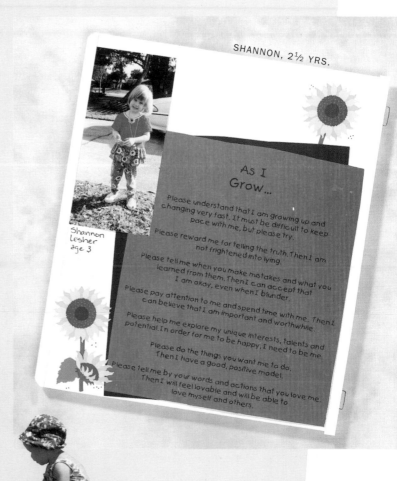

SHANNON, 2½ YRS.

Shannon
Lesher
age 3

As I Grow...

Please understand that I am growing up and changing very fast. It must be difficult to keep pace with me, but please try.

Please reward me for telling the truth. Then I am not frightened into lying.

Please tell me when you make mistakes and what you learned from them. Then I can accept that I am okay, even when I blunder.

Please pay attention to me and spend time with me. Then I can believe that I am important and worthwhile.

Please help me explore my unique interests, talents and potential. In order for me to be happy, I need to be me.

Please do the things you want me to do. Then I have a good, positive model.

Please tell me by your words and actions that you love me. Then I will feel lovable and will be able to love myself and others.

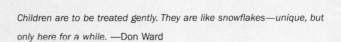

EMILY, 2½ YRS.

CLAIRE, 11 MOS.

Lettering Patterns & Page Title Ideas

Use these convenient lettering patterns to add a fun finishing touch to your toddler and preschool pages. Simply photocopy the lettering pattern, scaled to the size you need, and trace onto your page in pencil using a light table or window. Retrace and color in pen color of your choice. Or make your own patterns from the page title ideas listed by theme.

A DAY IN THE LIFE
A day in our life
It's toddler time!
Just hangin' out...
Our day in review
Simple pleasures
Welcome to our zoo

MEALTIME
Finger lickin' good!
Floor food's the best
My favorite foods...

BATH
Bathing beauty
Bubble, bubble, toil and trouble...
You clean up well!

SLEEPING
Going, going, gone....
I'll sleep anywhere, any time
Rise & shine!
Sweet dreams

MINIATURE MAYHEM
Caught in the act
It's the smile that keeps me out of trouble
My name's "No No," what's yours?
Pantry raid
Spoiled rotten
The original rugrat

JUST FOR FUN
Born to be wild
Clownin' around
Drama king or queen
Kids do the darndest things
Laughter is the best medicine
Monkeyin' around
The fun starts here
The streak
You're unbelievable!

CHILD'S PLAY
Backyard fun
Beep, beep, coming through
Boy toys
Boys will be boys
Everything a girl needs
Hide-n-seek
I love my blankie...
Just a swingin'
My dollhouse
My lil' Picasso
Painting is fun
Peek-a-boo!
Slip, sliding away
Toys R Me
Vrooom...

ALL IN A DAY'S WORK
Future careers
Hard at work
It's a guy thing
Just my size
Mommy's or Daddy's little helper
Monkey see, monkey do

FAMILY
A hug to remember
Brotherly love
Count your blessings
Family reunion
Family ties
Grandma's garden
Home, sweet home
It takes somebody special to be a daddy
It's all relative
Kissing cousins
Love lives here
Mommy's angel
My Grandpa & me
Sibling rivalry at its best
Sisters are forever
We are family!

FRIENDS
Best buddies
Best of times
Forever friends
Friendship blooms
Girlfriends forever
My new friends
Two peas in a pod

GOING PLACES
A day at the zoo
Do you see what I see?
Farm fun
Gone fishing
Mall adventure
On the go
Picnic at the park
Planes, trains, and automobiles
Pumpkin patch
State fair

TRIPS & VACATIONS
Away we go
Beach boys
Life's a beach
Road rules
Sea princess
Wish you were here

nothing a little
SOAP
and water
won't cure

I spy...

UH-OH!

100% GIRL

PRESCHOOL & SOCIAL ACTIVITIES
1st day of preschool
Born to dance
Graduate of the year 2018
Kindergarten, here I come!
Little ballerina
My favorite teacher
Preschool graduation
Put me in coach, I'm ready to play!
You're an all-star

RECORDING GROWTH
Growing by leaps and bounds
How does your garden grow?
Little calendar girl
Look at me now!
Watch me grow

BIRTHDAYS
A party for you
Birthday bash
Birthday boy or girl
Hooray for birthdays

MILESTONES
Atta boy
I can do it all by myself
It's potty time
Once upon a potty
Potty training 101
Snip, snip, snip
The big boy bed
What a big girl

artist
AT WORK

ROLLING ROLLING ROLLING ROLLING

NO! NO! NO!

FIRSTS
My 1st big bed
My 1st bike
My 1st camping trip
My 1st dental visit
My 1st eye exam
My 1st fishing trip
My 1st ice cream
My 1st nightmare
My 1st sleepover

PORTRAITS
100% doll
Cute as a bug
Cute as a button
Here's looking at you, kid!
Hollywood smile
Our shining star
Purr-fectly posed
Put on a happy face
Say cheese
Sew cute
Smile
Unbearably cute
What a doll
You ought to be in pictures

Here Comes TROUBLE

   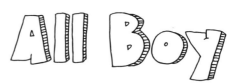

Project Patterns

Use these helpful patterns to complete specific scrapbook pages featured in this book. Photocopy and enlarge the patterns as needed to fit your photos and/or page size.

AUSTYN POTTY TRAINING, PAGE 362

PLAYTIME, PAGE 296

NIGHT NIGHT ZORYANA, PAGE 275

ENLARGE AND REDUCE AS NEEDED TO CREATE DIFFERENT-SIZED RINGS.

PLAYTIME, PAGE 296

PLAYTIME, PAGE 296

I LOVE TO EAT, PAGE 279

WHEN THE MOMMY CAT'S AWAY, PAGE 290

Interactive Photo Paper Piecing Patterns

To make your own interactive photo paper-pieced designs, photocopy and enlarge or reduce the patterns below to fit your selected photo. Cut the pattern pieces apart, transfer pieces to colored papers, and cut out. Reassemble all elements, adding a silhouette-cropped photo to complete the design.

PAGE 297

PAGE 302

PAGE 349

PAGE 286

PAGE 305

PAGE 269

PAGE 312

PAGE 306

PAGE 323

PAGE 335

PAGE 321

Charts

Our ready-made charts make it easy to begin a family tree, favorite things, or growth scrapbook page. Simply photocopy and enlarge to 115% (for an 8½ x 11" page) or 130% (for a 12 x 12" page), color as desired, and add cropped photos and journaling.

My Family Tree

My Favorite Things

Age	Subjects	My Favorites
	Animals	
	Adults	
	Books & Stories	
	Drinks	
	Foods	
	Games	
	Places	
	Rhymes	
	Songs	
	Friends	
	Sports	
	Toys	
	TV Characters	

Growth Chart

Age	Height	Weight	Clothes	Shoes
18 months				
24 months				
2 1/2 years				
3 years				
3 1/2 years				
4 years				
4 1/2 years				
5 years				

Instructions & Credits

title page
Colin Christine Cooley, Vancouver, Washington

page 260
Blanketed in Love
Treasured handmade blankets provide warmth, security, and companionship for Michele's three children. Begin with a four square of patterned papers (Hot Off The Press, MPR Assoc.) trimmed with a polka dot border (Hot Off The Press) cut from ¼" strips. Freehand crop photos into wavy blanket shapes; mat on polka dot paper. Cut title from template (C-Thru Ruler Co.). Complete with journaling. Photos Joyce Feil, Golden, Colorado and *Memory Makers'* Michele Gerbrandt

pages 262-266
Supplies used Background papers (Keeping Memories Alive, Paper Fever, Sandylion); mat papers (Imaginations); sticker letters (Making Memories); ABC cut-outs (*Déjà Views*° stencil by C-Thru Ruler Co.)

page 268
A Day in the Life
Cheri found a way to document everyday life events with a quick-and-easy filmstrip layout. First crop photos into 3½" squares. Cut 4" by 11" strips of paper in various colors. Punch filmstrip holes (Fiskars) along edges of strips. Either cut 3¼" square "frames" and mount photos behind frames, or simply mount photo squares atop filmstrip giving illusion of frames. Layer filmstrips on background paper. Finish with title and journaling; mount on page.

page 269
Adam Madaline Becker, Jonesborough, Tennessee

page 272
Morgan Jennifer McInnes, Coarsegold, California

page 277
Marissa
Sharon's granddaughter loves reading and being read to. Add depth and dimension to your photos by using any combination of complementary colored papers, decorative scissors, a decorative corner punch, and a ⅛" round hand punch to create a multi-layered photo mat. Sharon LaCroix, Orem, Utah; *Today's Top Ten Best-Loved Toddler Books*

courtesy of The Chinook Bookshop, Colorado Springs, Colorado, and the Pikes Peak Library District

page 280
Cheerios° are a registered trademark of General Mills, Inc.

page 281
David Donna Ecker, Thornton, Colorado

page 285
Band-Aid° is a registered trademark of Johnson & Johnson

page 286
Jenna Anita Hickinbotham, Mansfield, Ohio; *A little girl is...* quote by A. Beck; Brandon Janice Blackwelder, Greensboro, North Carolina

page 288
Mercedes Ken Trujillo, Thornton, Colorado

page 289
Derek Becky Smith, Lima, Ohio; *Head & Shoulders,* song copyright unknown

page 291
The Family Circus © 1998, Bil Keane, Inc., Distributed by King Features Syndicate

page 294
I Am a Child at Play
Karen captured her daughter's playful spirit on a beautiful page with just one photo and a poem (author unknown). Start with ½" border strips snipped into a "V" at the ends. Layer on three sides of page; mount. Triple mat photo, leaving ½" borders, trimmed with decorative scissors (Family Treasures). Write poem with white gel pen; trim with decorative scissors. Adhere title letters (Creative Memories).

page 295
Hannah
Marilyn's little fairy floats in sweetly crafted magic wands. Mat freehand or template cut stars; trim with decorative scissors (Fiskars) and mat again. Mount silhouette-cropped photos on stars. Add freehand-cut bow and paper strip for wand stick. Finish with pen stroke stitching. Marilyn Garner, San Diego, California

page 297
Reagan Kristen Melby, Steelville, Missouri; Mitchell & Spencer Carole Gentry, Tallahassee, Florida; Brittany Freehand cut a mud puddle; adhere to green paper. Add freehand cut splashes, grass blades, leaves, assorted punched flowers and saying to complete. Charla Campbell, Springfield, Missouri

page 302
Elise Stephanie Kirkessner, Lancaster, Pennsylvania; Play-doh° brand is a registered trademark of Hasbro, Inc., Pawtucket, RI 02862 USA. All Rights Reserved.

page 305
Jessica Laura Honeycutt, Winter Park, Florida

page 306
Zach Sarah Lyons, Highlands Ranch, Colorado

page 309
Mitchell Renee Bergman, Groveport, Ohio

page 310
Colin Crop photo, round corners and mat. Freehand cut dollar sign. Finish with journaling and memorabilia. Christine Cooley, Vancouver, Washington

page 312
Theo Diedre Tansy, Smithers, British Columbia, Canada

page 320
1999: A Year of Family, Friends & Fun! Photos of friends and family from a year to remember come together in Kelly's colorful stained-glass design. Mat all cropped photos on black paper. Layer and mount on page, leaving room for title and journaling blocks. Cut colored paper into geometric shapes to fit between photos, mat on black paper and mount. Print title numbers on black paper, cut out and embellish with tiny colored paper scraps to look like stained glass. Mat printed title and journaling on black paper, then again on mosaic matting. Create mosaic matting with tiny colored paper scraps mounted on black paper, leaving space between each piece.

page 321
Lyndsey & Tyler Shelley Littlefield, E. Taunton, Massachusetts

page 323
Ben Susan Brisson, Manchester, New Hampshire

page 326
Grandpa Johnson & Derek Christine Cooley, Vancouver, Washington

page 328
Lauren, Mitchell, Megan Nancy Phillipy, Huntington Beach, California

page 329
He Ain't Heavy Sidney Russell and Robert Scott © 1977, Harrison Music Corp., Jenny Music (ASCAP)

SEAN, 4 YRS.

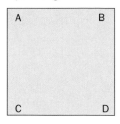

1. *Start with a square of paper.*

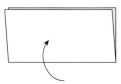

2. *With pattern side facing up, fold C and D to A and B, and crease.*

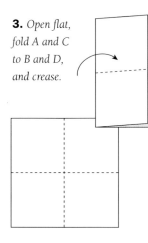

3. *Open flat, fold A and C to B and D, and crease.*

4. *Open flat and turn paper over with pattern side down.*

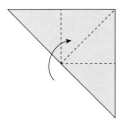

5. *Bring A to D, forming a triangle, and crease.*

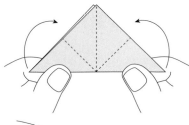

7. *Holding folded corners in either hand, push fingers toward center, forming a pocket opening, then move the corner in your left hand to the back and the corner in your right hand to the front, forming a layered triangle as shown.*

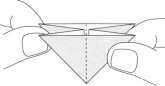

8. *Bring top right flap perpendicular to center fold.*

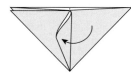

9. *Use a pencil to open the edges of raised flap.*

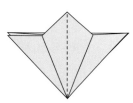

10. *Keeping center creases aligned, remove the pencil and press flat, creasing both sides of the new kite shape. Turn the piece over and repeat.*

page 331
Best Friends
Follow steps at left to make the large flower and corner embellishments. Assemble flower by holding two triangles with closed points facing same direction, slide top flap of one triangle between two flaps of the other triangle, snugging them up tightly and secure with adhesive. Continue until you have a full circle. For more paper folding techniques, see *Memory Makers Memory Folding*.

page 334
The Park
Kelly borders a page full of playtime photos with stamps that are made to look like a child's crayon drawings. Begin by stamping (Biblical Impressions) a border scene. Crop photos with decorative scissors (Family Treasures); mount on page. Write title with colored pen and add journaling.

page 335
KEVIN Plane pattern from German book, *Maeusekinder*, ISBN 3-7724-1787-6. Ilona Friedemann, Rialto, California; BRANDON Janine Blackwelder, Greensboro, North Carolina

page 338
McDonald's® Playlands and PlayPlaces are registered trademarks of McDonald's Corporation

page 347
JAKE MaryJo Regier, Littleton, Colorado; JORDAN Rebecca Collier, Riverside, California; LARISA Linda Crosby, Phoenix, Arizona; MADISON Janice McNamara, Macomb, Michigan; PAIGE Sarah Swanson, Maplewild, Minnesota; PATRICK Jenna Beegle, Woodstock, Georgia

page 348
Mackenzie, 18 Months
Karen captures her daughter's vivacious personality on a page with punched flowers created to look like the design on her dress. To begin, mat photos on solid colors, trimming some layers with decorative scissors (Fiskars). Stamp foot and hand prints with pigment ink; silhouette to shape. Cut journal block; punch (McGill) top and bottom border before matting on solid paper. Layer flower designs using large flower, small sun, small circle punch (all McGill) and small spiral punch (All Night

Media) out of solid colored paper. Layer and adhere all elements. Draw creative title lettering with black pen; color with pencils.

page 349
JACK Melissa Fagan, Hanford, California

page 352
EMILY Jan St. Marie, Carlsbad, California; MERCEDES Ken Trujillo, Thornton, Colorado

page 354
Look at Me, Me, Me! Song from *Barney®*, a registered trademark of Lyons Partnership

page 356
Blue's Clues © Viacom and Nickelodeon.

page 367
NICO Angela Gonzalez, Sacramento, California

page 371
SHANNON Idea and photo Julie Lesher, Longwood, Florida; EMILY & CLAIRE Jan St. Marie, Carlsbad, California

page 379
SEAN Debra Helm, Tewksbury, Massachusetts

Sources

The following companies manufacture products featured in this book. Please check your local retailers to find these materials. In addition, we have made every attempt to properly credit the trademarks and brand names of the items mentioned in this book. We apologize to any company that we have listed incorrectly or the sources were unknown, and we would appreciate hearing from you.

3L Corp. (800) 828-3130

AccuCut® (800) 288-1670

Amscan, Inc. (800) 444-8887

Art Accents (877) 733-8989

The Beary Patch (877) 327-2111

Biblical Impressions (877) 587-0941

Boston International (800) 637-5061

Canson (800) 628-9283

Carl Mfg. USA, Inc.
(847) 956-0730

Carson-Dellosa Publishing Co., Inc.
(800) 321-0943

Close To My Heart® (888) 655-6552

Cock-A-Doodle Design, Inc.
(800) 262-9727

Colorbök (800) 366-4660
wholesale only

Colors By Design (800) 223-3130

Craf-T Products (507) 235-3996

Crafty Cutter (805) 237-7833

Creative Imaginations (800) 942-6487

Creative Memories® (800) 468-9335

The C-Thru® Ruler Company
(800) 243-8419

Current® (877) 665-4458

Cut-It-Up™ (530) 389-2233

Dayco Ltd. (877) 595-8160

Delta Technical Coatings, Inc.
(800) 423-4135
Design Originals (800) 877-7820

DMD Industries (800) 805-9890

Dover Publications
(800) 223-3130

EK Success™ (800) 524-1349

Ellison® Craft & Design
(800) 253-2238

Emagination Crafts, Inc.
(630) 833-9521

Ever After Scrapbook Co.
(800) 646-0010

Family Treasures, Inc. (800) 413-2645

Fiskars, Inc. (800) 500-4849

Frances Meyer, Inc.® (800) 372-6237

Glad Tidings (800) 527-5214

Hallmark Cards, Inc. (800) 425-6275

Hot Off the Press (800) 227-9595

IMSI
(800) 833-8082

Karen Foster Design (801) 451-9779

Katee's Kut-Ups (858) 679-2132

Keeping Memories Alive™
(800) 419-4949

Lenderink, Inc. (616) 887-8257

Marvy® Uchida (800) 541-5877

Masterpiece® Studios (800) 447-0219
wholesale only

McGill, Inc. (800) 982-9884

me & my BIG ideas (949) 589-4607
wholesale only

Memories by Design (801) 775-9380

Michel® & Company (800) 533-7263

Microsoft Corp.
www.microsoft.com

MPR Associates, Inc. (336) 861-6393

Mrs. Grossman's Paper Co.
(800) 429-5459

My Mind's Eye™, Inc. (801) 298-3709

NRN Designs (800) 421-6958
wholesale only

Paper Adventures® (800) 727-0699

The Paper Patch® (800) 397-2737
wholesale only

Peaceable Kingdom Press
available at Windemere Bergmont
(816) 822-1944

Pebbles In My Pocket®
(800) 438-8153

Posh Impressions (800) 421-7674

Preservation Technologies, L.P.
(800) 416-2665

PrintWorks (800) 854-6558

Provo Craft® (800) 937-7686

Sandylion Sticker Designs
(800) 387-4215

Stampendous!
(800) 869-0474
wholesale only

Stampin' Up! (800) 782-6787

Stamping Station, Inc. (801) 444-3828

Stickopotamus® (888) 270-4443

Suzy's Zoo® (619) 282-9401

Westrim Crafts
(800) 727-2727

Xyron® (800) 793-3523
wholesale only

Bibliography

Brott, Armin. *The New Father: A Dad's Guide to the Toddler Years.* New York. Abbeville Press. 1998

Eisenberg, Arlene, Heidi Murkoff and Sandee Hathaway. *What to Expect: The Toddler Years.* New York. Workman Publishing. 1994

Fitzhenry, Robert I. *The Harper Book of Quotations.* New York. HarperResource. 1993

Kutner, Lawrence, Ph.D. *Toddlers and Preschoolers.* New York. William Morrow and Company, Inc. 1994

Miller, Karen. *Things to Do With Toddlers and Twos.* Massachusetts. Telshare Publishing Co. 1984

Solo, Dan X. *Bold Script Alphabets: 100 Complete Fonts.* New York. Dover Publications, Inc. 1989

Spencer, Paula. *Parenting Guide to Your Toddler.* New York. Ballantine Books. 2000

Stoppard, Miriam Dr. *You and Your Toddler.* New York. DK Publishing, Inc. 1999

I am a child at play

...who dances like a bouyant kite
caught up by a mischievous breeze.
I dart and drift and glide and soar.

Then I stop sometimes abruptly,
motionless a moment,
delighting in the heady atmosphere...
Savoring the peaceful view
spreading out before me at
these heights of freedom.

How to **organize** your
scrapbook workspace

storage solutions for any budget

MEMORY
MAKERS
BOOKS

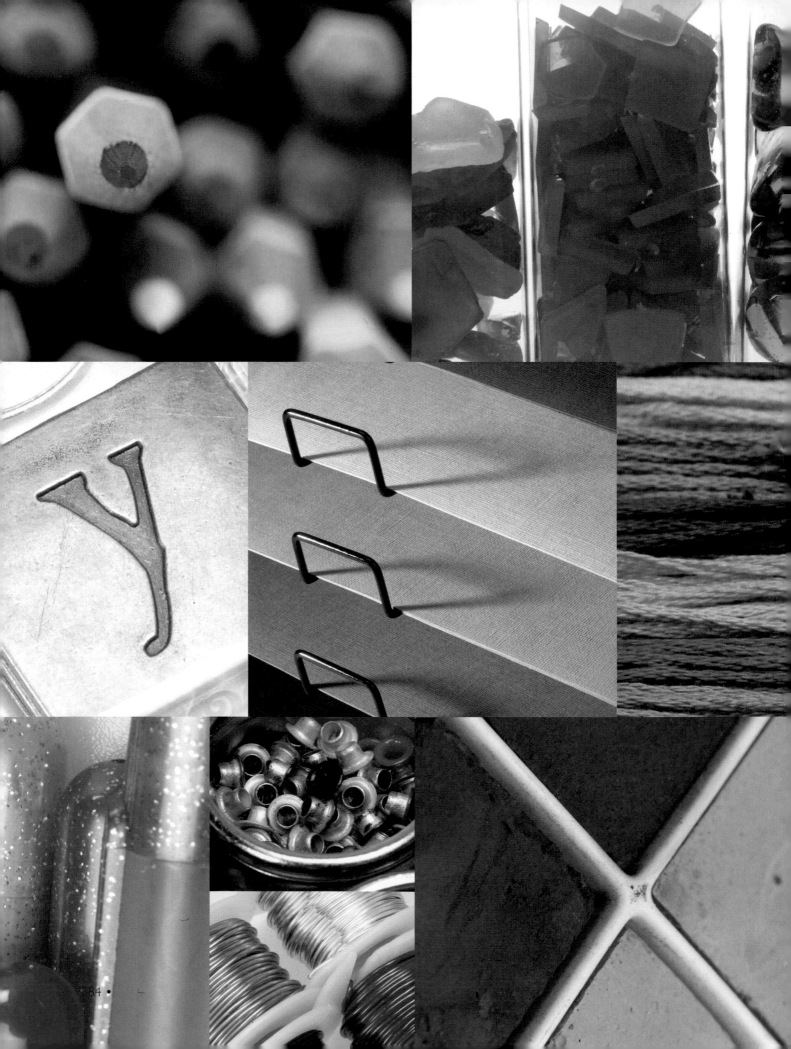

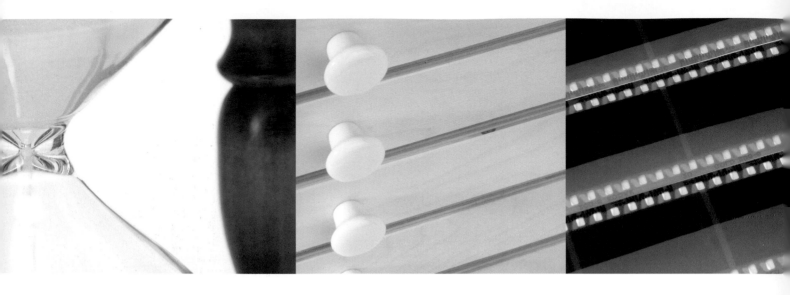

TABLE OF CONTENTS

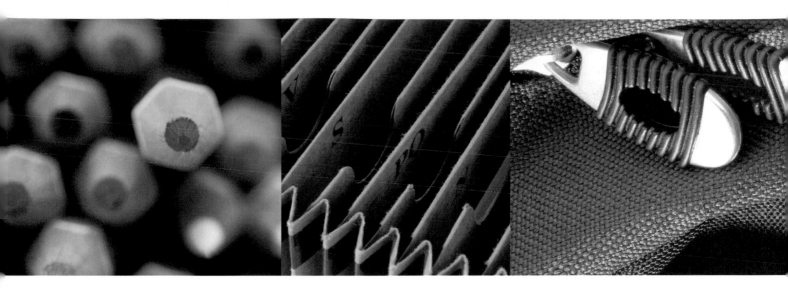

Introduction

The hobby of scrapbooking brings with it an immense amount of tools and supplies, with appealing new stuff appearing in the stores almost daily. And regardless of how we currently store our scrapbook "stuff," we always feel the need to be better organized. Like me, perhaps you need better scrapbook organization or workspace planning solutions. Maybe your photos and negatives are in such disarray that it's hard to settle on the next scrapbook page to make. Or maybe your papers, stickers and embellishments are stacked on every horizontal surface and the clutter overcomes your urge to crop. If you have the desire to get organized "someday," realize that someday never arrives without a commitment to take those first steps at getting organized. Take the initiative and start your organizational project today!

This book is designed so that you can set your own pace. You can either work through it in front-to-back fashion to organize absolutely everything you own or you can pick and choose which areas or items need work the most. You will learn how to create a plan of action, take stock of your available space options, plan for small spaces and plan storage that is right for you, undertake budget considerations, create a personalized floor plan, organize your scrapbook tools and supplies, efficiently plan page kits and discover solutions for streamlined and effective cropping on the go. Further, we explore countless storage products and containers from product manufacturers who are as dedicated as we are to helping you get and stay organized.

In addition to the pull-up-your-shirt-sleeves, nuts-and-bolts organizational know-how, we've included some really fun and unique ideas, too. I think you will love our section on room colors for enhanced creativity, ideas for the ergonomic workspace, how to host a swap, frugal flea-market finds, antiques in the workspace and storage that can be found around the house. You'll find one of the most revealing ideas in our section on trading scrapbook workspaces. Once they thought their workspaces were organized, we challenged two scrapbookers to trade workspaces for a day and create a page. Both women came away with organizational ideas that they have since implemented for their own workspaces as well as advice for one another on things they could do differently to streamline efficiency. It's an idea that you may enjoy doing with one of your own scrapbook buddies; it's quite a telling and rewarding experience!

Start at the beginning of this book or wherever you need the most help. It is all up to you. Take a look through the Table of Contents as an overview of what is available. Once you work through all the chapters of this book, you will definitely be a more organized and efficient scrapbooker! Whether you have a small nook or a large studio, these tips will help you get your scrapbooking act together. Working toward your goals for as little as ten to fifteen minutes a day will yield fantastic changes over time. Every scrapbooker wants to feel organized and productive as she creates a legacy for her family. This book is a tool that will help you become more productive and keep your workspace clutter-free.

Michele

Michele Gerbrandt
Founding Editor
Memory Makers magazine

Finding Time to Get Organized

The late, great singer Jim Croce hit the nail on the head: "There never seems to be enough time, to do the things you want to do, once you find them." A counterproductive—albeit far-too-true—lament in today's busy lifestyles where spare time is a commodity. However, by purchasing this book, you made a conscious decision to overcome the obstacles of clutter and chaos in an effort to be more productive. Ironically, in order to get organized, you have to find time in your busy schedule to commit to the process of getting organized. Squeeze more time out of every day with the following ideas.

ANALYZE HOW YOU SPEND TIME

Keep a time log for a week to identify vacant blocks of time or look back at a monthly calendar to determine the best time to get organized. Early birds may prefer rising thirty minutes earlier each morning whereas night owls tend to work best later in the evening. When are you willing to devote time to getting organized?

Once you have defined the best time to work, identify how you or others may be wasting your precious time and try to avoid those time wasters during your organizational phase. Typical time wasters include misuse of, or straying on, computer time, lengthy phone calls, inability to say "no" to people, frequently allowing interruptions, reading junk mail and watching too much television. In addition to avoiding time-wasting traps, perhaps hire someone else to do light house-keeping, baby-sitting, even laundry. Don't try to do it all. Use every available resource to squeeze spare moments from each day.

WAYS TO FIND TIME

According to Joe Peraino, Ph.D., in *Improving Productivity by Getting Organized*, "One minute of planning saves five minutes of execution." These methods will enable you to be five times more productive:

SET SIMPLE, OBTAINABLE GOALS

Start by setting realistic goals for yourself and determine how often you can devote time to getting organized. Are you realistically able to spend time once a day, week, or month? Make a deadline such as, "Within three months, my workspace will be organized." Make time for getting organized—and later remaining organized—a regular habit.

BEGIN BY PICKING A PROJECT

Looking at "the big picture" can be overwhelming. Select one project with which to begin. Your choices may include setting up your workspace with furniture, lighting and the essentials; sorting years of photos and negatives; or organizing non-consumable or consumable tools and supplies.

BREAK THE PROJECT INTO SMALLER PIECES

Even though you probably understand that the big picture includes organizing your entire scrapbook workspace, this book will help you achieve success by breaking the task into smaller, more manageable chunks. Isolate one area in which to begin. Collect everything in a large, open space where you can leave things out undisturbed for a couple days, if necessary.

ATTACK AND HAVE FUN

The good news is that this process can be fun once you begin to see the advantages of getting organized. Get the most out of your time by eliminating distractions. Turn off the phone. Organize in a quiet place out of the main runway of the home. By investing time, you will actually be able to gain time to scrapbook. One thing that you cannot recycle is wasted time, so get started today!

Finding time to get organized involves making a commitment to the task at hand. Use a calendar to plot out a general time-frame in which to get fully organized—even if it's just 30 minutes each day—and try hard to stick to it. Before you know it, you'll have more time for scrapbooking!

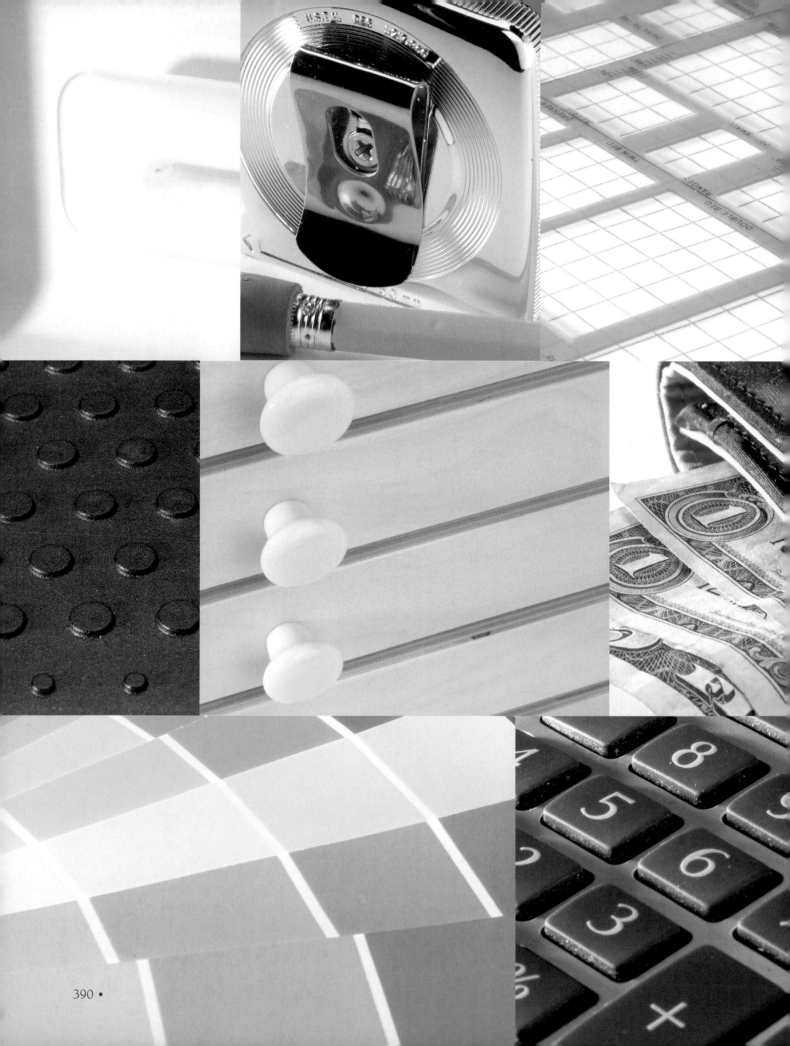

CREATING A PLAN OF ACTION

Every scrapbooker needs a place, even if it is a small one, to work on her scrapbooks at home. This highly rewarding hobby brings with it a lot of tools and supplies. Enough so that when they are unorganized and in disarray, it takes the fun out of the hobby. For a brief time, let us ignore the supplies and truly analyze the workspace itself. Start by taking stock of the physical space, furniture, shelving and lighting and if what you have is or is not working for you. Take notes as you work through the sections of this book. This will help you focus on the personalized needs of your workspace.

Scrapbook spaces can range from a scrapbook tote in the closet all the way up to a large artist-style studio with all the perks. Surprisingly, the mark of a productive scrapbook area is not purely a size consideration. Organization and efficiency are more important than square footage. Most scrapbookers have to carve out a space in their homes to call their own.

In this chapter, you'll learn how to start with an honest assessment of your space needs and continue working through every problem area in your scrapbook workspace. You will soon be well on your way to a functional workspace solution. Keep in mind that you want to start by changing small, but definite areas of your workspace. Whether you need to create a new space, declutter and consolidate the current one, or just rearrange the work area, the key is to do a little at a time.

Organization is more than just cleaning up again and again or putting things out of sight. It is creating a system that works for you in the long term. It takes time to create an effective workspace, but it is worthwhile. Tackle a section of your space or a chapter of this book at a time. Make informed decisions. Even if you are in chaos now, soon you will have a plan for your space and all your tools and supplies that suits your budget and the way in which you work.

Are You Ready for Change?

Something has got to give! New scrapbook supplies find their way home in bags that get piled behind doors. Papers are here and scissors are there. Adhesive cartridges are empty and in need of refilling. Inspirations, torn from magazines, overflow from their designated spot in an absolute symphony of disarray. And don't even look in the sticker box or the embellishments drawer! Unorganized scrapbook supplies can be overwhelming. You simply can't scrapbook when you spend all of your time pawing through bins, drawers and bags looking for stuff. If you're reading this book, and if your scrapbook workspace looks even remotely like the one shown below, you have obviously reached the point where you are ready for change.

Well-stocked chaos is the hallmark of an extremely busy scrapbook artist, as witnessed in this photo of Torrey Miller's (Thornton, Colorado; 2003 Memory Makers Master) scrapbook workspace. Even if you feel organized, there is always room for improvement. Assessing when and how you scrapbook—or rather, would like to scrapbook—can provide useful insights into effective changes that need to be made in your scrapbook workspace. For the record, Torrey's workspace has since been restored to its highly organized and efficient splendor.

Where to Start

What is driving you most crazy? What changes would you like to make in your scrapbook work-space? Start by taking stock of the problem. Get out a pen and paper and make a "problems" list. Dream a little. Is your work surface too small? Does your back ache after sitting in your chair for an hour? Do you have enough drawer space? Enough adequate storage units? Have you made the best use of your existing floor and wall space? Does the arrangement of your furnishings coincide with the way you work? Are you tired of feeling cramped? Is that cupboard door with a loose handle bugging you? Write it down! Order the problems from the most annoying to the least annoying, and tackle the most problematic areas first.

HOW DO YOU SCRAPBOOK?

What is the sequential order in which you create a scrapbook page? Do you work very methodically, taking lots of time to concept your pages and gather the appropriate materials before you begin? Do you skip the page concepting altogether and jump right in to page design, drawing materials from here and there on the fly? Do you work from right to left or left to right? Do you spend a lot of time switching from sitting to standing? Or moving your chair from side to side or forward and back-ward in order to gather scrapbook materials? Do you find that you go out into the living room to match papers to photos because the lighting is better there? Do you brush scraps to the floor and vacuum or sweep later or do you brush stuff into a trash bin as you go along? Recognize that even the tiniest of changes to your workspace may greatly enhance the time you get to spend on scrapbooking!

WHEN DO YOU SCRAPBOOK?

When do you tend to scrapbook the most? If you can't seem to find the time, ask yourself when you might best fit it in. Are you a loner who gets things done in the middle of the night? Or are you a busy mom who needs her sleep? Do you work outside the home and view your space as a refuge? Do you scrapbook only at crops or do you scrapbook in random 30-minute sessions at home? Do you like the whirl of activity in the family room? Or do you need a weekly "silent hour" or two alone to work? If you hate being alone, a large solitary studio will not be a fun place for you. If you can't think when the television is on, a workspace in the family room may be a bad choice. *When* you scrapbook will give you the largest clue to *where* you should scrapbook.

Rewards

If you feel intimidated by the task ahead of you, plan to reward yourself in small ways for the progress you will be making. Refrain from shopping for or buying any new scrapbook tools and supplies at this point; you'll only compound the matter of chaos. Instead, make a list of ten weeks of "treats" that you would like as small rewards, one after each week of dedicated orga-nizational work. Here are a few ideas:

- Light some scented candles for ambiance
- Take a well-deserved nap
- Rent a movie you've been longing to see
- Take someone special out for dessert
- Purchase that awesome set of earrings or shoes you've had your eyes on
- Take a leisurely walk with an old friend

- Call someone special long distance
- Get a soothing manicure; you may need it
- Load your CD player with your favorite recording artists and blare the music until everyone runs from the house
- Take a long, steamy bubble bath
- Go to bed two hours early, shut and lock the door, and read something really good

Sizing Up Your Workspace Options

Take stock of what you currently have available for workspace. Are you happy with it? If you are truly happy, you can probably skip to chapter 2. If not, examine your home for a nook or area where you might work happily. Think about your personal preferences. Ask yourself if you prefer to be in the room with the action or do you just want peace and a little music to help you create? Be practical! Many scrapbookers with large designated scrapbook rooms have found they miss the interaction with the family in the family room. Choose a space that will fit your hobby goals and your personal needs. Bring all of your scrapbook supplies into that area and keep them close to your work table. Being able to retrieve your items in seconds will speed the creation of your pages. You do not want to have to walk to another room for each item you use in this "getting organized" phase or when scrapbooking.

WHERE CAN I SQUEEZE IN A SCRAPBOOK AREA?

Look at all the rooms in your home. How are they being used? Is there a room that was originally designated for one activity but is no longer needed in that capacity? Formal dining rooms, lofts, billiard/pool rooms, dens, libraries, extra bedrooms, three-season porches, home gyms, "catch-all" rooms and basements are often underutilized spaces. Belongings and junk stored in these rooms can be moved elsewhere to create a few feet of space for your scrapbook area. Forget what the builders designed a room to be—make it what you need it to be!

WHAT KIND OF STORAGE WILL A NEW AREA REQUIRE?

Once you have selected a potential spot, look at the area as a professional organizer would. Do you have room for a full-fledged desk? Do you have room only to tuck in a folding card table or drop-down, hinged shelf-desk? Furnishings should be comfortable and inviting as well as functional. If a chair is too stiff to sit in for long periods of time, it is inappropriate for scrapbooking. A desk or plain pine door sitting atop two unfinished night stands can function well as a workspace if it is the right height for you. There should be a balance of actual desktop workspace and storage space. Too much of one without the other will leave you frustrated and unproductive.

Examine under-utilized areas of your home for potential spots to carve out a scrapbook workspace. MaryJo Regier (Memory Makers Senior Book Editor) considered converting a three-season porch to a workspace, but Colorado's winter cold dissuaded her. Her second and final option was to get rid of two older computers on an upstairs loft and claim it for scrapbooking. The loft is a shared space (see page 398) and a pathway between bedrooms; furniture that closes up to conceal its contents was an important factor. The ability to see over the railing to the front door, two different family rooms and the entire upstairs from the loft was also important for this busy mom of four.

Planning for Small Spaces

With scrapbooking, it's not the size of the space that counts most; it's what you do with it that really matters! When you look at a small space, close your eyes and then open them again. Ask yourself, "Where is the dead space?" Has every inch of space been used, including areas over doors and around windows? Put up shelves and labeled baskets (which keep the stacks and supplies out of sight) or put up cabinets with semi-clear, semi-frosted doors (which keep supplies in sight so you use them but not so visible that clutter is obvious). Vertical storage means wall shelving or cupboards or over-the-window shelving. Move things around. Put the knickknacks higher up and the tools closer to you. Take down a picture from the wall if it means you can add a cupboard with twelve more linear feet of shelving. If you have children underfoot while you scrapbook, adopt a technique that architects have used for centuries—get a drafting table and work standing up! This keeps the stuff out of reach from most little ones. During this early phase of getting organized, refrain from buying any supplies you will not use within two months! Let the stores dust and keep your paper until you need it. In the meantime, get out the tape measure and note the size of your actual floor and wall space. Then jot down things like how many linear feet of idea magazines and books you own or how big the paper cutter and the Xyron™ really are. Knowing the physical size of your tools and supplies will help you make informed storage purchases.

SOLUTIONS FOR SMALL WORKSPACES

Use these helpful hints to maximize useable space in smaller areas:

- Measure all available floor and wall space, as well as current furnishings. Create a floor plan (see pages 411-413) to help you visualize how furniture and shelving might fit together in a new configuration.

- Base the arrangement of furnishings on the sequential order in which you scrapbook to ensure that what you need most is within easy reach.

- Go vertical with shelving.

- Look for "recovered space" like that under the bed or in closets (see pages 396-397). Store magazines in a window seat or bench shelving.

- Surround windows with shelving and use the window ledge for storage.

- Make decor pull double duty as storage. Measure your supplies so you know what will fit where. Like an artist on a small canvas, make every decorative stroke count!

- Use your corners. Most rooms have four of them. Use triangular storage units to make the most of your corners.

- Use color. Light colors make rooms look larger and dark colors make them look cozier and smaller (see page 402-403).

- Buy only what you need.

- Purge and let go—often! Clean out drawers, files and closets as often as possible. Keep only the best; let go of the rest.

Rule one in small spaces is to go vertical, as Shawna Rendon (Memory Makers Magazine's Idea Editor) has done in her workspace using modular, compartmentalized shelving that extends almost to the ceiling.

To gain a few needed inches of floor space, Jodi Amidei (Craft Editor for Memory Makers Books) cleverly removed her closet doors to accommodate the rolling carts that now fit comfortably in the closet.

Recovering Space From Other Places

Don't forget those under-used rooms or storage areas! Make every inch of your home count so that you have room for your hobby. Shuffling out-of-season items to under-used spaces may free up part of a room elsewhere in the house. Even freeing up a few square feet of space in an unused area of the attic could mean that you now have room to store clutter that had been filling the spare bedroom. Keep an eye out for extra space in every room. Space under stairways can be organized to fit rolling short stack bookcases or shelving. Attics and garages or outbuildings can often be revamped and cleared to make more storage spaces. Some attics and garages have even proven to be airy scrapbooking nooks themselves. Landings, bay window seats, and even large closets can be transformed into places for a scrapbook desk! New closets can be carved out of existing walls with a little elbow grease and carpentry skills. Glean space between existing shelves; excess room between shelves wastes space and decreases the shelves' storage capacity. Rolling under-bed boxes can store multitudes of supplies. Putting the bed up on bedrisers will also give you additional room under the bed. Folding tables can fit behind a headboard or under the bed. Hang pocketed bags behind doors for small tools and punches. No room in the room? Cleaning out a walk-in closet could grant just the space needed for a small desk and a few plastic drawer carts. Look around with a discerning eye. There is space to be had!

Cathy Calvetti's (Eagle River, Wisconsin) scrapbook workspace was formerly an attic in her 1930s saltbox-style home. The sloped ceiling is the perfect height for storing bookcases and shelving beneath it.

When Diane Eppestein (St. Louis, Missouri) and her husband converted a bedroom into a home office, she "staked claim" on the closet for her scrapbook workspace. The closet itself is 90" wide and 24" deep, but the door opening is just 47" wide, leaving about 20" on each side of the bi-fold doors that can be difficult to access. A clever recovery solution for those extra 20" was narrow shelving to store photos, negatives, slides and seldom-used tools. To accommodate the narrow doorway, a drafting table on wheels can be rolled out when access to the shelving is needed. A magnetic board on the back wall holds tools in magnetic baskets as well as photos and pages. Convertible hanging file folders adorn the doors for easy paper access. Diane relies on an Ott-Lite for quality lighting in her small, recovered workspace.

Gabrielle Mader (Whittier, California) recovered two-thirds of the garage from her husband's workspace to call her own. Her husband built her scrapbook workspace from scraps, with all of the comforts of home. The room includes heating and air conditioning, an inlaid light box, a TV, a stereo and a refrigerator. Corkboard surrounds the room where her young daughters often join her to scrapbook. The garage-turned-scrapbook-workspace overlooks the backyard, where Gabrielle can keep an eye on her girls when they're outdoors. Her husband's finishing touch is the under-counter fishing pole "rod" that holds spools of ribbon for scrapbooking and gift wrapping.

Shared or Common Spaces

When your workspace is in the dining room, bedroom, family room or hallway closet, you need to get creative. Think invisible! Invisible means hiding things in baskets, under ottomans, and behind curtains in this shared or public space. Hide what you can from sight for a crisp clean decor. Drawer unit carts and file cabinets that roll away into closets or under desks when not in use are a good bet. Make sure the casters are large and can handle a lot of weight; paper, idea books, punches and rubber stamps are heavy. Armoires are also a popular choice for hiding supplies away from sight. Make empty containers do double duty. Box collections, tins, hat boxes, baskets, jars and linen chests can all be put to work. Storage containers can look like ordinary home decor but *you* will know the truth. Get twice the functionality out of furnishings you already own. A dining table can be your desk. A window seat can be your cozy seating if you add a collapsible card table when needed. Half-empty entertainment centers can store baskets of supplies.

Shared spaces often mean someone will be keeping you company while you work. Keep her comfort in mind. If she likes to scrapbook, make sure there is table space for her and a comfortable extra chair. Keeping a snack or two on hand is nice as long as things don't get messy. A favorite toy and nice floor mat might be a nice addition if your scrapbooking buddy is a child. Scrapbooking harmony in shared spaces might be easier than you think!

SAFETY CONSIDERATIONS

Keep safety considerations in mind when moving your scrapbook supplies into a shared space. Keep potentially harmful items—such as adhesive remover, embossing powders, preservation sprays, stamp cleaners, glitter and sharp tools—out of reach of small children. Secure wire racks and bookcases to the walls. Use ventilation when working with heat embossing and sprays. Heat guns and corded tools should be unplugged and put away on upper shelving after each use. Heavy tools like paper trimmers and die-cut machines need to be away from countertop edges so they don't get pulled down by accident. Look at your space and tools just as you would a garage, workshop or kitchen. Keep it safe, particularly where children are concerned.

DISGUISING YOUR SCRAPBOOK WORKSPACE

Do you want to disguise your scrapbooking space? Curtained shelving and roll-top units disguise the mess for you. They also keep busy little hands off your work between sessions. Floor screens or wall dividers can help set room boundaries and hide clutter at the same time. Try to get file cabinets and shelving in the same wood tones as other furnishings in the room. For example, if you scrap in your dining room, and your dining table is cherry, go for a cherry finish on the paper or tool drawer units. Maintaining the same tones in wood finish lessens the visual impact of your "work" furniture in a "non-work" room.

Tracy Wynn's (Truro, Nova Scotia, Canada) closet scrapbook workspace shares common ground with her home's spare bedroom/computer office—a fairly common scenario. To conceal her workspace from the rest of the multi-function room, Tracy simply draws the curtains closed.

Christy Baker's (Pleasant Hill, Missouri) multipurpose basement playroom/scrapbook workspace live together harmoniously thanks to Christy's great organizational skills for both her "toys" as well as her children's. Christy didn't have to spend a lot to get organized; much of her furniture and shelving was either salvaged from trash, recycled from other areas of the house or handmade by her husband. And with such a colorful and well-stocked play area, the kids have no need to get into Christy's scrapbook supplies!

Jenna Beegle's (Woodstock, Georgia) kitchen scrapbook nook sits at one end of the busiest room in the home. The kitchen's dining area was converted to functional workspace with kitchen cabinets and countertop to match her existing fixtures. Jenna's chair is on the other side of the countertop. Shelving was built into the window seat to increase storage space.

Three storage products that work great in shared spaces are Lifetime's® Personal Table that folds, Charming Ideas' clip-on Table-Pal™ that rolls up and Jokari's 24-pocket Scrap'N Stor™ over-the-door system.

Office-type hutches that close after you're done scrapbooking are a fine solution for scrapbooking in shared spaces. Simply open the doors, pull up a chair and you're ready to scrapbook. Shown are For Keeps Sake's Creation Station and two rolling companion KeepsSake Carts. Collectors Cabinets also produces a line of pine and oak cabinetry that blends well with other furniture in shared spaces.

Workspace Essentials

Scrapbookers vary in what they feel are the absolute essentials for an effective workspace. However, some basics seem to be universal. You can adapt this list as you see fit. Make sure your work area has what you need on hand, in good supply and that supplies and tools are within arm's reach if possible.

Once you know what the basic workspace essentials are, evaluate the furnishings that you own. Will they provide you with the space you need to work? Is there room for growth? Will you be comfortable sitting for long periods of time? Is the lighting adequate? Will you have enough shelving? Answering these and other questions will help you make wise decisions when determining if you need to purchase additional furnishings to make the space work for you. Use the ideas that follow as a starting point for creating a comfortable workspace with room for growth.

A productive scrapbook workspace features essential basics like those shown here: Sturdi-Craft modular cabinets, drawer units, pegboard and ample work surface and shelving; Daylight's Scrapbook Lamp™; The Board Dudes' combination cork/magnetic bulletin board; Ergonomic Services' ergonomically correct chair and Rubbermaid's trash can.

DESKTOP

Tabletop or desk workspace surface should measure at least three square feet but the bigger the better. Keep in mind that you can store seldom-used tools such as large paper trimmers, adhesive application machines and die-cut machines on separate countertops or sturdy tables elsewhere. Get in the mindset that your desk should stay clear except for the page you are currently working on. The surface should be smooth and easy to wipe clean. If possible, leave room for a friend to work beside or across from you. Sometimes it is nice to crop with a buddy.

FILING

You will need some sort of filing system. A file cabinet, a desk drawer, or a portable accordion file or rolling cart will all store idea sheets, poems and quotes, receipts, sticker sheets, page additions and other 8½ x 11" paperwork in file folders.

LIGHT

Let there be light, and plenty of it! Good lighting can increase your productivity from 10 to 40 percent and can decrease neck strain, mistakes and headaches. Good lighting allows you to accurately see photo colors and select papers and page accents that will coordinate beautifully. Light also affects your mood. You will need good light not only in the daytime but at night, too. Make sure the lighting you have is clear, natural light. Several light manufacturers make this kind of bulb, which is readily available at hobby and discount stores. Good light is especially important in northern climates, in the evening hours or if you have seasonal affective disorder. Everyday lamps and fixtures are fine—just make sure they have the right kind of bulbs in them. Ideally, your work light should come from above your shoulders or from the side onto your work surface. Avoid glare by changing the angle of the light or decreasing the wattage of the bulb. Counteract direct sunlight that causes glare with sheer curtains or semi-sheer blinds.

POWER

Where are the power outlets? Where is the phone? Orient your workspace around some of these important elements. Cords should not run across walking paths. Generally, it is good to have at least one outlet within five feet of your space. Electricity should be accessible for both accent room lighting and your tools. Easy access to other electronics, such as a computer or radio, are also important considerations.

SEATING

Most scrapbookers sit while they work. Get a good chair that is right for you. An adjustable chair is best so that you can change it to suit your height. This will help you avoid neck strain and backache. Cushions are nice; swivels are optional. If your room is carpeted and you want to use a rolling chair, consider getting a plastic office floor mat like those used in office settings. Test drive a chair in the store before you buy it. Make yours as comfortable as possible.

SHELVING

Give every tool its own place. Use shelving or space for paper, books, tools, and other supplies. Shelving comes in all shapes and sizes, from wood bookcases to wire cubes. Make sure you have the size and space you need and that the shelves will bear the weight and suit the dimensions of your intended stock items. Measure first, buy or build second.

TRASH CAN

Not only does scrapbooking come with a lot of tools and supplies, it tends to create a lot of refuse. Keep your work area clean by having a trash can or trash bags handy.

VENTILATION

Safety is of primary importance. Ventilation and heat are also important aspects to consider. Fumes and excessive heat are not good for you or your photos and paper.

WALL SPACE

Posting notes, ideas, and small supplies up on a bulletin board or pegboard in front of you will save table space and keep clutter off the work surface. Invest in a bulletin board or pegboard if you have space for it.

Quality, natural lighting provides true color rendition when matching photo colors to those in paper, pre-made page accents, embellishments and colorants. It's also easier on the eyes when scrapbooking for an extended period of time. Some favored scrapbook lamps include (left to right): Verilux's HappyEyes™Floor and Desk Lamps, Daylight's Compact Lamp and Ott-Lite® Technology's TrueColor™ FlexArm Plus Lamp. Be sure to check out these manufacturer Web sites as models and styles differ widely to suit your personal workspace needs.

Room Colors for Enhanced Creativity

If you are fortunate enough to have an entire room dedicated to scrapbooking, one of the most fun aspects of getting organized can be selecting the color for your walls. Two key points to consider when deciding the color of your workspace are your personality and the work that you'll be doing in the room.

Choosing a color sounds simple enough, but many people don't realize the impact the color of a room can have on the work that's done there. So when poring over the endless palette of paint chips and color swatches at your local paint store, keep in mind that the primary color you select could possibly act as a "creative enhancer" for your workspace. Whichever colors you choose to personalize your workspace, remember that it's *your* space and should reflect your personality while inspiring you to be creative.

WHITE

White lends itself to, and blends with, the countless moods and colors used in scrapbooking. Don't fret about white being dull or lifeless. Rather, it can be fresh and crisp one moment and pure and soft the next. White represents freshness and a clean slate. A white background offers no distractions to the project at hand. This "non-color" makes walls appear to recede, giving the illusion of a larger room. With white as a base color, you'll be able to change accent colors as often as you like.

COLOR INSPIRATION

Walk through your home, spending some time in each room—particularly in your favorite places. Observe your feelings, then notice the colors around you. You'll find that certain colors inspire specific emotions. Check out some books on using color in the home to better understand the energy created by different colors. With these insights you're ready to choose the colors to accent your workspace while staying true to your personality. Here's more color for thought:

The white walls of Kimberly Ling's (Fresno, California) scrapbook room make her tools, supplies, mementos and trinkets "pop" from their perches on the walls for quick visibility and access. Note Kimberly's interesting use of her desk's keyboard tray; she uses it to store punches!

COOL COLORS

A splash of blue soothes and relaxes with its optimism. Pale and dusty blues appear delicate, while cobalt, turquoise and aquamarine can bring a room electric vitality. Some blues, however, can give a room a chilly effect. Green, nature's neutral, forms a refreshing, almost spiritual backdrop for a scrapbook workspace. Easy-going green provides a quick pick-me-up in many of its countless shades. Purple infuses sporty playfulness in its various shades and hues.

Katie Schwetz's (St. Louis, Missouri) cool (in many ways!) blue and green scrapbook workspace sings with invigorating expectancy. Even the painted pegboard seems alive and ready to help!

WARM COLORS

Flashy and dramatic red lends passion, energy and vitality to a workspace. Darker reds emit timeless elegance, while pale pinks add a touch of gentle femininity. Bright reds and hot pinks can be overpowering; use in small doses. Shades of orange can bring a warm robustness and excitement to the workspace, while peach provides a sense of peacefulness. The optimistic attitude of yellow raises the spirits and brings a sense of warmth and joy to help you stay focused.

Debby Schuh's (Williamsville, New York) bright, rose-red walls give her workspace spirit and spunk while Gina Will's (Arlington Heights, Illinois) yellow workspace glows with cozy, welcoming ambiance.

The Ergonomic Workspace

We've all heard of tennis elbow, but what about cropper's elbow? Or cropper's neck, back, hands and eyes, for that matter. If you spend even a few hours at a time cropping, you've no doubt endured crop-related pain. That pain can slow you down, or worse, develop into a chronic injury.

Croppers are susceptible to several injuries that can affect the hands, wrists and back. Incorrect posture and repetitive and forceful tasks cause tendons, muscles and nerve tissue excessive wear and tear.

Croppers typically practice risky postures while crafting: hunched shoulders; bent/flexed wrists; repetitive hand, arm and shoulder motions; long reaches for materials; long periods of sitting and on nonadjustable chairs; working with the neck bent and using pinched grips on pens, pencils and cutting tools.

The good news is that simple changes in your posture and workspace or workstation setup will make noticeable differences, says Brian Foxhoven, certified ergonomic evaluator and owner of Ergonomic Services, Inc.

When Foxhoven evaluates a workstation, he identifies factors that put people at risk of injury and then recommends the proper adjustments. He pointed out the following factors and suggested changes after observing and evaluating scrapbookers at work.

This is an ergonomically correct cropper. Take note of the following:
1. *The lumbar area, or lower back, is supported, and the cropper exhibits neutral back, shoulder and neck posture.*
2. *The crop station is at forearm level to keep wrists straight and neutral.*
3. *The hips are slightly higher than the knees.*
4. *The knees are bent at a 90-degree angle.*
5. *Feet are flat and a footrest is utilized to compensate for short stature.*
6. *Task lighting exists to reduce eyestrain.*

POSTURE

Posture-related changes will almost instantly make your body feel better, Foxhoven says. "Ergonomics is fitting the workstation to the body, so evaluating posture is key," he says. "The workstation or workspace setup will be different for everyone."

Height and weight determine the correct workstation setup. Guidelines for correct crop-station posture are as follows: The back should be straight with a slight, supported curve in the lumbar, or lower back, region. The neck and wrists are straight. Shoulders are relaxed. Hips are parallel to the floor, and knees are bent at a 90-degree angle. Feet rest flat. The work surface sits more or less at forearm height. All furniture is big or small enough to suit the individual's stature.

REPETITION

Repetition is the hardest risk factor to control when constant cutting, craft-knife work and trimming need to be done. It can increase strain and pressure on the joints, tendons, blood vessels and nerves. Repetitive movements can lead to injuries like Carpal Tunnel Syndrome, which causes tingling, numbness and weakness in the wrists. The most effective way to reduce repetition is to vary your tasks and to take breaks, Foxhoven says. Set an egg timer to remind yourself to switch jobs, or better yet, take frequent breaks—10 minutes each hour.

Breaks also increase productivity. Use precut products, die-cut titles or torn-paper accents to reduce the amount of cutting and trimming.

FORCE

Narrow tools, like a craft knife, and slick work surfaces cause one to naturally increase force. Force tightens muscles that then decrease the blood flow to tissue, causing lactic acid buildup.

If your knuckles turn white when you cut with your craft knife, something needs to change. Alter your grip or try using rubber grips on your knives, pens and pencils to reduce finger force. The Pencil Grip's grips (shown below) increase a narrow tool's surface area, making it easier to hold.

Several companies create products with an ergonomic edge to help reduce force (see below). The McGill Strongarm is a press that reduces the amount of force necessary to activate a punch, thereby enabling children and arthritics to punch easier.

The Quickutz Personal Die-Cutting System acts like a desk press. By resting the hand tool in a cradle, scrapbookers use their weight to precision-cut letters and shapes.

You can also reduce force by performing tasks such as punching and stamping while standing to use stronger muscle groups.

Ergonomic scrapbooking products

1. Tutto Bag Tylenol and the Arthritis Foundation bestowed a design award on this bag for being back-friendly. It's easy to pull and maneuver, and it's versatile and durable.

2. Footrest Shorter croppers can keep their feet flat with a footrest, like this one from McGill, Inc.

3. Pencil/knife grips Grips increase the contact area on narrow tools, like pens and craft knives. These are from The Pencil Grip.

4. Lumbar pillow Strap this lumbar pillow to a chair to support the lower back. Check back stores and the Internet for one that suits you.

5. Daylight Task Light Proper light reduces eyest rain and promotes good posture. It also eliminates glare and shadows.

6. Strongarm Punch The Strongarm from McGill reduces the amount of force needed to punch.

7. Fiskars scissors Soft Touch scissors are spring-loaded to ease the force used for repetitive cutting action.

8. QuicKutz To operate this personal die-cutting system, place the tool into the desk cradle and use body weight to precision-cut letters and shapes.

DESIGNING THE ERGONOMIC WORKSPACE

Your scrapbook workspace should be designed to fit your body in its most neutral position. A neutral position exists at the halfway point in a joint's range of motion. Use the following tips to adjust your workstation to fit you.

The chair is the best tool for addressing posture, so it's worth it to invest in a quality chair. Look for a chair with adjustable height (a pneumatic lift) and adjustable back tilt. A few dollars today translates into pennies for a lifetime of proper sitting.

The chair's seat pan should be shallow or deep enough to fit your body. When sitting back, two or three fingers should fit between the back of the knee and the edge of the seat. Also, get a chair without arm rests. Arm rests hinder cropping and promote unnatural arm posture, causing stress on the shoulders.

When seated at the workstation, pull the chair as close to the table as possible to keep the lumbar region supported. If you are going to a crop and cannot bring your chair, try a lumbar-support pillow that straps onto the back of the chair, or a rolled-up towel.

While maintaining the natural curve of the spine, sit at a slight forward angle, Foxhoven advises. You can sit on a pillow to increase chair height or use a seat wedge pillow that also promotes the slightly forward posture recommended for scrapbooking.

A secondary risk factor related to posture is contact stress. Contact stress occurs when an object presses into the body, cutting off circulation and causing discomfort. Shorter legs may go numb because the seat edge inflicts contact stress on dangling legs. A footrest will keep feet flat. McGill makes a heated footrest. Telephone books can also serve the same purpose.

Using a task light instead of overhead light also promotes good posture by reducing eyestrain. Overhead light, or indirect light, either hits the back of the head and casts shadows over your work or bounces off the work surface and causes a glare. A task light provides direct light over your work, reducing eyestrain and the need to hunch over in order to see your work. Beware of bright, natural light from windows. This also causes glare.

If possible, work on an angle to reduce glare. Portable, angled desk easels that rest on top of your crop table raise work a few inches, making it easier to keep your neck and shoulders straight. You can set the desk easel aside if a certain task requires a horizontal surface.

Redesign tasks to suit your neutral posture. For example, if trimming with a craft knife, position the paper so you are cutting toward your body with your wrist straight, instead of cutting in the direction across your body with a bent wrist. The same can apply when using a paper trimmer.

Use these practical solutions to improve your posture and to cut back on repetitive movements and the use of force. By reducing the risk factors, you increase your productivity, which leads to another solution: More pages in less time!

Keep supplies around you in a semicircle—within the Easy Reach Zone. Supplies used most frequently should be the closest to you; supplies seldom used should be farthest. Organize tools and supplies from left to right, or right to left, in the order in which you use them.

Top ten tips for healthier scrapbooking

1. Vary tasks and take breaks to increase productivity. Set a timer to remind you to take short breaks.

2. Incorporate stretches and exercises into your crops. Visit ctdnews.com/suffer/CTDprevent.html for a list of easy and effective exercises. Build up muscle groups that feel the effects of scrapbooking, like the shoulders and hands.

3. Use tools that decrease force whenever possible.

4. Support the lower back with a lumbar pillow or rolled-up towel.

5. Use a footrest or phone book to help keep feet flat.

6. Increase task lighting to alleviate eyestrain.

7. Use different workstations for different tasks. Use sitting stations for precise work, like beading, and standing stations for force-intensive work, like punching or stamping, to permit more efficient use of the upper body.

8. Keep often-used tools and supplies within the "swing space," or within the Easy Reach Zone (see above illustration).

9. Orient your work to suit you whenever possible. Redesign the task to keep your body in a neutral position.

10. Work at forearm level to keep arms, neck and shoulders relaxed and wrists straight and neutral.

Budget Considerations

Even if you're on a tight budget, you already have four assets to help you acquire the space you need and the storage solutions you crave. Don't underestimate the following resources.

ATTITUDE

If you're willing to change, you must be willing to work. The first resource you need is attitude, which will drive how successful your organizational efforts turn out to be. Don't delay! Make time for this project and get started. Ensure organizational success with these tips:

- Get ready to change what is needed—inside and out.

- Make a plan. This book will give you the tools you need to complete the task and do it right. Purchase items you need so your budget doesn't take a big hit all at once.

- Be realistic. Perfection is not the goal. Gaining an efficient workspace and a method of organization that works for you is the goal. Just because you can't afford $3,000 built-in shelves doesn't mean you can't start getting organized. Begin with small things and persevere. Bit by bit it will all get done.

- Do your homework. Assess your budget. What funds, if any, are available for this project? Use the convenient products and ideas featured in this book as a starting point and check on their prices. You'll find the companies that manufacture these products listed in the Source Guide at the back of this book.

- Keep your system going. For most, this means simply putting things back in their places. Doing a little every day goes a long way to feeling organized. Maintaining the system you set up is more important than unlimited budgets or highly specialized containers.

BUDGET

Is the sky the limit? Probably not. But do take stock of your organization project budget and the monetary resources available. What changes can you truly afford to make? What solutions can be saved for someday in the future? Can you use a secondhand desk until the next pay raise? Will a set of bookcases from the basement do in the short term? Make a list of what work items you truly need right now and what can wait (see page 28). Consider nice-looking modular furniture or shelving to which you can add units over time. Search out easy-to-construct shelving plans online or in simple woodworking books. A little elbow grease goes a long way toward creating a space you will use and love.

Truly assess your budget and the monetary resources you might have as well as determine what furniture and storage containers you have and those you need for a logical approach to getting organized without "losing your shirt."

If you are on a budget, plan your expenditures. Create a budget work sheet or use the one on the following page, then do your homework and save. A few dollars set aside a week will soon add up to buy your larger items. There are still plenty of ways to organize your space using what you have on hand. Do-it-yourself options abound for workspaces. Don't be put off by the high cost of special furnishings or organizational solutions. Simply ask yourself whether you have a container that will fit certain supplies. If the answer is yes, go get it and start using it now. You can always make a list of items you want to buy later on. Don't let tight finances stop you from finding solutions—even if they are short-term solutions.

UNDERUTILIZED FURNISHINGS

You may already own home furnishings that will work in your new space. Most families have an extra dresser, table and chair in storage somewhere just waiting to be called into use again. Check attics, garages, basements and each room in the home for little-used items that can be used in your scrapbook workspace. Ask friends and family to see if they have something useful. A few common furnishings "found" around the house might include bookcases, bulletin boards, chairs, desks, file cabinets, lamps, shelving and tables. See pages 88-89 for "found" storage containers.

PEOPLE

Take stock of the human resources around you. Can you put these resources to work for you? Do you have time to do the organization yourself or would you gladly pay someone to plan and organize your space? Does your dad work in a cabinet shop? Is your cousin a closet organizer? Is your spouse a great woodworker? Maybe your mom is available to baby-sit weekly, freeing you up to tackle organizational chores. Ask them to help you or trade their expertise for some of your own. Perhaps someone you know would gladly make you a shelf unit in exchange for getting his or her photos organized chronologically. It doesn't hurt to ask!

Scrapbook Workspace Budget Considerations

This work sheet can help you create and track a workspace-improvement budget. Fill in the blanks as you do your planning and research. If estimated costs are higher than actual costs on certain items, consider saving these purchases for a later date as more funds become available.

BEGINNING DATE		
ENDING DATE		
PERSONAL BUDGET		
WORKSPACE NEEDS	**ESTIMATED COST**	**ACTUAL COST**
DESK		
CHAIR		
LIGHT		
BOOKCASE		
SHELVING		
TOTALS		

Paring Down

By now, you have analyzed your workspace options. You have a good idea of what workspace essentials involve: a large work surface, quality lighting, a comfortable chair, wall and shelf space, and filing space. You've examined potential room colors for enhanced creativity and understand what constitutes an "ergonomically safe" workspace. You have even worked out any budget considerations. With all of this "homework" completed, now is the time to pare down any plans that may prove too costly including new furniture and large-item storage container purchases. Determine the first changes you will make to your physical workspace. The work sheet on the following page will help you with this phase of getting organized.

Begin by reviewing your Budget Consideration work sheet. Use a critical decision-making process before acquiring any new furnishings. Collect magazine and Internet photos of furniture or storage items that you like and note their precise dimensions. The worst thing you can do is to buy something that will not fit your budget, your workspace or your belongings.

Decide what additional pieces and changes you need to make in order to function better in your scrapbook workspace. The general storage rule of thumb is that you usually need at least twice as much storage space as you believe.

There are a number of things you can do to pare down your workspace plans if they seem too far-fetched. Empty and clean newly acquired used furniture, shelving and file cabinets. Even if you don't like the look of these items, they can serve their purpose in the interim. Put off building those cabinets for now and give yourself time to save money for them. Consider purchasing modular furniture and storage units that you can add to over the course of time.

Remember to keep your focus on organization, not acquisition. Make only those necessary furnishings purchases that will help you achieve your goal. All in good time, your dream space will emerge.

ScrapNCube's flexible furniture, including its line of Cubit! modular units, can be configured in a myriad of ways. The units can be purchased all at once or a little at a time as your budget allows and your supplies grow.

Display Dynamic's modular furniture components can also be combined in various configurations as budgets allow. Shown are the company's Scrapbook Station (above) and Mobile File with Slide-Out Tray (right).

Developing a Step-by-Step Plan of Action

Based on what you have learned in the previous pages, analyze and evaluate your existing workspace situation and belongings to discover what you need in order to make immediate progress in getting organized. These questions will help you strategize and create a specific plan of action.

1. Do you like the furniture you have and why?	7. What kind of furniture would you like to add?
2. What kind of space do you have to work with?	8. What changes would you like to make?
3. What does your furniture contribute to the way you scrapbook?	9. Do you want to have your computer right on your scrapbook workspace?
4. Do you have adequate shelving or room to add shelving?	10. If there's not enough room, where else might you put the computer so it's still handy?
5. What furniture do you want to keep?	11. What changes can you afford to make?
6. How would you describe the quality of your workspace lighting?	12. What changes do you plan for the future?

How to Create a Floor Plan

Whether you have a shared space or an entire room devoted to scrapbooking, it can be beneficial to create a floor plan (or drawing) early in your organizational project. A floor plan helps you visualize a room before you start moving furniture around. Desks and cabinets can be heavy, so before you lift and move them, it's nice to know ahead of time their best placement.

A floor plan also contains essential facts that will prove useful on shopping trips to scrapbook, craft and furniture stores. With a floor plan and a tape measure, you will be able to measure and select new furnishings and storage vessels to ensure they will fit into your workspace scheme.

Floor plans are so useful that learning how to draw them is among the first things taught in many interior design classes. Drawings of your scrapbook workspace needn't be beautiful and artistic renderings; simple sketches—drawn to scale—will do fine. Move paper cutouts that represent your furnishings around on a scaled drawing of your workspace. It's fun, easy and quite informative!

SKETCH

Begin by sketching a rough drawing of your scrapbook workspace's floor or wall dimensions. You needn't worry about scale yet; simply draw a representation and rough sketch of the room. Show the approximate shape and size of the space, together with any connecting doors, closets, hallways, or permanent fixtures, such as built-in bookcases or shelving.

MEASURE

Using a steel tape measure, begin at one corner of the room or space and measure the distance to the opposite corner. Record that measurement on your rough sketch. Continue measuring each wall of the workspace and recording measurements. Measure twice and record once for accuracy. If your tape measure slips or moves, ask a spouse, child or friend to help, or use masking tape to hold the tape measure securely in place.

Next, measure any connecting doors, hallways, or permanent fixtures, such as built-in bookcases or shelving, as well as the height beneath windows if these spaces will be used for storage or furniture. Measure closet dimensions if you plan on outfitting a closet for storage.

SCALE

Now transfer your workspace or room to ½" scale using quad-ruled (4 squares equal one-half inch, which equals one foot of actual space) graph paper, a pencil or pen and a clear plastic graphing ruler. Some interior designers draw floor plans in ¼" scale (¼" on paper equals one foot of actual space) and there are office and home furnishings templates available in ¼" scale if you prefer working in this smaller size. At ½" scale size, you can fit most rooms on a single sheet of graph paper with enough room in the margins to make notations. This latter scale size is easier to work with if you've never created a floor plan because the drawings are larger.

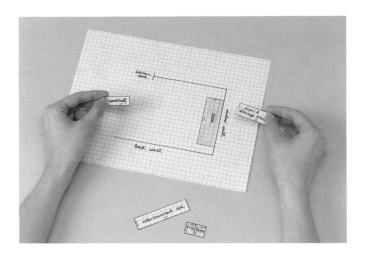

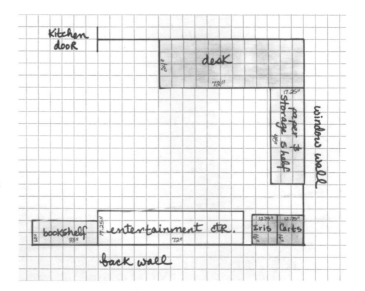

By moving representational paper cutouts of furniture around on a scaled-down drawing of your scrapbook workspace, you will get a good visual idea of which arrangements are worth trying (top). When you shuffle the paper patterns around until you feel comfortable with the organization of the furnishings, a working blueprint develops for the workspace (center). The blueprint plan then springs to life as you arrange your furniture and shelving according to your floor plan (bottom). Scrapbook workspace photo courtesy of Cori Dahmen (Portland, Oregon).

Use the graphing ruler to create straight lines on the graph paper, to help maintain 90-degree angle corners and to draw accurate line length. Keep in mind that two grid boxes on the quad-ruled graph paper represent one foot of actual space.

It can be difficult to mark inches or anything less than one foot on your scale drawing. For these, you will have to mark portions of grid boxes on the graphing paper, perhaps even "eye-balling" it before marking. For example, at ½" scale, two inches would be one-third of a grid box. Strive for accuracy whenever possible to ensure that the furnishings you have and those you intend to purchase will actually fit in your workspace.

Record any connecting doors, hallways, or permanent fixtures, such as built-in bookcases or shelving, as well as the height beneath windows if you plan to use the space for storage or furniture. Transfer closet dimensions if you plan on outfitting a closet for storage as well.

FURNISHINGS

Use a tape measure to measure the width of any furniture or storage units that will go along the walls of your workspace. In your measurements, allow for room between units or for walkways if needed. In addition, measure the height of any furniture or storage units that will go beneath windows and the depth of any storage units that you may be placing in a closet. Before you make any new storage unit purchases, make a trip to the store to get their measurements.

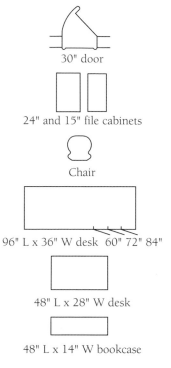

Furniture & floor plan shapes

30" door

24" and 15" file cabinets

Chair

96" L x 36" W desk 60" 72" 84"

48" L x 28" W desk

48" L x 14" W bookcase

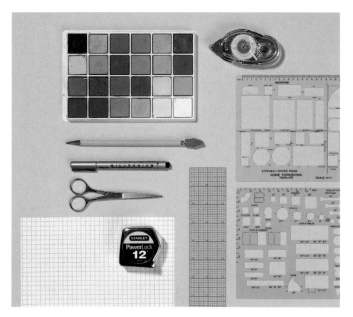

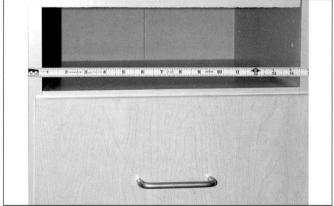

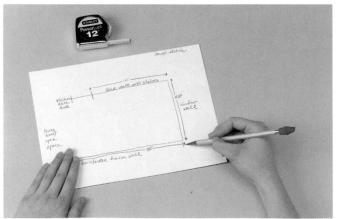

To create a floor plan, you'll need the following tools (above): quad-ruled (4 squares = 1") graph paper, a pencil, an eraser, a clear graphing ruler and a tape measure. Use the key above to freehand draw furniture and room shapes or use office and home furnishings templates (C-Thru Ruler Company) to create shapes for placement on your floor plan. Use a tape measure to measure the width and depth of furniture (above right) as well as the physical floor space of your area. Use the scale of ½" equals 1' of actual size to create the floor plan. Before making a scaled-down floor plan, sketch a rough drawing (right) of the room's shape, jotting down the measurements of any walls, windows and doors that will be part of your workspace.

Use additional graph paper to create the paper cutouts representative of the furniture and storage containers you intend to keep in your scrapbook workspace, transferring your measurements as accurately as possible to the grids on the graph paper. Trace around the shapes in black pen and color with chalk if desired. Use scissors to cut out the paper shapes of your mock furniture.

CREATE THE FLOOR PLAN

Now for the fun part! Move the paper cutouts around against the walls of your paper floor plan. Think about how you scrapbook as it applies to the intended use of the furniture and storage units, and arrange the items accordingly. Leave plenty of room for pathways, moving your chair side to side or forward and back, opening file drawers and closet doors, etc.

Take your time. And don't be discouraged if you don't get it "just right" on the first attempt. When you discover the perfect arrangement, you'll know it.

When you're happy with a final arrangement, use a removable adhesive to glue the paper cutouts in place on the floor plan. That way, if you discover some inaccurate measuring or something just doesn't fit like you had hoped, you can move the shapes around on the floor plan again.

Put your plan into action by physically moving the furniture and storage units you have on hand into the places noted on the floor plan. Then take your floor plan and a tape measure shopping with you to buy new furniture or storage units.

With a plan like this, you're sure to create a functional and effective workspace with minimal backache and budget pain!

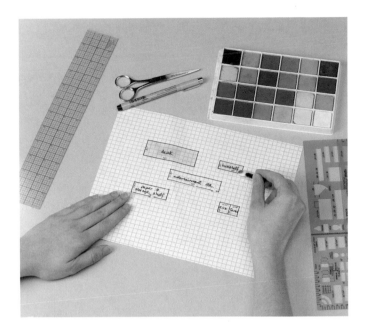

Again, using the scale of ½" to equal 1' of actual size, use a pen and graphing ruler to freehand draw (or use the furnishings templates to trace at ¼" scale) the paper pattern cutouts to represent your furnishings. These paper patterns don't have to be precise, but getting them as close to accurate as possible will ensure that your furnishings actually fit into your workspace in the way that you envision them. Taking accurate measurements will help achieve this goal.

Recommended spacing

Use the following spacing guidelines to help you create a functional floor plan that maximizes your space yet still gives you room to move about as freely as possible:

Foot-traffic walkways

36" in busy, shared spaces; 24" to 30" in private or seldom-used spaces

Chair pull-back and side-to-side space

About 36" to 40"; 42" if the space is also a foot-traffic walkway

In front of desks

36" for standing room while opening drawers; 42" to 60" for pulling back chair

Between desk, cabinets, bookshelves

These items can butt up against each other or you can leave room to squeeze bins, racks or drawer units between them

In front of filing cabinets

Allow enough room for drawers to extend fully

In front of closets and bookshelves

36" to view contents if doors slide or fold open; width of closet doors if they swing open

Between wall shelves

Height between shelves should accommodate the tallest items you will store on the shelves; allow head space so you don't bump your head when standing

TAKING STOCK I: NON-CONSUMABLE TOOLS & SUPPLIES

Getting organized may seem like a less daunting task now that the workspace itself is more in order and ready to receive your tools and supplies. You may be surrounded now by messy piles of photos, memorabilia and scrapbooking tools. Perhaps your digital files are out of control as well, making it time-consuming to search for the fonts and images when you need them. Take heart, step back for a minute and breathe.

In this chapter, you will be gathering, sorting, cleaning, repairing and labeling your non-consumable items. Perhaps you'll even decide to purge, donate or sell items you no longer use. You will learn how to master the "divide & conquer, clean & label" theory. It is a process that you will repeat over and over again while getting organized, regardless of the type of tool or supply you are getting under control.

The time you spend now will ensure that these items serve you for a long, long time. Keep what works for you. Do a little at a time. Gradually it won't be such a daunting task to look at that photo stack or that tool bin. You will know exactly where every item is when you need it. Each step along the way will bring focus back to your scrapbooking area and to your goals for the hobby.

The "Divide & Conquer, Clean & Label" Theory

This theory is a simple process that will help you get organized. Use this "plan of attack" regardless of what type of tools or supplies you are organizing. You will first gather all of one type of item together. Then you will divide it into piles for "keeping" and "getting rid of." Next, you will clean and repair the keepers and either donate, sell or regift the unwanted items. Before storing the keepers, be sure to label the items as well as the drawer, box or bin they will be stored in. That way, you will know where they are at a glance and any item that might accompany you to a future crop will be labeled with your name or your initials.

Empty storage areas, bins and drawers of scrapbook supplies and gather in one place. Sort and group like items; determine what to get rid of. Clean and label the keepers so they're ready for use and for cropping on the go.

Keep a good supply of labels, index cards and dividers, binder dividers and sticky notes handy for labeling your "keepers." Dymo's Letra Tag QX50 is a user- and cost-friendly labeling system that can help you create a unified look among your labeled tools and supplies.

Top five ways to rid yourself of unwanted tools & supplies

Donate them

Give your tools and supplies to a charitable organization, such as a school, church group, baby-sitting co-op, the Picture Me Foundation, Girl or Boy Scouts of America, a nursing home or a children's hospital.

Swap them

Set unwanted items aside for a future in-home or Internet swap (see following page).

Sell them

Sell the items at a garage sale or the flea market. List items in a local newspaper ad or sell them on an Internet auction. For a minimal fee, some local scrapbook stores may allow you to display your wares on select days.

Regift them

Give the items to your children to help them foster a love for preserving memories or wrap the items up for a special scrapbooking friend.

Discard them

If the items are simply beyond repair, toss them out for good.

How to host a swap

As you go through the process of dividing, conquering, cleaning and labeling, you'll inevitably run across items perfect for a swap. Swapping one unwanted item for an item you will use can help you recoup some of your original cost. You can also make an outright sale of your item at the swap if you can't find anything to trade for that you will use. Don't bring home any swapped items that you won't use. For a successful swap, try these tips:

In-Home Swaps

- Send out invitations at least 2-3 weeks in advance.
- Create plenty of open space with comfortable seating.
- Provide large tables for displaying supplies. Supply price tags and pens.
- Offer refreshments.
- Provide tally sheets for guests to keep track of trades or purchases.
- Make the atmosphere festive with table decorations and music.

Internet swaps

- Join an online group and be a part of the fun.
- Determine the style of the swap; for example, try a "round robin" swap.
- Select the type of items to be swapped; for example, swap page additions or, perhaps, cutting tools.
- E-mail information regarding your intentions to host a swap to interested parties.
- Provided a complete set of rules to all swappers.
- Remind participants to include correct postage on their swap parcels or shipping boxes.
- E-mail sender a notice of confirmation upon receipt.

- Regularly post the status of the swap on the appropriate Internet bulletin board.
- Be punctual in sending swapped materials to participants.
- Check out these Internet Web sites for more information on swaps: www.scrapbook.com, www.havilandtelco.com, www.ourlittlesiteontheweb.com and www.twopeasinabucket.com.

Swapping one unwanted item for an item you will use can help you recoup some of your original cost. Just don't trade for or bring home any swapped items you won't use or you'll set yourself back in the goal of getting organized.

Taming Our Most Prized Possessions

Scrapbooking involves getting your most prized possessions, such as photos, negatives and memorabilia—even slides, computer files, digital images, audio and visual images and sounds—into safe storage environments so that you can utilize and enjoy them for years to come. While these cherished and irreplaceable possessions are the heart and soul of scrapbooking, they are also the most difficult to get under control because of the sheer volume of these items. Over the years, the "piles" get bigger and bigger. With a good organizational system, even an unruly mountain of memories can be tamed.

Photographs

Negligence harms photos the most. Left in piles and bundles and crammed into drawers, they crumple and get brittle. Unsorted photos get lost. Undocumented photos get thrown away. Each year that photos are left unattended and unsafe, their demise is hastened. With some sound advice, your photos will become easily accessible while stored in the safest of all possible environments.

CARE

To care for your photos, you must recognize—and avoid—the top threats to photo longevity. You can deal with each threat in a positive way. Each photo care challenge has its own solution.

Sooner or later, we all have a stockpile of unorganized photos, negatives and memorabilia just begging for organization and, ultimately, to be put in a scrapbook album so their stories can be told.

- Humidity can wreak havoc on precious photos. Emulsions shift, mildew grows, photos start to warp, and pages stick together. According to the Library of Congress, humidity is the greatest enemy of photographic materials. The ideal storage humidity is between 20-50 percent humidity. If your rooms exceed this, you can purchase desiccant crystals from major photo suppliers. These crystals will absorb excess humidity from a room.

- Consistent storage temperatures are important. Ideal conditions for photo storage is in the range of 60-75 degrees Fahrenheit. If you have a cool basement that is not humid, this is ideal. Never store photos in an attic. Attics are the worst rooms in the home for temperature fluctuation. Steady temperature is especially important to color photographs because of their chemical compositions. Repeated cold temperatures make photo chemicals less stable. Try not to let your photos freeze. Do not leave them in the car if you live in excessively cold, hot and/or humid climates.

- pH levels are also important. In chemical terms, acid also harms photos. A severe base compound would also be harmful. Photos want to be neutral. The safe range for photos is 7.5-8.5 pH level. Use only albums, papers, pens and embellishments that are made from durable and chemically stable materials. Paper should also be acid- and lignin-free. Check with a pH acid testing pen if in doubt about any scrapbooking or storage product.

- Avoid unsafe plastics. These will outgas over time onto the photos. Don't use items that have polyvinyl-chloride (PVC) plastics. Use plastics that are specifically labeled safe for archival storage and photo use. Safe plastic products are made with polypropylene or polyethylene.

- Consider extreme compression. The pressure of weight and gravity is not good for photos. Store your photos in an upright, vertical position. Do not stack them lying flat.

- Watch out for chemical reactions. Store photos separately from negatives. Not only is this a good idea in case of a disaster, it keeps the varied chemicals from interacting between the two mediums. Wooden boxes or containers like wooden baskets are not good for storage of photos. Do not store photos in rooms with a lot of chemical interchange, such as kitchens, garages, shops or laundry rooms.

- Hands carry body salt, oil and dirt that cannot be seen or detected. These contaminants transfer to the photos with handling. Wash hands before working with photographs. Wipe the photo with a clean, nonabrasive cotton cloth after you handle it. After scrapbooking, wipe the page gently when you finish it to decrease this risk. There are also hand lotions developed to neutralize hand oils. Some scrapbookers wear gloves while handling photos and scrapbooking. Use page protectors available for your album style. Decrease handling risks whenever possible.

- Keep your photos away from bright light and sunlight. Continuous light fades photos. Rotate photos that are hung on walls so that no one photo is exposed to direct light more than one year. Keep photos out of ultraviolet light as much as possible, including black lights.

ORGANIZATION

Sort your photos chronologically regardless of how you plan to scrapbook them later. If you can find the photo, you can pull it out later for specialty albums or emotion and sentiment pages. Our minds think chronologically. When you think of a photo, you naturally recall when it was taken. You remember how old the child was, or when the vacation was, in the context of your personal history. Use that personal chronological timeline as a basis for your photo filing system.

WHAT YOU'LL NEED

- 4 x 6" index cards in several colors OR the photo work sheet on page 423

- One or more large photo storage boxes

- Black journaling pen

- Negative holders if sorting negatives (see page 424) at the same time as you sort photos

- Page protectors or a large box if sorting memorabilia (see page 426) at the same time as you sort photos

- Time and table or floor space to work on this project over the course of a few days

- All of your loose photos (and negatives and memorabilia)

- Sticky notes for journaling

- Any calendars you have saved to help identify photo dates and events

ORGANIZATIONAL HOW-TO

Gather up all the photos from around the house. Bring them into one room. Make a work sheet or an index card for each year. You may also make cards for each event if you have enough photos to warrant it. Later, sort by month. Finally, sort by event, if needed. While sorting, jot down memories the photos trigger involving events and people in the photos. If you are unsure when the event in a photo took place, estimate the time frame based on clues in the photo. Ages of children, hairstyles, cars, skirt lengths, hats, shoes and clothing styles all help pinpoint various eras. File these photos and their negatives in a separate container to investigate at a later time. Storing photos in chronological order will now be easy. Use photo storage boxes, files, or slip-in-sleeve type albums to store photos by date until you are ready to scrapbook.

STORAGE

Photo storage options abound. How you store your priceless pictures will depend on how often you want to view them, how much work you want to go through to showcase them, and how many of them you have to work with. Do you want all your photos in scrapbooks? Or do you feel the majority can go into sleeve albums or boxes while saving the scrapbooking for the most special photos? Regardless of what you choose for storage, keep in mind that photos are best stored at 60-75 degrees Fahrenheit for optimal longevity.

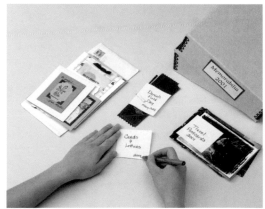

Before you file your organized photos and memorabilia away in chronological order, be sure to jot down pertinent information on index cards or a photo work sheet for future reference when scrapbooking. Tag or mark any accompanying memorabilia for future scrapbooking as well.

PLASTIC BOXES & TOTES

These are often called photo supply boxes or photo totes. These come in varying sizes and styles. Sort your photos first to determine the number and size you need. Plastic boxes should be made from polypropylene, acrylic or polyethylene. Some fit under the bed and have handles and rollers. New research suggests that wooden boxes may not be best for long term photo storage. Even treated wood contains acid and lignin which can release gas over time. Choose an alternative to wood if possible.

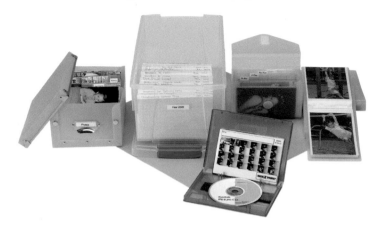

Among the popular, archival-plastic photo storage containers are (left to right): Kokuyo's large E-Z Snap storage boxes, Rubbermaid's photo and media storage boxes, and un-du's PhotoKeeper™, which can hold photos, negatives and a CD-ROM. For transporting sets of photos to crops for scrapbooking, try Generations' Foto Friend™ accordion wallet with Velcro® fastener or Kokuyo's photo storage albums with sleeve cases. To store photos and negatives until you can scrapbook, try Pioneer's Space Saver™ albums with cases (above right) or Leeco/Cropper Hopper's Photo Case (right).

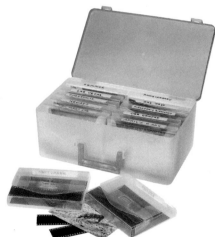

Acid-free, archival-safe cardboard photo storage can be an inexpensive but effective way to store photos. Some of today's popular choices are (left to right): Generations/K & Co.'s Photo Express, Pioneer's Photo Box, Highsmith's Photo Chest and Photo Keepers, and Colorbök's the Perfect Scrapbook™ Memory Storage box and photo folders. Try Jotter's Pocket Jotter™ for noting memories about photos before storing them.

ACID-FREE CARDBOARD BOXES & KEEPERS

These are most often made for 4 x 6" photos or smaller, but there are some available for enlargements and panoramic photos. Certain cardboard photo storage containers come with dividers, or you can use index cards to label the years. Other units have drawers to accommodate decades of photos, while still others have handles for portability.

RECYCLE PHOTO DUPLICATES

Sort and label duplicate photos and then let a family member store them for you in an archival photo storage box. This will ensure that if natural disaster strikes your home, you will have photos elsewhere. Duplicates that you no longer care about may be given to family members or friends. Or consider using them to make a "year in review" scrapbook page spread—or a calendar, greeting cards or gift tags.

If you save photo scraps to crop and use as page accents, sort them by color regardless of theme, and store in an accordion-style plastic folder such as Caren's Crafts' Scrap-N-File™ mini accordion file, which has elastic bands to keep photo scraps snug and organized.

Polaroids

Polaroids need basically the same care as regularly developed photos with a few added elements.

- The main hazard of Polaroid prints is before they are fully developed. Handle all parts with care. The processing jelly, which contains sodium hydroxide or potassium hydroxide, can be highly caustic. It remains at a high pH on the discarded portion (the non-image and negative area) for up to two hours. It is highly corrosive to the skin, eyes and mucous membranes. Avoid skin or eye contact with residual processing fluid. If children chew or ingest film, flush with water and contact a poison control center.

- Dispose of wet negatives in a closed waste container to prevent further contact.

- Leave Polaroid "integral" prints intact. An integral print, noted for its thickness and ¾" lower white border, contains chemicals that can leak out when the edges are cut open. Peel-apart prints are safe to cut because the chemical-containing negative is separated from the positive print.

- Do not use adhesives on Polaroids. The chemicals in the glues may react with the backing and chemicals of the photograph. A safer storage solution for Polaroids is to use large photo corners to hold the photo in place on a scrapbook page. You may also place photos in plastic memorabilia sleeves or pockets.

Advantix

- Store unexposed film and disposable cameras at 70 degrees Fahrenheit or cooler. Always store film (exposed or unexposed) canisters in a cool, dry place.

- Process film as soon as possible after exposure.

- Advantix negatives never leave their canisters. Special organizer boxes can be purchased for holding these negatives that look like film canisters.

- Do not disassemble the Advantix negative cassette. Store the cassette in a cool, dry place with its index print. Label both for ease in later identification

Pioneer's Advanced Photo Case™ and Advanced Photo Storage Box™ provide the perfect archiving environment for Kodak's Advantix™ film and corresponding index prints.

Slides

- Archival slide holder sheets are available that hold up to 20 slides. These are then labeled and stored in notebook binders by subject or by date. These slide sheets can also be hung from hanging file slide rods and stored in file cabinets.

- Good labeling is key. Ensure that you can find what you want by labeling accurately. Create an index sheet that lists the slides' topics and dates; store chronologically or by theme.

- Do not store slides in daylight conditions. Cases for storage binders are available or store the slides in the slide reels in which they came inside an acid-free box. Or store them in the semi dark of the file cabinet as hanging files. Keep in mind that the original slide reel boxes are probably not archival.

- Sturdy slide storage boxes are available from photo supply houses. These can hold up to 200 slides each. Label and store at a moderate temperature around 75 degrees Fahrenheit.

Try Kokuyo's Color 'N' Color Collection three-ring binders, outfitted with Pioneer's archival-quality slide protector sleeves and an index sheet, to organize and store slides.

Audio- & videotapes

With the advent of the camcorder, family videos abound. Learn to care for your family videos so they last as long as possible. The shelf life of family camcorder and homemade video movies is much shorter than originally thought. Consider having them transferred to longer-lasting DVDs.

- Keep recordings free of dirt, dust and mildew.

- Play as little as possible. Each playing depletes some of the quality and the lifetime of the recording.

- Videotapes last between 10 and 30 years. Treating cassettes and videotapes carefully should increase their life span.

- Handle cassettes and videotapes as little as possible. Never touch the tape section with your fingers.

- Avoid extreme heat and humidity.

- Play and rewind sound recordings and family videos as little as possible. Each time you rewind a tape it traps dust and debris between the layers, which can scratch the tape's surface and impede the quality of its playback.

- Do not smoke near your cassettes and videotapes.

- Avoid pausing your cassettes and videotapes too long or too often. Pausing stretches the tape.

- Keep all electronic and magnetic storage (like videos and floppy disks) away from magnets.

- Store in temperature-regulated areas of the home.

- Store cassettes and videotapes upright or on end.

- Do not store in the attic or garage where heat can be a great enemy of vinyl recordings, audiotape and videotape.

- Humidity is dangerous to audiotape. The tape actually absorbs the water from the air and degrades the recording.

- Video storage boxes and tubs are available to control dust and humidity.

Archival-quality storage boxes for videocassettes—such as Pioneer's lidded video storage boxes with index cards—can add life to these precious taped memories.

Work sheet for sorting photos

YEAR: _____

JANUARY	**JULY**
FEBRUARY	**AUGUST**
MARCH	**SEPTEMBER**
APRIL	**OCTOBER**
MAY	**NOVEMBER**
JUNE	**DECEMBER**

Source: Barbara Tolopilo, Family Treasures, Inc.

Negatives

The secret to preserving your treasured negatives is to handle them as little as possible. Place them in archival-safe containers or albums. Store these collections in the coolest environment in your home. Keep them away from large variations in temperature and humidity.

CARE

- Wash and dry your hands thoroughly before handling negatives. Keep your hands free of oils, body salts and moisture while handling negatives. Dust your work surface before laying down negatives.

- Wear cotton gloves when previewing negatives to prevent scratching. Hold the negatives on the outer edges only. This prevents smudging.

- Avoid cutting negative strips when organizing or reordering reprints. Cutting a negative ruins the emulsion, thus ruining the negative. Cutting negatives also means you have handled them again and added to the risk of fingerprinting or permanently scratching the small surface area.

- Clean dirty negatives with a negative-cleaning solution, such as PEC-12.

- Like your photos, keep your negatives away from dust, bright light, excessive heat and high humidity.

- Consider storing negatives "off site." In the event of a disaster, they'll be safe.

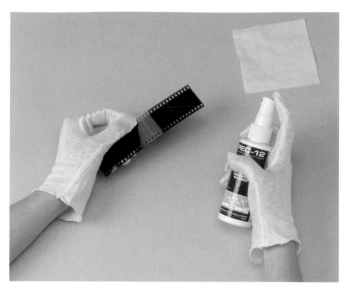

*Clean negatives, if needed, with Photographic Solutions' PEC-12® Emulsion Cleaner and PEC*PAD® Non-Abrasive Wipes. Handle clean negatives with Highsmith's lint-free cotton gloves to prevent skin oils from transferring.*

ORGANIZATION

As you sort the photos into safer environments, sort your negatives as well. Organize your negatives just as you do your photos. Sort them chronologically, by subject matter or by theme. It will be easier to understand a chronological-order system for those who inherit the negatives. Taking the time to sort negatives now translates into more efficient scrapbooking later on. The two basic storage systems for negatives that scrapbookers use with success are the binder or the box system.

BINDER SYSTEM: WHAT YOU'LL NEED

Binders are a convenient and economical way to organize and store negatives. For this type of negative storage system, you will need:

- Binder-style, three-ring notebook

- Archival negative sleeves

- Unsorted negatives

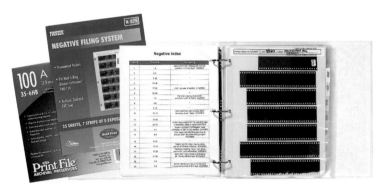

Store clean negatives in Pioneer's three-ring binder albums, outfitted with the company's Negative Filing System archival sleeves, a correlating index sheet, and notebook tab index dividers to separate months or years. Print File® is another quality company that manufactures archival, PVC-free negative preserver sleeves.

Keep the negatives in complete strips and in chronological order. Archival negative sleeves hold one strip of negatives per row. The sleeves should be labeled with date, event, and people in the photo. Be consistent in your labeling. Always put the full date on the negative sleeve where you can see it. Then add the event name and the person's name. If exact dates are not known, give your best estimate. Place the filled negative sleeves into a three-ring binder and create tabs for various months or years. Add an index sheet at the front of the binder with a listing of the photo events in that binder. Label each binder on the spine for quick reference.

BOX SYSTEM: WHAT YOU'LL NEED

Negatives may also be stored in boxes as long as the boxes are archivally safe and there are acid- and lignin-free strips of paper between the negatives to prevent sticking. You'll need:

- A negative storage box

- Acid- and lignin-free paper strips or negative pockets a little larger than the negatives

- An archival pen that will write well on paper or plastic

- Negatives that need sorting

Keep the negatives in complete strips and in chronological order. Negatives that are sliced into small sections are too easily lost or damaged and are hard to file. Label the strips of paper with data about the negative. Keep your writing on the white slip at the top of the paper so as not to affect the negative film filed in front of it. Be certain to add a strip of acid-free paper between negative strips to prevent them from sticking together. Label the box with full dates. Add an index sheet of dates and events related to each box of negatives.

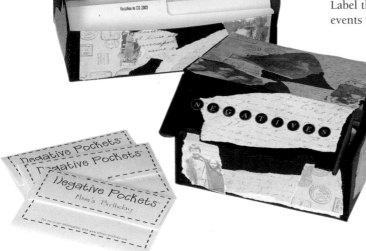

Some popular archival cardboard negative containers include Highsmith's Acid-Free Photo Tote and Acid-Free Negative Box, which can be decorated. Or, try Light Impressions' FoldLock™ negative sleeves stored inside their negative storage boxes. The Sentimental Playground manufactures acid- and lignin-free Negative Pockets™, which are a convenient way to organize and label your negatives once the companion photos have been put in albums.

STORAGE

- Use only 100% acid-free, lignin-free, and PVC-free negative sleeves, storage binders and storage boxes. Buy from reliable brands and sources.

- Store in a climate-controlled area. Avoid extremes in chemical vapors, lighting, heat and humidity.

- Store negatives in temperatures between 65-70 degrees with about 30 percent humidity. Humidity over 60 percent is harmful. Use anti-desiccant canisters or room dehumidifiers if necessary.

- The best place for negative storage is in a safe place out of your home such as a bank vault, safe-deposit box or with a family member. If natural disaster strikes, it is unlikely it will hit both homes at the same time.

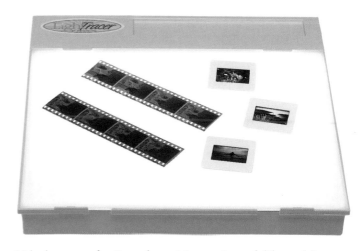

Make the process of sorting and organizing negatives and slides much faster by viewing them on Artograph's budget-friendly Light Tracer® light box.

Memorabilia

Memorabilia, also called "ephemera," are other treasured possessions that accumulate through the years. Memorabilia can include anything from lockets of hair and sports patches to brochures and newspaper clippings. With proper care, organization and storage, memorabilia can be easily accessible for scrapbooking.

CARE

As the family scrapbooker, it is up to you to treat these documents and memorabilia so that they will last as long as possible. Many of these documents—such as construction paper art and newspaper—tend to disintegrate quickly. Newspaper articles, school artwork and many other private documents are not created on acid-free papers or archivally safe products. Items like these need to be preserved for their genealogical and historic value as well as family sentiment. Try these handy preservation suggestions:

- Make second copies of irreplaceable documents by copying them onto acid-free, archival-safe paper stock. You can store or scrapbook the original and have a backup copy on a more stable type of paper. Consider photocopying historic documents on oatmeal-colored paper to preserve the antique look.

- Spray documents with an acid-neutralizing spray. Most family and legal documents are not created on archival papers. It is a good safety measure to spray them with an archival spray to stop the acidic decomposition.

- Store newspapers separately. Never store newsprint with other non-newsprint documents. The acidic nature of the newsprint may contaminate other documents. Place the newsprint in page protectors or memorabilia keepers after it has been treated with an archival spray.

For acid-free cardboard storage of memorabilia, try (left to right): Highsmith's Acid-Free Memory Boxes, Generations' Memory Express™, General Box Co's. Tower of Boxes, or for large artwork, maps, etc., Light Impressions' TrueCore™ Drop-Front Box. Decorate as desired to identify the type of memorabilia stored in each box.

- Store documents and memorabilia in a climate-controlled environment. Pick a cool, dark and dry place for the storage of these family treasures.

- Use acid-free, archival-safe materials to encapsulate questionable memorabilia before adding to a scrapbook. Polypropylene sheet protectors and memory keepers are useful for this purpose.

- If your item is too large or you have space limitations, consider photographing the items and getting rid of the original. This is a particularly good idea for 3-D school projects, sports trophies, band uniforms, military uniforms and bulky, homemade items of only slight sentimental value (see next page).

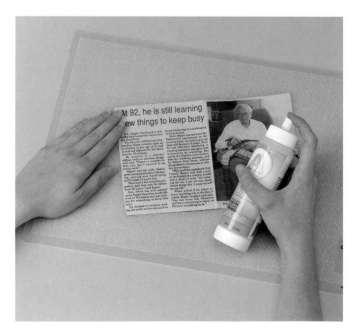

De-acidify memorabilia with a spray such as EK Success' Archival Mist® before adding it to a scrapbook page. An alternative to spraying is to photocopy the newsclipping or document onto acid-free paper.

ORGANIZATION

It is a good idea to sort and organize your memorabilia at the same time that you are sorting photos and negatives. This will make it easier to "match up" memorabilia with any corresponding photos when scrapbooking. Organize memorabilia by theme, such as home, military, baby, school, sports, etc., then organize it chronologically. Index what is in each box, page protector or pocket, and label accordingly. Label memorabilia by box or bag number. Be sure to note the number on your photo index cards or photo work sheet of any corresponding memorabilia so that you'll know where to find it. Keep your memorabilia files up-to-date. Make two copies of your index. One copy is for you to have as a reference. The other copy is to keep in/on the actual storage device as a content index. For example, glue one listing on the outside the storage box and put the other copy with your organized photos. You'll then be able to locate the items quickly by using the reference.

STORAGE

Common cardboard boxes are not a safe solution for document and memorabilia storage. Plastic boxes should be made from polypropylene, acrylic or polyethylene. Invest in a few high-quality archival boxes for your important family documents. Consider implementing one or a combination of these useful memorabilia storage options:

BAGS

Polyethylene bags of all sizes are available. Sort by date, type of event, theme or person. There are also specialty zipper-type bags for this purpose that are archivally safe.

BOXES

These are often called rare-book boxes or portfolio boxes. Memorabilia boxes can be purchased at scrapbooking and archival supply outlets. Dry cleaners often have access to acid-free boxes in larger sizes. More recently, some of the scrapbooking vendors have created under-the-bed models from safe plastics, cardboard and other materials.

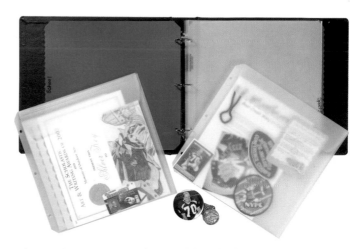

If you prefer storing organized memorabilia in binders, Generations' Memorabilia Pockets, separated by their Memory Album Dividers, work well in 12 x 12" binders or albums from Collected Memories.

ACCORDION FILES

Make sure these are acid-free and archival-safe. Ordinary cardboard office supply styles are generally not archival quality.

HANGING FILES

Set up a labeled folder for each year and file your memorabilia accordingly. Break it down by month if needed.

SCRAPBOOK ALBUMS

Scrapbooks come in sizes ranging up to 15 x 18" along with archival page protectors to fit. This size accommodates most larger items and documents.

THREE-RING BINDERS WITH PAGE PROTECTORS

These will store most small paper and flat mementos. Label the spines with the items and dates included.

Photographing memorabilia

- Outdoors, use 200-speed film and flash; shoot in open shade or soft sunlight.
- Indoors, use 400-speed film and flash; shoot in well-lit location or late in the day for a nostalgic effect.
- Arrange memorabilia on floor or tabletop in an eye-pleasing display.
- Fill the frame with your arrangement when you look through the camera's viewfinder.
- Get as close as possible to accurately record words and numbers.
- Snap many photos from different angles, rearranging memorabilia as needed for visual appeal.
- For a photography alternative for flat memorabilia such as ribbons and certificates, scan the item(s), either alone or in collage-style, reduce the size and print on acid-free paper of choice.

Computer Files & Digital Images

The Information Age has impacted scrapbooking in a big way, creating the need to care for, organize and store computer files and digital images. From font CDs, downloaded fonts and digital photographs to favorite Web site "bookmarks," computer files can quickly become hard to find because of sheer volume. The first rule when storing digital images and computer files is to back up your data. Make at least two copies and store them in different places. One copy can be on your hard drive but make sure another copy is elsewhere. You just never know when tragedy might strike! Use these tips to help you keep your computer files and digital images in tiptop shape.

Computer files

- Online storage is not recommended for exclusive or long-term storage of your images. However there are online services that will store your digital images for a monthly fee. Be warned that some of these companies have clauses that protect them from lawsuit should they go out of business and/or mistakenly delete your files! Be sure to back up any online photo storage with real prints or CDs.

- Hard drive storage of images is only recommended for very short-term storage until you can burn a CD of the image files.

- Upload items from the hard drive as soon as possible to photo processing sites and order prints or print them at home with archival ink and acid-free papers.

- Keep your hard drive folders sorted and be sure that the names accurately reflect the contents. Trash folders on a regular basis when you find that you never use them.

- Make it a point to regularly file and sort through your computer bookmarks. Many no longer function after six months. Create a subfolder within your "bookmark" or "favorites" folder and drag all scrapbooking-related Web sites to that folder.

- Use a font organizer program. Fonts can be addictive. They can also overload your system if you have too many. Weed through duplicates that can be deleted. Font organizers help you see which fonts need installing and what they look like. You can print out a hard copy to use as a reference.

Keep your CD-ROMs and floppy disks in tip-top shape by storing in jewel cases in a tower or in Light Impressions' Slimline CD Album with CD pages. For a collection of floppy disks, try Kokuyo's small E-Z Snap storage box.

CD-ROMs

- All photographic images can be scanned or converted to electronic images and stored on CD. You can make electronic slide shows or photo albums. This medium may not last forever but it is a good secondary storage device at the moment.

- Store your image master CDs "off site" in a safe-deposit box as you would negatives.

- Keep the temperature normal and humidity low. According to a major CD manufacturer, writable CDs will have a data lifetime of greater than 200 years if stored in the dark at 60 degrees Fahrenheit and 40 percent relative humidity. When stored in a 70-degree Fahrenheit home environment, the lifetime of a writable CD should be at least 100 years or more.

- Even though CDs normally have a long shelf life, they can be damaged. Do not drop, scratch, warp or heat a CD.

Digital images

- Store your digital data in more than one place, more than one copy and more than one format. Make a hard copy if possible for anything irreplaceable in your digital files like heritage photos, genealogy documents or family portraits.

- Regularly upload your camera to your hard drive and save your images on the hard drive to a writable CD. Do this at least monthly.

- Use a folder system to organize the computer storage of images.

- Sort photo uploads by date but also add something in the folder title that describes the event or subject. Example: 2/03/01 Nana Jones' birthday party and gifts.

- Make a date with your computer. Regularly upload images to photo sites and have them printed or print them yourself.

- Once a CD has several months' worth of photos on it, take it in to be developed at a photo center. Many photo centers develop directly from the CD.

- A CD can store up to 700 MB. Just a handful of CDs can store your entire photo collection. Just make sure they are in folders and labeled with, at minimum, the chronological dates.

If you work faster on a computer than you do manually, you may find that software programs for scrapbooking organization are just what you need. Try LNS Software Solutions' Organized Expressions™ for Scrapbooking (for MS Windows) or Handango's MyCraftCompanion by C. Cirelli Palm-Pilot®-style organizer shareware.

Scrapbooking software

Digital scrapbook gurus will be happy to know that there is an organizing software—Organized Expressions™ for Scrapbooking—available from LNS Software Solutions. The MS Windows™-based program allows you to keep track of your supplies, swaps, page-layout ideas and more. For Palm-Pilot® users, there's Handango's MyCraftCompanion by C. Cirelli—a shareware organizer program. It allows you to track supplies, page submissions, entry deadlines, swaps and more even when you're on-the-go. Even if you don't create digital scrapbook pages, these user-friendly software programs can help you get organized.

Top eight good reasons to do a backup

Power surges
A sudden oversupply of electric power can damage the files on your hard drive.

Hard drive crashes
Your files can be lost due to a network system or electrical failure.

Human error
You accidentally drop the hard drive, delete a file or reformat a disk.

Hackers
Someone could tamper with the information on your computer.

Theft
Someone can copy or delete information from your computer or steal the entire unit.

Natural disasters
A natural disaster could destroy your computer and hard drive.

Magnetic interference
Your floppy disk could come in contact with magnetic material, erasing files.

Electronic viruses
Your hard drive or disks could become infected, compromising their data.

Non-Consumable Tools & Supplies

What is a hobby without tools? Non-consumable tools and supplies are those that keep on giving and giving until they eventually break or wear out. Your tools are some of the most important aids to creativity during the page-making process. Misplacing a tool, breakage and duplicate purchases can all add to the chaos of an unorganized workspace. This can be avoided if you know what you have, where it is located and how to care for it. Gather up all your tool supplies from around the house. Check the totes, bins, bags and even the car! Sort tools by type. Keep like items together. Get rid of any tool that you never intend to use (see pages 416-417). Once you've weeded out the chaff, clean and label supplies and determine what kind of containers you will need to store them. Transparent and labeled containers and bins, and notebooks with labeled dividers can make it faster to locate the items you need.

Brayers & crimpers

- Keep your crimpers and brayers as clean and dust free as possible. Serious dust buildup can cause roller jams.

- Keep fingers out of the way of the rolling bar on brayers and crimpers.

- These types of tools are generally used less frequently than others. Store labeled in a clear, lidded bin, in the drawer of a cart or on hooks on pegboard.

- Crimpers, brayers and other "T-shaped" tools can also be stored on hangers or stands designed for paint rollers and rakes.

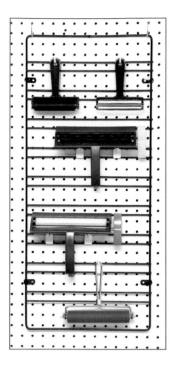

Brayers and crimpers are happy hung on Sturdi-Craft's pegboard and pegboard hooks. Pegboard on a wall is a great solution for hanging tools that aren't used as often as others.

Create an inventory notebook

While dividing, conquering, cleaning and labeling your tools and supplies, make a tool inventory in a scrapbook inventory notebook. These are sold commercially (see left) or you can make your own. A scrapbook inventory notebook allows you to keep track of what you own in each tool category. Don't buy duplicates ever again!

- Get a notebook or binder in a size you like. If you plan to take it shopping, it should be a small planner size of binder with plenty of blank pages.

- Make a full listing of each tool category. Include details such as the names of decorative scissor blades, pen colors and brands, and letter template font names and sizes. The more tool details you include the better.

Artfully Scribed's Scrap-A-Log™ is a handy little notebook that comes with preprinted pages for cataloging your tools and supplies. The log also helps keep track of page layout ideas, web sites, store information, publications and wish lists.

- Keep in mind that papers such as cardstock and printed pattern papers do not need to be inventoried because they get used so quickly. Creating an inventory of all your papers would be time-consuming and nearly impossible to keep up to date. Instead, inventory your more permanent, non-consumable items like the tools featured on the following pages.

- Take your notebook shopping. You will know for a fact whether you have a particular decorative scissor, die, punch or stamp.

Craft knives

- Keep them sharp; replace the blades often.

- Use an emery board to sharpen larger blades periodically.

- Clean blades with rubbing alcohol or un-du® to remove any adhesive residue. Dry thoroughly.

- Store out of the reach of children.

- Store blades inside of protective sheaths.

- Always store your knives in the same easy-access location. This is one often-used tool you don't need surprising you later if misplaced in the wrong bin, drawer or caddy.

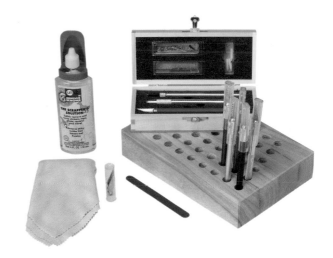

Armada Art's solid oak blocks provide a great little home for craft knives or scissors if you prefer desktop storage. Hunt Corporation's X-ACTO knives come in their own utility case. Use un-du's adhesive remover to clean knives and sharpen with an ordinary nail file or sharpening stone or replace with new blades.

Croppers & cutters

- Cropping tools like shape cutters need fresh blades regularly. If you try to save a few pennies on a new blade but end up ruining a photo with a dull cutter, where are the savings?

- Clean blades and bodies with alcohol or un-du® to remove any residue. Dry thoroughly.

- Store out of the reach of children.

- Cutters and blades should be stored in tightly closed containers for safety.

- If you use your paper trimmer frequently, tuck it out of view from children when you are not scrapbooking.

Shape croppers and mat cutters generally store well in lidded containers, such as this Rubbermaid® unit, to keep them dust-free. If you keep your paper trimmer on your desktop, dust occasionally with a soft towel or feather duster. Replace blades as necessary.

Dies & die-cut machines

- Remove any paper bits, particles or dust from dies and machines, using tweezers if needed to get into tiny crevices.

- Organize dies alphabetically or by theme, depending upon the size of your collection.

- Store dies in commercially made wooden-box racks or corrugated storage compartments, specialty binders from the manufacturer or specially made spinning racks.

- Die-cut machines can be bulky and heavy. If you don't use the machine daily, store it away from tiny fingers.

Store standard-sized dies in Accu-Cut's laminate towers (available in many sizes) or for smaller dies, try Sizzix/Provo Craft's Die Storage System. Store QuiKutz' dies in the company's EZ-Store Sheets and Storage Binder.

Miscellaneous tools

Many scrapbook tools have metal and movable parts. Care should be taken to maintain the metal so it remains in prime condition. Because these tools are used quite frequently while scrapbooking, you'll want to keep them handy—preferably on the desktop. Good care will maintain the lever action of movable parts. Proper care and storage will give you years of use for these kinds of tools: metal straightedge and graphing rulers, hammer, eyelet setter, tweezers, piercing tool, embossing stylus, button-shank remover, round needle-nose pliers and scissors. Keep tools and their handles dry, dust free and clean of adhesives and colorant residue. Store in a desktop caddy, tool box or in handled totes or zippered bags for cropping on-the-go.

Convenient desktop tool caddies include The Pampered Chef's Tool Turnabout, Westwater Enterprises' Canvas Craft Caddy, Armada Art's Small Art Supply Caddy, Inventor's Studio's Fold 'N Hold's mesh caddy, Twin Ray's Organize-Up clamp-on Craft Space Organizer or ArtBin's Solution Boxes.

Punches

- Punches should be kept dry and out of humidity to prevent rusting.

- Remove jammed paper from the punch with tweezers. If that doesn't work, place punch in the freezer for 20 seconds. The metal will contract for easy paper removal.

- Temperatures below 32 degrees Fahrenheit may be harmful to the plastic casings. Repeated cold temperatures make plastics brittle before their time. Try not to let your punches freeze. Do not leave them in the car overnight if you live in a cold climate.

- When dull, punch through heavy-duty aluminum foil.

- When a punch sticks, punch through wax paper several times to re-lubricate.

- Use un-du® to clean off adhesive residue left by stickers, tape and self-adhesive paper. Simply squirt the solution on the underside of the punch. Punch through scrap paper until all of the solvent has evaporated.

- Keep track of which punches you own. Punch a sample from black paper and mount it onto white cardstock sheets. Label each with name, size and brand. Add this reference to a scrapbook inventory notebook (see page 430).

- Store punches in a dry place and protect against moisture and dust. Clear containers have the added advantage of

Dull and sticking punches can be sharpened and lubricated with heavy-duty aluminum foil and wax paper. Create a quick reference guide by filling a small notebook with each punched shape from your collection. Organize pages by size, type or theme.

visibility. If possible, label your storage containers in the same manner that you label your punch reference guide.

- Store in over-the-door pocket organizers, bins, toolboxes or plastic drawer units. For cropping-on-the-go, take punches in special totes, bags and carryalls made specifically for this purpose.

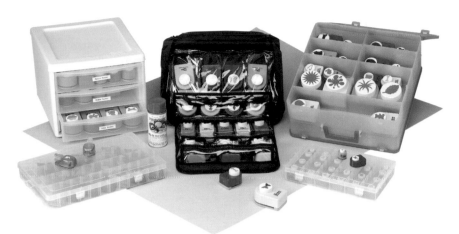

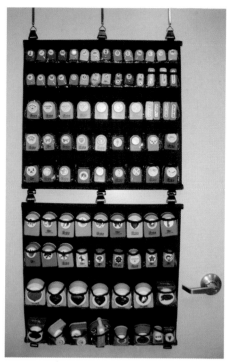

Punch storage comes in a wide array of sizes and styles. Try storing punches in ArtBin's Clear View boxes, Sterilite's drawer towers, McGill's Punch 'N Go tote or Leeco/Cropper Hopper's Supply Case. Tutto offers a Punch & Stamp Holder™ carrying tote and Crop In Style® provides an over-the-door Punch Pal™ that can grow as your punch collection grows.

Scissors

- Clean all metal blades, both regular and decorative, with adhesive remover after you cut through adhesive-backed papers.

- Decorative scissors are hard to sharpen professionally. Cut through heavy-duty aluminum foil to bring back their edge.

- Straightedge scissors can be sharpened professionally at any hardware or fabric store. Or you can do it yourself with a sharpening stone. Hand-held stones are often sold in the scissor section of fabric stores.

- Add a drop of lubricating liquid when scissor levers get stiff. Wipe well with a clean cloth before using on paper.

- Store scissors either horizontally in bins or drawers or hanging with the tips downward.

- Store out of the reach of children.

Scissor storing solutions include Tutto's scissor holder tote and Plaid's Creative Gear™ scissor holder tote. Crop In Style® makes the tri-fold Scissor Caddy. Armada Arts' Paper Shapers™ come in their own solid oak stand and Novelcrafts offers a triangular spinning rack for scissor storage.

Stamps

- Clean rubber stamps after every use. Use warm soapy water or a commercial stamp cleaner and a sponge or small tray and flat rubber scrubber.

- Dry completely with a lint-free cloth to avoid mildew on the rubber. Blot stamps gently on towel instead of rubbing them.

- If you have a large stamp collection, sort and organize stamps by design theme or style, artist, brand or alphabetically.

- Keep inventory pages or index cards in a notebook of all the stamps you own for quick identification and to avoid duplicate purchases. Rubber stamp each image on paper and sort the pages by theme.

- Store stamps in stamp travel cases or totes or in commercially manufactured stamp storage units made of wood or corrugated cardboard.

- Store rubber side down so you can see the image on the handle. Do not stack rubber stamps.

- Unmounted stamps can be stored in 3 x 5" or 4 x 6" slip-in-style, photo-sleeve page refills. File these pages by theme or by manufacturer in a three-ring binder. Unmounted stamps can also be stored in CD-ROM jewel cases.

Stampin' Up! offers Stampin' Scrub and Stampin' Mist Cleaner pads and refills to help keep stamps clean. The company also makes Powder Pals™ trays and brushes to assist in embossing powder recovery.

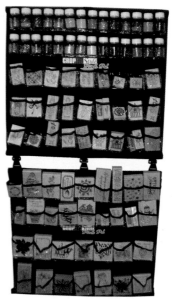

Keep stamps ready for use with Traffic Works' plastic boxes for smaller stamp collections, Highsmith's Stamp Storage Chest & Totes, Eagle Affiliates' Stamp Case, Rubbermaid's wide array of bins or Westwater Enterprises' Craft Pockets.

Crop In Style's Punch Pal™ (above) works nicely for stamps as well, and the company's stackable Stamp Store storage trays work great for stamping on-the-go. Try ArtBin's clear Prism™ boxes or Quick View carrying cases for stamping on-the-go with smaller stamp collections.

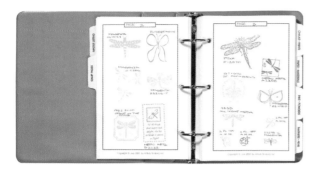

Artfully Scribed's Stamp-A-Log™ provides ultimate rubber stamp inventory organization in a three-ring binder format.

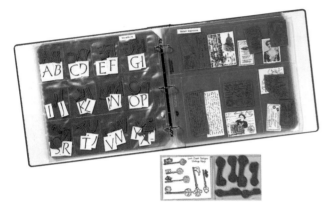

For unmounted stamps, try storing them in a Collected Memories album outfitted with C-Line Products' Memory Book® Page Protectors, Generations' Memory Album Dividers and the stamped image on paper. You can also store smaller unmounted stamp collections in CD jewel cases with the image stamped on scrap paper.

For quick and easy template, stencil and ruler identification, try these handy storage products: Kokuyo's photo albums with cases or Crop In Style's Binder Buddy™ with the company's page refills and binder dividers. For Coluzzle™ Nested Templates, Provo Craft offers its own organizer tote.

Templates & decorative rulers

- Wash plastic templates and rulers with warm soapy water and pat dry with cotton or paper toweling. Wash brass templates and stencils with plain warm water. Do not use soap unless you need to do so. Soap may discolor the brass and accelerate tarnishing. Dry thoroughly with cotton or paper toweling.

- Wipe off all templates and rulers with paper towels after each shape or letter is traced. It takes a minute or less for some inks to dry so wipe frequently.

- Remedy swivel-knife nicks in the plastic of graduated or "nested" templates as soon as you can. Many can be sanded horizontally using slight pressure with a fine emery board.

- Organize templates, stencils and decorative rulers into one of these categories: envelopes; tags and windows; frames; geometric shapes; letters; page-makers; puzzles; theme designs and decorative motifs. If desired, you can subdivide designs and motifs into holidays, seasonal, sport, travel, etc.

- Store all of your stencils, templates and embossing patterns in a three-ring binder, preferably a 12 x 12" binder so that all of your templates and stencils will fit together. If desired, insert templates into 12 x 12" page protectors or just insert them into the binder using the three holes punched into them. Label notebook dividers with the above categories.

- Insert a plain white paper between templates to prevent snagging and bending. Trace the template or stencil image onto the paper so you know which ones go where after each use.

- Smaller templates and stencils can be tucked into page protectors in the same binder.

- Brass templates and tiny stencils can be placed into baseball-card sleeves or mini photo albums for easy viewing and storage.

- Store binders flat.

TAKING STOCK II: CONSUMABLE TOOLS & SUPPLIES

With your physical workspace now in order, those chaotic scrapbook supply piles should be shrinking a bit. Your tools are organized and your photos, negatives and memorabilia are sorted. Now tackle the rest of your scrapbooking stash. Get started gathering, sorting, purging, labeling and storing those consumable supplies by type. For easy retrieval, keep like items with like items.

Goods such as albums, adhesives, embellishments, fibers, paper, pens and stickers are all items that come and go as you use them up. Storage for these should be flexible and have the ability to grow and shrink as your supplies regularly grow and shrink. Weed out consumables that you don't like. Keeping items you do not care to use takes up space and mental energy every time you must look for "the good stuff."

Keep in mind that what is trendy in scrapbooking today may not be in fashion next year. Keep only what you will love and will honestly use, and then tailor your storage to suit your personal needs. By whittling these types of supplies down to the essential "keepers," you will be able to scrapbook more rapidly and with less guilt and less debate. Every supply you keep should be a joy to use.

Consumable Tools & Supplies

In addition to non-consumable tools and supplies, the hobby of scrapbooking also brings with it consumable tools and supplies. Consumable supplies are those products that will have to be replenished over the course of time. Consumable supplies include adhesives, albums, cleaners, colorants, embellishments, sources of inspiration, paper and pre-made page additions—which include die cuts and stickers. Retail scrapbook and hobby stores are filled with aisles and aisles of these mesmerizing products. We buy all of the "gotta have 'em" items that we can afford. At home, we plunk the shopping bags down wherever there's room, only to paw through them and rediscover the items later while looking for something else. So now it's time to gather up all of your consumable tool and supplies from around the house. Sort and group the items, keeping like items together. Weed out those items that you're fairly certain you'll never use and get rid of them (see pages 416-417). Once you've determined all of the "keepers," decide what kind of containers you really need. Containers that will comfortably hold your current collections, plus a little room for growth, are ideal. Transparent and labeled containers and bins and notebooks with labeled dividers will make it easier to find just what you need.

Adhesives

Scrapbookers have access to a wide range of glues and tapes that make it quick and easy to attach photos, memorabilia, accents and embellishments to pages. Select only products that are acid-free and photo safe. Start by dividing your adhesives into two categories: wet and dry.

- Always put the cap back on wet adhesives; they dry out very quickly.

- Use a pin or piercing tool to unclog the spouts of bottled adhesives; wipe around tip with a damp cloth to keep clean.

- If you end up with adhesive where you don't want it, use adhesive remover or a white eraser to remove the surplus.

- Check wet adhesives every two months to see if they are still fluid and usable.

- Store dry adhesives in their original packages when not in use to prevent unraveling or sticking to other items.

- Buy tape runner cartridge refills as needed to avoid the cost of purchasing an entire new tape dispenser.

- A convenient time to remove residue from an adhesive application machine such as a Xyron™ is when you're changing adhesive cartridges. Use adhesive remover and a cotton swab to wipe residue away. Use a dampened cloth to wipe grime from the unit's body.

- Store all adhesives away from heat sources and out of sunlight.

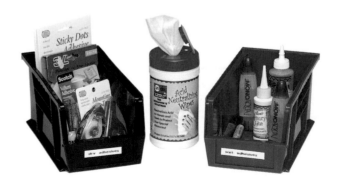

Store sorted adhesives in rapid-access containers such as Rubbermaid's Slim Drawer or Quantum™ Storage Systems' 4-Drawer Tilt Bin or Stackable or Hangable bins. Keep your Xyron™ machine clean by removing any sticky residue with an adhesive remover and keep hands clean with un-du's Acid Neutralizing Wipes.

Albums

Photo albums should be acid- and lignin-free, and the page protectors in them should be made of polypropylene or polyethylene plastics. Spine choices should also be considered for longevity. For example, steel closures always last longer than simple adhesive or sewn fiber bindings. In addition:

- Albums range in size from 5 x 7" up to 12 x 15". Shelves or bookcases should be deep enough so that the albums do not hang over the edge. This avoids needless bumping and tipping.

- Store upright on a shelf, leaving a tiny bit of "breathing room" between albums. Excessive compression of albums will crush photos and page accents over time.

- Do not store albums long term in a horizontal manner. Papers and photos will be crushed and compressed over time.

- Use a lightly dampened cloth to wipe excess grime from fabric and vinyl covers. Use a clear dust jacket to protect the album's cover from hand oils, dust and pollutants.

- Ideal storage conditions are the same as those for photos.

- If storing albums on open shelving, avoid sunlight and keep albums as dust-free as possible. Large computer monitor dust covers, available at office supply stores, can cover multiple albums.

- Spines should be labeled and facing outward so you can read them.

- Avoid the use of magnetic photo albums with static, liftable sleeves. They may be labeled "archival," yet these have been shown to be hazardous to photos.

Make it a point to remove photos from magnetic albums during your "getting organized" project. Remove photos by slipping a slender knife or dental floss beneath a corner to lift. If photos are firmly stuck, try using un-du's PhotoCare™ Solution. If the album's plastic overlay is stuck to your photos, consult a conservator. Never force a photo from a page. If photos have already begun to deteriorate, consider investing in reprints rather than attempting to remove. Never use heat to loosen photos.

Store albums upright on open shelving or in bookcases that are deep enough to accommodate the albums' width. Avoid packing the albums tightly together; excessive compression can damage pages and bindings over time. These beautiful 12 x 12" albums are from Colorbök.

To keep album covers dust-free, try Crop In Style's Protective Album Covers—available in 12 x 12" or 8½ x 11".

Keep albums dust-free with Highsmith's acid-free cardboard Album Cases. You can decorate the album case to identify the album type, if desired.

Cleaners

Cleaners, sprays and solvents need special care, particularly if there are small children in the home. If possible, keep cleaners in a locked toolbox for safety's sake. More helpful tips:

- Keep caps on tightly when products are not in use. Some cleaners evaporate rapidly and fumes can be overwhelming.

- Do not mix chemicals. Allow time for complete drying between chemical processes such as spraying with an archival fixative, using un-du® or inks, heat embossing, or applying liquid lacquers.

- Be careful with cleaners, sprays and solvents near a heat embossing gun. Do not use flamable archival sprays, adhesive remover or spray fixatives in the same room and at the same time as a heat gun. Read all label cautions when using these products indoors.

If possible, keep cleaners in a locked toolbox for safety's sake. Read all label cautions and warnings to be on the safe side, especially when using these products indoors.

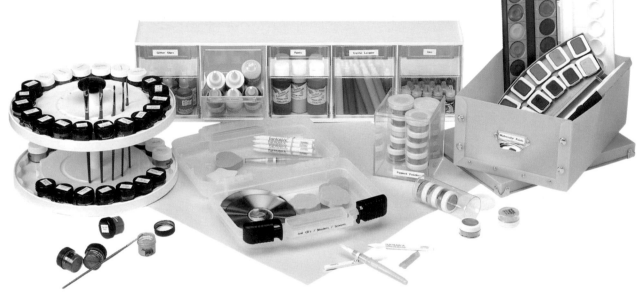

There are many good products available for storing enamels, lacquers and paints. Try Paintier Products' Paintier 40 Carousel, Quantum Storage System's 5-Drawer Tilt Bin or Kokuyo's large E-Z Snap storage box. Store sponges, water brushes, water pens and extra CD "palettes" in ArtBin's Quick View Carrying Case. Flex Products' Flexinizers™—available in many shapes and sizes—work great for stacking pearl powder pigments.

Colorants

Colorants are increasingly finding their way into our scrapbooks and overrunning our scrapbook workspaces. The selection of colorants for scrapbookers has expanded beyond basic pens, markers and ink pads to include chalks, paints and pigment powders, to name a few. Each colorant has its own distinct characteristics and unique properties, which impacts its own care and organization needs. These ideas should help you tame your coloring tools and supplies.

ENAMELS, LACQUERS & PAINTS

Paints are a dynamic medium that come in a spectrum of radiant colors and for different uses. Keep them in ready-to-use condition by following these guidelines:

- Keep watercolor paint palettes in good condition by mixing different paints on an old CD rather than on the paint palette.

- Add a few drops of water to pearl pigment powders on a CD to mix the medium. Do not mix the pigment powders and water in the original container. You are not likely to use all of this type of colorant in one sitting and premature mixing will only waste it.

- Pearl pigment paints never dry on plastic. You may store them in plastic however.

- Store acrylic and stencil paints right side up. Use within a year.

- Keep paintbrushes clean and store carefully to prevent damage to brush tips.

- If you use sponges to apply paint, be sure to wash them out with warm, soapy water and allow to air dry up to 48 hours before storing in a closed container.

- Close clear and crystal color lacquers tightly after use. Even a little air flow will dry the liquid. Use a sewing needle to unclog the lid dispensers of lacquer bottles.

- Store lacquers upright in their jars. This reduces dehydration and decreases leaks.

- Lacquers dry to a shiny, watery effect. Tap applied lacquer to see if it is dry after 24 hours before storing a scrapbook page. If it is firm, it is dry. Store lacquers upright and use within two years.

- Wipe the nozzles of glitter glues and glitter paints with a damp rag before capping. Unclog nozzles with a sewing needle or pin.

- Store enamels, lacquers and paints in their original containers.

- Organize enamels, lacquers and paints by grouping together by brand, type, color or frequency of use.

- Jars can be stored on a spinning rack made to hold small bottles or in bins, totes or drawers.

For large collections of jewel, acrylic or stencil paints, try Canvas Collectibles' over-the-door or wall mounted creative storage solution.

Store clean paintbrushes in ArtBin's Essentials Brush Box or Tutto's Brush Holder tote.

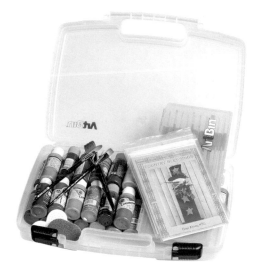

Here's just one of ArtBin's Quick View carrying cases. The company manufacturers a wide array of storage solution boxes and totes are perfect for colorants and other scrapbook tools and supplies.

EMBOSSING POWDERS & ENAMELS

Embossing powders, used primarily with stamping inks and embossing pens, come in a dazzling array of colors and textures, such as "ultra thick," pearl, tinsel and foil. Get the most out of your investment with these tips:

- Seal tightly after use.

- Sprinkle powders onto your art and catch any excess with a sheet of paper or recovery tray. Pour excess powder back into jar to avoid wasting it.

- Beware of the fumes. When heated, embossing powders release fumes as they turn from a solid to a liquid state. Do not inhale fumes or allow them in your eyes.

- Organize embossing powders and enamels by manufacturer, color or type.

- Store away from heat, moisture and water.

- Store in original jars on spinning racks, in trays, in stamp caddies, in bins or drawers. Storing powders upside down will enable you to see the powder colors easier.

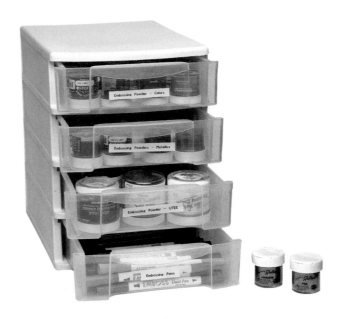

For ease in identification, sort embossing powders by type and then store upside down so that you can view the colors. Ours are stored in a Sterilite desktop drawer unit.

Whenever possible, store pencils in their original containers to be able to differentiate between standard and watercolor pencils. Organize by color grouping for quick access. For pencils that don't come in their own packaging, try storing in Armada Arts' Twist Tube or Kokuyo's small E-Z Snap storage box.

PENCILS

Probably the most under-utilized yet highly effective scrapbook colorant, pencils, are simple to care for, organize and store.

- Keep pencils dry, clean and sharpened.

- Do not drop. Lead is brittle and cracks easily.

- Organize pencils in rainbow-color groupings in original packaging, to be able to differentiate between ordinary color pencils and watercolor pencils.

- Water pens or brushes, used to wipe across watercolor pencils for a painterly effect, should be stored nearby for easy access.

- Store in pencil boxes, desk pen holders, flat-pack caddies or zippered pouches.

PENS FOR BLENDING

- While not a colorant, blender pens are used quite frequently to blend colorants. Keep close at hand for using to blend colorants.

- Before changing colors, wipe the blender tip clean on a scrap piece of paper.

- If the blender brush tip is frayed it can be replaced. Just pull the nib out and replace it with a new nib brush.

- Clean by wiping on clean paper or cloth.

- When your blender pen gets dry, pull the end cap off. Add several drops of blending fluid to refill.

PENS & MARKERS

Make sure your pens are the best possible choices for journaling and drawing in scrapbooks. Pens should be acid-free, fade- and waterproof pigment ink. In addition:

- Don't lose the caps. The minute you open a pen, you are in a race against evaporation. Keep caps on between uses.

- Use your pens regularly at least once a week. This keeps the ink flowing and the tips mobile.

- Avoid excessive writing on the backs of photos. Writing directly on photos may exert too much pressure on the back of the photo, creating visible indentations from the front.

- Many pens are not safe for writing on photo backs. If you want to write on your photos, do so in an inconspicuous place such as a corner. That way it will not affect the photo quality should the ink bleed through to the photo front.

- If you use a spray bulb to splatter ink from pen tips onto your scrapbook pages, immediately wipe the bulb tip with a damp cloth after each use to keep the tip color-free.

- Sort your pens regularly and toss out those that have dried out.

- Sort your pens by color, by type or by brand. Various types of pen points include calligraphy, brush, writer, scroll, bullet and chisel.

- Keep an inventory of what pens, tips, brands and colors you own to prevent duplication.

- While pen manufacturers vary in opinion on whether horizontal or vertical storage is best for pens, we recommend you store pens horizontally at least 90 percent of the time.

- Store pens upright in pen caddies or horizontally in shallow pen cases, boxes, bins or drawers.

- Store pens away from heat registers and drafts. Air movement speeds evaporation—even with the caps on!

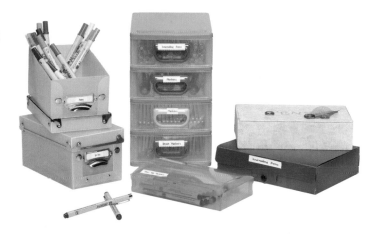

Pen storage options are many. Try Kokuyo's Kaddy™ supply tote (below) or small E-Z Snap storage boxes, Lion Products' Estima desktop drawer unit, General Box Company's Decorate Me™ boxes (we decorated ours!) or Traffic Works' wide array of plastic storage boxes.

For pen totes, try Plaid's Creative Gear™ Pen & Marker Holder or Tutto's Maker Holder tote. Crop In Style offers a 75-Pen Caddy, which stands up or folds flat (left). ArtBin's clear Prism™ and translucent Solutions™ boxes (below) have dividers for keeping pen types separate.

CHALK

Chalk—an inexpensive and popular scrapbook colorant because of its ease of use and versatility—needs special care.

- Keep chalks as dry as possible.

- Avoid dropping chalk cases; chalk palettes are fragile and break easily.

- Clear off extra dust from your chalks by blowing gently or rubbing the surfaces with cotton swabs.

- When using a chalk palette, do not press or twist your applicator into the chalk. Instead, sweep it lightly across the surface to keep chalk in good condition.

- Cover your work surface with paper towels before working withchalk.

- If you use a blender pen with chalks, use plain water so it will dry out evenly and not create an oily residue on top of your chalks.

- Keep a white eraser with your chalk. Chalk mistakes erase with ease.

- If you apply chalk with sponge-tip applicators, keep them clean with warm, soapy water. Allow to dry up to 48 hours before storing in a closed container.

- Spray chalked artwork with a fixative to prevent chalk particles from scattering.

- Store chalks in their original, compartmentalized containers inside zippered sandwich bags or in small supply cases with or without handles.

- Store gel metallic rub-ons closed. Wash all tools immediately after use to remove the fine colorant film.

INK PADS & INK DAUBERS

Make sure your ink pads are safe for your albums. Stamping inks and daubers should be acid-free, fade- and waterproof pigment ink. Available in rich and vibrant hues, ink pads and daubers last longer if you follow these tips:

- Make sure lids are on ink pads securely prior to storing.

- Ink pads should be stored horizontally. Some schools of thought believe that ink pads must be stored upside down.

- Use ink pads regularly to keep the ink sponges saturated.

- Dauber caps tend to fall off easily. Make sure they are secure to prevent dehydration.

- Sort and organize ink pads by color, ink types or brand names for easier identification.

- Ink refill bottles should be stored upright. Keep the caps on tightly.

- Store ink pads in special racks made of wood or corrugated cardboard made specifically for ink storage or in shallow bins, drawers, supply cases or totes.

Keep chalks and metallic rub-ons in their original palette containers. Store colorant applicators in Provo Craft's Bradletz Drawerz. Larger chalk palettes and rub-ons can be stored in Kokuyo's large E-Z Snap storage boxes. Store Craf-T's chalk enhancers and spray fixatives with cleaners, if possible.

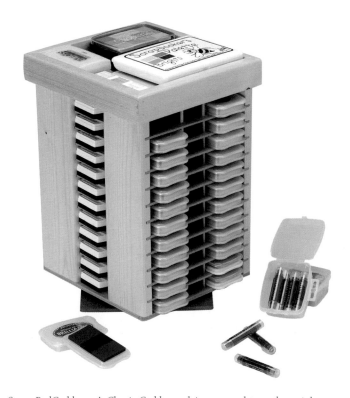

StampPadCaddy.com's Classic Caddy revolving carousel tower keeps ink pads organized and visible, with extra storage at the top for more pads. Tsukineko's ink daubers fit perfectly in TidyCrafts' rectangular Snappy Craft Containers. Other companies that make stamp pad storage include Last Dollar Designs and Port-a-Ink by CDJ Designs, LLC.

Embellishments

The boom in scrapbook embellishments has brought unique beauty and texture to pages along with a storage quandary for the scrapbook workspace. Because these items vary in size and bulk, it can be challenging to arrange them for easy access. How do you sort, organize and store all these baubles and trinkets? Don't fear! Solutions for taming all of your embellishments are right at hand.

METALLICS

Metal embellishments lend a shiny luster or masculine touch to scrapbooks. Metallics include bookplates, brad fasteners, charms, embossing metals, eyelets, frames, hinges, jewelry-making components, nailheads, photo corners, tags, wire, wire mesh, chains, penny nails and washers. Though tough and resilient by nature, metallics do require a little tender loving care where storage is concerned.

- Store all metal embellishments in low humidity. Flexible metals have alloys which can rust, as can those metals with iron in. (Test with a magnet. If a magnet can pick it up, it has iron in it.)

- Keep all metals dry and wiped free of hand oils which contain body salts. Salt, water, and other chemicals can lead to the corrosion of metal. Make sure you wipe all fingerprints and hand oils from metals before you encase them.

- Aluminum can oxidize, turning black over time. Make sure aluminum-coated or rimmed tags are not touching your photos.

- Copper oxidizes when exposed to air and gains a green patina or coating. This patina can flake off much. Keep copper items like tags, embellishments, copper eyelets and pennies encased and separated from your photos on the page.

- Label your eyelet hole punches with the size of hole it creates. Use a permanent marker to write S ($\frac{1}{16}$"), M ($\frac{1}{8}$"), and L ($\frac{1}{4}$") on the tip itself.

- Carry a sample of each eyelet color and size when you shop; to prevent buying duplicates. String one example of each color and style onto a large safety pin or a length of wire and tuck it in your handbag.

- Memorabilia keepers are great for encapsulating coins or heritage metal objects. This limits air flow, human contact and humidity changes.

- Sort such embellishments by type of item and then by color.

- Choose storage solutions that suit either your desktop, travel tote or both. Consider storage that effectively contains your organized embellishment collection, plus has a little room for growth to accommodate new items that attract your eye.

- Store in compartmentalized units, nut-and-bolt drawer organizers, watchmaker tins, compartmentalized trays, craft cases, a carousel outfitted with round containers made specially for craft supplies, stackable clear canisters, clear and flat compartment organizers and carrying cases with handles and tight-fitting lids.

For keeping metallic embellishments organized, try ScrapKings' aluminum cases with matching tins; Uniek's clear, round dispenser; Quantum Storage Products' 9-Drawer Tilt Bin; Provo Craft's Bradletz Drawerz; SCS/Hemline's compartmentalized Storage Organizer and Craft Storage Stackers, TidyCrafts' rectangular Snappy Craft Containers, and Making Memories' 18-compartment Sortables box and Stackables jar towers. For at-a-glance identification and shopping ease, add one type of each eyelet you own on a wire and twist ends to secure. And for a unique container that can mount under a desk or cabinet, try TidyCrafts' Eclipse™ container with six Shuttle Cups tucked inside (below).

BAUBLES

Baubles add an ornamental flair to scrapbook pages. These items include beads, buttons, confetti, gems, glitter, punched shapes, sequins, tiny glass marbles and more. All should have their own homes. These mini wonders add so much to your pages but are easily misplaced. To find what you need in a hurry:

- • If the baubles are made of glass, stone or fired ceramic, they contain no acid and will not harm photos or scrapbooks.

- Plastic items are suitable as long as they do not contain PVC. If you're not sure whether a bauble is photo-safe, encapsulate it or place it away from photos.

- Remember that baubles are hard objects that can potentially scratch your photos; don't place photos opposite these items on a facing page.

- To avoid adding excess bulk to a page, use small and flat objects whenever possible.

- Sort such embellishments by type of item and then by color.

- Store in containers with clear bodies and/or lids that permit you to see what's inside, allowing for easier identification.

- Use containers that give your fingers easy access, close tightly and allow you to pour easily into a tray for further sorting.

- Choose storage solutions that suit either your desktop, travel tote or both. Consider storage that effectively contains your organized embellishment collection, plus has a little room for growth to accommodate new items that attract your eye.

- Store in compartmentalized units, nut-and-bolt drawer organizers, watchmaker tins, compartmentalized trays, craft cases, a carousel outfitted with round containers made specially for craft supplies, stackable clear canisters, clear and flat compartment organizers and carrying cases with handles and tight-fitting lids.

To contain baubles, try Eagle Affiliates' The Bead Tray, Flex Products' Flexanizers™, Magic Scraps' jar tower, TidyCrafts' round Pony Craft Containers, SCS/Hemline's round Craft Storage Stacker, Crop In Style's Itty-Bitty Box and Darice's The Ultimate Bead Box & Band. Beadalon's Mini Bead Tray works great for corralling and pouring tiny baubles.

TidyCrafts' Deluxe Carousel Craft Organizer with Pony Craft Containers provide quick-view access, as do Flambeau Products' ArtBin's Clear View Storage Boxes and Leeco/Cropper Hopper's Embellishment Organizers. TidyCraft's Tidy Trays also provide easy corralling and pouring of tiny baubles.

TEXTILES

From embroidery threads, fibers and jute to raffia, ribbon and yarn—textiles add a finishing touch to scrapbook pages. If you have ever had to stop scrapbooking to untangle a softball-sized tangle of fibers and embroidery threads, you understand the special storage needs that textiles present. Read on to learn how to restrain unruly yard goods.

- Fibers manufactured from natural materials—such as cotton ribbons, threads, hemp, jute and raffia—need to be kept dry for longevity. Moisture invites mildew and rot.

- Both natural and synthetic textiles may contain fugitive dyes. Test for color permanence by applying a moist cotton swab to the textile to see if the color spreads onto the swab.

- Some fibers last longer if you spray them with archival sprays. These include wood-product fibers, hemp and raffia.

- If a textile holds sentimental value, such as a ribbon from a wedding gown or baby booties, it should be encapsulated to protect if from adhesive, light, dust and moisture.

- Sort and group textiles by color family for easier access. For example, keep red fibers, ribbons, embroidery threads and yarn together on the same cardstock "bobbin" or on separate bobbins in the same container.

- Some scrapbookers prefer to separate the individual color strands of fibers that come in multi-packs, while others prefer to keep them together as packaged. Use the method that best suits your scrapbooking style.

- Try not to bunch textiles which makes them wrinkle. Winding them around a bobbin or cardstock square is a better option.

- Floss boxes come with embroidery floss winding cards or bobbins. Wind one fiber type on each card. File these mini cards in the floss box by color. Each box can hold dozens of these small, fiber-wrapped cards. You can also place the bobbins in sticker sleeves in binders.

- Store textiles in compartmentalized boxes or cases, pocketed totes or in binders inside sticker protectors.

Eagle Affiliates' The Cross-Stitch Case and SCS/Hemline's Embroidery Thread Organizer help tame fibers when used with Uniek's plastic or SCS/Hemline's cardboard "bobbins." For quick winding of fibers onto bobbins, try Westex Corporations' Floss Winder.

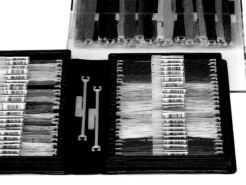

Keep embroidery floss sorted and under control with DMC's StitchBox™ Floss Holders, stored in the company's Organizing & Storage Binders and Cases (above). Plaid's Creative Gear™ Floss & Bobbin Holder tote provides on-the-go floss containment.

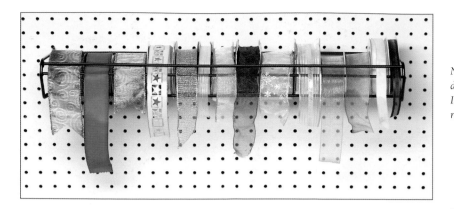

Novelcrafts' sticker dispenser for pegboard pulls double-duty keeping rolls of ribbon organized and ready for use. It's great for keeping large rolls of stickers organized and ready for use, too!

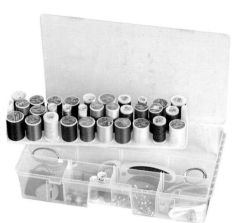

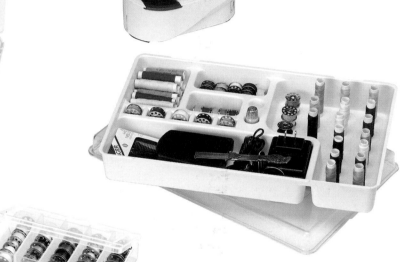

If you stitch on scrapbook pages, either by hand or by machine, you'll appreciate SCS/Hemline's Sewing Supplies Organizer (right), ArtBin's Sew-Lutions™ (above) and Bobbin Boxes. Tutto's Bobbin & Needlecraft Holder tote makes it easy to travel with threads.

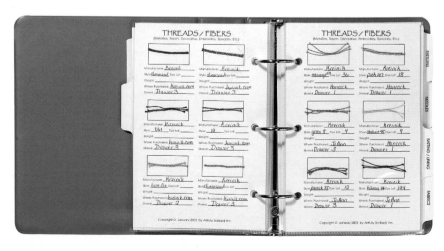

Use Artfully Scribed's Stitch-A-Log™ to help organize your fiber, floss and thread collections. The pre-printed three-ring binder even has a section for recording your favorite "master" stitches.

ORGANICS

Organic materials add a touch of nature to scrapbook albums. However, care and storage of organic materials—like cork sheets, feathers, pressed flowers, sand, shells, skeletonized leaves and tree bark—are an ongoing challenge. But these natural elements are definitely worth the extra effort. Here are some tips to help guide you.

- Keep all natural materials dry.

- Encase flowers and loose petals in vellum envelopes, plastic memorabilia envelopes and pockets or in separate areas where they will not harm photos if they crumble or shed seeds.

- Allow flowers to dry at least three months in open air before placing them in a storage container or scrapbook so that any tiny insect eggs can hatch and any microscopic insects will leave the organic matter.

- Shells, sand, twigs, bark and other organic items should be encapsulated in memorabilia pockets, plastic envelopes, or well-sealed shaker boxes.

- Shells should be allowed to dry naturally for two months in open air before you store them in containers or use them in a scrapbook. This allows the body of the animal to decompose inside the shell and not cause odors.

- Twigs and bark may cause staining of page elements due to wood tannins. If you use them in scrapbooking, allow them to dry for at least two months before storage or use. Keep them at least 4" away from photographs.

- Sort and group like items together.

- Whenever possible, keep organic materials flat and stable. Many are delicate and will break in too large storage containers that allow excessive movement.

- Store organic materials in zippered bags, flat boxes or cases or memorabilia keepers until you are ready to use them.

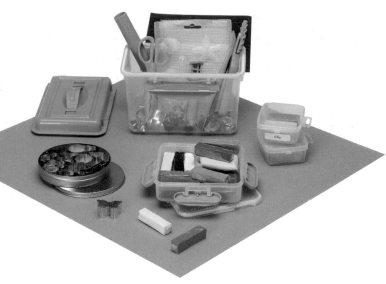

If you use clay in your scrapbooks, you'll appreciate Provo Crafts' Makin's Clay's Airtight Storage Boxes for clay and tools. Also, try TidyCraft's rectangular Snappy Craft Containers for storing small bars of clay.

For storing organic scrapbooking materials, stick with containers that provide little movement of materials as many organics are delicate. We like Akro-Mils' Craft Organizer Caddy, Flex Products' Flexanizers™ tubes and boxes, 3L's Memorabilia Pockets and C-Thru Ruler Company's Déjà Views® 3D Keepers.

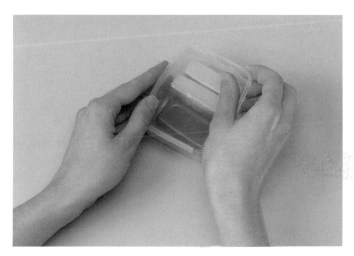

Keep your clays soft, supple and ready to use by "burping" containers to remove any excess air in them before closing tightly.

Inspirations

The inspirations and ideas that you rely on for scrapbook page design, page titles and journaling come in many forms and from many sources. Scrapbookers find inspiration from books, magazines, Internet Web sites, calendars, greeting cards, fabric or wallpaper swatches, napkin designs and the world around them. Some inspirations are printed from the computer, photocopied, photographed or simply torn from magazines. Other forms may include . Learn how to make a molehill out these "paper prompter" mountains. Knowing exactly where your page ideas are filed will save you half the time when you need to do the actual page layout. Being able to retrieve the idea when you need it is the secret to good organization.

IDEA BOOKS & MAGAZINES

Books and magazines can accumulate rapidly, especially if you are an avid subscriber. There are things you can do to stay on top of these types of inspiration.

- Avoid letting new idea books and magazines stack up in piles for "later." Later is an elusive beast often hard to find. Go through books and magazines within a week of receiving them and affix sticky notes only to the pages you really want to re-create.

- To easily identify a page theme, try color-coding page ideas with different colored sticky notes. For example, use pink or blue to tag baby pages, yellow to tag travel pages, green to tag Christmas, orange to tag autumn pages, etc. Use the same color coding system to tag other sources of inspiration, such as those listed on the following pages.

- Some magazine publishers' Web sites have indexes for the past year's article topics. Print these out and store them with that year's magazines for quick reference.

Store punch art, theme, technique and general interest scrapbooking books in Highsmith's Colorful Magazine Files, which can be decorated as you wish to identify the different types of books you have.

- Some scrapbookers opt to avoid the storage of periodicals altogether by simply tearing out the ideas or techniques they like. Ideas are then pasted on a sheet of typing paper and sorted, organized, labeled and inserted into a binder. They then pitch the magazine.

- If color-coding pages with sticky notes or tearing magazine pages out is not for you, try scanning page ideas that you want to re-create. Print them out as 4 x 5" images in black-and-white. File in an index-card file or keep them in a binder sorted, organized and labeled by theme or season . Label with a reference to the issue date, number and page so you can find the original if needed.

- Do not keep a "miscellaneous" file section. It will get too big and too broad to be useful.

- Regardless of the organizational system you choose for books and magazines, file the ideas right away. Keep only the layout concepts you know you will use in due time.

Avoid letting new idea books and magazines stack up in piles for "later." Some magazine publishers manufacture specialty binders in which to store their scrapbook magazines.

- Sort and organize magazines by month, year or publisher. Some scrapbookers store their magazines in groups by month regardless of publisher, which enables them to find seasonal ideas quickly.

- Try organizing a year's worth of magazines in chronological order. Then photocopy each index page and file all twelve of these in the front of the yearly section.

- Create a database in a word-processing program that indicates your favorite page layouts and which pages they are on in certain books or magazines.

- Sort your magazines yearly. You will be surprised how your tastes change over time. Do not keep every magazine you buy. If you have outgrown everything in a magazine, gift it to a new scrapbooker, sell it on an Internet auction or at a garage sale.

- Store magazines in publisher-manufactured three-ring binders in bookcases or on open shelving.

- Sort and organize idea books by topic. Group theme books (wedding, baby, toddler, school, travel, heritage, etc.), how-to technique books (paper crafts, photo cropping, punch art, rubber stamping, etc.) and general interest (basic scrapbooking topics, like this book) together for storing.

- Books should be stored on end with spines facing you.

- Take your favorite "used often" idea books to an office-supply store and have them spliced and spiral bound. This allows them to lie flat without harming the spine.

POEMS, QUOTES & SAYINGS

Poems, quotes or sayings may link your mind to a set of photos you already have or photos you would like to take. These inspirational words easily become page titles and journaling blocks. If you enjoy researching and saving these words of wisdom, put a good organizational system in place so you can find them when you need them.

- Use a word-processing program to keep a database file in your computer and add quotes you like to it. Sort the lists by season and theme.

- Keep a section in a scrapbook inventory binder (see page 48) for your poems, page title ideas, quotes and sayings, or keep them in a separate binder.

- Print poems, quotes and sayings that you love immediately onto vellum as a 4 x 5" size. File these "ready to use" vellum words by theme with your other pre-made page additions. Use as you would other pre-made sentiments, sticker poems and titles for quick pages.

- Print poems out as simple text documents and file in hanging files by topic. You can later retype them in fonts you prefer.

- Use a diskette or reusable CD to store poetry you find online. Keep it near the computer and update it as needed. You can also create a CD for each season. Add all the Christmas, valentine and snow poems to the "winter poetry" CD. Retrieve them from the CD as needed.

- Keep a "poems, quotes and sayings" notebook in your own handwriting, divided by season or theme.

Store sorted poems, quotes and sayings by theme in Kokuyo's Color 'N' Color Collection three-ring binders. Use notebook dividers to separate theme categories.

PAGE SKETCHES

If you're one of those talented scrapbookers with the artistic ability to sketch out page design layouts, the following ideas may help keep them organized.

- Sketch your own layout ideas on blank paper or index cards.

- File idea index cards according to either theme, supplies used, or number of photos used. Use the same type of labeling system if storing ideas in a binder.

- Tack sketches up on large bulletin boards or room divider screens for quick reference if you intend to create the page in the very near future.

PERSONAL MEMORIES

Personal memories and notes about events from your life and the lives of loved ones are numerous. Use these ideas to help preserve and document these memories, with the ultimate goal of getting these memories into a scrapbook album to share with others.

- Keep a daily journal or a journal that you write in after each photographic event. Note the date, place, and people as well as any emotions, happy or sad happenings, or memories from the event. Jot down your thoughts. You don't have to use all of this information in a family scrapbook but it will be a good device to jog your memory when you do make the scrapbook page.

- Keep a "snapshot log" with your camera. Each time you return the camera to its storage spot, jot down notes from the snapshot session just completed.

- Tape recordings, recorder buttons and videotapes are great devices for recording the elder generation. Interview them at length and transcribe the notes for later. See page 40 for care, organization and storage of audio- and videotapes.

- Keep computer text files in a word-processing program. Memories can either be verbose or simple; from rough notes to elegant essays. Keep track of the feelings behind the events. You can even import poems, quotes or images into the file for later use.

Page sketches on index cards store nicely in General Box Company's Decorate Me™ boxes, decorated how and wherever your whimsy takes you.

- Jot short blurbs down on sticky notes and attach them to the backs of photos as soon as they are printed.

- Never throw away your annual calendars or day planners. They hold a wellspring of information about the events of a year. Get in the habit of recording as much information about daily life as possible on a calendar and store the calendar with that year's photographs to help jog memories about dates, times and events.

OTHER SOURCES OF INSPIRATION

Wherever you find words, shapes, color and texture, you will find page design inspiration! You can find "photos to take" ideas, journaling or graphic concepts in advertisements, billboards, cartoons, catalogs, children's story books, clip art, clothing, coloring books, gift wrap, greeting cards, t-shirts, wall paper and borders. Keep track of these noteworthy inspirations for quick reference.

- Trim tear sheets with scissors.

- Sort and group these inspirations by themes or topics.

- Paste ideas onto index cards and store in an index-card file or on notebook paper stored in a binder.

- Label card file or notebook dividers as you label any other source of information, color-coding as needed to keep your organized inspiration system easily identified and united.

To help with journaling on scrapbook pages, get in the habit of keeping a daily journal, saving annual calendars and attaching sticky notes right away to the backs of photos when you get the prints from your photo lab.

If you collect design and quote inspirations from sources like greeting cards, catalogs, etc., you'll find it helpful to trim them down and paste on index cards by theme. Then use file card dividers to keep them sorted by theme. As you tear out new inspirations, immediately paste them on the cards to avoid clutter.

Paper

Paper is one of the most important staples in a scrapbooker's arsenal of tools and supplies. It comes in hundreds of colors, patterns, textures and weights and is sold by single sheet or in packets, pads or booklets. Paper plays a vital role in scrapbook page design and it is one of the most enjoyable items to shop for at the store. You may have a lot of paper or a just a little. Either way, you need to know how to take care of it so that it gets from the store to the completed scrapbook page in good condition.

- Keep your paper in a clean, dry place away from direct sunlight.

- Ideal temperatures for paper storage are between 65 to 80 degrees Fahrenheit, with low to moderate humidity.

For small or portable paper collections, try Kokuyo's Paper Kaddy (available in two sizes), Leeco/Cropper Hopper's Paper Organizer, Mochalatte's Scrapping & Accessories Organizer, Caren's Crafts' Scrap-N-File Photomate™ and Scrap-N-File™ Original, Generations' 12 x 12" Scrapfolio™ or Plaid® Creative Gear's Expandable File.

- To be photo-safe, paper should be pH neutral (acid-free) and lignin-free.

- Many varieties are buffered, which is preferable for scrapbooking projects.

- Keep insects away from your papers.

- Pets and small children can cause a lot of turmoil with a paper stack. Keep your paper out of reach of children and family pets.

- Sort and group solid-colored paper and cardstock using the "ROYGBIV" rainbow order. This is Red, Orange, Yellow, Green, Blue, Indigo and Violet. Add black, gray, white, cream, brown and tans to the front or the back end of the filing spectrum.

- Sort and group patterned papers by design theme (see list on page 455) for easier access.

- Not all vellum, mulberry, metallic or handmade papers are archivally safe and, as such, should not be allowed to directly touch photos and memorabilia on a scrapbook page or be stored with acid-free, archival-safe papers.

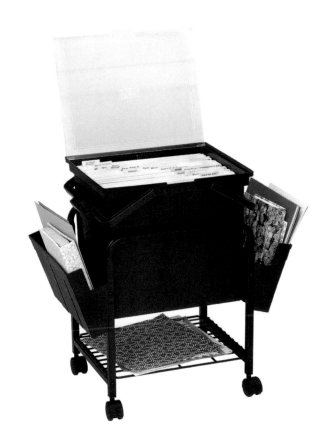

Plastic paper totes come in mainly in two styles: those with and those without dividers, as in the case of Leeco/Cropper Hopper's 12 x 12" Paper Organizers.

If you prefer vertical paper storage, Leeco/Cropper Hopper's 12 x 12" Heavy Duty Workstation allows for simple sort-and-drop filing. The unit holds over 4,000 sheets of paper.

- If you have a significant collection of vellum, mulberry, metallic or handmade papers, sort by color and/or theme. Otherwise, a simple folder or drawer for each paper type may suffice.

- For booklets of paper, you have a number of organization options. You can keep the paper bound in the booklet until ready to use and just organize the booklets on a shelf or in a 12 x 12" binder by theme. Or tear the patterned sheets from the booklet and incorporate into the rest of your sorted patterned or specialty papers.

- When you identify papers you no longer wish to use for scrapbooking, they can be used for wrapping small gifts, making greeting cards or other craft projects.

- Create a "give-away" folder filled with papers you no longer care for anymore. When the folder is full, give it to a charity or a scrapbooking friend.

- Store your paper in a manner that makes it easy for you to find it again. If you like to work by manufacturer, sort that way. If you work by theme, sort your patterned papers that way.

- Paper can be stored in a wide variety of ways. Store paper horizontally whenever possible. For horizontal storage, store paper flat in corrugated cardboard, wire, wood or acrylic paper racks, trays or shallow drawer units.

- For vertical storage, store paper upright in magazine file boxes, accordion files, hanging files in cropping bins or file drawers, or in paper cases and totes. If storing paper vertically, keep it snugly filed so it does not curl or "hunch" over.

- When storing paper on wire racks, make inexpensive dust covers from bed sheeting. Fasten fabric to wire racks with heavy-duty glue dots.

- Secure tall racks to the wall, if possible, to prevent toppling.

- Take a sample sheet of scrapbooking paper along with you when you shop for storage containers. You can test the fit before you buy.

- Keep a 12 x 12" paper keeper in your car for unexpected shopping trips to keep the paper in tip-top shape until you get it home.

There are many options, styles and sizes available for wire paper storage solutions, including Novelcrafts' Scrapbook Displays (black) and Caren's Crafts' Stack-N-File™ Hanging File System. Take precautions to ensure that small children cannot climb on or topple over tall paper racks and towers.

Patterned paper categories

You'll find that you can sort, group and/or organize most all of your patterned paper into the following theme categories. As a general rule, the more paper you have, the more precise you'll need your categories. The less paper you have, the more broad your categories can be. Perhaps you'll find themes or categories that we haven't even thought of!

Amusement Park/Carnival	Patriotic
Animals or pets	Picnic/BBQ
Autumn	Plaids
Baby	Pool
Beach	Religious
Birthday	School
Camping/fishing	Scouting
Celebrations	Seasonal
Chanukah	Snow
Characters	Sports
Christmas	Spring
Disney	Stripes
Dots	Summer
Easter	Swirls
Feminine	Teen
Floral	Texture
Gardening	Thanksgiving
Halloween	Travel
Heritage/Victorian	Wedding
Holidays	Winter
Masculine	Zoo
Nature and outdoors	

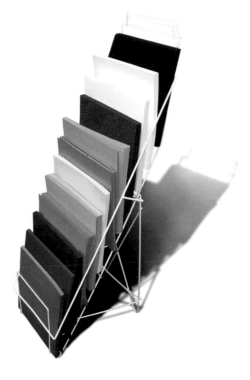

DMD's 12 x 12" Paper Pack Rack provides upright paper storage. It is also available in an 8½ x 11" model.

Specialty papers

You'll find that most of your specialty papers will fall into one of the following categories:

Handmade	Suede
Metallic	Vellum
Mulberry	Woodgrain

For those who prefer acid-free cardboard paper storage, a couple of options include Highsmith's 12 x 12" Supply Chest (left) and 8½ x 11" Paper Keeper (center). For smaller or specialty paper collections, try Generations' Memory Express™. For the fun of it, all can be decorated and embellished to suit your personal style.

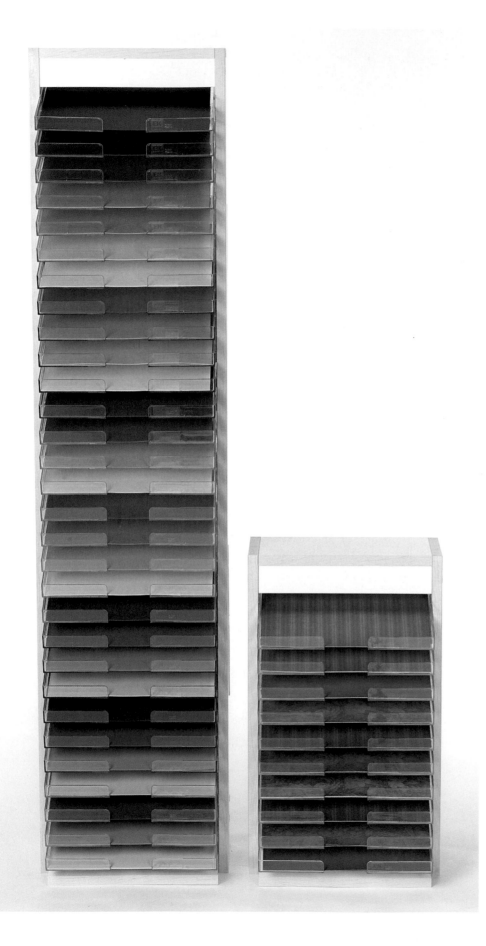

Another paper storage option is Display Dynamics' flexible, stackable clear plastic paper trays and wood laminate towers. The Paper Station has enough space to hold 30 trays, while the Paper Station Mini can accommodate 10 trays. Both models are available in 12 x 12" and 8½ x 11" sizes. The stations can stand on floors, desktops or anywhere you keep paper. Display Dynamics' also has free-standing, stackable trays in both popular paper sizes. With tall paper racks and towers, take precautions to ensure that small children cannot climb on them or topple them over.

PAPER SCRAPS

Scrapbooking generates a lot of bits and pieces of paper scraps. Those little scraps come in awfully handy for creating punch art, photo corners, mats, journaling blocks and other page accents. Keeping paper scraps organized will ensure that they get used thus getting the most bang for your scrapbook buck.

- Dump out your entire lot of scrap papers. Use a pair of scissors to trim off any frayed, bent or awkward edges to make containment easier.

- As if you're dealing a deck of cards, sort scraps into piles by color family. It isn't necessary to separate out solid and patterned papers. Simply "deal" each scrap into the following piles: white/white patterns, black and black/gray patterns, brown/brown patterns, cream/cream patterns, red/red patterns, orange/orange patterns, yellow/yellow patterns, green/green patterns, blue/blue patterns and violet/violet patterns.

- Sort specialty papers by group (see type categories on page 455) or intermix types and sort by color. Remember not to store archival papers with specialty papers.

- Once all scraps are sorted determine the most suitable-sized storage container for your scraps.

- Paper scrap storage options include drawer units, vertical hanging file folders and accordion files. Be sure to label each category of paper color for at-a-glance locating.

- If desired, cut scraps into 3 x 3" or 4 x 4" journaling squares, 4½ x 6½" photo mats and 2" squares. Punch jumbo and mega squares and circles for future use in page titles or accents. File these precut paper blocks in rainbow-color order with your pre-made page accents (see following page).

- Throw away paper scraps that are no larger than 2 x 2".

You'd be amazed at how much additional use you can get out of paper scraps when they are organized. Store in accordion-style keepers such as Caren's Crafts' Scrap-N-Sticker Border File™ (which also works great for stickers!).

PRE-MADE PAGE ADDITIONS

Next to paper and embellishments, pre-made page additions are likely to be your largest collection of mass chaos among your scrapbooking supplies. There's a reason why these collections grow so fast; they look smashing on scrapbook pages and help make scrapbook page design quick and easy. That is, of course, if you can find your page additions.

A pre-made page addition comes in many forms and can include anything that you add to a page as a decorative accent, design element, title or journaling block, border, frame or corner design. See the list on the next for paper items that could be considered a page addition.

For scrapbooking efficiency, organize all of your page additions by theme—not by type of supply or by product manufacturer. For example, when you create a winter page layout, find all of your "winter" accents quickly in the "winter" section of your page additions or use the patterned paper categories on page 455. These tips will help:

- Store page additions flat, either horizontally or vertically. Possible storage containers include accordion-type files, large envelopes, file folders, plastic drawer units, or binders outfitted with page protectors.

- Glue die cuts or other page additions onto blank sheets of paper by theme with removable/repositionable adhesive. Store these sheets by theme category in page protectors within binders.

- Use a 12 x 12" or 8½ x 11" three-ring binder for page addition storage. Binders with page protectors and photo sleeves will fit all sizes of page additions or die cuts. Your binder can be stored in your file drawer, large tote or bin, or on the desk.

- Store paper die-cut shapes in boxes, accordion files, hanging files, tilt bins, binders, plastic zippered sandwich bags held on a ring, or inexpensive 4 x 6" photo albums—sorted and organized by theme.

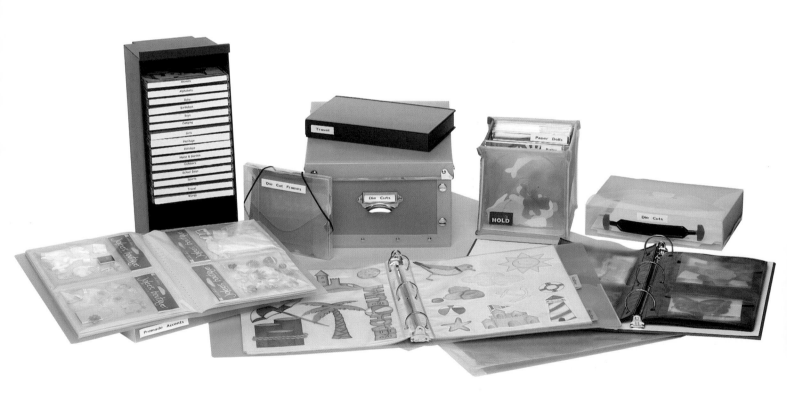

There are many ways to store organized pre-made page additions and die cuts. Try Kokuyo's photo albums with cases, Leeco's Media File Bin outfitted with jewel cases, Traffic Works' corded storage boxes, VHS "clamshell" cases, Kokuyo's large E-Z Snap boxes, Inventor's Studio's Fold 'N Hold mesh caddy outfitted with CD jewel cases, Traffic Works' handled storage boxes, Light Impressions' Slimline CD Album with protective sleeves or Kokuyo's Color 'N' Color Collection binder with page protectors.

WHAT'S A PRE-MADE PAGE ADDITION?

- 3-D stickers
- Blank journaling boxes
- Border accents
- Decorative elements
- Die cuts
- Frames
- Handmade page accents
- Laser-cut frames
- Page "toppers" and titles

- Paper dolls
- Paper piecings
- Paper-folding patterns
- Paper-piecing patterns
- Preprinted poems
- Punch art or punched pieces
- Stickers
- Tags

PAGE ADDITION THEMES

Finding an element quickly is the object of page-addition organization and sorting by themes is one of the most efficient methods. Divide your page additions into at least four seasonal categories. The more page additions you have, the more theme categories you will need. Keep your theme categories in alphabetical order. If you have more than 10 pages of one theme, break it into subcategories. For example, Autumn can become Halloween, Thanksgiving, Autumn Activities, etc. Or Winter can be broken down into Christmas, New Year's, Wintry Activities, and so on. Pick and choose from these suggested themes, depending on what best describes your page-addition collection, or use the themes on page 455 for sorting.

- Animals/Pets/Zoo
- Baby/Small children
- Bible/Religion
- Birthday/Celebration/Party
- Camping/Hiking
- Christmas
- Computers/Technology
- Disney
- Eras—1970s, 1980s, 1990s, etc.
- Fall/Leaves/Halloween
- Floral/Garden
- Food/Dishes/Teapots
- Hearts
- Heritage/Victorian

- Hobbies/Scrapbooking/ Quilting/Tools
- Holidays (Choose the holidays that suit your family)
- Music/Stage/Dance
- Paper dolls (Blank and not dressed—no theme yet)
- School/Artist/Graduation
- Scouting
- Sports
- Summer/Sun/Sandals
- Trees/Large Shrubs
- Travel/Vehicles
- Water/Beach/Pool
- Wedding
- Winter/Snow

For large die-cut and page-addition collections, Quantum Storage Systems' special Die Cut Centers come in two varieties: wall-mounted or mobile, like the one shown at left.

Stickers can be an immense part of your scrapbooking supply collection. They vary in theme, size and style and can pose an organizational challenge. There are, however, some great ways to organize and store the stickers you have without crushing or damaging them. Once you get your stickers and page additions organized, you'll know just where to find them for photo mats, borders, page accents, journaling blocks, corners, on pop ups, and inside large die-cut cardstock letters. Follow these convenient tips for taming your sticker collection:

- Sort your stickers into themes.

- Use the right-sized storage device. Stuffing a 12" inch sticker into an 11" space will end in crushing and crumpling your supplies.

- Put away stickers promptly after purchase or scrapbooking to prevent damage or loss.

- Give each theme and size of sticker its own home within your filing system.

- Store your letter and number stickers separately from your theme and picture-style stickers.

- Sliding your stickers into page protectors or slip-in sleeves of some kind will protect them better than having them loose in a file system where edges will catch and sticker strips will come loose and adhere to their neighbors.

- Sticker storage containers include sticker binders produced by sticker manufacturers; storage cases with index cards as dividers; page protectors in three-ring binders; slip-in, sleeve-style photo album refill pages for 4 x 6" and 5 x 7" photos (for smaller stickers); accordion-style file organizers or hanging files in cabinets.

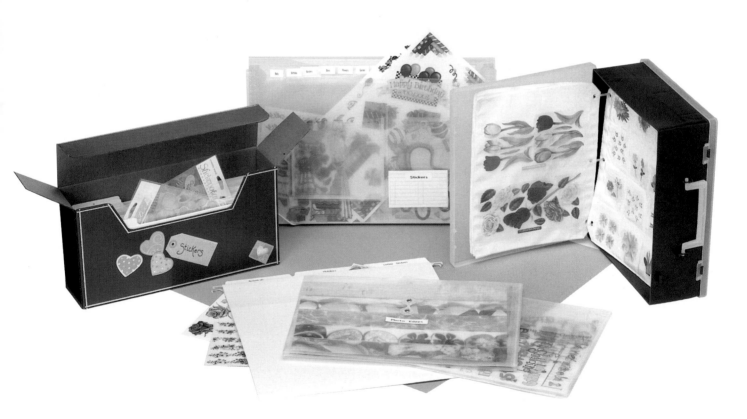

Sticker storage options include Highsmith's Sticker Keeper, ready for you to decorate; Caren's Crafts' accordion-style Scrap-N-Sticker Border File™; Leeco/Cropper Hopper's Sticker Case and Generations' Craft Keeper pockets, to name a few. For "drop system" storage, try Making Memories' hanging file folders.

Uses for extra stickers

When sorting stickers, you may come across a few you no longer like for scrapbooking. Use them in a variety of ways around the home.

- Spruce up plain gift bags and plain butcher paper by adding stickers. Vary the theme for each gift bag or sheet of gift wrap.

- Give them to your youngster. He or she will love playing with them.

- Donate them as a scrapbooking door prize at the next crop you attend.

- Make greeting cards. It only takes a few stickers and a few pieces of cardstock to make an elegant card.

- Place the stickers on reward charts or chore charts for your children or grandchildren.

- Add them to the school carnival prize bucket.

- Place them on your outgoing bills and letters to brighten a mail handler's day.

- Swap, donate or sell them (see page 416).

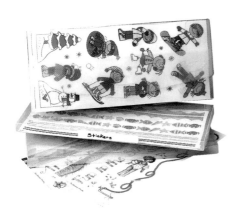

Crop In Style's zippered Paper/Sticker Binder (PSB), outfitted with the company's acid- and PVC-free inserts, is sure to fit your sticker storing needs.

Leeco/Cropper Hopper manufactures a number of sticker storage options, including a 7 x 12" Expandable Organizer and an Oversized Organizer. The company's 12 x 12" Hanging Sticker Sheet Variety Packs drop right into their 12 x 12" Heavy Duty Workstation for vertical sticker storage.

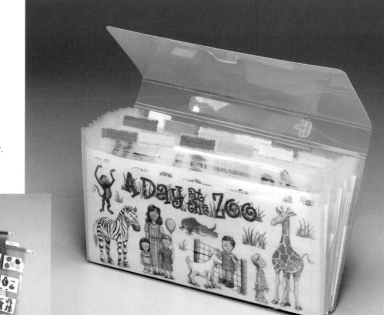

ALTERNATIVE WORKSPACE & STORAGE OPTIONS

You now have fairly good exposure to the wide variety of wonderful storage products and units designed specifically for scrapbookers. While a visit to the local scrapbook or container store will reveal a plethora of storage and containment ideas, there are plenty of less-expensive substitutes as well if you are on a fairly tight budget.

Selecting the right storage unit can be an overwhelming task at first, but if you have experience organizing a household or an office, many of the same principles apply. In fact, many of the same storage materials that you use to organize household and office supplies come in handy in a scrapbook workspace.

In this chapter you will learn about a variety of places where you can find frugal yet effective storage solutions. You will discover how to comb a flea market for inexpensive storage supplies. You will also find suggestions for incorporating antiques into your workspace and tips for converting ordinary household items into sensational storage containers.

In no time at all, you will have a place for everything so that you can finally put everything in its proper place!

At the flea market, bring lots of small bills and be prepared to wade through aisles and aisles of boxes, bins and booths in search of storage containers. Don't get sidetracked by all of the other stuff. Stay on goal.

Frugal Flea-Market Finds

Flea markets can be a storage and container "treasure trove." Flea markets can also be a financial downfall if you are a spontaneous shopper who loves to buy anything fun that catches your eye. The key to successful flea-market shopping is to stay focused on finding products you truly need.

To prove that an effective workspace can be pulled together quickly and economically, three *Memory Makers* staffers—Senior Book Editor MaryJo Regier, Executive Magazine Editor Debbie Mock and Staff Photographer Ken Trujillo—visited a local flea market to test their shopping prowess. Their mission? To stock a complete workspace for $100 or less.

PREPARATION

To get the very best deals possible, staffers made the following preparations before hitting the flea market. These ideas will help you be more successful at the flea market as well.

- First they assessed their scrapbooking tools and supplies and storage containers and needs (see shopping list on following page).

- Then they set a budget and agreed to bargain as much as possible in an effort to spend $100 or less.

- The workspace area's height, width and depth were measured and recorded. The measurements and a tape measure were taken to the flea market to avoid the frustration of purchasing an item that would be too big for the space.

- The team decided to take MaryJo's van for hauling purchases back to the office.

STAYING FOCUSED

Our staff shoppers put on their proverbial "horse blinders" before walking down the flea market aisles. The team had to resist the temptation to purchase paintbrushes, make-up sponges, etc.—many of which cost less than a dollar—and focus on the goal at hand: to find items in which they could store their scrapbooking supplies. "If you keep repeating 'store and contain' over and over to yourself, it will help you stick to your mission of finding organizational containers," says MaryJo.

Don't be too shy to get right in there and dig down into a seller's wares. Sometimes the best storage treasures are hidden deep!

FINDING PERSPECTIVE

Our staffers found that not everything at the flea market was a bargain. Some items could be found at a lower price at discount or office supply stores. In other cases, the quality of the products at the flea market was compromised and purchasing these items new at a store, even if they cost a little more money, made sense. As Debbie explains, "If you can pick up a sturdy new table at a home store for $50, it will probably be a better investment than a wobbly $15 table from the flea market."

HAVING PATIENCE

Shopping a flea market is not the fastest process, but it can reap huge rewards. Staffers wore their best walking shoes so that they were prepared to walk the entire market. Oftentimes they found an item that seemed almost right but not perfect. Rather than purchasing it on the spot, they moved on, noting where in the market the item was located, in case they decided to return later on.

BEING PERSISTENT

Things at the flea market were not always organized. Staffers made sure to dig into bins and to scan each booth to make sure they didn't overlook any shelves or tables. Sometimes the biggest treasures were hidden deep

Debbie and MaryJo examine countless containers, weighing how functional and useful they would or wouldn't be in a scrapbook workspace. If an item is not going to be useful and solve an immediate storage problem, don't buy it. You'll just add to your existing clutter.

Flea market shopping list

Here's the preliminary shopping list the team took to the flea market:

- Card table to be used as a work surface
- A lamp or light
- Makeup case for embellishments and tools on-the-go
- Cigar boxes for pens
- Silverware cases, trays or caddies for embellishments and tools on-the-go
- VHS "clamshell" cases for die cuts or pens
- CD-ROM jewel cases for die cuts, stickers or "punchies"
- Plastic or clear containers with lids—preferably stackable; some compartmentalized—for punches, decorative scissors, colorants, tools, pens, stamps or embellishments
- Stackable spice jars for embellishments

- Small, compartmentalized toolbox for tools or cleaners
- Baskets for idea books and magazines
- Wooden compartmentalized cabinets or shelves for stamp storage
- Kitchen utility carousels or spoon holders for most commonly used work surface tools
- Office storage pieces or bins to place atop, beneath or beside work surface
- Small file cabinet
- Small bookshelf
- Small sheet of pegboard with hooks
- Bulletin board
- Any container or caddy with handles for cropping on-the-go

ASSESSING POTENTIAL

Before purchasing any item, staffers asked themselves several questions. Is the item in good condition (or can it at least be easily fixed)? Is it large enough for my needs or will I outgrow it quickly? Will it work well with other containers I already have? Will it have an immediate impact on my mission of getting organized? If they answered "no" to any of these questions, they moved on to the next booth.

HAGGLING

Staffers kept a "cool head and a poker face," says Debbie. They carried cash in small bills so that they could make quick and easy purchases. They kept in mind a price they were willing to pay for an item and were not afraid to haggle or to walk away if negotiations were not successful.

THE FINAL INVOICE

At the end of the day, the team triumphantly returned to the office with everything they needed to create a highly functional scrapbook workspace. Here's a list of MaryJo, Debbie and Ken's expenses for the day, including flea-market admission, shopping cart rental and lunch. The final cost of their shopping spree? Just $68.50—well under their starting budget of $100.

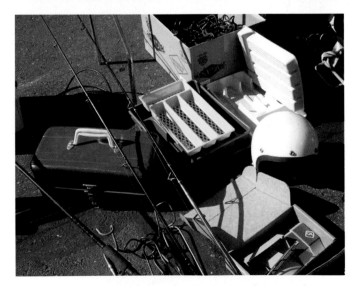

Negotiate on prices and walk away if a seller is not ready to come down. Perhaps he'll change his mind later. And when a storage product is just perfect, you'll know it—such as these old spice racks, a "lazy susan" turntable and a straight-sided silverware tray.

Our flea market finds	
Budget	$ 100.00
Flea market admission	3.00
Shopping cart rental	2.00
Lunch	14.75
Folding table	5.00
Sm. fabric-covered caddy	1.00
Sign (impulse buy)	.75
Nuts and bolts drawer unit	2.00
Crisscross accordion hanger	1.00
4 mini Rubbermaid containers	1.50
Polka-dot bag on wheels	4.00
Over-the-door hanger	1.00
Yellow multipurpose caddy	1.00
Wood/acrylic wall-display shelves	1.00
Old wooden crate	7.00
Brown office chair	8.00
Lazy Susan	1.00
Paper storage compartment	1.00
Decorative jars	1.00
Two 3-ring notebooks	1.00
Silverware tray	.50
Wooden cigar box	1.00
Large tackle box	5.00
CD tote	4.00
Portable paper file	1.00
Total spent	$ 68.50

Before:

What a mess! When tired staffers arrived back at the office, they triumphantly piled up their purchases, but the workspace was far from ready to crop in. With a little elbow grease, cleaning and decorating...

After:

...the frugal flea market finds became a functional workspace. Everything has been labeled and organized supplies have been stocked in the containers. One could just sit down and make a scrapbook page!

Antiques in the Workspace

While the primary purpose of a scrapbook workspace is functionality, there is no reason why it cannot be beautiful as well. Many scrapbookers depend on the clean lines of contemporary, modular furniture for scrapbooking, but other scrapbookers prefer a more traditional look to blend in with their home decor.

Sound expensive? Antiques don't have to be. Survey your home for older furniture, or shop local flea markets and secondhand thrift stores. You might even inherit a piece or two from other family members.

Here's how some of our readers have incorporated used-but-not-abused and hand-me-down furniture into their scrapbook workspaces.

Betsy Bell Sammarco (New Canaan, Connecticut) uses a piece of historic American furniture—the Hoosier cabinet—as a workspace and to organize her scrapbooking supplies. Hoosier cabinets were commonly found in early 20th-century kitchens. They were multifunctional—serving as pie safes, kitchen tables, cutting boards and dough boards. Many had drawers, hooks, spice racks, sugar jars and flour sifters as well in order to to make a housewife's job easier in the kitchen.

The top doors of Betsy's cabinet open to a shelved area which holds her magazines and idea books. To the left of these doors is a metal flour sifter, which she uses as a trash can. The outside of the sifter holds her "to do" lists and other notes with magnets. Hidden behind a center panel is a little shelf and a lot of room for storing punches, pens and scissors. The porcelain tabletop pulls out to become a large work surface. Under the tabletop to the left is a large bottom cabinet which holds her albums, paper, cutting mat and other large supplies. She hangs supplies from the metal bracket hanging from the inside door. To the right of this cabinet are three drawers. The top one is sectioned and holds her rulers, pencils and other supplies. The middle drawer holds stickers and the bottom drawer is large and perfect for larger size supplies. Betsy says that one of the best things about the cabinet is that it can be closed up when she is done working to conceal its contents and return to its glory being a beautiful antique in her home.

In Tricia Renner's (Leawood, Kansas) dining room at right is an optician's cabinet dating back to the early 1900s. The cabinet contains eighteen small, shallow drawers and ten large, shallow drawers—all of which are numbered. It was originally used to house a wide variety of eyeglass lenses, but nowadays it stores Tricia's paper, stickers and supplies. Tricia says that the cabinet is a super place for organization of supplies and doubles as a great piece of furniture.

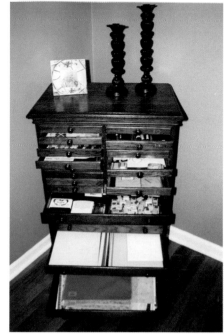

Connie Mieden Cox's (Westminster, Colorado) workspace is a wonderful combination of contemporary and used furniture. Mixed in with the plastic modular storage units are two antique library card-catalog cabinets and an art-deco-style kitchen cupboard that she purchased at an antique store. She created a scrapbook-themed bulletin board by refinishing an ornate antique picture frame that she found at a flea market. An old air-drying clothes rack has been given new life as a hanger for large sheets of paper. And her favorite antique spice racks now store beads, baubles and other tiny embellishments.

Found Around the House

If you're in a budget quandary, you often need not look further than your own home to find a container in which to stash supplies. A quick survey of your kitchen, bathroom, home office and other rooms will provide organizational storage opportunities. Want to make your workspace personalized as well as functional? Use your well-honed scrapbooking skills to decorate "found" storage containers with stickers or patterned papers. Here's just a few ideas:

ADHESIVES

• Baskets

CROPPING-ON-THE-GO

• Cosmetic bags

• Large makeup cases

• Tackle and tool boxes

DECORATIVE SCISSORS

• Belt and tie racks

EMBELLISHMENTS

• Baby food jars

• Clear, empty film canisters

• Small, compartmentalized tackle boxes

• Small drawer units

• Seven-day pill organizers

• Snack-size plastic baggies with zippered closings

• Spice rack with jars

IDEA BOOKS & MAGAZINES

• Crates

MISCELLANEOUS TOOLS

• Magnetic kitchen utensil rack

• Plastic bins

• Plastic food storage containers

• Silverware caddy

PAPER AND PRE-MADE PAGE ACCENTS

- CD-ROM "clamshells"
- Empty, clean pizza box
- Kids' baseball card holders
- Letter size accordion files
- Plastic milk-crate box filled with letter-size folders
- Under-the-bed storage box

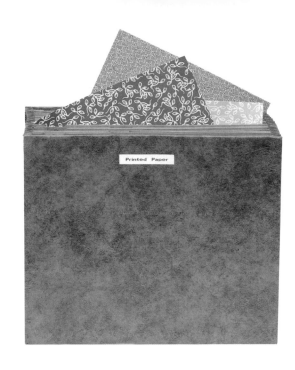

PENS, PENCILS & MARKERS

- Canning jars
- Coffee mugs
- Flowerpot with drainage hole plugged
- Old make-up bags
- Pencil cases
- Revolving office supply caddy
- Straight-sided silverware-drawer organizers
- Vases
- VHS tape "clamshell" cases

PUNCHES & STAMPS

- Clear and deep acrylic picture frames with the backing removed
- Compartmentalized tackle or tool boxes
- Emptied-out silverware case
- Large plastic storage containers with lids

472 •

MAINTAINING WORKSPACE EFFICIENCY

Congratulations! What an accomplishment! Hopefully by now you have carefully inventoried your supplies, purchased economical storage units and stashed away your materials in an orderly fashion. And now you are eager to start using your space to create more scrapbook pages—the ultimate reward! But what happens once you begin to actually crop in your newly designed workspace? Or when you return from a shopping trip with a bag of new supplies? How about when you return home from cropping-on-the-go? These three activities—page creation, shopping and cropping-on-the-go are culprits when it comes to turning an orderly workspace back into disarray. But if you make a concerted effort to maintain your workspace after each page creation or shopping or cropping trip, you'll be blessed with a fresh start each time you sit down to scrapbook.

In this last chapter you will find guidelines for developing helpful organizational habits to help you maintain your scrapbook workspace, as well as tips for reviewing, rotating and replenishing supplies. You will discover how to get organized for efficient cropping-on-the-go, including how to make "page kits" for streamlined scrapbooking. You'll see numerous totes and carry-alls designed just for scrapbookers to help make your scrapbook trips comfortable and carefree. And as a grand finale, gain insight from two scrapbookers who traded scrapbook workspaces for a day and learned to view their own workspaces through fresh eyes.

Like a fine-tuned automobile, an effective scrapbook workspace requires ongoing maintenance. A little organization and few good habits will help you to go the distance!

Maintaining Your Workspace

Whether you scrapbook on a folding table, a kitchen counter or customized scrapbook station, maintaining your workspace is the best way to ensure unhampered creativity. These tips should help.

Tips for Staying Organized

CLEAR YOUR DESK

Before you start any scrapbooking session, make sure that your work surface is clutter-free.

TAKE OUT ONLY WHAT YOU NEED

Leave all unneeded tools and supplies tucked away so you have room to spread out. If you are working on a birthday page, place only your balloon print paper and cake die cuts in front of you. If you are working on punch art, take out your punches and cardstock.

CLEAN AS YOU GO

Keep a trash can next to your desk or tape a paper bag to the side of your table. As paper scraps pile up, be sure to deposit them. Upon finishing with each tool, put it back in its place. As you complete individual pages, place them in page protectors and file them away.

WRAP UP WITH A CLEAN SWEEP

When done scrapbooking, clear off paper scraps, wipe down your work surface, vacuum and take out the garbage.

SUPPLY REVIEW & ROTATION

As your scrapbooking style evolves, so too will your supply needs. Tools that were once essential may become obsolete. And items you once thought you'd never use may become staples. Periodically review and rotate your supplies to ensure maximum potential.

BE FLEXIBLE

It takes time to determine your scrapbooking requirements and trial and error to identify which supplies you really need. Don't hesitate to make changes when necessary.

FOR EVERYTHING, THERE IS A SEASON

Think of your supplies as your scrapbooking wardrobe. Change them with the seasons. Place out-of-season items in long-term storage until next year.

After you are done scrapbooking, clear off any random items, refile useable paper scraps, wipe down your work surface, vacuum up paper scraps from the floor and take out the garbage. Wrap up with a clean sweep!

SWAP WITH YOURSELF

If you have participated in a swap, you know the excitement of receiving a package filled with brand-new goodies. Experience that same excitement on your own. Instead of keeping all your embellishments close at hand, box some of them up and place them in a closet. Every few months, "swap" with yourself by taking some new items out of the box and putting others away.

WHEN IN DOUBT, THROW IT OUT

Don't hold onto supplies that you won't use. If something has been in storage for more than a year and you haven't wanted or needed it, then sell it, trade it or give it away.

Replenishing Supplies & Smart Shopping

One of the most enjoyable activities in scrapbooking is shopping, whether replenishing those supplies that have been used up, or purchasing just-on-the-market products. But in order not to clutter your workspace with unnecessary impulse purchases, it is important to balance what you want with what you truly need. These smart shopping tips will help:

BUDGET YOURSELF

Determine a budget and stick to it. This will help cut down on impulse purchases.

MAKE A LIST; CHECK IT TWICE

Before shopping, create a list of essential items you must replenish. Purchase these items first. Buy yourself a treat with money left over.

COMPARE PRICES

Shop around. Search catalogs, the Internet, and watch for sales for the best bargains.

WHAT'S IT WORTH TO YOU?

Before purchasing a new item, consider its price and usefulness. That paper punch may only cost $10, but if you use it just twice, each use costs $5. On the other hand, if you use that $100 personal die cut machine 100 times, the investment pays off.

CLIP COUPONS

Many craft stores offer coupons which allow you to purchase products for up to 50% off. Mark the expiration date of coupons on your calendar and shop before the store promotion expires.

BUY IN BULK

Purchase staples, such as cardstock, in bulk. You will pay less money in the long run. You may also wish to chip in with a group of friends to share the discount and the product.

SHOP OFF THE BEATEN TRACK

Office supply stores, discount warehouses, dollar stores and online auctions often carry scrapbooking supplies at lower prices than specialty stores. Check them out.

So that you do not clutter your workspace with unnecessary purchases, it is important to practice smart shopping strategies that will help you balance what you want with what you truly need.

PATIENCE IS A VIRTUE

Don't purchase the latest trendy product on a whim. Start a "wish list" and wait to see if the item you want today is the item you still want next week or next month.

BECOME A FREQUENT SHOPPER

Ask if your favorite store has a preferred customer card. You'll save money while indulging your passion for shopping.

Cropping-on-the-Go

Scrapbooking at a friend's house, a crop party, a scrapbooking store or retreat presents even the most organized scrapbooker with unique challenges. Decisions must be made in advance regarding which photos and supplies to take. Oftentimes the impulse is to bring everything just in case you need it (and you most likely won't). A little planning will help lighten your load.

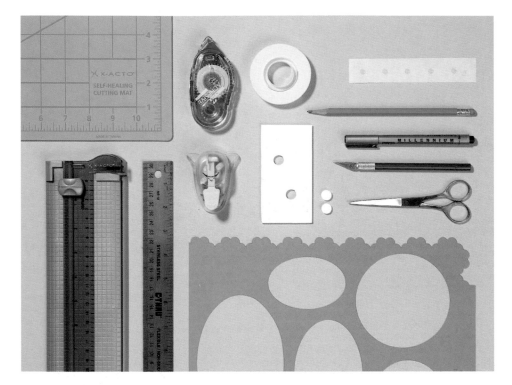

Make a travel cropping kit of basic scrapbooking supplies that you know you will need no matter where or when you crop. This way, even if you receive a last-minute invitation, all you have to do is grab your cropping kit and go!

Getting organized for a crop

Make a travel cropping kit filled with basic scrapbooking supplies that you are sure to need no matter where or when you crop. This will make it possible to "grab and go" even if you receive a last-minute invitation. Include the following:

- Adhesives
- Basic shape template
- Black journaling pen
- Blank scrapbook pages
- Corner rounder punch
- Craft knife
- Metal straightedge ruler
- Page kits (see right)
- Page protectors
- Paper trimmer
- Pencil with eraser
- Scissors
- Small assortment of colored cardstock
- Small cutting mat

If you have extra room in your basic cropping kit, you may also consider bringing:

- A couple of pairs of decorative scissors
- Colored pencils, pens or markers

What's a page kit?

When cropping on-the-go, consider bringing along "page kits" in addition to your basic supply kit. A page kit is a packet filled with materials you intend to use to make a specific scrapbook page. For example, a page kit compiled in anticipation of the creation of a child's birthday celebration spread might include party photos, themed patterned paper, birthday page accents or embellishments. It might also include memorabilia such as birthday cards, a napkin or gift wrap samples. If you plan to work on a scrapbook technique—such as stamping, setting eyelets or creating punch art—you will also need to pack the tools and supplies needed to accomplish the task.

The key to making page kits is to do as much planning as possible before leaving home in order to insure a more productive cropping session while away.

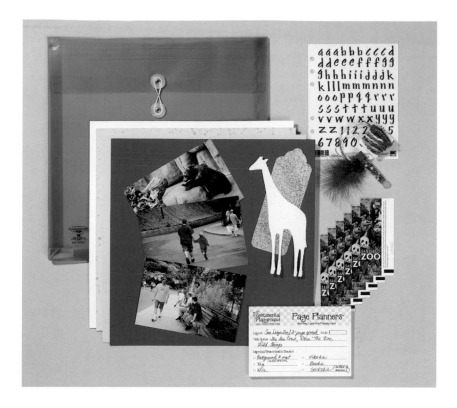

Page kits make for quick and easy cropping-on-the-go. This page kit began with zoo photos. Appropriate background and accent papers, letter stickers, embellishments and memorabilia make the page kit complete. Our page kit is contained in a Generations' Craft Keeper™, which comes in 12 x 12" and 8½ x 11" sizes. Fill out and tuck in The Sentimental Playground's Page Planner™ to keep your page plans on target.

How to make a page kit

DETERMINE CONTAINMENT

Store your page kit in an empty page protector, zippered plastic bag, box, accordion file or other keeper large enough to hold 12 x 12" papers and any page additions. Plan on one "container" for each page kit to keep each photo layout separate and protect the selected supplies. Several companies make products that are perfect for containing individual as well as numerous page kits for cropping-on-the-go.

SELECT PHOTOS

Spread out your pictures. Select high quality photos that truly speak to you. Place one to five photos for each proposed scrapbook page into each page kit container. Toss out or give away photos you don't care for any longer and file away your negatives. Add any correlating memorabilia to the page kit.

CHOOSE PAPERS

Use paper colors that are consistent with the mood, and work well with the hues, in your photos. Choose primary and complementary colors. Select both background and patterned accent papers. Add papers to the page kit and include appropriately-colored paper scraps to use for photo mats or title and journaling blocks.

DECIDE ON PAGE ADDITIONS & COLORANTS

Add pre-made page accents (see pages 458-461) and other embellishments (see pages 448-449) to kits for each layout. Place smaller items like fibers and eyelets in snack-sized zipper baggies before adding them to the larger protectors. If embellishments require special tools, make these beforehand so you don't have to bring the tools themselves. For example, fill a bag with pre-cut punchies so you don't have to transport paper punches. Select and include special colorants (see pages 440–444) that you wish to use on accent your page.

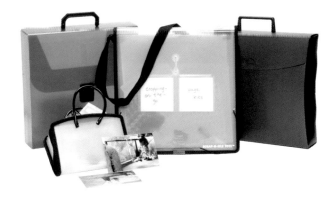

Many manufacturers make totes to contain a number of page kits for easy travel. Try Mochalatte's Super Tote Box, General Box Company's Crop 'N Go™ tote or Caren's Crafts' Scrap-N-File Tote™, to name a few. If you prefer to keep your photos stored outside of the page kits, keep them organized in an accordion-style tote such as Generations' My Generation™ Sassy Scrapper™.

ADD JOURNALING NOTES & PAGE DESIGN INSPIRATION

Place journaling notes (see page 450-452), scratch paper on which you jot down page sketches, potential page titles and journaling ideas into page kits.

INCLUDE TITLE MATERIALS

Include title lettering templates, sticker letters or pre-made titles.

On-The-Go Storage Solutions

If you are an on-the-go scrapbooker, you will need a portable storage unit. While there are many portable storage units on the market specifically designed to hold scrapbooking supplies, general art supply storage products are also useful.

Customized options for the scrapbooker range from backpacks and shoulder bags to cases on wheels and plastic storage totes. Many of these carry-alls have designated compartments and pockets for safely storing tools and supplies—such as punches, stamps, decorative scissors and pens. Many have special compartments for toting 12 x 12" and 8½ x 11" papers and sturdy compartments for storing heavy 12 x 12" albums. Add a luggage identification tag with your contact information for a measure of security, should you and your tote become separated.

Here and on the following pages, we feature a wide array of travel totes for scrapbooking and carrying art supplies. However, companies are continually expanding their product lines to meet the needs of today's scrapbooker, so be sure to check out their Web sites (see our Source Guide) for new offerings.

Immediately after a crop, unpack your travel tote and put tools and supplies away in their storage bins and compartments. Trim paper scraps and file them. Sort and store unused photos and negatives. Add finished pages to scrapbook albums or in a designated "holding container" until you're ready to place them in an album.

Generations' Weekender™ Backpack and Scrappack's Scrappack™

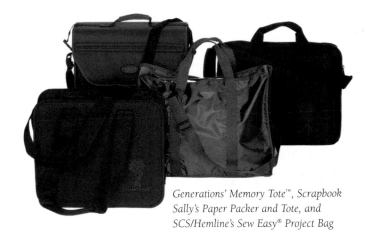

Generations' Memory Tote™, Scrapbook Sally's Paper Packer and Tote, and SCS/Hemline's Sew Easy® Project Bag

Most product manufacturers produce several different types of totes and carry alls for scrapbooking "on-the-go." From backpacks and shoulder bags to handled totes on wheels—you're sure to find exactly what you need to suit your scrapbooking style. Check out the manufacturer web sites (listed in our Source Guide) for each company's latest and greatest offerings.

Generations' Crop Station™ and Plaid's Creative Gear™ Wheel Cart & Craft Tote

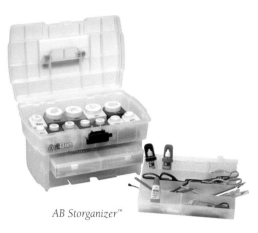

AB Storganizer™

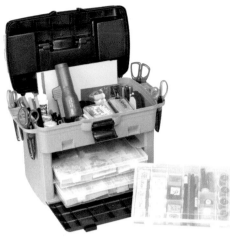

AB Easy View I

AB Quick View™

ArtBin has an extensive line of plastic and canvas totes, tray boxes and carrying cases in an enormous array of styles and sizes. You're sure to find just the size you need for storing your on-the-go tools and supplies—whether it's a little or a lot!

AB Tote 'n Go

AB Mega Tote

AB Tote Express™

AB Quick Tote

AB Ultimate Solutions Tote™

CIS Paper Taker

Crop In Style, as well as other companies, designs high-quality travel totes and wheeled "pulls" with the scrapbooker in mind. Whether you're looking for a simple backpack, a shoulder tote or a full-fledged suitcase on wheels—even a portable scrapbooking table—there's a lot to choose from! Crop In Style also manufactures a wide array of storage components that fit inside their traveling totes. These storage products can be added to your scrapbooking repertoire over time as your collection grows and your budget allows. Their most recent addition to their growing line: a backpack with wheels, a pulling handle and its own rain poncho (see far below on the right)!

CIS Back Pack

CIS Na Navigator LTD

Crop In Style's XXL

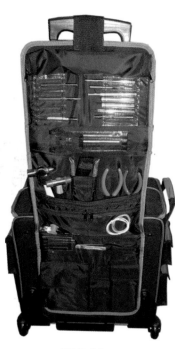

CIS Tool Bag

CIS Na Navigator LTD with Tote Table

CIS Stamp Store

CIS Not Just For Kids Back Pack

Jokari's Scrap'N Stor Carryall™ is a versatile little tote that has a hook for hanging; a shoulder strap for carrying; and an adjustable, rotating stand for desktop or desk-side access while cropping-on-the-go.

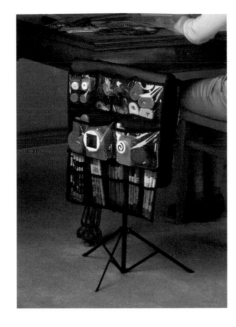

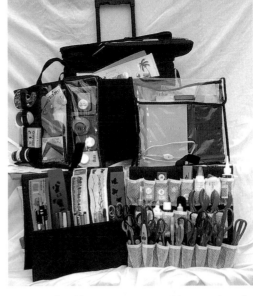

Canvas Collectible's components are sold separately and fit into their square tote in background. Storage elements include Ditty Plus, Protect 'n' Store, Double-Sided Insert and Accessory Insert.

Besides its many smaller totes, Tutto offers Crafts on Wheels™, which you can read more about on page 405.

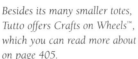

Crop With This' Paper Express provides ample room for paper on-the-go or to store paper in the workspace.

Besides their wide array of plastic paper and sticker totes and cases, Leeco/Cropper Hopper also manufactures a line of on-the-go organizers including The All Terrain Bag (ATB), Scrapbook Tote Bag and the Flat Pack™ Organizer.

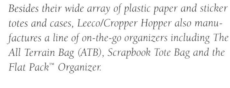

Trading Scrapbook Workspaces

Just when you think you "have it all together" in your scrapbook workspace, try "trading" your workspace with a scrapbooking friend to see how your organizational abilities stack up.

The concept is simple. Create a scrapbook page within a set amount of time—such as three hours—in a friend's scrapbook workspace. You may bring with you only one set of photos. Your friend will do the same in your scrapbook workspace. Invariably, the space swap will give you great organizational ideas to incorporate into your workspace once you return home. Try it! This is guaranteed to be among the most fun and educational times you've spent scrapbooking.

The scrapbookers

We found two scrapbookers—Julie Labuszewski and Maureen Behnke—who were willing to take our *Trading Scrapbook Workspaces* challenge. They were instructed not to discuss the theme of their photos or details about their workspaces with each other prior to the swap. Our staff documented the fun, foibles and frustrations the women experienced while visiting each others' homes.

Julie Labuszewski, of Centennial Colorado, invades Maureen's home and personal scrapbook workspace to see just how easily she can create a scrapbook page outside the comfort of her own workspace.

JULIE'S PERSPECTIVE

"I liked the spacious, uncluttered room. Maureen's Memory Garden theme, so beautifully executed, made the space pleasant and inviting. I liked working next to a large window. The natural light, which was gentle on my eyes, illuminated the desktop perfectly. I liked the display of product on the shelves behind me. The colorful selection of glitter, beads and embossing powder inspired me.

"I liked how Maureen utilized and labeled her storage units. There was a storage unit filled with 12 x 12" solid paper, a unit for scrap paper and another storage unit for printed paper. She labeled each smaller folder inside the unit, so finding a specific color of paper was quick and easy.

"I liked seeing labels on the stack of purple interchangeable drawers designed to fit inside a travel tote. I quickly found most of the supplies and tools I needed.

"I liked not having to get out of my chair to get supplies, tools and paper. Everything was conveniently within arm's reach.

"I liked the high-quality office chair. It provided back support and comfort. I won't be attending any more midnight crops where I'm expected to sit in a metal folding chair for three or four hours.

Julie's first stumbling block was trying to find the perfect shade of golden yellow cardstock to pull out the striking color in her photos. There was no match, however.

After selecting a different set of photos to scrapbook, Julie quickly found the paper, tools and supplies she needed to work on a scrapbook page. Having everything within arm's reach made it easy!

As time runs out, Julie's frustration grows as she tries three different black pens to trace over her penciled journaling. The pens were dried out! The fourth pen was a charm and journaling was completed. The last hurdle: no sewing needle or thread to be found for her button embellishments.

"I liked seeing Maureen's work elegantly displayed on the wall in two wooden 12 x 12" frames. I absolutely loved the Sizzix die cut machine. Maureen had a die-cut for every letter of the alphabet. In less than five minutes, I had the headline for my page punched out. I may incorporate this machine into my workspace. Usually, I hand letter all my headlines, which takes time. With three children running around the house, I am going to have to scrapbook faster. A Sizzix machine would be a great solution. It would even give me an opportunity to use up my surplus of patterned paper."

RECOMMENDATIONS FOR CHANGE

Julie's first hurdle: a limited selection of solid-colored papers. "When I showed up at Maureen's house, I brought along some great photos of my son and a thumbnail sketch of the page I had planned on creating. I wanted to find paper to match the striking background color in these photos. I looked though her solid papers but couldn't find the color I needed—a golden yellow. I considered using other colors for the page but I could see they wouldn't work, so I decided not to execute my initial page idea. Fortunately, I had a few photos of my son in the tub. I found a sheet of cobalt blue. Now I was on a roll. In summary, I would have liked a larger selection of colored paper to choose from."

Dried-out pens were another stumbling block for Julie. "When I finished journaling the text on my page in pencil, I looked for a black pen to go over the pencil lines. I found three black pens. Unfortunately, each one had dried-out ink. I was getting frustrated and my time was running out. When I turned around and discovered a complete set of ZIG pens on the shelf behind me, I was ecstatic."

Julie's final impediment included a needle and thread that were nowhere to be found. "I chose to embellish my page with yellow buttons. Usually I sew on buttons. I think this looks more authentic. I wanted to sew on the buttons but I couldn't find a needle and thread. I ended up using sticky dots. Later that day, Maureen showed me where she keeps her needle and thread."

Julie was pretty fond of Maureen's labeling on everything, which made it easy for her to identify and find things quickly. She also liked Maureen's high-quality chair for its great back support and comfort.

Maureen Behnke, of Littleton, Colorado, enters Julie's home with photos in tow to embark on her own adventure of discovery.

MAUREEN'S PERSPECTIVE

"I liked the atmosphere in Julie's office. The café theme invited me to come in and relax and take a moment for myself. Julie even had cappuccino and cookies set up in the entrance hall!

"Another thing I really liked was her 12 x 12" paper rack. The first thing I do when making a page is pick out my background paper. Julie had a tall 12 x 12" paper rack that made selecting just the right color a snap!

"I could tell that organization was a priority in Julie's workspace. She labeled large baskets with all the necessary supplies. For example, she had a basket of adhesives, a basket of cutting tools, a basket of punches, another for stamps and yet another for embellishing tools. Plus, they were all within arm's reach from the work surface."

Playing with Julie's "toys" was to Maureen's liking. "It was fun exploring all of her tools. I used her small alphabet stamp set to make custom tags for my layout. I also enjoyed her selection of punches, which were easy to use with her Power Punch accessory."

Julie's reference materials proved to be handy as well. "I used Memory Makers Quick & Easy Journaling to help me with adjectives to spice up my journaling. Julie even had a thesaurus and a dictionary which came in handy for my page title "Bubbley", which became "Bubbly" in the nick of time!

RECOMMENDATIONS FOR CHANGE

Julie's lighting's got to go! "Julie has a window in her office, but it was an overcast day. The ceiling and small desk lights were not bright enough for detailed work like stamping and embossing. I would invest in an Ott Light or some other craft lighting.

Maureen appreciated Julie's corralling and organization of her supplies, making it easy for her to find just the right adhesives and more.

Julie's cafe theme was inviting, but Maureen confessed that her lighting "has to go!"

THE AFTERMATH

After trading spaces, Julie and Maureen talked about the experience. "I recommend this to anyone who wants to make significant improvements in their workspace. It forced me to think differently about my workspace. For the first time, I began to think about my workspace objectively—from an outsider's point of view," says Julie. "As a result, I came up with new, creative and more efficient organizational strategies.

"I tossed out my old push-pin bulletin board and purchased a few new magnetic ones. They're the perfect choice because with a magnet you never have to poke a hole in a favorite photo again!

"It was fascinating to hear about Maureen's experience working in my office. For example, since I usually hand letter my headlines, I don't have any lettering templates, lettering stickers or lettering reference books. This drove her crazy! She also couldn't find the blades for my circle cutter. Frankly, I'm still looking for them too. In the end, we found the feedback valuable," adds Julie.

"Oh yeah, the lettering thing," Maureen winces. "Julie is a master at freehand lettering. I, on the other hand, need all the help I can get, thus my Sizzix machine. I had to go beyond my comfort zone and hand letter my title. Sticker letters, which are not my first choice, were in short supply."

And then there's the awkward feeling of working in someone else's kitchen. "This is not something Julie could change, but something built into the experience," says Maureen. "Sometimes I felt like I was an Italian chef working in a Chinese restaurant. The tools were different, the paper was different, even the music was different! Julie and I have different personal styles, which are evident by our offices. I would say Julie's office is more upbeat and chic, whereas I have a more warm, homey office. I did not expect my creativity to be affected by the space I was working in, but my page turned out to be very much like a page Julie would do!"

Both women agree on one thing: "This was a wonderful experience and we would highly recommend it!"

Once past the awkward feeling of working in someone else's workspace, both scrapbookers settled in to complete their task at hand. The ladies met afterward to discuss the day's events. Maureen and Julie are still best scrapbooking buddies and both agree that trading spaces was a wonderful learning experience.

Gallery of Efficient Workspaces

Many scrapbookers have already discovered the joy of scrapbook workspace organization and have reaped the benefits of increased productivity. Let their beautiful workspaces inspire you to begin working on your your own!

Linda Lawrence's (Palm Beach, Florida) husband, Gene, gets all of the credit for designing her highly functional workspace. Besides its sheer spaciousness, the room's other quality traits include lots of closet storage, over-the-door punch pockets on both sides of the door and built-in shelves behind the closet door that are the perfect depth for storing 12 x 12" albums. Linda's quite fond of her sticker and die-cut binders, tilt bins and plastic storage drawers. The self-proclaimed scrapbook addict offers this advice: "Label, label, label," says Linda. "And always be flexible: Out with the old and in with the new!" Way to go, Gene and Linda!

Kathy Gleason's (Crete, Illinois) well-stocked and organized workspace features an astounding array of storage shelving, drawers, slots and racks. Kathy holds monthly crops where guests are amazed how easy it is to find everything—even if it's their first time there! Her best productivity advice? "Label everything so you don't waste time looking for a certain item," says Kathy. "Always put things away after scrapbooking, so you don't waste time cleaning the next time you scrap." We really like Kathy's idea of displaying her die-cut shapes on the wall. Each time she buys a new die, the shape goes up on the wall!

Barbara Gardner (Scottsdale, Arizona) is a professed fanatic about having a place for everything and everything in its place. "My scrap room was designed so most of my supplies are out-of-sight in drawers or on shelves behind doors," says Barbara. Her tidy workspace boasts 40 feet of running countertops, and lots of quality light. "Good lighting is paramount," says Barbara, whose workspace is illuminated by a north-facing window, two skylights, six recessed halogen ceiling lights and under-cabinet lights spaced 2' apart. The 12 x 12" cardstock trays, made by her husband, are "priceless." We adore this room as much as her Persian cat, Jasmine—who sits on the shelf atop the computer and listens to classical music while watching Barbara scrapbook. Very nice!

Linda Owens' (Camarillo, California) 30 square feet of counter space; wire paper racks; custom-made, 300-stamp wall organizer and ample work surfaces dominate the highlights of her efficient workspace. "Excellent lighting is very helpful," says Linda. "And having plenty of work space and a designated place for every item are my best organizational tips." Love that stamp organizer, Linda!

Angie McGoveran (Festus, Missouri) employs side-by-side drawer units beneath an inexpensive countertop for valuable storage space. Pre-fabricated bathroom cabinets and an antique file cabinet round out the storage capacity of her well-organized workspace. Angie used to want an entire room devoted to scrapbooking, but has fallen in love with her shared space at the end of her family room. "I can be a part of what my family is doing while I am scrapbooking," says Angie. Her organizational advice: "Put things away as soon as you bring them home. If things pile up, it becomes a huge job. It's less overwhelming to put stuff away 10-15 minutes at a time." Nice job, Angie!

Kelly Angard's (Highlands Ranch, Colorado) scrapbook workspace features white-laminate modular furniture with plenty of storage shelves and work surfaces. The painted walls (inspired by SEI patterned paper) burst forth with creative energy. We're a bit partial to the wall art, which is fitting for this loyal Memory Makers Books art contributor and writer. Bravo, Kelly!

Additional Resources

If you need even more in-depth help organizing your workspace, there is help available. Whether you like to gain inspiration reading quietly on your favorite sofa or if you prefer to be online with an insightful group of thousands of other scrapbookers, you may find these additional resources useful.

WEB SITES

123 Sort It

Advice and forms to print for organizational use in residential homes and the office.

123sortit.com/toc.phtml

15 Uses For...

interiordec.about.com/library/bl_15uses.htm

Club Mom

Free organization checklists for all areas of the home.

clubmom.com

HGTV Trash To Treasure

hgtv.com/hgtv/trash_to_treasure/0,1792,HGTV_3912,00.html

I Need More Time

ineedmoretime.com

Katie Leckley's Grand Plan for Home Organization Room by Room

members.aol.com/bullseye57/webtest/geto/grandplan.html

Organize Tips

Tips for helping you get organized in your daily life.

organizetips.com

Organized Home

Free advice and printable organizer notebook sheets for home and scrapbooking organization from Cynthia Tower Ewer.

organizedhome.com

Organizing From the Inside Out

Web site and book advice from a professional organizer on how to develop an organizational style that suits you.

juliemorgenstern.com

Picture Me Foundation

An organization that gladly accepts surplus scrapbooking tools and supplies.

pictureme.org/newhome.html

Scrappers Challenge

An e-mail loop at yahoogroups.com that provides free daily reminders and monthly challenges to help you keep your focus on organizing your scrapbook workspace. Moderated by Kathleen Aho, one of the contributing writers for this book.

groups.yahoo.com/group/Scrappers Challenge/

Sidetracked Home Executives: From Pigpen to Paradise

Pam Young and Sydney Craft Rozen

shesintouch.com/index.html

Sink Reflections

Flylady groups, products and advice for week-by-week home cleanup from Marla Cilley.

flylady.com/index.asp

BOOKS & PUBLICATIONS

Balance Magazine

The magazine about getting and staying organized.

livinginbalancemagazine.com

Clutter's Last Stand by Don Aslett

Good Things for Organizing by Martha Stewart

How to Get Organized When You Don't Have the Time by Stephanie Culp

Improving Productivity By Getting Organized by Joe Peraino, Ph.D.

Is There Life After Housework? by Don Aslett

It's Here . . . Somewhere by Alice Fulton and Pauline Hatch

Lighten Up by Michelle Passoff

Office Clutter Cure by Don Aslett

Organizing Plain and Simple: A Ready Reference Guide With Hundreds of Solutions to Your Everyday Clutter Challenges by Donna Smallin

You Can Find More Time for Yourself Every Day by Stephanie Culp

Additional Credits

Reader photos

All reader photos appearing in this book were shot with Kodak HD High Definition 400-speed film, made possible by a generous donation from the Eastman Kodak Company of Rochester, New York.

Sources

The following companies manufacture workspace and storage products featured in this book. Please check your local retailers to find these materials, or go to a company's Web site for the latest product. In addition, we have made every attempt to properly credit the items mentioned in this book. We apologize to any company that we have listed incorrectly, and we would appreciate hearing from you.

3M Stationery
(888) 364-3577
3m.com

AccuCut®
(800) 288-1670
accucut.com

Akro-Mils
(800) 253-2467
akro-mils.com

Armada Art, Inc.
(800) 435-0601
armadaart.com

ArtBin by Flambeau
(800) 232-3474
www.artbin.com

Artfully Scribed, Inc.
(703) 787-8267
artfullyscribed.com

Artograph, Inc.
(888) 975-9555
artograph.com

Avery Dennison Corporation
(800) 462-8379
avery.com

Beadalon®
(866) 423-2325
www.beadalon.com

Board Dudes, Inc., The
(800) 521-4332
boarddudes.com

Canvas Collectible's, Inc.
(866) 633-TOTE
canvascollectibles.com

Caren's Crafts
(805) 520-9635
scrapbooking4fun.com

C-Line Products, Inc.
(800) 323-6084
c-lineproducts.com

Collected Memories
(866) 483-9391
collectedmemories.com

Collectors Cabinets
(715) 484-5025
collectors-cabinets.com

Colorbök™, Inc.
(wholesale only)
(800) 366-4660
colorbok.com

Crop In Style®
(888) 700-2202
cropinstyle.com

C-Thru® Ruler Company, The
(800) 243-8419
cthruruler.com

Darice®
(866) 432-7423
darice.com

Daylight Company, LLC
(866) 329-5444
daylightcompany.com

Display Dynamics, Inc.
(908) 231-1132
displaydynamics.net

DMC Corporation, The
(973) 589-0606
www.dmc.com

DMD, Inc.
(800) 805-9890
dmdind.com

Eagle Affiliates
(800) 643-6798
eagleaffiliates.com

EK Success Ltd.
(800) 524-1349
eksuccess.com

Ellison Craft & Design
(800) 253-2238
ellison.com

Ergonomic Services, Inc.
(303) 904-8333
ergonomicservices.net

Fiskars, Inc.
(800) 500-4849
fiskars.com

Flex Products
(800) 526-6273
flex-products.com

For Keeps Sake
(801) 967-6664
for-keeps-sake.com

General Box Company
(912) 283-5716
generalbox.com

Generations®
(314) 542-5400
GenerationsNow.com

Handango™
handango.com

Highsmith®, Inc.
(800) 558-2110
highsmith.com

Hunt Corporation
(800) 879-4868
hunt-corp.com

Inventor's Studio, The
(800) 799-3653
inventorsstudio.com

Jokari/US, Inc.
(800) 669-1718
jokari.com

Jotters
(877) 568-8371
jotters.net

K & Company
(888) 244-2083
kandcompany.com

Kodak Corporation
(800) 235-6325
kodak.com

Kokuyo
(877) 465-6589
www.kokuyo.co.jp/english

Leeco Industries, Inc.
(800) 826-8806

Lifetime® Products, Inc.
(800) 225-3865
lifetime.com

Light Impressions®
(800) 828-6216
lightimpressionsdirect.com

LNS Software Solutions, LLC
(253) 850-2457
LNS-software.com

Magic Scraps™
(972) 385-1838
magicscraps.com

Making Memories
(801) 294-0430
makingmemories.com

McGill Inc.
(800) 982-9884
mcgillinc.com

Media Group/Sewing Genie™
(203) 406-1000
www.sewinggenie.com

Novelcrafts
(514) 582-3208
novelcrafts.com

Ott-Lite® Technology
(800) 842-8848
ottlite.com

Pageframe Designs
(877) 55-frame
scrapbookframe.com

Paintier Products, LLC
(586) 822-7874
paintier.com

Pampered Chef®, The
(800) 266-5562
www.pamperedchef.com

Pencil Grip, Inc., The
(888) 736-4747
thepencilgrip.com

Photographic Solutions, Inc.
(800) 637-3212
photographicsolutions.com

Pioneer Photo Albums, Inc.®
(818) 882-2161
pioneerphotoalbums.com

Plaid Enterprises, Inc.
(800) 842-4197
plaidonline.com

PrintFile, Inc.
(407) 886-3100
printfile.com

Provo Craft®
(800) 937-7686
www.provocraft.com

Quantum Storage Systems
(800) 685-4465
quantumstorage.com

QuicKutz, Inc.
(888) 702-1146
quickutz.com

Rubbermaid
(888) 895-2110
rubbermaid.com

Scrapbook Sally
(866) SB-SALLY
scrapbooksally.com

ScrapNCube
(800) 216-4992
scrapncube.com

Scrappack
(866) 228-1458
scrappack.com

Scrapptopia
(408) 846-9144
scrapptopia.com

SCS USA/Hemline
(800) 547-8025

Sentimental Playground, The
(207) 655-7109
sentimentalplayground.com

Sizzix®
(877) 355-4766

Tutto®
(800) 949-1288
tutto.com

TwinRay
(323) 939-9059
twinray.com

un-du Products, Inc.
(888) 289-8638
un-du.com

Uniek, Inc.
(800) 248-6435
www.uniekinc.com

Verilux, Inc., "The Healthy
Lighting Company"
(800) 454-4408
healthylight.com

Westex Corporation
(908) 624-0093

Xyron, Inc.
(800) 793-3523
xyron.com

Sources II

The following companies donated products used to decorate boxes featured in this book. Check your local retailers to find these products, or go to a company's Web site for the latest information.

American Traditional™
Designs
(800) 448-6656
americantraditional.com

Clearsnap Inc.
(888) 448-4862
clearsnap.com

Delta Technical Coatings, Inc.
(800) 423-4135
deltacrafts.com

Design Originals
(800) 877-7820
d-originals.com

Hot Off The Press, Inc.
(800) 227-9595
CraftPizzaz.com

Plaid Enterprises, Inc.
(800) 842-4197
plaidonline.com

Sources III

The following companies manufacture scrapbook supplies that were used to stock the storage containers featured in this book. Please check your local retailers to find these supplies, or go to a company's Web site for the latest product.

Page 416
Label maker (Dymo), Pens (American Crafts, EK Success, Sakura), Post-It® notes (3M), labels and dividers (Avery), adhesive (Hermafix), punches (Hyglo, McGill).

Page 417
Stamps (EK Success), punch (Hyglo), pens (EK Success).

Page 420
Acrylic paints (Delta), Mod Podge® (Plaid), transfer (American Traditional).

Page 421
Film border punch and square punch (Family Treasures), Film (Kodak).

Page 425
Patterned paper (Design Originals), letter stickers (EK Success), Mod Podge® (Plaid).

Page 426
Acrylic paint (Delta), Mod Podge® (Plaid), stamps (Hero Arts,Inkadinkado, Plaid, PSX Design, Stampabilities, A Stamp in the Hand, Stampin' Up!), ink (Clearsnap, Tsukineko), stickers (Karen Foster Design), ribbon (Garden Gate Designs), stencil (American Traditional), fibers (Rubba Dub Dub).

Page 430
Crimpers (Fiskars), brayers (source unknown).

Page 431
Cutters (Carl, Fiskars, Lion, Puzzle Mates, Shaping Memories, X-acto).

Page 433
Scissors (Armada Arts, Family Treasures, Fiskars, Provo Craft), punches (All Night Media, Carl, EK Success, Emagination Crafts, Family Treasures, Hyglo/American Pin, The Punch Bunch).

Page 434-435
Stamps (Club Scrap, Design Originals, EK Success, Hampton Art Stamps, Hero Arts, Limited Edition, Magenta, PSX Design, Rubber Stampede, Stampin' Up!), Unmounted Stamps (Design Originals, Lost Coast Design, Oxford Impressions, Wordsworth), Mod Podge® (Plaid), floral napkins (Plaid), acrylic paint (Delta).

Page 435
Templates, stencils, and decorative rulers (C-Thru Ruler, Dream Weaver Stencils, Lasting Impressions, Scrap Pagerz).

Page 438
Adhesives (3L, 3M/Scotch, American Tombow, Art Accents, Duncan, EK Success, Glue Dots, Paper Mate, Pioneer, Ranger, Suze Weinberg, Therm O Web, US Art Quest); adhesive application machine (Xyron).

Page 439
Wallpaper cut outs (Wallies), stickers (Stickopotamus).

Page 441
Paints (Angelwing Enterprises, Chartpak, Delta, Duncan Enterprises, Ranger Industries, Sakura Hobby Craft), applicators (EK Success, Loew-Cornell, Tsukineko).

Page 442
Embossing powders (Ranger, Tsukineko, Suze Weinberg), embossing pens (Tsukineko) pencils (Chartpak, Staedtler).

Page 443
Pens and markers (EK Success, Sakura, Staedtler), stamps (Clearsnap, Hero Arts), ink (Clearsnap, Stampin' Up!), organics (Hot Off The Press).

Page 444
Chalk (Craf-T Products, EK Success), metallic rub-ons (Craf-T Products), applicators (Craf-T, EK Success, Tsukineko), ink pads (Clearsnap, Hero Arts, Ranger, Tsukineko), Dauber Duos (Tsukineko).

Page 445
Metallics (Artistic Wire, Biblical Impressions, Eyelet Co., Global Solutions, Halcraft, Making Memories, Provo Craft, Rubba Dub Dub, Scrap Yard 329).

Page 446
Shaved ice and tinsel (Magic Scraps), buttons (Blumenthal Lansing), tiny glass marbles (Halcraft, Magic Scraps), sequins and confetti (Westrim), beads (Bead Heaven, Blue Moon Beads, JewelCraft).

Page 447
Fibers (On The Surface, Rubba Dub Dub, Scrapbook Sally); floss (DMC).

Page 448
Sewing Genie™ and threads (Media Group, Inc.), ribbons (Offray).

Page 449
Organics (All Night Media, Colorbök, Hot Off The Press, Magic Scraps, Rubba Dub Dub, U.S. Shell), Clay (Provo Craft, Sculpey by Polyform Products).

Page 450
Binders and books (Memory Makers).

Page 452
Acrylic paint (Delta), letter stickers (PSX Design), Mod Podge® (Plaid), patterned paper (Provo Craft).

Page 454-456
Cardstock (Bazzill, DMD), patterned papers (Design Originals, Hot Off The Press, Karen Foster Design, PSX Design).

Page 455
Mod Podge® (Plaid), clip art (Dover Publications), ink (Clearsnap), patterned paper (Design Originals, Karen Foster Design, Magenta), stickers (EK Success, Club Scrap), acrylic paints (Delta), paper accents (EK Success), colored pencils (Prismacolor), stamps (A Stamp in the Hand), label holders (Anima Designs), ribbon (Offray), and hemp string (Pulsar).

Page 458
Pre-made page additions (Colorbök, Deluxe Cuts, Design Originals, DMD, EK Success, Ever After, K & Company, JewelCraft, Westrim Crafts).

Page 460
Stickers (EK Success, Me & My BIG Ideas, Mrs. Grossman's Paper Company).

Page 476
Cutting mat, paper trimmer and X-acto knife (Hunt Corporation); templates and ruler (C-Thru Ruler); scissors (Mrs. Grossman's Paper Company), vellum adhesive (3M), corner punch (EK Success), tape runner (American Tombow), foam dots (Ranger), glue dots (Glue Dots International).

Page 477
Stickers (Stickopotamus), wire (Artistic Wire).

frolicking   Malibu, California - 2002

Let a joy keep you. Reach out your
hands and take it when it runs by.

~Carl Sandburg

The material in this compilation appeared in the following previously published Memory Makers Books, and appears here by permission of the authors. (The initial page numbers given refer to pages in the original work; page numbers in parentheses refer to pages in this book.)

Editors of Memory Makers	Scrapbook Embellishments © 2003	Pages 1, 4–127 (5–130, 494–495)
Editors of Memory Makers	Cutting Edge Photo Cropping for Scrapbooks © 2003	Pages 1, 4–127 (131–255)
Editors of Memory Makers	Toddler Scrapbooks © 2001	Pages 1, 4–127 (256–382)
Editors of Memory Makers	How to Organize Your Scrapbook Workspace © 2003	Pages 1, 4–111 (383–493)

Other fine Memory Makers books are available from your local bookstore, craft store or direct from the publisher.

09 08 07 06 05 5 4 3 2

Big Book of Scrapbooking / edited by Memory Makers Books—1st ed.
       p. cm.
     ISBN 1-892127-62-8 (hc.: alk. paper)

Cover Designer: Marissa Bowers
Production Editor: Jennifer Ziegler
Production Coordinator: Kristen Heller